I

Photo Credit: Jenna Sammon

The History Of
CORPUS CHRISTI
CATHOLIC CHURCH
Deerfield, Steele County, Minnesota

Ronald F. Eustice & Carla (Maas) Brady
2024

ABOUT THE AUTHORS

Ronald F. Eustice

Carla (Maas) Brady

Ronald F. Eustice was born September 24, 1945 in Waseca, Minnesota. He is one of four children born to Donald F. and Alice Mae (Perron) Eustice. The Eustices purchased 160-acres on the Steele-Waseca County line in 1947 and moved to Deerfield in early 1948. They were active members of Corpus Christi parish for many decades.

Ronald became a Mass server in 1953 and continued to serve for the next ten years. He attended a one-room country school in Deerfield Township and graduated from Owatonna High School in 1963. He enrolled at the University of Minnesota and earned a degree in Agricultural Journalism in 1968. His career in International agriculture and the cattle industry has taken him to more than 80 countries with foreign assignments in Uruguay (1967-68), Mexico (1970-72), and Indonesia (1987-1990). He served as executive director of the Minnesota Beef Council from 1990 until retirement in 2012.

Since then, Ronald has pursued a second career in writing with particular focus on his lifelong interest in history. In addition to this volume, he has written more than 20 books on various aspects of agriculture and family history.

Ronald has been united in marriage to Margaret McAndrews since 1975. They are the parents of three children; Kevin, John (1979-2013) and AnnMarie.

Carla T. (Maas) Brady was born June 21, 1958, to Francis and Georgette (Babos) Maas on a farm northwest of Medford on the Rice/Steele County line. She has 4 older brothers and 4 younger sisters, and she was truly the middle child.

She attended Christ the King Church and Medford Public School. While, growing up she was active in the church choir. With 4 older brothers, she did not help on the farm; she was her mother's helper, learning to cook, clean, bake, garden, and do laundry. In the summer, one day she would do laundry, the next gardening, the third baking bread, and then cook. It prepared her well for her future in life.

Her first job was in bookkeeping in the banking world at 1st National Bank, Faribault. She married Byron P. Brady on June 17, 1977, at which time she became a member of Corpus Christi Church Deerfield. She continued at the bank advancing to head bookkeeper and resigned to become a stay-at-home mom in 1980. She is the mother of five children (Erin, Byron F., Moggie, Emerson, Anna). She farmed along side her husband; milking cows, raising calves, chickens and a few pigs. In 1994, she returned to banking with Faribault Federal Savings Bank, getting the job through Jean Gillis. While there, she attended South Central Community College in Faribault and received her AAS degree in accounting. She continued her banking career retiring in 2021, as a Commercial Relationship Manager with an emphasis on agricultural lending at US Bank.

Over the years Carla taught religion, was a long-time member of the Corpus Christi choir (1977-2016), CCW President from (2001-2016) and continues to serve on the Finance Council (2002-present) at Christ the King Church. She assists her husband Byron, caring for Corpus Christi Church and still organizes Oratory activities as they come up.

FOREWORD

Rev. James E. Starasinich

Dear Brothers and Sisters in Christ Jesus the Lord,

When I arrived in the Diocese of Winona-Rochester, I had never been to the southern part of Minnesota. I was formed to serve as a Diocesan Missionary presbyter (the correct term for "priest" as found in the documents of the Second Vatican Council), and that is how I arrived here, as a missionary to serve in two parishes and an oratory within this Diocese.

Shortly after serving here, I began to understand my formation and appreciate it even more. Ronald Eustice has written on page 18 in this book: "Considering the vast area and the sparse population, we must assume that attending Mass and the Sacraments was irregular at best. Put your imagination to work as you visualize a few families coming together for the awaited arrival of a priest. Religious formation had to be completed in a short span of time. Now that we are well into the 21st century, we might do well to copy their zeal and determination."

Indeed, zeal is necessary today to spread the Gospel. Pope Francis recently gave his Wednesday catechesis entitled, "The passion for evangelization: the apostolic zeal of the believer." It also took zeal to build a house to worship in and that is what the first Catholic settlers in Deerfield set out to do. Reminiscent of the movie "Field of Dreams", when a voice is heard saying, "If you build it, he will come." Yes, build it they did, and He did come! The parish would be incorporated a few years later within the Archdiocese of St. Paul. Sixteen years later the new Diocese of Winona would be formed.

The Parish of Corpus Christi goes beyond the quaint white chapel that stands as a landmark to the residents of Deerfield. I recall my first meeting at Christ the King in Medford, discussing the future of the "oratory" of Corpus Christi. I had never ventured west to see the property, the building, and the cemetery. Someone suggested bringing the stained-glass windows from the old church and make a small addition at Christ the King, utilizing these precious works of art. Another spoke of demolition. I simply stated that as pastor I had just arrived and would like to see this poor structure and have a say in it myself. What I found was something beautiful and well maintained, not worthy of destruction. It spoke well of the parishioners and that said everything to me.

The church is not a building but a people, anointed through baptism and growing in faith through the Sunday celebration of the Eucharist. It is an ongoing maturation in the Holy Spirit, being formed to be an icon of Christ, a child of God. Nourished through the Sacraments, we grow in love of God and in love of one another.

In these pages you will find the stories of ordinary men and women who drew their strength from Christ at this sanctuary in the countryside. The words of St. Peter ring true about the origins of this community of believers, gathered together: "Come to him, a living stone, rejected by human beings, but chosen and precious in the sight of God, and, like living stones, let yourselves be built into a spiritual house to be a holy priesthood to offer spiritual sacrifices acceptable to God through Jesus Christ (2 Pt 2:4-5).

The Oratory of Corpus Christi is indeed a place of prayer and still gathers the faithful on special occasions to celebrate Mass and gather afterwards, continuing to live up to the name "Corpus Christi", The Body of Christ. Jesus is the Head, and we are the members, continuing the mission some two thousand years later, transmitted down the generations by simple folk who believe in God's love for them. Let us pray that the Spirit that keeps the Oratory alive will also bring priests to serve Her once again as a Parish.

Sincerely in the Crucified and Risen Savior, Jesus Christ the Lord,

Rev. James E. Starasinich
Rev. James E. Starasinich, Pastor
St. Joseph Parish, Owatonna
Christ the King Parish, Medford
Corpus Christi Oratory, Deerfield

PREFACE
By Ronald F. Eustice

My family moved to a farm in Deerfield Township in 1948. One of the very first actions that my parents took was to become members of Corpus Christ Catholic Church in Deerfield. A list of Corpus Christi parishioners for 1947 lists my father Donald F. Eustice as a parishioner but we did not actually move to the farm in Deerfield until early spring in 1948.

My father had a green Chevrolet 3/4 ton pickup truck; our only vehicle. Attending Mass at Corpus Christi was a priority and always a family affair. Mom, Dad, and three little boys crowded into that pickup truck until my sister was born in 1950. We never missed Mass but sometimes we were late and then we crowded into the "crying room," an annex attached to the church on the west side. The crying room was popular and always crowded.

Father Raymond Snyder was serving as Assistant Pastor at Sacred Heart Church in Waseca when he was assigned to serve as the pastor at Deerfield. He brought enthusiasm and excitement to a parish that had been closed from about 1935 until 1938. It was a sad day in 1942 when parishioners learned that Father Snyder had been re-assigned to parishes in Fountain and Wykoff, but there was rejoicing when he returned a year later. Father Harold Mountain replaced Father Snyder at Corpus Christi in 1952. He remained at Deerfield until 1968, the year I graduated from the University. Fr. Harold Mountain was a man of great integrity and an important influence on my life.

Those were formative years in my life. Every Saturday morning during the school year catechism classes were taught by the Dominican Sisters of Sinsinawa from Bethlehem Academy in Faribault. We learned about our Catholic faith from the Baltimore Catechism. In early June, the School Sisters of Notre Dame came to Deerfield for two weeks to teach religion and prepare us for the sacraments. Soon after I made my first communion, on June 14, 1953, the sisters prepared me to serve Mass. In those days, before Vatican II, the entire Mass, except for the readings and the homily was in Latin. I can still recite most of the Latin responses to the prayers. *Ad Deum qui laetificat etcetera*...I was an altar boy for the next ten years until I went off to college.

In those days, most of the parishioners lived on farms; small family farms usually with a small dairy herd, a few pigs and a small flock of chickens. The main crops were corn and soybeans. No one got rich financially but there was a great spiritual wealth. Everyone seemed to live comfortably and religion was an important part of our lives. Families were large; several very large with ten or more children.

Growing up on a farm was a unique experience. In those days, Deerfield seemed remote; a long way from everywhere. I often felt that I missed out on some of the experiences city kids had, but through the years I have begun to appreciate the useful things I learned on the farm which prepared me for later life. Corpus Christi parish, our one-room country school, 4-H club and FFA work helped to make me the person I am today. I feel fortunate and very blessed.

By Carla (Maas) Brady

It was by default that I came to be co-author of this book. I was on the food committee for the final celebration. The church closed in 2016, and the plan was for a history of the church to be captured in a "book" for our parish families. Names, checks (never cashed) and cash were taken at our final celebration for those that would be interested in the Corpus Christi history. It started out to be a compilation of the old church books, with memories from families that had attended over the years, and additional pictures from the final celebration. Renee Thompson from our parish began to work on the book, but due to circumstances the book was sidelined. She had done great work up to that point. Ron Eustice met with Jackie Dulas, who told him to contact Carla to see what happened with the book. This began the co-writing of the final book over the past couple of years. Thank you to all who contributed.

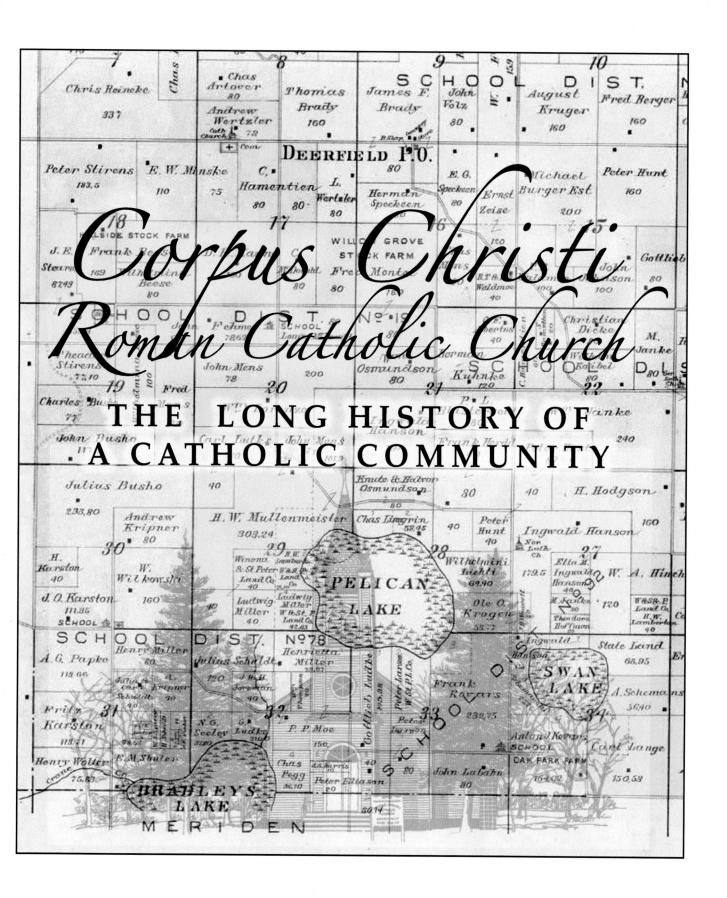

Corpus Christi
Roman Catholic Church

THE LONG HISTORY OF
A CATHOLIC COMMUNITY

Entrance to Corpus Christ Catholic Church on September 13, 2023. These doors have welcomed the Faithful Catholics for more than 160 years. (Photo credit: Jenna Sammon)

As we celebrate the history of Corpus Christi Parish, we are grateful to the pioneers who came to this area over a century ago. It is due to their courage, determination, faith and hard work through many decades that we are able to share this remarkable story.

CORPUS CHRISTI CATHOLIC CHURCH
DEERFIELD TOWNSHIP,
STEELE COUNTY, MINNESOTA

1856-2016

INTRODUCTION

Records show that Father George Keller of Faribault traveled to Deerfield to perform marriages as early as 1855. Such visits were infrequent since Father Keller also traveled as far as the Iowa border to meet the spiritual needs of Catholics in a wide area of Southern Minnesota.

In 1875 Father Francis Pribyl became the first resident pastor at Owatonna with Corpus Christi as a mission until 1879. His successor, Father Walter Raleigh, a convert, served the people until 1885. Father John Solnce then became pastor holding the office until 1889. It appears from the directory, that the faithful from Deerfield were attended from Faribault during the pastorate of Father Solnce at Owatonna. In 1891, Father John Pivo became the pastor of Sacred Heart, Owatonna, and of Corpus Christi. With the exception of the years 1894-1896, when it was attended by Father Patrick Kiernan of St Joseph's parish, Owatonna, Corpus Christi was served by Father Pivo until 1903. In that year Corpus Christi became attached to the Claremont parish.

The following pastors from Claremont served until 1938; Father John Meyers,1903-1909; Father James Cotter, 1909-1916; Father Thomas McCarthy 1916-1921; Father H. H. Forkenbrock, 1921-1923; Father Frank Schimek, 1923-1929; Father Robert Jennings, 1929-1932; Father John Misiak, 1932-1935; Father Alfred Frisch, 1935-1938.

During the first half century, the priests traveled to Deerfield by horse and buggy or on horse back and only came to Deerfield at intervals of weeks or months.

The priests came the day before and stayed overnight with one of the families. Later, a small house was erected north of the church where the priest stayed when in residence and was available for confessions, and other sacraments.

During the pastorate of Father McCarthy, 1916-1921, some improvements were made on the Corpus Christi church and the choir loft was added. The stained glass windows were probably installed around 1940. One of the windows lists A. J. Larscheid of Minneapolis is identified as the artist, no year is given.

In 1938 Bishop Francis Kelly of Winona was the guest speaker at the Knights of Columbus banquet in Waseca and that night he announced that Corpus Christi, Deerfield, was to be the mission of Sacred Heart, Waseca, and that Father Raymond Snyder then at St Hyacinth's, Owatonna, was to be the assistant pastor at Waseca. Pastor Msgr. James J. Treanor, then entrusted the care of the Deerfield congregation to Father Snyder, who offered the first Mass there on Pentecost Sunday June 5, 1938. Sister Assisi and the Junior Choir of Waseca sang at the Mass.

As soon as a sizable congregation was established, Father Snyder began the groundwork for renovating the church.

In 1938/39, under the supervision of Julius Kohlmeier, a contractor from Owatonna, the church was moved back north and west from the road right of way to higher ground. During moving of the church Mass was said in the cemetery.

In 1942, Father Snyder was appointed to a pastorate at Fountain and Wykoff in southeast Minnesota and and Father Alois Quillan, assistant at Waseca, attended Corpus Christi.

Six months later the parish of Christ the King, Medford, was established in 1943 and Father Snyder returned to assume the new pastorate of Medford and Deerfield until he was transferred in 1952.

Father Harold Mountain then was the pastor from 1952 until 1968 when Father Francis Glynn was appointed the pastor.

The new organ was purchased in 1968 and that same year parishioner William Francl made and donated the small outdoor grotto of the Blessed Virgin.

Father Warren Ryan succeeded Father Glynn in 1976 for one year and then Father John Cody became the pastor assisted by Father Raymond Snyder until the latter retired the following year. Father Cody was pastor of both parishes in 1979-1985. Fr. Ed Mountain came in 1985-89, followed by Fr. Milo Ernster, 1989-92 and Fr. Robert Herman until the parish was closed in 2016.

TABLE OF CONTENTS

Corpus Christi Church: 160 Years of Faith, Family & Friendships has been published during 2024 in the United States of America and printed by CreateSpace, a division of Amazon. Additional copies of this book can be purchased directly at Amazon.com or from Ronald F. Eustice, 7040 North Via Assisi, Tucson, Arizona 85704; phone: (612) 202-1016; email: reustice@gmail.com and website ronaldeusticepublications.com.

The Covers:
Front Cover: An aerial view of Corpus Christi church taken by Scott Cody with a drone.
Back Cover: The crucifix located in the Corpus Christi cemetery. Photo by Ronald Eustice (2022).

CHAPTER I

BEFORE THERE WAS A PLACE CALLED DEERFIELD

BEFORE THERE WAS A PLACE CALLED DEERFIELD

In 1803, the United States purchased 828,000 square miles of territory from France. This acquisition was known as the Louisiana Purchase.

In return for fifteen million dollars, or approximately eighteen dollars per square mile, The Louisiana Purchase extended United States sovereignty across the Mississippi River, nearly doubling the nominal size of the country.

The purchase included the portion of Minnesota west of the Mississippi River and included what was to become Steele County.

However, France only controlled a small fraction of this area, most of which was inhabited by Native Americans. Effectively, for the majority of the area, the United States bought the "preemptive" right to obtain "Indian" lands by treaty or by conquest, to the exclusion of other colonial powers. Thus began a complicated process involving a series of treaties as well as hostilities between settlers and the Native Americans who had occupied the land for many centuries.

In 1850 the area of what is now Deerfield was a vast land of heavy timber and rolling prairies inhabited by roving bands of Dakota (Sioux) Indians, large herds of buffalo, deer and other wildlife including wild turkeys and even passenger pigeons (now extinct).

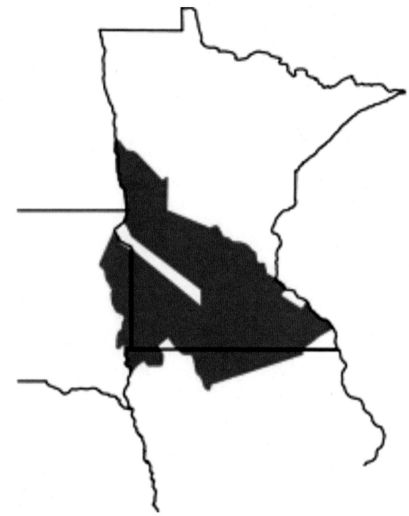

The area shown in red, almost 30,000 acres, was ceded by the Dakota Indians to the US Government in 1851 under terms established by the Treaties of Mendota and Traverse des Sioux.

In 1851, the four Dakota bands signed an agreement with the United States Government ceding their lands west of the Mississippi River in exchange for a reservation along the Minnesota River and annual payments.

The Treaty of the Traverse des Sioux, signed July 23, 1851, was an agreement with the Sisseton and Wahpeton Dakota. The Treaty of Mendota, signed August 5, 1851, was an agreement with the Mdewakanton and Wahpekute Dakota.

The Dakota chiefs were reluctant to sell their land, but felt as if they had little choice. If they had not agreed to sell, they might have lost their land and been left with nothing. Unfortunately for the Dakota, the terms of the treaties were rarely met or were unfavorable.

Wahpekute territory was largely located in the "big woods," a large strip of deciduous forest that originally covered about two-thirds of Rice County in dense forests of ash, basswood, elm, oak, and maple trees.

The Treaty of Traverse des Sioux (1851)

Painted around 1905 by Francis Millet, The Treaty of Traverse des Sioux, depicting the treaty signing, was inspired by Frank Blackwell Mayer's sketches of this historic event near present-day St. Peter, Minnesota, on July 23, 1851. This document, between the United States and the Sissitunwan and Wahpetunwan bands of the Dakota Oyate (Nation), was one of 12 treaties signed with the Dakota between 1805 and 1858.

Living in the "big woods" set the Wahpekute apart from many of the other Dakota people, who were more accustomed to living on the open plains. This land was ideal due to the intersection of the Straight and Cannon Rivers, which provided easy transportation for the tribe, and the abundance of small game for food.

This is where the name "Wahpekute" originated from, meaning "Shooters Among the Leaves." This was a reference to the forests of which the Wahpekute regularly traversed and hunted for game.

The Deerfield area included three small lakes, known as Pelican Lake, Swan Lake and Bradley Lake. all in the southern part of the township.

Although these lakes no longer exist due to drainage, changing climate and farming practices, for centuries they were a refuge for wild life and fish for the native peoples. Indian artifacts such as arrow heads have been found on the dry lake beds.

The land ceded in the Louisiana Purchase was more than 30 million acres and included nearly all of southern and western Minnesota, parts of Iowa and South Dakota. It is hard to imagine that Deerfield was once claimed by France

By 1849 there was great demand for the lands of the Dakota to be acquired by the United States. Dishonest traders often inflated their claims and found ways to obtain the money promised to the Dakota.

Some white colonists had begun squatting on unceded Dakota lands. A tide of western migration was close at hand, and the Dakota lands were attractive to land speculators.

While Steele County was part of the Louisiana Purchase, the United States only bought the "preemptive" right to obtain "Indian" lands by treaty or by conquest, It was not until the Treaty of Traverse des Sioux and the Treaty of Mendota in 1851 that the fertile lands of Deerfield and Steele County became available for settlement.

Steele County got its legal existence during the sixth session of the St. Paul legislature in 1855.

BEFORE THERE WAS A PLACE CALLED DEERFIELD

The Wahpekute Dakota people settled around what would later become Rice and Steele Counties, establishing semi-permanent villages around Cannon and Cedar Lakes. The area provided abundant food in the form of fish and wildlife.

Young Wahpekute Dakota Woman

Wahpekute Dakota Indians in Native Dress

Wahpekute Chieftains

Deerfield Creamery (1900).

The Deerfield Creamery Association was officially organized on March 17, 1898. Corpus Christi parishioner Peter Stirens was elected president and served as manager. The Deerfield Creamery began receiving cream on April 1, 1898. By September 1898, the creamery was receiving 7,211 pounds per day. About this time, James F. Brady Jr. also a Corpus Christi parishioner was hired as butter maker. In 1942, there were 54 farmers delivering cream to the Deerfield creamery and 148, 343 lbs. of butter was produced. Many of these were Corpus Christi parishioners. The Deerfield creamery closed in the fall of 1944. Up to that time, very hot water was poured into cream cans at the creamery and hauled to the Corpus Christi picnics and festivals to make coffee.

Arriving at Corpus Christi by horse and buggy for Sunday Mass.

CHAPTER II

FROM THE BEGINNING: DEERFIELD & CORPUS CHRISTI CATHOLIC CHURCH

Scene from Deerfield Township during the early 1900s.
(Edith (Kniefel) Hoffman is at far left. Her parents Edward and Ella (Hartle) Kniefel are holding the other horses).

In 1850, the area now known as Deerfield was a vast land of heavy timber and rolling prairies inhabited by roving bands of Dakota (Sioux) Indians, large herds of buffalo, deer, and other wildlife.

Deerfield Township was first created on April 6, 1857, and reorganized into its current configuration in the spring of 1858. The first claims in Steele County were made in the summer of 1853 in what later became Medford Township, and the first cabins were erected that fall. In 1854 more settlers came and by 1856 all parts of the county were inhabited.

The first settlement in Deerfield township was made May 12, 1855, by Edward McCartney, who came from Illinois with his family. He located on the northwest quarter of Section 8 in Deerfield Township, on land later owned by Louis and Lucille Pirkl, a short distance northeast of where Corpus Christi church is located.

There were no roads in this territory, only trails. Wolves howled about the log cabins at night, and it was very common to encounter native American peoples as they hunted and fished along Cannon Lake, the Straight River and Crane Creek.

Within a year or so later the following settlers came and staked claims: Andrew Wuertzler, Nicholas Stirens, Conrad Reineke, E Crandall, John and James Condon, E. J. Lilly, H. Hodgson, Arthur MacMillen, John H. Morse, Washington Morse, Charles Birch, Mr. Austin, L. Anderson, E.I. Stocker, Shephard Moses and others. In 1857 Deerfield Township had a population of 192 persons; in 1885 this had grown to 863.

Deerfield was attractive to European immigrants because of fertile soil, abundant timber and access to water; sometimes in excess. There was a wide belt of timber, bordering on Crane Creek, and more timber along the Cannon and Straight rivers on the east and to the north.

Times were very challenging during those early years. Supplies required a four-day trip to St. Paul or Hastings. Many times, corn or wheat was boiled and eaten without being ground. As more settlers arrived, they cleared land, built cabins, made dirt roads and established a school in 1857.

The history of Corpus Christi Catholic Parish dates to 1857, before Minnesota became a state and prior to the establishment of the Winona Catholic Diocese.

Father George Keller was the first Catholic priest to hold services in Steele County. Records held at Divine Mercy parish in Faribault show that Father Keller traveled to Deerfield as early as 1859. At the time he lived in Faribault and had charge of the mission from there south to the Minnesota/Iowa state line. Father Keller traveled by horseback and Mass was said in private homes until the construction of the church. It is thought the Corpus Christi church was built in 1869, but the property was not officially obtained until August 27, 1873, and recorded on July 10, 1874, by Rt. Rev. Thomas L. Grace, Bishop of St. Paul. It was transferred to the Winona Diocese May 19, 1919, and incorporated on July 20, 1923.

The first marriage in Deerfield Township was that of Stephen Birch to Priscilla Cole. The ceremony was performed in June 1858, at the residence of the bride's father, by Washington Morse, a justice of the peace.

On January 8, 1859, Fr. Keller performed the marriage of John Woods, a resident of East Prairie to Ellen Conlin of Deerfield. The witnesses were Charles Chagnon and Mary Hogan. Another entry at Divine Mercy in Faribault, dated June 26, 1859, records the marriage of John Thoman and Elizabeth Stiren, both of Deerfield. John Bauer and Leonard Rauchenmeyer served as witnesses and Father George Keller was the celebrant. The first school in the township was taught in the summer of 1857, by Miss Elizabeth Hodgson.

Indians were friendly until the Sioux Uprising in 1862 when most of the settlers fled the area for a few days until hostilities subsided.

Father Keller of Faribault exercised pastoral care of the few pioneer families in this area from 1865 until he was transferred to another parish in 1869. The Directory lists his successors at Faribault serving Deerfield. They were Father Clement Scheve, 1869 - 1870; Father Arthur Hurley, 1870 - 1874; and Father Lawrence Wiesler, 1874 - 1875.

The federal Homestead Act of 1862 gave 160 acres free to any head of a household, widow, or single person, who was at least 21 years old and a citizen of the U.S., on the condition that the homesteader would improve the land (with crops and a minimum 12' x 14' dwelling) and reside on it for a minimum of five years. The homesteader also had the option of purchasing the acreage at $1.25 an acre after living there for six months.

The Homestead Act initially applied only to land that had been surveyed, but in 1880 non-surveyed public land was also included. Most land available to homesteaders was located in Minnesota, South Dakota, North Dakota, Nebraska, and Kansas because the majority of public land in states east of the Mississippi River had already been transferred to private ownership by 1862. The free land offered by the Homestead Act was a great enticement for settlers to move west to Minnesota and the Dakota Territory from states farther east.

The early Deerfield families were subsistence farmers. They grew just enough food to feed themselves and their farm animals, with some left over to trade for things they needed. It was a hard life, with little money, meager tools, crude homes, and few household goods. Without roads or motorized vehicles, the one reliable means of transportation was to ride horseback or hitch the horse to a buggy or wagon to accommodate the family. The settler's priority was to plow a few acres of open land to get seed in the ground followed by clearing the wooded land to make more farmable acres.

The major crop planted in Steele County before 1875 was wheat. It did not require much money and was easy to grow. Despite its appeal, wheat had its risks. It depleted nitrogen from the soil very quickly. Yield could vary greatly from year to year.

By the late 1850s, competition from farmers in Iowa and Wisconsin and low-quality crops brought the price of wheat down. Disaster struck in the 1860s, when tiny insects known as chinch bugs began devouring Minnesota wheat crops. Chinch bugs are tiny, hard-to-see insects that cause crop damage which can often be confused with drought stress.

Farming in the Steele County began changing in the 1880s. Wheat farming was on the way out. Faced with the many challenges of growing wheat, farmers began experimenting with alternative crops. Feed grains, rather than cash crops, were better suited to Minnesota's climate and soil.

EARLY HISTORY OF CORPUS CHRISTI PARISH

During the early years farmers increased their herds of livestock. The number of dairy cows increased quickly. By 1899, more than 90 percent of Minnesota farms raised dairy cows. By 1900, Steele County had 24 creameries and was considered the "Butter Capital of the World."

Andrew Wuertzler (1821-1900) a native of Bavaria, moved his family to Deerfield from Elgin, Illinois about 1850 and homesteaded the land on which Corpus Christi Church is located. The site for the church was donated by Andrew Wuertzler. The property for the cemetery was donated by John and Veronica Loemer. The church cost $300 to build and it was most difficult to raise the money. Logs were hewn and the interior was not finished. It is believed that Corpus Christi Church was built in 1869 but the property was officially obtained by the Diocese of Winona on August 27, 1873, and recorded on July 10, 1874 by R. Rev. Thomas L. Grace Bishop of St.Paul.

The first priest to say Mass in Corpus Christi church was Fr. Slevin who came from Faribault by buggy or on horseback. A small house was erected just north of the church, where the priest could spend the night. He would then be available for confessions, baptisms, marriages etc.

In 1875, Father Francis Pribyl became the first resident pastor at Owatonna with Corpus Christi the mission until 1879. His successor, Father Walter Raleigh, a convert from the Episcopalian faith, served the people until 1885. Father John Solnce then became pastor holding the office until 1889.

It appears however, from the old parish directory, that the faithful from Deerfield were attended from Faribault during the pastorate of Father Solnce. In 1891, Father John Pivo became the pastor of Sacred Heart, Owatonna, and of Corpus Christi. With the exception of the years 1894-1896 when it was attended by Father Patrick Kiernan of St Joseph's parish, Owatonna, Corpus Christi was served by Father Pivo until 1903. In that year it was attached to the Claremont parish. The following pastors from Claremont served until 1938; Father John Meyers, (1903-1909;) Father James Cotter, (1909-1916); Father Thomas McCarthy (1916-1921); Father H. H. Forkenbrock, (1921-1923); Father Frank Schimek, (1923-1929); Father Robert Jennings, (1929-1932;) Father John Misiak, (1932-1935); Father Alfred Frisch, (1935-1938). During the first fifty years most of the priests traveled by horse and buggy and only arrived at intervals of weeks or months.

During the pastorate of Father McCarthy, (1916-1921), some improvements were made on the Corpus Christi church and the belfry was added. The stained-glass windows may have been installed at this time, too.

In 1938 Bishop Kelly of Winona was the guest speaker at the annual Knights of Columbus banquet in Waseca and that night he announced that Corpus Christi, Deerfield, was to be the mission of Sacred Heart, Waseca, and that Father Raymond Snyder of St Hyacinth parish, Owatonna, was to be the assistant pastor at Waseca.

Pastor Msgr. James J. Treanor of Waseca, then entrusted the care of the Deerfield congregation to Father Snyder, who offered the first Mass there on Pentecost Sunday, June 5, 1938. Sister Assisi directed the Junior Choir of Waseca which sang at the Mass.

In 1942 Father Snyder was appointed pastor at Fountain and Wykoff and Father Alois Quillan, assistant at Waseca, then served Corpus Christi. Six months later the parish of Christ the King, Medford, was established and Father Snyder returned to assume the new pastorate of Medford and Deerfield until 1952. Father Harold Mountain then was the pastor from 1952 until 1968 when Father Francis Glynn was appointed the pastor. The new organ was purchased in 1968 and that same year William Francl made and donated the small outdoor grotto of the Blessed Virgin.

Father Warren Ryan succeeded Father Glynn in 1976 for one year and then Father John Cody became the pastor assisted by Father Raymond Snyder until the latter retired the following year.

The village of Deerfield no longer exists but by 1897 included a post office, blacksmith shop, creamery, and store. The Deerfield milk skimming station was built in November 1893 in Section 9 of Deerfield Township by the Golden Rule Creamery Association. James F. Brady Sr., a Corpus Christi parishioner, gave one-acre of land where the creamery was built. The creamery began receiving cream on April 1, 1898.

By September 1898, the creamery was receiving 7,211 pounds per day. About this time, James F. Brady Jr. was hired as butter maker. Butter from the creamery was entered into competition at the 1898 New York State Fair and received a score of 97.5. Butter production in 1942, was 148,343 pounds. There were 54 patrons delivering cream to the Deerfield Creamery which was closed in 1944.

Early Corpus Christi parishioners included Irish families such as Brady, Condon, Fitzpatrick, Hackett, Morgan and O'Neill families, as well as German speaking families from Bavaria, Prussia, Bohemia and Alsace-Lorraine. Many of the early priests serving Corpus Christi were fluent in German and Czech as well as English.

Although the Diocese of Winona came into existence in 1889, it was not until May 19, 1919, that the property was officially obtained by the Archdiocese of St. Paul and it was incorporated on July 20, 1923. Corpus Christi functioned as a mission church until 1935. Corpus Christi was mostly inactive as a parish during the Depression from about 1935 until 1938.

On its simplest level, the Great Depression was an economic crisis. Between 1929 and 1933, the average family in the United States saw its income drop by more than one third. The national jobless rate, which stood at about three percent in October of 1929, reached at least twenty-five percent less than four years later. The numbers in Minnesota and Steele County were comparable to other parts of the country.

When Father Snyder was assigned the mission of Corpus Christi, he contacted all of the Catholics in the area urging them to attend it. Mrs. Lawrence (Easter) Kvasnicka tells of the first time they attended mass there, Leo Mullenmaster Sr. swept down the cobwebs before serving the mass which was attended by about a half dozen families.

People were reluctant to leave their parishes for the uncertain future of Corpus Christi, but Father Snyder's persistence paid off and gradually more and more families began to attend Mass there regularly. A news article from 1938 reported that 43 families had become members of Corpus Christi by June 1938.

As soon as a sizable congregation was established, Father Snyder began the groundwork for renovating the church. Under the supervision of Julius Kohlmeier, a contractor from Owatonna, the church was moved back north and west from the road right of way to higher ground. Note that Julius Kohlmeier had lost a leg in an accident. While he couldn't move mountains, he still could move churches. The basement was dug by using horses and a walking plow to break up the soil which was then removed with a scraper.

The church was moved onto the new foundation by winching it with horses on a stump puller. The frame of the church, cut from hand-hewn logs, was crooked and caused considerable difficulty by crushing some of the blocks in the foundation and it had to be jacked up and redone several times. All of the work was done by volunteer parish labor and some of the men spent the entire summer working on the project.

A wood burning stove was installed in the basement to replace the big stove that had stood under the choir loft with a stove pipe extending to the front of the church.

The janitors of those early years, Peter Stirens and Henry Hager, had their work cut out for them getting the furnace stoked up in advance of Sunday morning Mass.

A regular event in those years was the wood-cutting bee to stock pile enough wood to supply the need for the coming year. A wood shed stood directly north of the church until the oil-burning furnace was installed in the 1960s. It was replaced by a gas furnace in the early 1980s which is in use today. In 1976, the custodial duties were taken care of by Sylvester Dulas.

During the renovation of 1939, the interior of the church was redone with wall and floor tile, the pews refinished, kneeling benches added, electric lights installed, and on Christmas Eve, 1939, the first midnight Mass was offered in the newly completed church. The weather was perfect, and the large crowd not only filled the church but the church grounds as well. A brightly lighted Christmas tree was placed on the altar.

Once the church itself was finished attention focused on the lawn. It was graded, seeded, and extensive landscaping was done under the supervision of Father Snyder's brothers who owned a nursery in Charles City, Iowa.

In 1938, Father Snyder began an intensive campaign to raise funds to pay for remodeling the church by asking someone to host a parish "picnic." Mr. and Mrs. Wm. Kvasnicka offered their place thinking of an ordinary picnic. To their surprise, it proved to be a huge fund raiser. Tables were set up under the big trees in their spacious yard, equipment borrowed from wherever available. A bountiful chicken dinner was served by the ladies and all types of games and gadgets were employed to entice spending.

There were games of chance, raffles, trap shooting, even airplane rides, a barn dance and free movies to keep the crowd there. Hundreds of people attended, and a tidy sum was realized. After it was over the exhausted workers took time only to put the leftover food away leaving the clean-up for the next day. Mrs. Kvasnicka had shut her chickens up during the picnic, but being a hot night, she opened the hen house door before going to bed. The next morning, she looked out to see her chickens walking among the floral bouquets on the white linen tablecloths eating the crumbs off the tables.

Mr. William Kvasnicka died the following spring, so they did not care to have another picnic and it was held in Mullenmaster's pasture. Just after dinner a tornado suddenly swooped down beside the picnic site sweeping the dishes off the table and creating a havoc that abruptly ended the picnic. In 1940 it was decided that it was too risky weatherwise to hold such a large affair in the open, so a circus tent was rented from a business out of Mason City, Iowa.

For the next five years the picnic was again held under the big tent on the Kvasnicka farm.

In 1942 Father Snyder was appointed to a pastorate at Fountain and Wykoff and Father Alois Quillan, assistant at Waseca, attended Corpus Christi. Six months later the parish of Christ the King, Medford, was established in 1943 and Father Snyder returned to assume the new pastorate of Medford and Deerfield until 1952.

In 1946, the parish picnic was moved to the church grounds and the tent set up on the west side of the church. This was not satisfactory due to lack of space. The next year an area was cleared east of the cemetery where electricity was installed and a well dug beside the church.

The picnics continued to grow and provided the major source of income for the parish until they were discontinued in 1951.

Every man, woman and child was pressed into service at these picnics and outside help was welcomed. A typical list of items each family was expected to donate included six fried chickens, dressing from two loaves of bread, one peck of peeled potatoes, two quarts of gravy, two cans of corn, two cans cranberries, one lb. of butter, one quart of cream, one pint jam, one bunch of celery or carrots, five pounds of tomatoes, one quart of pickles, five pies, a cake, and articles for the bazaar. Most of these picnics were held during World War Two when rationing was in effect and supplies had to be eked out of allotments. Three or four days of advance preparation were required as well as clean up afterwards.

The coffee was made in ten-gallon milk cans by putting in cheese cloth bags and taken to the Deerfield creamery until 1944, where the cans were filled with boiling water. The comradeship and teamwork engendered by these picnics remains in the parish to this day.

In addition to the picnics, activities included ice cream socials on the cemetery lawn where the ice cream was made from real cream in freezers cranked by hand. There were contests in which a man from the north and the south parish boundaries competed to see who would get their ice cream frozen first. Those not competing often played soft ball while they waited. The frozen delicacy was served with berries in season, with cake or pie.

For many years an outdoor Corpus Christi procession was held on the feast day of the Corpus Christi, with the people singing hymns and praying as the Blessed Sacrament was carried to three altars, ending with Benediction, a guest speaker, and then a social hour.

Rosary groups were active during World War II with the north, south, east and west groups meeting in homes weekly to pray the rosary for peace. May Crowning was another annual event. The Corpus Christi Parish activities included study clubs, the annual Christmas program with Santa and treats, card parties, Bingo, pot luck dinners, the Knights of Columbus picnic, mission breakfasts, etc, some to raise money and some purely social.

An active sewing group made over two hundred quilts plus many other articles for the missions for many years. There were painting bees, lawn raking bees, and woodcutting bees in the church woodlot for winter fuel.

In the early 1940s, several men donated their spare time during the winter finishing off the basement ceiling and walls to cover the rough logs and pipes and building kitchen cabinets.

In 1943 the Medford parish of Christ the King was established, and many members of Corpus Christi transferred to the new parish. They were missed, but the two parishes maintained a close relationship through the years.

After the convent was built in Medford, the Notre Dame Sisters arrived to help with the religious education of the young people and assisted with other parish activities.

The Cemetery:
The Corpus Christi cemetery land was acquired at the same time as the church land in 1873 but nothing was done and graves were dug in a haphazard fashion, most were unmarked, and no records kept for over sixty years during which time the lots were given away. In 1953 Bishop Fitzgerald of Winona required all church cemeteries in the diocese be platted, a cemetery association formed, and financial records sent to the chancery. The Articles of Association for Corpus Christi Cemetery were signed in March 1954. At that time the old part of the cemetery was set aside, and new lots were platted

In 1958, William Francl made and donated the small outdoor grotto of the Blessed Virgin which stands just west of the church entrance.

on the west side. The grounds have been enlarged and are well kept. In 1950 an altar and large crucifix were erected which added much to the cemetery nestled against a wooded background. The statues were purchased in 1951 for $358.00.

Mrs. Leo Sammon (Margaret Fitzpatrick) was baptized with her twin sister Agnes Fitzpatrick at the church in April 1907, and continued to be a faithful member until her death in 1981. She tells of torrential rain the night before her baptism that made the mud roads so impassable that her chosen sponsors could not get to church, so her father picked sponsors from the few people that did get there.

Thomas Swintek and Margaret Bruzant were the first to be married in Corpus Christi after it was reorganized; Lawrence Kvasnicka and Easter Pelky, the second in 1939. Leo Mullenmaster Jr. was the first baby baptized and Billy Kvasnicka the second.

Credit must be given to the faithful custodians, Peter Stirens (1938 - 1950), Henry Hager (1951 - 1975) and Sylvester Dulas (1976-2006), Joel and Jackie Dulas (through 2008, Deb and Paul Sontheimer (2009 -2016) who unlocked the doors, kept the church warm, shoveled the walks, mowed the grass, trimmed the shrubs and kept a watchful eye on every detail. Jean Larson cared for the altar linens.

HARPER'S WEEKLY.

A JOURNAL OF CIVILIZATION.

Vol. XI.—No. 563.] NEW YORK, SATURDAY, OCTOBER 12, 1867.

Well before roads were built or motorized vehicles invented, the only reliable means of transportation were to walk or travel by horse and buggy or ride horse back. Early priests traveled on horseback to Deerfield from Faribault, Owatonna and Claremont. The image above appeared on the cover of Harper's Weekly on October 12, 1867 which is about the same time Corpus Christi was established.

During the visits which were weeks or months apart, the priests would stay in the family's home, hear confessions, baptize infants, conduct marriage ceremonies and funerals or memorial services.

Records show that Father George Keller of Faribault traveled to Deerfield to perform marriages as early as 1855. Such visits were infrequent since Father Keller also traveled as far as the Iowa border to meet the spiritual needs of Catholics in a wide area of Southern Minnesota.

In 1857 Deerfield Township had a population of 192 persons; in 1885 this had grown to 863. In 1875 Father Francis Pribyl became the first resident pastor at Owatonna with Corpus Christi as a mission until 1879. His successor, Father Walter Raleigh, a convert, served the people until 1885. Father John Solnce then became pastor until 1889.

It appears from the directory, that the faithful from Deerfield were attended from Faribault during the pastorate of Father Solnce at Owatonna. In 1891, Father John Pivo became the pastor of Sacred Heart, Owatonna, and of Corpus Christi.

Considering the vast area and the sparse population, we must assume that attending Mass and the Sacraments was irregular at best. Put your imagination to work as you visualize a few families coming together for the awaited arrival of a priest. Religious formation had to be completed in a short span of time. Now that we are well into the 21st century, we might do well to copy their zeal and determination.

Traveling priests, also known as "circuit riders," were tasked with overseeing the spiritual needs of Catholics in a specific area. Circuit rider priests would travel by horseback or in a buggy in between each site, stay a few days with a family in each place and then travel to the next location.

Chapels in the home would come in various forms from using the hall or hallway on the ground floor depending on how the house was designed, to transforming the parlor into a temporary chapel, to having a special room dedicated to serving as a chapel if the house was large enough.

DEERFIELD TOWNSHIP PLAT MAP (1879)

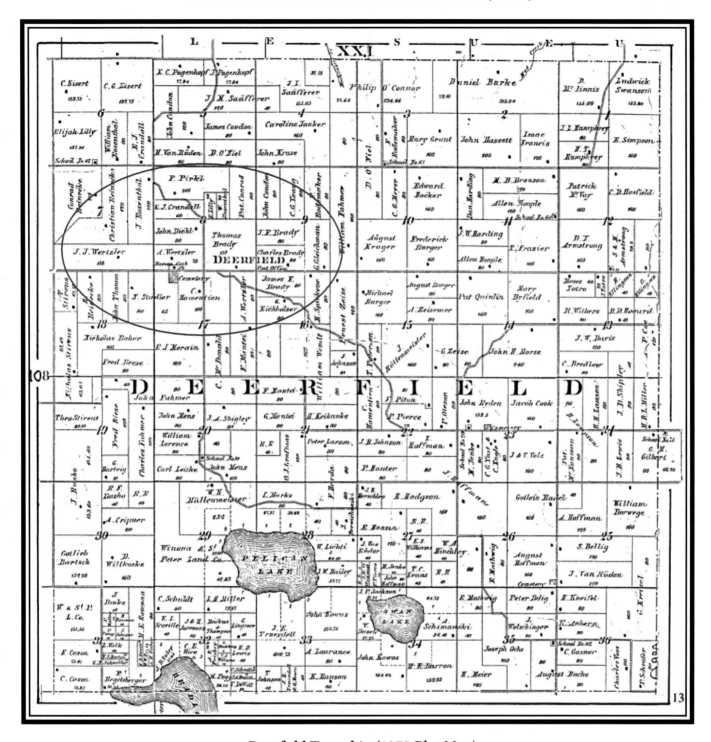

Deerfield Township (1879 Plat Map)

Construction began in 1869 on the present Corpus Christi church building. The site for the church was donated by Andrew and Mary Wertzler, Bavarian immigrants who came to Deerfield from Elgin, Illinois in 1850 and homesteaded the land. The plot for cemetery was donated by John and Veronica Loehmer on November 14, 1873 to the Archdiocese of St. Paul for the sum of $1.00. Mrs. Loemer's daughter was Anna Schmidt/Smith Stadler, wife of Nickolas Stadler. The Corpus Christi property was officially obtained from the Wertzlers by the Archdiocese of St. Paul on August 27, 1873 and recorded July 10, 1875 by Rt. Reverend Thomas L. Grace, Bishop of St. Paul.

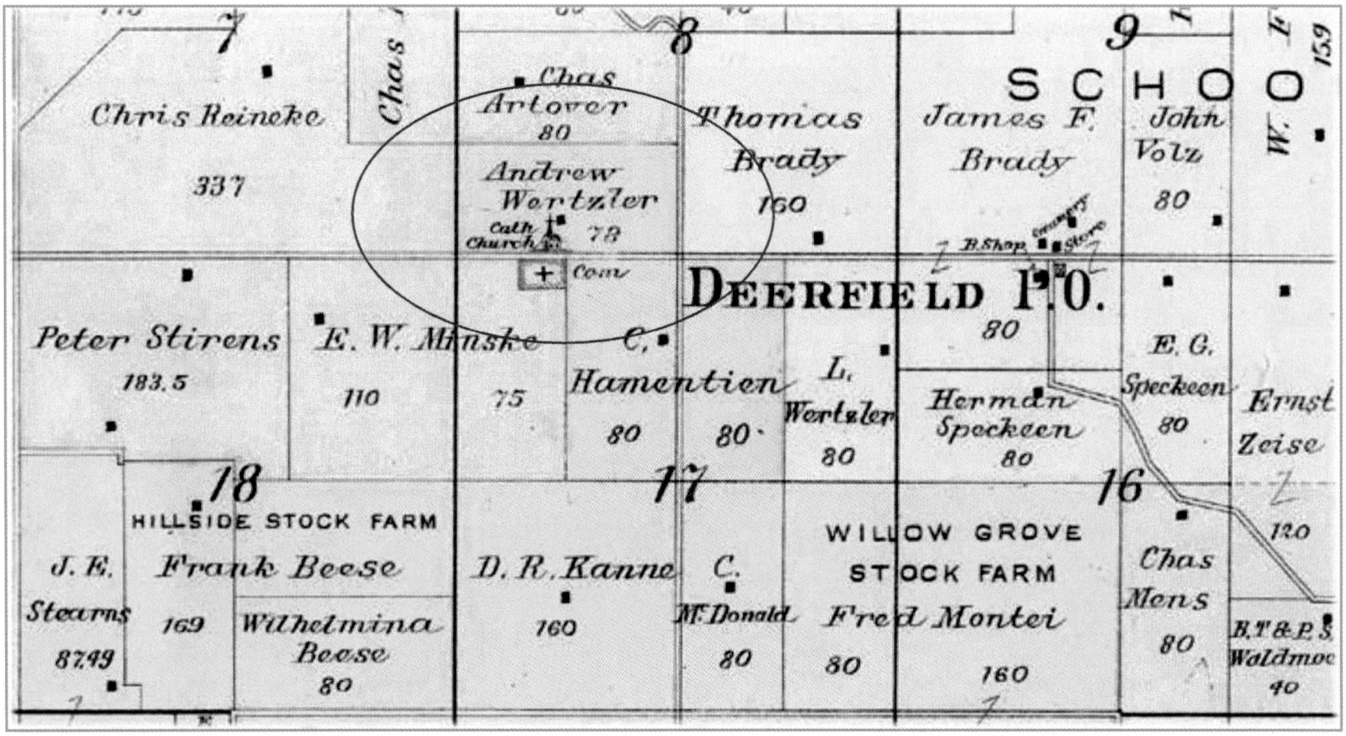

The map shows a plat with sections numbered 7, 8, 9, 18, 17, 16. Named landowners include:

- Chris Reineke 337
- Chas Artover 80
- Andrew Wertzler 78 (Cath Church)
- Thomas Brady 160
- James F. Brady
- John Volz 80
- S C H O O... (W)
- Peter Stirens 183.5
- E. W. Minske 110
- C. Hamentien 75, 80
- L. Wertzler 80
- Herman Speckeen 80
- E. G. Speckeen 80
- Ernst Zeise
- DEERFIELD P.O. 80
- HILLSIDE STOCK FARM
- J. E. Stearns 8749, 169
- Frank Beese
- Wilhelmina Beese 80
- D. R. Kanne 160
- C. McDonald 80
- WILLOW GROVE STOCK FARM
- Fred Montei 80, 160
- Chas Mens 80
- B.T.&P.S. Waldmoe 40
- 120

The village of Deerfield no longer exists but by 1897 included a post office, blacksmith shop, creamery and store. The Deerfield cream skimming station was built on land donated by James F. Brady in November 1893 in Section 9 of Deerfield Township. The land for the church was donated by Andrew Wertzler in Section 8 in 1873.

Marion W. Savage, owner of the race horse Dan Patch, planned an electric railroad that would connect the Twin Cities to his farm and stables south of the Minnesota River. Savage purchased Dan Patch for $62,000 (a fortune in 1902), then lavishly promoted his equine protégé.

Savage and his backers chose 54th and Nicollet, at the time the Richfield-Minneapolis border, as the starting point for the new railroad. Minneapolis' Nicollet streetcar line ended at that spot, so passengers could easily transfer to the adjacent Dan Patch system.

Its owners named their new firm the Minneapolis, St. Paul, Rochester and Dubuque Electric Traction Company, but no one used the full name.

Instead, they preferred the nickname "Dan Patch Line." Construction began in 1908, eventually reaching Northfield in late 1910. Grading began on an extension to Faribault in 1911. The proposed line would extend from Faribault to Deerfield (as shown on the map on the facing page) and then branch to Owatonna and Waseca. The company never secured an entrance into Faribault and abandoned the project.

Life would be very different if the line had reached Deerfield as a destination. The Dan Patch Line's original intention was for transporting passengers while freight mostly consisted of produce from local farms going to markets. That changed when the Dan Patch Electric Line went into receivership and the Minneapolis Northfield & Southern Railway (MN&S) took over in 1918.

The proposed line would have extended from Faribault to Deerfield.

20

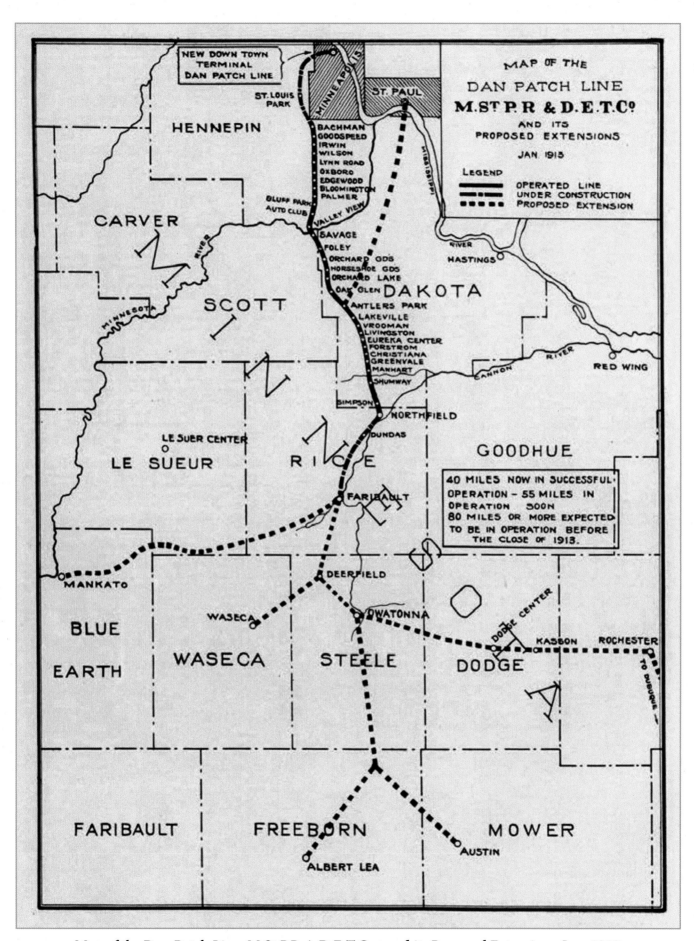

Map of the Dan Patch Line, M.St.P.R & D.E.T.Co., and its Proposed Extensions, Jan. 1913.
(Perry-Castañeda Library Map Collection).

21

TYPICAL PIONEER FARMS IN SOUTHERN MINNESOTA (c1890-1910)

Deerfield Creamery and the James F. Brady Farm, Deerfield, (c1900).
(This beautiful painting is by Evelyn (Maas) Brady, a talented artist and wife of James M. Brady.)
The Deerfield Creamery was located on the James F. Brady farm and began receiving cream on April 1, 1898.
By September 1898, the creamery was receiving 7,211 pounds per day. About this time, James F. Brady Jr. was
hired as butter maker. Butter produced by James F. Brady competed with the best butter makers in contests in
Steele County and throughout Minnesota. In 1939, he was one of 100 farmers awarded a trip to the World's
Fair in New York City as a guest of the Firestone Company. In 1942, there were 54 farmers delivering cream to
the Deerfield creamery and 148, 343 lbs. of butter was produced. Many of these were Corpus Christi parishio-
ners. The Deerfield creamery closed in the fall of 1944.

A typical Southern Minnesota farm (c1900).

CHAPTER III

SOME EARLY
CORPUS CHRISTI FAMILIES

ANDREAS "ANDREW" & MARY EVA (BRAUN) WUERZLER/WERTZLER

Andrew Wuerzler/Wertzler was born November 27, 1821 in Bavaria. He first emigrated to Illinois and moved to Deerfield, Minnesota in 1856 and homesteaded on Section 8 on January 3, 1863. At the time of Andrew's birth, his father, Michael Wuerzler, was 23 and his mother, Catharine Elizabeth Lang, was 22. He married Mary Braun/Brown, daughter of Andrew and Laura (Lang) Braun (whose mother or grandmother's maiden name may have been Schlaster) who also arrived from Germany in April of 1865. Mary Braun/Brown was born in 1819. Andrew and Mary were the parents of six children, two sons and four daughters with Mary Eva Braun. Mary died in 1878. Andrew then married Barbara Eberle Smyde on December 22, 1882, in Steele County. He was serving as the postmaster in Deerfield during the 1870s and 80s. He died December 29, 1900 in Deerfield Township, having lived a long life of 79/80 years.

Andrew Wuerzler Obituary (1900)

Andrew Wertzler (1821-1900)
& Mary (Braun) Wertzler (1819-1878)
Early Burial at Corpus Christi Cemetery

Mariane (Braun) Wertzler (1820-1878) headstone.

24

ANDREW & MARIA EVA (BRAUN) WERTZLER FAMILY

Leonard Wertzler
(1858-1938)

Mary Eva Wertzler
(1853-1934)

Mary Eva Wertzler was born on January 3, 1853, in Illinois. She married John Peter Becker on 2-1874 at St. Lawrence Church in Faribault. They lived at Medford and later moved to Faribault where she died on May 18, 1934 at the age of 81, and was buried there.

Leonard Wertzler was born in February 1858 in Deerfield Township. He married Johanna Hennessy on November 23, 1897. She was born in Wisconsin on January 23, 1861, her father being born in Ireland and her mother in Indiana. Her mother died of stomach cancer. Johanna died on October 23, 1913. Leonard Wertzler later married the former Rose Glodfelty who had three children: Mary (May), Henrietta and Joseph. Mary married Arley Rauchman and died giving birth to a son on September 23, 1939 at St. Lucas in Faribault. Henrietta married Arthur Fratske of Faribault.

Leonard farmed in Deerfield until his retirement in 1923. He then resided at 727 1st Ave. N.W., Faribault until his death on July 20, 1938. He and his first wife, Johanna Hennessey are buried in Corpus Christi Cemetery at Deerfield.

Johanna Wertzler (1861-1913). (Wife of Leonard Wertzler)

Rosina Marischka, wife of Theodore Stirens.

Standing is Caroline A. Stirens (Mrs. Pierce Hackett); Seated is Rosina Marischka Stirens, wife of Theodore Stirens. Seated on chair arm is Rose Mary Hackett, daughter of Pierce and Caroline (Stirens) Hackett. (Inscription on back of picture dated June 10 1910).

SOME STIRENS FAMILY MARKERS AT CORPUS CHRISTI CEMETERY

Theodore Stirens Headstone
Corpus Christi Cemetery, Deerfield Township

Theodore Stirens was born in Prussia May 18, 1820. He married Rosina Mariscka, a native of Bohemia about 1861. Theodore Stirens died at Deerfield May 11, 1906 at age 86 and is buried in Corpus Christi Cemetery. Theodore and Rosina were the parents of at least eleven children.

Maria Stiren (1873-1888)
Inscription in German Reads:
Hier Ruhet (Here Rests) Maria Stiren
Geboren (Born): 13 Januar(y) 1873
Gestorben (Died): 21 November 1888

Ambrose Stirens
(May 16, 1910- May 25, 1914)

Gertrude Stirens
July 17, 1905- August 15, 1905)

Peter & Anna (Fait) Stirens

Peter Stirens was born February 16, 1866, in Deerfield Township. He had a twin brother John Joseph. Their father, Theodore, was 45, and their mother, Roseanna, was 33. Peter married Anna Fait on November 24, 1897, in Waterville, Minnesota.

Anna Fait was born on June 7, 1879, in Austria and arrived in the US with her family at New York on May 31, 1881 from Bremen. Peter and Anna had eight children in 13 years. All of the children were born in Deerfield. Peter Stirens Sr. died on December 11, 1938, in Deerfield at the age of 72. Anna died October 30, 1942 at Deerfield. Both Peter and Anna are buried in Corpus Christi Cemetery.

PETER & ANNA (FAIT) STIRENS FAMILY

Peter & Anna (Fait) Stirens Family
Front row: Peter Sr., Sylvester Lawrence, Margaret P., Ambrose L., Anna (Fait).
Back row: Peter Leo, Theodore Vincent, Joseph John.

The large barn on Peter Stirens' farm near Deerfield was destroyed by fire Monday afternoon at about 3 o'clock. Mr. and Mrs. Stirens were in Owatonna at the time and on their return it was to their great sorrow that not only the barn and its contents burned, but that their youngest son, a child about four years old, had perished in the flames. The little fellow was left at home with two older boys, and while they were doing some duties about the farm the barn got on fire. It is not known how the fire got started or how the little boy happened to be in the barn. The remains of the boy, when recovered were badly burned, almost beyond recognition. The funeral was held at the house on Tuesday afternoon. A large amount of hay and several head of stock were also burned. *Rice County Journal (June 3, 1914).*

Josie Fait, sister of Anna (Fait) Stirens and Ray Arndt. son of Bertha (Fait) Arndt, also Anna's sister. (Photo taken at the Peter & Anna Stirens farm.)

THEODORE STIRENS

Funeral services for Theodore Stirens, 78, were held Monday, August 17, 1953 at 9 a. m. at the St. Lawrence Church, Faribault with the Rev. F. L. Tschann officiating. Burial was made at the St. Lawrence Cemetery. Mr. Stirens passed away at his home, 1336 Central Avenue, Thursday evening, August 13, following a two months illness. Pallbearers were Joseph Stirens, Jr., and Joseph Stirens, Sr., of Owatonna, and John Hackett, George Hackett, John Hartmann, and Frank Carey.

Theodore J. Stirens was born in Deerfield Township, Steele County, November 11, 1876, the son of Theodore and Rose Mariska Stirens. On December 2, 1922, he was united in marriage to Genevieve Garske, who survives him.

His father, mother, four brothers and five sisters preceded him in death. Mr. Stirens has lived in Faribault for the past 31 years and has operated a farm in Deerfield Township during that time. Attending the funeral services from away were: Mr. and Mrs. Ernst Roemhildt and Frank Kaupa, Elysian; Mr. and Mrs. L. E. Seewald, Mankato; Mr. and Mrs. Joseph Stirens and son, Owatonna; Mr. and Mrs. Martin Hackett, St. Paul; Mr. and Mrs. Ceril Mariska and Mr. and Mrs. Idan Haugen and family, Minneapolis; Mr. and Mrs. Sylvester Stirens, Waterville; Mr. and Mrs. Theodore Stirens, Morristown; Mrs. Mildred Stirens and family, Deerfield; and Mr. and Mrs. Bernard Menz, Fairmont.

Faribault Daily News (August 1953)

Stirens Family Marker
Deerfield Cemetery

Anna Fait was born on June 7, 1879, in Austria. She married Peter Stirens (1866-1938) and died October 30, 1942 at Deerifield.

31

Nicholas Martin Stirens was born on October 1, 1868, in Deerfield Township, Steele County. His father, Theodore, was 48 and his mother, Roseanna Marischka, was 36. He had four brothers and seven sisters. He married Harriet Bernice Gale on January 18, 1898 at Kilkenny, Le Sueur County. Nicolas Stirens died on August 1, 1937, in Minneapolis at the age of 68.

J. J. FOSTER, Montgomery, Minn.

Nicolas Sterins
Born: Oct. 1, 1868; Deerfield
Died: Aug. 1, 1937; Minneapolis

Susana & Caroline Stirens

33

CAROLINE STIRENS & PIERCE HACKETT

Caroline (Stirens) Hackett
Caroline (Stirens) Hackett was born October 14, 1871 at Deerfield. She died May 13, 1947 at age 75.

Pierce & Caroline (Stirens) Hackett

CAROLINE (STIRENS) HACKETT
1871-1947)

Funeral services for Mrs. Caroline Hackett, for 27 years a resident of Faribault who passed away at St. Mary's hospital in Minneapolis on Tuesday, May 13, were held this morning in the Immaculate Conception church with the pastor, the Rev. J. P. Foley officiating at 10 o'clock. Interment was made in Calvary cemetery. The pallbearers were four grandsons, George, Leo, Francis and Patrick Hackett and Francis and Harlan Pettipiece.

Caroline Stirens was born on October 14, 1871, the daughter of Theodore and Rose Stirens at Deerfield, Steele County. She spent her young lifetime in the Deerfield community where she attended the rural schools.

On June 11, 1895, she was united in marriage to Pierce Hackett at Owatonna. They made their home on a farm in Blooming Grove Township, in Waseca County where they resided for 24 years. In 1920, they moved to Faribault where they made their home. Mr. Hackett passed away 16 years ago, and she continued to make her home here until a short time ago when she was taken to Minneapolis for care after she became ill.

Mrs. Hackett is survived by four children, John and Theodore of Faribault, Martin of St. Paul, and Rose of Minneapolis, besides six grandsons. Two grandsons, Joe and John Hackett, are in the service of the United States armed forces and were unable to be present for the funeral service. She is also survived by one brother, Thomas Stirens of Faribault. Relatives and friends from out of town attending the service here today were Mrs. Sadie McNamara, Van Houdt, N. D.; Mr. and Mrs. Martin Hackett, St. Paul; Cyril Mariska, St. Paul, and Mr. and Mrs. Bernard Mentz of Owatonna.
Faribault Daily News (May 16, 1947)

Daniel & Susanna (Stirens) Devine

SUSAN (STIRENS) DEVINE OBITUARY

Mrs. Dan Devine died Sunday morning at the age of 72 years at the Walter Shannon home north of Waterville, where she had been cared for for some time. She formerly lived on a farm east of Elysian. She is survived by her husband. The funeral was held Tuesday morning from Holy Trinity Catholic church in Waterville. *Elysian Enterprise, August 11, 1944.*

*Note: Susanna Stirens, daughter of Theodore and Rosina (**Marischka**) Stirens, was born June 10, 1863 in Deerfield and passed away August 6, 1944 at Waterville. Susanna and Daniel/David Devine are buried at Calvary Cemetery, Waterville. Source: Dalby Database.*

NICHOLAS & ANNA (SCHMIDT/SMITH) STADLER FAMILY

Nicholas & Anna (Schmidt/Smith) Stadler
(50th Wedding Anniversary ---1922)

The Stadlers lived in Deerfield and were members of Corpus Christi parish from 1873 until 1889. All the children except Clara were all born in Deerfield.

Nicholas Stadler was born in 1850 in Germany and in 1857, at the age of seven years came to the US with his parents, Peter and Magdelena Mary (Sterin?) (Heber?) Stadler (1816-1902). Peter Stadler (1818-1908) was from Deudesfeld, Rheinland-Pfalz, Germany and emigrated to the US in 1857. *Some records show that Nicolas Stadler enlisted for service in the Civil War, however he would have been only 12.*

Nicolas Stadler married in Anna Schmidt/Smith on June 26, 1872. Anna was already living in Deerfield by 1870 with her mother and step father.

Soon after their marriage, Nicolas and Anna Stadler purchased 165 acres of land in Deerfield Township directly across from Corpus Christi church excepting the parcel of land of the Corpus Christi Cemetery on November 14, 1873 from John and Veronica Loemer. The Loemers had donated the parcel to Corpus Christi to serve as the cemetery.

The Stadlers and Loemer families lived next to each other and were related. Anna Schmidt/Smith Stadler's mother was Mrs. Loemer from a previous marriage. The Stadler family lived in Deerfield until 1889, when they moved to Walcott where they lived for 15 years and then went to Faribault on West Division Street where they lived out their lives.

Family of Nicholas & Anna (Schmidt/Smith) Stadler:

1). John Stadler, b.1873, d. 1885;
2). Katherine "Kate," b. 1875, m. J. F. Winkley, Porterville, Montana;
3). Peter Paul (b. 7 May 1877 Deerfield; d. 6 Jan 1946, Rice Benton County; m. Eleanor Rainey;
4). Nicolas Charles, b. 1879; d. 1975; m. Catherine Adams;
5). Elizabeth, b. 1883; d. 16 June 1915; Faribault;
6). Joseph, of San Diego, California;
8).Anna Maria, Mrs. Peter Weber, Walcott
9). Emma, Mrs. John Reichert, Faribault;
10). Clara, 1891-1919 (Died of Tuberculosis@32 yrs.)

Nicholas Stadler
(January 1, 1850-June 1, 1935)

NICHOLAS & ANNA (SCHMIDT/SMITH) STADLER FAMILY

FUNERAL SERVICES FOR N. STADLER, SR., CONDUCTED TUESDAY. Funeral services for Nicholas Stadler, Sr., who died Saturday at St. Joseph's Hospital, Mankato, at the age of 85 years, were conducted Tuesday morning at 10:30 oclock from the St. Lawrence Church. The solemn requiem Mass was read by the Rev. John Volz, assisted by the Rev. Valentine Schiffrer, pastor of the church. Interment was in St. Lawrence cemetery. The active pallbearers were the six grandsons of Mr. Stadler: Joseph Weber, Edward Stadler, Ernest Stadler, Frank Stadler, John Reichert and Peter Reichert.

Mr. Stadler was born in 1850 in Germany and at the age of seven years, he came to this country where he was married in 1873 to Anna Smith. To them nine children were born. During the Civil War, Mr. Stadler enlisted for service.

Surviving him are three sons, Joseph, San Jacinto, Calif., and Peter and Nicholas, Jr., Faribault; three daughters, Mrs. J. F. Winkley, Powderville, Mont., Mrs. Anna Weber and Mrs. John Reichert, Faribault; 48 grandchildren and 51 great-grandchildren. His wife, two daughters and one son preceded him in death.
Faribault Daily News; June 5, 1935.

Anna (Schmidt/Smith) Stadler (March 25, 1849-Sept. 27, 1926)

MRS. STADLER PASSES AWAY MONDAY EVE---WAS STRICKEN WITH HEART FAILURE WHILE VISITING AT HOME OF HER DAUGHTER.

Heart failure caused the death of Mrs. Nick Stadler of this city last evening at 7:45 o'clock. She died an hour and a half after being stricken at the home of her daughter, Mrs. John Reichert, in Wells township, where she was visiting for the day. She was 77 years old and had enjoyed good health until immediately before her demise.

Miss Anna Smith was born on March 25, 1849, in House 72, Dlouhá Trebová, East Bohemia (now Czech Republic), and came to the United States with her mother, Veronica Loemer (1826-September 13, 1900) at the age of 12 years. Veronica's mother was a Kubista.

The 1870 US census lists Anna Smith, age 20, a native of Bohemia, living in the home of Francis and Veronica (Froniga) Loemer. Following her marriage to Nick Stadler June 26, 1872, she lived in Deerfield for 17 years.

She then moved to Walcott and later to Faribault with her husband and has lived here ever since.

Besides her husband, she leaves six children to mourn her death. They are Mrs. J. F. (Kate) Winkley of Porterville, Montana, Peter Stadler of Faribault, N. C. Stadler of Walcott, Mrs. Peter (Anna) Weber of Walcott, Joseph Stadler of San Diego, Cal., and Mrs. John (Emma) Reichert of Wells. Forty-eight grandchildren and 15 great-grandchildren are also living. Funeral services will be held tomorrow morning at 9 oclock at the St. Lawrence church and interment will be at the St. Lawrence cemetery. Father Villman will officiate. Pallbearers will be six grandchildren, John, Albert and Frank Stadler, John Reichert, Jacob and Nicholas Weber.
Source: Faribault Daily News, Sept. 29, 1926.

JOHN F. STADLER
(1873-1885)

In 1885, as the story goes, while living on the farm in Deerfield, Nicolas Stadler saw an approaching storm and had a team of horses out in the field. Nicolas was yelling to his 12-year-old son John to get the horses into the barn. As John was bringing the horses in, he was struck by lightning and killed. John Stadler was the second burial in the Corpus Christi cemetery. When the family moved to Faribault in 1889, selling their land to E.W. Minske on March 22, John's body was exhumed and moved to the St. Lawrence Cemetery. His headstone from the Corpus Christi Cemetery was used as a cornerstone in the basement foundation of the farmhouse that Nicholas Stadler, Jr. built and is still there. The writing on the headstone with translation from German is as follows:

JOHN F.	*JOHN F.*
Sohn von	*Son of*
N & A Stadler	*N & A Stadler*
Gestorben den	*Died the*
8ten Juli 1885	*8th July 1885*
Alter 12 Jahren	*Age 12 Years*
14 Tage.	*14 Days.*

John F. Stadler Headstone

Pierce & Caroline (Stirens) Hackett Family
Top: Martin, Theodore, John; Bottom; Pierce, Rose, Caroline. Mrs. Caroline Hackett was the daughter of Theodore and Rosina (Marischka) Stirens.

PIERCE HACKETT
(1850-1931)

Funeral services for Pierce Hackett, a resident of Minnesota, for more than seventy-five years, who died at his home Monday morning were held Thursday morning at 9 o'clock at the Immaculate Conception church with Rev. Father J. P. Foley officiating. Burial was made in Calvary cemetery. Pallbearers included George Kaul, Phillip McCarthy, Dudley Geiger, A. C. Judd, Nick Schweisthal, A. C. King, Ed. Sammon, and Emmett Sammon.

Pierce Hackett was born at Janesville, Wis., June 12, 1850 and came to Minnesota with his parents in 1856, settling first on a homestead in Blooming Grove, Waseca County, where he remained until 1920 when he moved to Faribault. His wife, four children, John, Theodore and Martin of this city, and Rose Hackett of Fort Madison,Ia., are left to mourn his loss. Two sisters, Mrs. Julia Pettengill of Minot, N. D., and Mary Hackett of Stockton, Calif., and one brother, John Hackett of Manyberries, Alberta, Canada, also survive as do five grandchildren.

Those from out of town who attended the funeral services Thursday were: Mrs. Julia Pettengill, Minot, N. D.; the Misses Margaret and Ellen McCarthy, St. Paul, Mr N. M. Stirens, Minneapolis; Mr. and Mrs. Cyril Mariska, Mrs. Louis Mariska, Mr. and Mrs. James Lawlis, Mrs. Dan Devine, all of Waterville, Mr. and Mrs. George Brady, Mr. and Mrs. James F. Brady and family, Peter Stirens all of Deerfield; and Mr. and Mrs. Frank King and family of Morristown. *Faribault Daily News (12/Dec/1931).*

HACKETT FAMILY HISTORY

John Hackett was born in county Tipperary, Ireland in 1811. His wife, Margaret Phelan was born in county Kilkenny, Ireland in 1820. They came to Boston, Mass. in 1845 with one son, Martin. They moved to Rockford, Illinois, where John Hackett worked for a number of years with a team digging basements, etc.

In 1856 they moved to Minnesota via a Mississippi river boat from Galena, Ill., at Ninniger, Goodhue County, a village of about 500 population at that time. From there they came to Blooming Grove Township, Waseca County, where they took a homestead of 160 acres of land. They brought with them a team of horses and a number of cattle. They put up hay with a scythe and hand rake. There was timber on part of the land that had to be grubbed out. Potatoes and other vegetables were successfully grown. The first four acres of wheat were beat to the ground with hail. Cash was received from butter and eggs. They later raised sheep for wool and hogs for meat. Corn was grown for bread as flour was scarce. The closest town was Hastings, a four day round trip with team. Faribault was the nearest post office.

The Hacketts had 10 children: Martin, Pierce, Julia, John Jr., Mary and Margaret; 4 died in infancy. In 1895 Pierce married Caroline Stirens whose parents were natives of Bavaria, Germany. They had three sons: John, Theodore and Martin, and one daughter, Rose. Three others died in infancy. They farmed in Blooming Grove until 1920, then sold the farm and retired to Faribault.

On May 25, 1918, John Hackett was drafted and entered World War I. He returned in July 1919. He married Christina Stoeffel in November 1924.

They had seven children: George, Joseph, John Jr., Leo, Francis, Patrick and Mary. Pierce Hackett died December 7, 1931. Caroline died May 13, 1947. Theodore died March 1964. Martin died November 2, 1973. Rose died January 8, 1981. John J. Hackett, 84 years of age, lived out his life at St. Lucas Center in Faribault. Source - *RICE COUNTY FAMILIES. PUB. 1981*

Mrs. Margaret Hackett, whose maiden name was Phelan, is a native of County Tiperary, Ireland, and resided in that county until she attained her twenty-seventh year. One year previous to that she had been united in marriage with John Hackett. They sailed for America about a year after marriage, landing at New York City, and from there went to Milwaukee, but after a residence there of six months moved to Rockford, Ill., where they remained some eight years, he working by the day at any work that he and his team could find to do. In 1856 they came to Waseca County, settling on the place on section 13, Blooming Grove Township, where they now live. They have had ten children born to them: Martin, Pierce, Julia, Patrick, William, John, James, Mary, Maggie and William. Five of the children are living and five are numbered with the dead. Two boys are in St. Paul, Julia lives near Hastings, Minnesota, and two are at home with their parents. Source: *Book - History Of Steele & Waseca Counties, Mn., Published In 1887. Blooming Grove Township.*

****

Mrs. John Hackett, *nee* Phelan, died Sunday afternoon, March 8, at the home of her son, Pierce Hackett, in Blooming Grove. The cause of her death was pneumonia. The funeral was held from the Catholic church in Deerfield yesterday and the remains were placed in the vault at Calvary Cemetery. Mrs. Hackett is survived by two sons and one daughter --John and Pierce Hackett and Mrs. Peckengall, of Hastings. *Rice County Journal (March 11, 1903).*

Daniel & Susanna (Stirens) Devine (seated) with Pierce & Caroline (Stirens) Hackett (standing).

SOME HACKETT FAMILY OBITUARIES

MARTIN HACKETT
(1899-1973)

Martin A. Hackett, 74, of 1336 Central Ave., Faribault, passed away Friday, Nov. 2, at the Rice County District One Hospital. Funeral services will be held Monday, Nov. 5, at 10 a.m. from the Immaculate Conception church with the Rev. Gilbert DeSutter, officiating. Interment was at the Corpus Christi Cemetery in Deerfield. Friends and relatives called at the Kohl Funeral Home from Sunday afternoon until the hour of services Monday morning. the parish vigil prayers were recited Sunday at 8 p.m. at the Kohl Funeral Home. Members of the Faribault Aerie 1460, Fraternal Order of Eagles were requested to meet at the Kohl Funeral Home Sunday at 7 p.m. to pay their respects as a group.

Martin A. Hackett was born Sept. 8, 1899, in Blooming Grove Township, Waseca County, to Pierce and Caroline (Stirens) Hackett. He was united in marriage to Clara Harrison in 1935 at Kilkenny. She preceded him in death in 1959. Hackett is survived by one brother, John Hackett of Faribault; one sister, Mrs. Rose Zupfler of Ellsworth, Wis., and a number of nephews, nieces, and other relatives. *Faribault Daily News (November 3, 1973).*

MRS. MARTIN HACKETT
(CLARA HARRISON)
(1885-1959)

Funeral services for Mrs. Martin Hackett, 74, who died suddenly Saturday, Dec. 26, at her home, 138 11St St. N.W., were held Monday, Dec. 28, at St. Lawrence Catholic Church with the Rev. F. L. Tschann officiating. Rosary was recited Sunday evening at the Bold Funeral Home. Pallbearers were David Judd, Stephen Judd, Leo Judd, Hilary Sammon, Emmett Sammon and John Nagle. Interment was made in Corpus Christi church cemetery at Deerfield Township.

Clara Harrison, daughter of Patrick and Ellen Harrison, was born Dec. 27, 1885 in Shieldsville township. She was married to Martin Hackett. The St. Lawrence Rosary Society of which she was a member attended the services in a body.

She is survived by her husband; and by Mr. and Mrs. John Pemrick, St. Paul, Mrs. Tress Derkin, Milwaukee, Wis., Mrs. Gilbert Trytten, MIlwaukee, Wis., Mrs. Anthony Pemrick, Faribault, and Mrs. Catherine Sorenson, Faribault. Mrs. Hackett was the last survivor of the Harrison family. Relatives and friends attended the funeral from Kilkenny, Shieldsville, Faribault and the surrounding community. (*Faribault Daily News (December 1959)*

Clara & Martin Hackett Headstone at Corpus Christi Cemetery.

HACKETT BURIALS

SURNAME	NAME	BIRTH	DEATH	INSCRIPTION
HACKETT	INFANT 3 CHILDREN			CHILDREN OF P.& E. PIERCE HACKETT JOSEPH, BABY BOY & BABY BOY
HACKETT	CLARA H.	27/DEC/1885	26/DEC/1959	SP. MARTIN A. NEE: HARRISON. FDN. 26-30/DEC/1959. SEE OBIT FILE.
HACKETT	MARTIN A.	08/SEP/1899	02/NOV/1973	SP. CLARA HARRISON. PAR. PIERCE & CAROLINE STIREN HACKETT. MAR. 1935. FDN. 03/NOV/1973. SEE OBIT FILE.

GEORGE M. HACKETT
(1925-2009)

George M. Hackett, age 83, of Morristown, died Wednesday, September 16, 2009, at his home surrounded by his family from ALS (Lou Gehrigs disease).

Mass of Christian Burial was held on Saturday, September 19, 2009 at 10:00 a.m. at Christ the King Catholic Church in Medford. Interment was held at the Corpus Christi Cemetery in Deerfield.

George Martin Hackett, the eldest son of John and Christina (Stouffel) Hackett was born on December 4, 1925 in Faribault. He attended Faribault High School and graduated with the class of 1944. After graduation, George served his country during WWII in Japan. After his discharge from the service he graduated from Mankato Teachers College in 1950 with a Bachelors Degree in Education.

He was united in marriage to Catherine DeFrees on December 27, 1950 at the Sacred Heart Catholic Church in Faribault.

George Hackett first taught in Adrian, Minnesota for two years. He and Catherine moved to Mankato in 1953 where he taught science and math at Lincoln Junior High for 28 years.
He obtained his Masters of Science Degree from Mankato State in 1968. In addition to teaching and coaching, George farmed in Steele and Rice County from 1957 until 2007. After his retirement from teaching in 1981, George and Catherine moved to the farm near Morristown. George and Cathy enjoyed wintering in Arizona, most recently in Mesa.

He is survived by his wife of 58 years, Catherine Hackett of Morristown; by his six children Michael (Annie) Hackett of Faribault, Patricia (Niles) Batdorf of Duluth, MN, Christine (Rodney) LeVake of Faribault, Ann (Michael) Yungner of Maple Grove, MN, Mary (Allen) Peterson of Eden Prairie and Elizabeth (Jeffrey) Wickmann of Northfield; by 22 grandchildren and five great grandchildren; by brothers Leo (Arolyne) of Hastings, Patrick (Delores) of Chicago, IL, John of Polo, IL and sister Mary Valone of Lady Lake, FL.

He was preceded in death by his parents and two brothers Joseph and Francis Hackett. George Hackett's goal was to provide well for his children and grandchildren. He encouraged them in their education. His family is thankful for his deep quiet faith, work ethic, honesty, integrity, love and generosity. *Parker Kohl Funeral Home September 16, 2009.*

Hackett Infant Children

VINCENT & PHILOMENA (HONDLE) FAIT FAMILY

Vincent & Philomena (Hondel) Fait Family
Back Row: Bertha, Tony, Joe, Bill & Annie
Front Row: Josie, Mother Philomena, Father Vincent, Molly & Mary. Annie married Peter Stirens.

Vincent and Philomena Fait owned a small farm located in Blooming Grove Township, Waseca, County close to the Steele County line (Deerfield Township) line. They came to the United States in 1881 arriving in New York as passengers on the Ship: Weser, which departed out of Bremen, Germany with 1388 passengers: They are listed as Ving Fait, Philomena, Anna. Arrival on 31 May 1881, New York. By May 1, 1885 were in Blooming Grove. Both the 1900 and 1910 census show Vincent Fait as head, owner-free (without mortgage) of farm. The census also stated that he was a naturalized citizen.

The Faits farmed and raised family at Deerfield until they retired and moved to Owatonna. In the 1920 and 1930 census it is recorded that Vincent and Philomena could not, read, write or speak English.

By 1917, Vincent and Philomena lived at 416 Chestnut St, Owatonna. Philomena (Hondel) Fait passed away December 2, 1936. Vincent passed away February 24, 1939. Vincent and Philomena (Hondel) Fait are buried at Sacred Heart Cemetery, Owatonna.

SS Weser

43

Alice Fait
(Born June 22, 1895;
Died Feb. 19, 1902 at 6 years old).
Alice Fait was born on June 22, 1894, in Blooming Grove Township, Waseca County, Minnesota, her father, Vincent Fait, was 40, and her mother, Philomene Hondle, was 42. She had nine siblings. Alice died as a six year-old child on February 19, 1902 and was buried at Corpus Christi Cemetery, Deerfield. Vincent and Philomene Fait were immigrants from Bohemia.

Mrs. W. (Esther) Linder (1910-1941)

JAMES & LOUISE (PARSONS) BRADY FAMILY

James Brady (1848-1931) and Louise Parsons

James F. Brady was born in Canada, April 2, 1849. He came to Steele County, Minn., and located in Deerfield, September 1, 1856. Mr. Brady was married January 7, 1873, to Louisa Parsons. They have five children as follows: Charles, James F., Alice M., George and Arthur. Mr. Brady was a supervisor of the township and held various offices of importance including Steele County Commission. James and Louise Brady were early members of Corpus Christi parish.

James Brady was an excellent farmer with 240 acres, the most of which was under cultivation. Mr. Brady's father, Charles Brady, was still living in 1887 with James, at the advanced age of eighty-seven. The mother died July 20, 1885, of "lung fever," aged eighty-four. Mr. Brady was mentioned frequently in the book *History Of Steele & Waseca Counties, Mn., Published In 1887.*

James F. & Amelia (Dusbabek) Brady
Married May 2, 1902

BRADY MARRIES AT FARIBAULT.

Faribault, Minn., May 14.—(Times Special)—J. F. Brady of Deerfield and Miss Amelia Dusbabek were married yesterday morning at the church of the Immaculate Conception.

Minneapolis Daily Times (May 15, 1902)

James F. & Amelia (Dusbabek) Brady
Photo Taken at the Fiftieth Wedding Anniversary Mass on May 2, 1952 at Corpus Christi Church

SOME BRADY FAMILY BURIALS AT CORPUS CHRISTI CEMETERY

Catharine, Wife Of Thomas Brady (maiden name) Cocklin. With Charles T. & Rose (McGuire) Brady.

Charles & Rose (Mcguire) Brady; Parents Of Thomas Brady.
Charles Brady (1875-1949)   Rose (McGuire) Brady (1887-1969)

SOME BRADY FAMILY OBITUARIES

JAMES FRANCIS BRADY
(1876-1960)

James Francis Brady was born on November 22, 1876, in Deerfield Township to Louisa M. Parsons, age 20, and James F. (Francis) Brady, age 28. He married Amelia Johanna Josephine Dusbabek and they had six children together. James F. Brady, passed away September 29, 1960, in Deerfield at the age of 83. Burial took place at Calvary Cemetery, Faribault.

AMELIA (DUSBABEK) BRADY
(1881-1978)

Amelia Dusbabek was born on Nov. 15, 1881, in Shieldsville, Rice County. She married James F. Brady on May 2, 1902. He passed away September 29, 1960.

Mrs. James (Amelia) Brady, 96, of rural Medford, died on Friday, May 19, at the Owatonna Nursing Home. Services were held at 10:30 a.m. (today), Monday, May 22, at Christ The King Church in Medford. Interment was in the Calvary Cemetery in Faribault.

She was preceded in death by her husband, one son, two sisters and one brother. She is survived by three sons: James and Byron of Medford, and Arthur of Florida; two daughters: Mrs. Donald (Mary Alice) Karaus of Huntsville, Ala., and Mrs. Orvie (Evelyn) Jensen; two brothers: Wencl and Walter Dusbabek of Faribault; four sisters: Mary Hartle of Owatonna, Elvina Logghe of Faribault, Loretta Clemmon of Colorado and Edith Waite of California; 25 grandchildren and 38 great-grandchildren. *Faribault Daily News (May 1978).*

James Melvin Brady, son of James F. and Anna (Dusbabek) Brady. (Pictured on the Brady family farm about 1920).
Note: The color in the above photograph was enhanced by Kathleen (Brady) Sweeney, daughter of James and Evelyn Brady.

CHARLOTTE (LESCAULT) BRADY (1918-1967)

Mrs. Charles (Charlotte) Brady, 49, of 306 NW 7th St., passed away on Saturday evening, Aug. 26, at the Rice County District One Hospital. Funeral services will be held on Tuesday morning, Aug. 29, at 10 a.m. at the Sacred Heart Catholic Church, with the Rev. Donald Westhoff, pastor, officiating. Interment will be at Calvary Cemetery. Mrs. Brady is survived by her husband, Charles and her father, Charles Lescault of Faribault. Friends and relatives may call at the Kohl Funeral Home from after 2 p.m. on Monday afternoon until the hour of services on Tuesday morning. The parish vigil prayers will be recited on Monday evening at 8 p.m. at the Kohl Funeral Home. *Faribault Daily News (8/Aug/1967)*

CHARLES BRADY
(1919-2000)

Charles Thomas Brady, the son of Charles and Rose (McGuire) Brady, was born March 13, 1919, in Deerfield Township. He was raised in Deerfield Township and attended school in Medford. He was married to Charlotte Lescault; she preceded him in death on Aug. 16, 1967. He lived in both Faribault and Medford and worked for more than 10 years at Jerome Foods, Faribault.

Charles "Bud" Brady, 81, of Faribault and formerly of Medford, died Saturday, Sept. 23, 2000, at Infinia Faribault Care Center. Funeral services were held at 10:30 a.m. Wednesday at the Parker Kohl Funeral Home, Faribault, with Deacon Dan Wesley officiating. Burial was at Calvary Cemetery, Faribault.

He was survived by many cousins and friends.

BYRON BRADY
(1914-1991)

Byron Francis Brady was born Jan. 5, 1914, in Deerfield. He married Jane Ellingson Feb. 24, 1941 in Deerfield. Brady farmed until 1970. He worked at K&G Auto Parts in Faribault until he retired in 1976 and also was a school bus driver for Medford Public Schools. He was a Grand Knight of the Knights of Columbus Council 4090, a 4-H leader and served as a member of the National Guard Co. F of Owatonna. He was a 1933 graduate of Medford High School.

Byron Francis Brady, 77, Route 1, Medford, died Sunday, March 24 at St. Lucas Care Center, Faribault. Services will be 10:30 a.m. Wednesday at Christ the King Church, Medford, with the Rev. Milo Ernster officiating. Burial will be in Corpus Christi Cemetery, Deerfield. Visitation will be from 3 to 5 and 7 to 9 tonight at Brick-Postlewaite Funeral Home, 1603 Austin Road, Owatonna, with parish prayers at 4 p.m. and the Knights of Columbus reciting a rosary at 7 p.m.

Survivors include his wife, Jane; three sons, Byron of Medford, Kevin of Long Beach, Calif. and Charles of Maui, Hawaii; three daughters, Mrs. David (Sharon) Popowski and Mrs. Noel (Edie) Lange of Mankato, and Mary Brady of St. Paul; 10 grandchildren; a brother, James of Medford; and a sister Mrs. Donald (Mary Alice) Karaus of Huntsville, Ala. He was preceded in death by his parents, two brothers and one sister. *Faribault Daily News (March 26, 1991).*

*Byron & Jane (Ellingson) Brady Headstone
Corpus Christi Cemetery, Deerfield*

JANE (ELLINGSON) BRADY
(1920-2007)

Jane Ellingson was born in 1920 in Alberta, Canada, daughter of Henry and Edith (Harlan) Ellingson. Jane was a graduate of Ellendale High School in 1937. After high school, Jane attended and later graduated from Brady and Rogers School of Cosmetology in Minneapolis. After graduation, Jane worked as a beautician at Cinderella Beauty Salon in Owatonna for a few years. On Feb. 24, 1941, Jane was united in marriage to Byron Brady at Corpus Christi Church in Deerfield Township. Jane worked as a farm wife and a homemaker while raising her children. Later she worked as a therapeutic assistant at the Faribault State Hospital until she retired in 1980. She was a life member of the Catholic Daughters of America, St. Anne's Court of Medford/Deerfield, Corpus Christi Church, Senior Place. She was a volunteer at Cedarview for many years. Her life interests were painting ceramics, listening to music, especially country, traveling and camping.

Jane Brady of Deerfield Township, rural Steele County, died Dec. 26, 2007, in Owatonna. A Mass of Christian Burial is set for Wednesday, Jan. 2, 2008, at 10:30 a.m. at Christ the King Catholic Church in Medford, Minn. Interment was at Corpus Christi Cemetery in Deerfield Township. Visitation was on Tuesday, Jan. 1, 2008, from 4 p.m. to 7 p.m. at the Medford Funeral Home. There was a 4 p.m. Catholic Daughters of the America's Rosary, in addition to a 7 p.m. wake service at the funeral home on Tuesday. The visitation continued one hour before the funeral liturgy at the funeral home on Friday followed by a procession to the church.

Jane was survived by her children: Sharon (David) Popowski and Edie (Noel) Lange, both of North Mankato, Minn., Byron (Carla) Brady of Medford, Minn., Mary Brady of Minneapolis, Minn., Kevin (Marcela) Brady of Bellflower, Calif., Charles (Cheryl) Brady of Kauai, Hawaii; along with 15 grandchildren and 11 great-grandchildren. She is also survived by her sister, Phyllis Thielen of Emily, Minn. Jane was preceded in death by her husband, Byron, in 1991 and her brother, Emery. Memorials are preferred to the African Partnership c/o St. Olaf Catholic Church 215 S. Eighth Street Minneapolis, MN 55402.
Faribault Daily News (December 28, 2007)

Byron & Jane (Ellingson) Brady
(Married Feb. 24, 1941 in Deerfield).

FAMILY OF JAMES & AMELIA (DUSBABEK) BRADY

Evelyn Brady
(Married Orvie Jensen)

Mary Alice Brady
(Married Donald Karaus)

Arthur Brady
(Married Marcella Teresa Rollins)

James Melvin Brady
(Married Evelyn Maas)

James & Evelyn (Maas) Brady

EVELYN (MAAS) BRADY
(1923-2008)

Evelyn Maas was born the daughter of Jacob and Phyllis (VanDerputte) Maas in Walcott Township, Rice County. Evelyn attended Catholic school at Immaculate Conception in Faribault. Evelyn married James Brady on June 14, 1943 at Immaculate Conception Church in Faribault. The couple made their home on a farm in Deerfield Township. The couple raised six children. Evelyn was a full-time homemaker helping her husband in all aspects of the farm. They were members of Corpus Christi church in Deerfield and in 1981 they moved to Medford and became members of Christ the King Church. She was a member of Catholic Daughters of America and Steele County Historical Society.

Evelyn volunteered for many years as project leader for 4-H, Homemakers club of Deerfield and Christ the King Church. Evelyn will be remembered for her high energy level and her many creative talents. She was a wonderful self-taught artist who won awards for painting and sculptures. Sewing quilts for her family as well for the missions and collecting antiques plus repairing them were other passions of hers. She loved to share all of these activities with her grandchildren. Evelyn was a remarkable woman who touched so many lives and will be greatly missed by all who knew her. Evelyn M. Brady of Medford passed away October 4, 2008 at her home in Medford. Evelyn was survived by her sons Patrick Brady, Dennis (Theresa) Brady and James (Judy) Brady all of Medford, daughters Carolyn (LeRoy) Hoffman of Brookings, SD. and Kathleen (Bart) Sweeney of Scottsdale, AZ 14 Grandchildren, seven great grandchildren. One brother Albert (Florence) Maas of Medford, sisters Marion Van Den Boom of Faribault and Imelda Ellerbush of Burnsville. Evelyn was preceded in death by her husband James in 2005, son Melvin Brady, 2 brothers Francis and Henry, 2 sisters Elizabeth and Isabelle.

JAMES M. BRADY
(1916-2005)

Jim Brady was born on Aug. 25, 1916, in Deerfield Township, Rural Steele County, to James F. and Amelia (Dusbabeck) Brady. Jim was a member of the graduating class of 1936 in Medford. After high school he continued to farm on the family farm in Deerfield Township. Jim married Evelyn Maas on June 14, 1943, at Immaculate Conception Catholic Church in Faribault. The couple raised their family on the family farm, and Jim continued to farm until 1981. While farming, Jim was a beekeeper and enjoyed sharing the honey with friends. He was a member of Corpus Christi Church and later Christ the King Catholic Church, Medford Knights of Columbus, and the Sioux Honey Bee Association. His hobbies were fishing, enjoyed hunting, playing cards, and especially traveling and spending winters in Arizona. James M. Brady, 88, lifelong resident of the Medford area, died March 31, 2005, at St. Marys Hospital in Rochester. A Mass of Christian Burial is set for 10:30 a.m. Monday, April 4, 2005, at Christ the King Church in Medford. Interment will follow at Corpus Christi Cemetery in Deerfield Township. Friends may call at the Medford Funeral Home on Sunday from 3 to 6 p.m. There will be a 3 p.m. Knights of Columbus Rosary at the funeral home on Sunday. The visitation will continue from 9:30 a.m. to 10:15 a.m. on Monday at the Medford Funeral Home, followed by a procession to Christ the King Church. Jim is survived by his wife of 61 years, Evelyn of Medford; children, Carolyn (LeRoy) Hoffman of Brookings, S.D., Patrick Brady of Medford, Kathleen "KiKi" (Bart) Sweeney of Scottsdale, Ariz., Dennis (Theresa) Brady and James A. (Judy) Brady, all of Medford; 14 grandchildren; four great-grandchildren; sister, Mary Alice Karaus of Huntsville, Ala.; and other relatives. Jim is preceded in death by his parents; son, Melvin; and three brothers, Bernard, Arthur and Byron. *Faribault Daily News; April 1,2005*

JAMES M. & EVELYN (MAAS) BRADY FAMILY

James M. & Evelyn (Maas) Brady Family (1992)
L-R; Front, seated: Judy, Evelyn, James M., LeRoy, Carolyn, Kathy, Bart.
Back, standing: Jamie, Terri, Dennis, Patrick.

PATRICK BRADY (1947–2018)

Patrick Jacob Brady, age 70, lifelong resident of Deerfield Township, passed away peacefully on May 22, 2018 at Hennepin County Medical Center in Minneapolis surrounded by his children. Mass of Christian Burial was held Saturday, May 26 at Christ the King Catholic Church.

Pat was born November 12, 1947, the son of James and Evelyn (Maas) Brady. He grew up in rural Deerfield Township where he attended country school. He attended Medford high school where he was active in wrestling and FFA. In 1966, Pat graduated from the South-ern School of Agriculture in Waseca, MN. From there Pat went on to work on the family farm and later for several different construction companies. Pat was united in marriage to Connie Schmidt on Sept. 18, 1982. Together they had four children, they later divorced. He enjoyed fixing cars and spending time with his children and his younger brother Jamie.

His favorite pastime was attending auctions and finding hidden treasures.

Patrick was a member of the Medford Knights of Columbus and was a past Grand Knight. He was a devoted parishioner at Corpus Christi Catholic Church. He is survived by his children, Brent Brady, Marissa (Mike) Ewert, Kristin (Travis) Gunsolus, Brandon Brady (Renee Scheier); grandsons Giakobe Parker, Colin and Lucas Gunsolus; siblings Carolyn (Lee) Hoffman, Dennis (Terri) Brady, James (Judy) Brady; and many nieces and nephews. Pat is preceded in death by his parents James and Evelyn Brady, and siblings Melvin Brady and Kiki Sweeney.

SURNAME	NAME	BIRTH	DEATH	INSCRIPTION
BRADY	JAMES M.	25/AUG/1916	31/MAR/2005	SP. EVELYN M. MAAS. PAR. JAMES F. & AMELIA DUSBABEK BRADY. MAR. 14/JUN/1943. FDN. 01/APR/2005.
BRADY	EVELYN M.	1923	4/OCT/2008	SP. JAMES M. PAR. JACOB & PHYLLIS VANDERPUTTE MAAS. MAR. 14/JUN/1943. FDN. 05/OCT/2008.
BRADY	MELVIN J.	01/JAN/1944		PAR. JAMES M. & EVELYN M. MAAS BRADY. FDN. 24/JUN/1976
BRADY	CATHER-INE		2/APR/1919	WIFE OF THOMAS BRADY. NEE: COCKLIN. WITH CHARLES T. & ROSE BRADY
BRADY	CHARLES T.	06/MAY/1875	6/FEB/1947	SP. ROSE McGUIRE. PAR. THOMAS. FDN. 07-13/FEB/1947
BRADY	ROSE	23/JAN/1887	18/MAR/1969	SP. CHARLES T.; NEE: McGUIRE.

Elizabeth Niebels, William Henry Mullenmeister, and Gerhard (Jerry) Niebels

William Henry & Elizabeth (Neibel) Mullenmaster Family
Top Row: Oscar, Caroline, Henry, Anna, William. Center Row: Laura, William Sr., Arthur, Elizabeth, Winnifred, Bottom Row: Gertrude, Ella.

DEATH OF RESPECTED OLD CITIZEN
W. H. Mullenmaster Passes Away at His Home on Oak Street Monday Night.

W. H. Mullenmaster, an old and highly respected resident of this county, died at his home on Oak Street in this city Monday evening, after a short but severe illness.

William Henry Mullenmaster was born in Prussia December 20th, 1837. He came to this country with his parents in 1853, the family first locating in Wisconsin.

In July 1854, he was united in marriage with Miss Elizabeth Neibels of Rock River, Wisconsin who has been his faithful partner of his life's labors and survives to mourn his death. About 1867, Mr. and Mrs. Mullenmaster settled on a farm in Deerfield, where they lived for thirty years. Twelve years ago (about 1898), Mr. Mullenmaster retired from active farm work and they moved to Owatonna which since has been their home.

Besides the surviving widow, ten children mourn the loss of their kind father. They are Henry Mullenmaster of Cass Lake, Mrs. Madden and Mrs. J. McDonald of Minneapolis, Mrs. George Misgen of Faribault, Mrs. Vogel and Oscar Mullenmaster of Cannon Lake, Mrs. Charles Brady and William Mullenmaster of Deerfield, and Arthur and Gertrude Mullenmaster who live in the family home in Owatonna. The funeral was held at St. Joseph's church Friday morning at 10:00 am. *Owatonna People's Press (Friday January 21, 1910).*

Nomen Familiæ.	A. D. 1907 Die Mensis.	REGISTRUM MATRIMONIORUM.	Dispensationes et Notanda.
Mullenmaster & Cromer 38⁰	Oct. 1ᵉ	*Ego infrascriptus præmissis tribus denuntiationibus et mutuo contrahentium consensu habito, per verba de præsenti matrimonio conjunxi* Guilielmum. J. Mullen-Master *ex loco* Deerfield. Stele Co *Filium et* Ortillam . M. Cromer. *ex loco Filiam Præsentibus testibus* Arthurus. Mullenmaster Jennie Cromer. J. J. Slevin	

Marriage of William Mullenmaster and Ortillia Cromer at Corpus Christi on October 1, 1907.
Witnesses were Arthur Mullenmaster and Jennie Cromer.
(Recorded at Immaculate Conception Church, Faribault).

Nomen Familiæ.	A. D. 1907 Die Mensis.	REGISTRUM MATRIMONIORUM.	Dispensationes et Notanda.
Engel & Dusbabek 38⁰	Apr. 16ᵉ	*Ego infrascriptus præmissis tribus denuntiationibus et mutuo contrahentium consensu habito, per verba de præsenti matrimonio conjunxi* Joannem. W. Engel *ex loco* Deerfield. Stele Co. *Filium et* Annam. M. Dusbabek. *ex loco* hoc *Filiam Præsentibus testibus* Georgius. W. Engel Alvina Dusbabek J. J. Slevin	

Marriage of John Engel and Anna Dusbabek at Corpus Christi on April 16, 1907.
Witnesses were George Engel and Alva Dusbabek.
(Recorded at Immaculate Conception Church, Faribault).

Leo Mullenmaster & Creta Lonergan were married at St. Aidan's Catholic Church of Bath on September 22, 1938. Leo was the son of William and Ortillia (Cromer) Mullenmaster.

L-R: Rita Mullenmaster, Gertrude Lonergan, Creta Lonergan, Leo Mullenmaster, Paul Lonergan, John Mullenmaster Leo and Creta Mullenmaster were long-time Corpus Christi parishioners and raised a family of 16 children which were born between 1939 and 1960; Leo Jr., Colette, Ann Marie, Mary, William, Larry, Candace, Coleen, Elaine, Greg, Monica, Tom, Brian, Mark, Maurice, Scott. All of the children were baptized at Corpus Christi church and many made their first communion there also.

Leo & Creta (Lonergan) Mullenmaster Family (1954)
L-R: Bottom: Candace, Coleen, Elaine, Cleta holding Monica, Leo Sr. holding Greg, Larry.
L-R, Standing, Top Row: Mary, Ann, Leo, Colette, Bill.
This photo was taken at the time the Mullenmaster Family was chosen as the Catholic Family of the Year by the Diocese of Winona and published in the Courier, the diocesan newspaper.

Leo Cyril Mullenmaster, son of William Theodore and Ottilia Mary (Cromer) Mullenmaster, was born Sept. 2, 1913, in Deerfield Township. Leo graduated from Owatonna High School in 1930. He married Creta Irene Lonergan Sept. 22, 1938, at St. Aiden's Catholic Church in Bath Township, Freeborn County. Leo and Creta farmed for many years in Deerfield Township. They moved to Mille Lacs County near Onamia, where they farmed for several years before retiring to Waseca. Over the years, Leo was a very active church member. He was former member of Corpus Christi Catholic Church in Deerfield and was a current member of the Sacred Heart Catholic Church in Waseca. He was a longtime member of the Knights of Columbus. Leo was an avid outdoorsman. He also enjoyed singing and dancing, playing cards and gardening. He was known as a man of solitude and a person with a great sense of humor.

Leo C. Mullenmaster Sr., 87, of Waseca, died Monday, April 16, 2001, at the Waseca Medical Center. Mass of Christian burial was held April 20 at Sacred Heart Catholic Church with Fr. John Kunz officiating. Interment was in the St. Aiden's Catholic Church Cemetery in rural Ellendale. He was survived by eight sons and seven daughters.
Source: Mille Lacs Messenger (April 25, 2001).

Creta Lonergan was born April 26, 1921 in Berlin Township, Steele County. She attended rural Steele and Ellendale public schools.

On September 22, 1938, she married Leo C. Mullenmaster at St. Aiden's Catholic Church, Bath. The couple farmed in Deerfield Township until 1968 when they moved briefly to Bloomer, Wisconsin, then to Isle and to Onamia. While in Isle and Onamia, Mrs. Mullenmaster was employed in nursing homes. In 1981, Mr. and Mrs. Mullenmaster retired and moved to Waseca. Mrs. Mullenmaster was a member of Sacred Heart Catholic Church, Waseca and a former member of the Catholic Daughters and WCCW.

Creta Mullenmaster, age 69, passed away Monday June 18, 1990 at Waseca. She was survived by her husband, Leo; seven daughters, and nine sons.

Leo & Creta (Lonergan) Mullenmaster Family
Seated Front; R-L: Greg, Elaine, Candace, Leo Sr., Creta, Monica, Coleen, Mark.
Standing Back, L-R: Maurice, Bill, Ann, Thomas, Larry, Colette, Brian, Mary, Leo Jr., Scott.

CLAUDE & ANN MARIE (MULLENMEISTER) HAMENTIEN FAMILY

Claude Hamentien was born May 18, 1832 in Alsace-Lorraine then part of France. He was the son of Anthony and Margaret (Luther) Hamentien. Claude Hamentien married Ann Marie (Hannah) Mullemeister about 1862. Ann Marie was the daughter of William Henry and Ann Marie (Schorn) Mullenmeister. Anna Maria (Hannah) Mullenmeister and her twin sister Mary Eva were born on December 19, 1843, in Birkesdorf, North Rhine-Westphalia, Germany.

The Hamentiens arrived in Deerfield soon after their marriage and most of their 15 children were born in Deerfield between 1863 and 1888.

The 1897 plat book shows that the Hamentien family owned 160 acres in Section 17 of Deerfield Township adjacent to the Corpus Christi cemetery and across the road from the church. Claude Hamentien also owned 80 acres in Section 22 of Deerfield. They were still living in Deerfield when Ann Marie (Mullenmeister) Hamentien died at age 60 on August 1, 1904. She is believed to be buried in Corpus Christi cemetery, Deerfield. Their oldest son Joseph, died at age 22 on May 26, 1886 and is buried in Corpus Christi Cemetery.

Claude Hamentien died on February 8, 1923, in Hennepin County, Minnesota, at the age of 90.

FAMILY OF CLAUDE & ANN MARIE (MULLENMEISTER) HAMENTIEN;

1). Joseph; born at Deerfield on August 23, 1863; Died at Deerfield on May 26, 1886, not married;

2). Mary Eva; born October 17, 1865 at Deerfield; She married Frank Rademacher (1855–1913) on August 5, 1884 at Winona. Mary died at Winona on July 4, 1955. The Rademachers had four children.

3). Margaret; born in November 1869 at Deerfield; She married Leopold Radel on 11 Oct 1893 in Steele County. Margaret Radel, age 40 was living in Deerfield Township with her brother Henry in 1910. Leopold Radel died in Des Moines, Iowa on April 22, 1952. There is no mention of Margaret in his obituary.

4). Henry William; born in Somerset Township on May 4, 1870. He married Mary McGough on October 25, 1916 at St. Canice Church, Kilkenny. He died April 19, 1943 in Wilton Township, Waseca County.

5). Elizabeth Caroline; born December 13, 1872 at Deerfield; died June 20, 1843 in Minneapols. She married John Hopkins (1869-1927). They had four daughters.

6). Emma; born March 27, 1876 in Deerfield; she died at age 92 on August 1968 at Chicago, Cook County, Illinois. She married James Hopkins on June 9, 1906 in Winona.

7). Catherine "Katie;" born about 1878 in Deerfield. She appears on 1885 Minnesota census; No further record found.

9). Rose; born December 19, 1881 at Deerfield; she died in Minneapolis January 30, 1962. She married Clyde T. Glodfelty who died in 1910. They had three children. Rose then married Leonard Wertzler (1858-1932).

10). Theresa; born about 1884 in Deerfield; She married Clark Fitz-Simmons (1886-1972). They were the parents of Carlotta FitzSimmons (1909-1971).

11). Anna; born at Deerfield in June 1885; She died at Shell Lake, Wisconsin in 1922. Anna Hamentien married Peregrine "Perry" Matzke at Owatonna on April 11, 1899.

12). Louise; born September 1888 at Deerfield. No further record found.

13). Isabelle; born October 18, 1892; died February 1980 at Sleepy Eye, She married George Vernon Schaup (1891-1980).

Joseph Hamentien Headstone
Inscription in German as follows: Joseph Hamentien
Geb(oren) (Born) 28 August 1868, Gest(orben) (Died) 26 Mai (May) 1886
Alter (Age) 22 Jahre (Years) 9 Monat (Months)

FRANZ & ROSINA (HOLUB) PIRKL FAMILY HISTORY

Franz Pirkl (1825-1897) son of Johannes Pirkl and Juliana Schmid was born February 10, 1825 in Horní Dobrouc, East Bohemia, now Czech Republic. He married Rosina Holub in Bohemia.

Based on 1900 Census records, Franz (Frank) and Rosina (Holub) Pirkl arrived in the USA in 1864. They appeared to have settled on a farm in section 8 of Deerfield Township, sometime around January 18, 1864.

The land seems to have been the same acreage that Deerfield Township's first resident, Edward McCarthy lived on. It is unclear whether Frank and Rosina Pirkl moved onto land with buildings or whether they had to construct their own living facilities.

There is a small creek, lined with woods, running through the land, so it had the capability of supporting a family building their homestead.

Frank and Rosina Pirkl had one girl and six boys. Rosa, their only daughter stayed in Bohemia or died at a young age. Two other sons, Johann and Franz, died at a young age before the family left Bohemia.

Franz and Johann, who were obviously named after their deceased brothers, came with their parents on the long journey.

Hubert and Peter were born on the farm in Deerfield Township. In the May 1 1885 Census, Mary Arnold age 10 was living with Franz and Rosalia. Mary was born in Bohemia.

Leo Pirkl, the little five year old son of Mr. and Mrs. John Pirkl, last week Thursday afternoon, September 24, 1914 fell into a cistern on his father's farm in Deerfield and was drowned. The cistern had been left open in order to get water from it, the pump being out of order, and the little fellow evidently lost his balance while satisfying his curiosity by a peek into the open hole. He was missed and a search made for him finally resulted in the discovery of his hat floating on the water in the cistern, which immediately told the sad story of the tragedy.
Rice County Journal (Sept. 30, 1914)
Note: Original article says Martin Pirkl, a twin brother to Leo.

Family of Franz (Frank) & Rosina (Holub) Pirkl:
1). Rosa Pirkl; Died young or remained in Bohemia),
2). Johann Pirkl; (Died young),
3). Franz Pirkl; (Died young),
4). Franz Pirkl (1859-1924) married Mary Benesch (1868-1930) on January 30, 1888. They had 10 children.
5). John Pirkl married Rosa Langer in 1895 and was living on 80 acres of land on section 8 in Deerfield Township and later moved to a farm located west of Owatonna on old Highway 14. John and Rosa had eight children.
6). Hubert Pirkl married Louise Santo and had three children.
7). Peter William Pirkl married Justina Langer, the sister of Rosa Langer, John Pirkl's wife. Peter and Justina (Tina) had 3 children and took over the 150 acre "home place" in Deerfield Township.
Research by Paul Pirkl

FRANZ PIRKL
(1825-1897)

Residence: 1895 in Steele County, Minnesota.
Death: 07 Oct 1897 in Deerfield Township, Steele County, Minnesota.
Burial: Owatonna, Steele County, Minnesota
Cause Of Death: Prostatitis and Acute Nephritis
Occupation: Farmer
Residence: May 1, 1885 in Steele County, Minnesota.

Rosina Holub was born February 24, 1826 at Horní Dobrouc, East Bohemia, (now Czech Republic) and died November 25, 1909 in Deerfield Township, Steele County, She married Franz Pirkl (1825–1897) who was born at Horní Dobrouc, East Bohemia, Czech Republic on February 10, 1825. Franz Pirkl was the son of Joannes Pirkl and Juliana Schmid/Schmied. He died October 7, 1897 at the home farm in Deerfield Township, Steele County. *Photo courtesy of Rosemary Pirkl Meyer*

Frank & Mary (Benesch) Pirkl
(Married January 30, 1888)
Frank Pirkl was born November 2, 1859 and died October 2, 1924. Mary Benesch Pirkl was born May 2,
1868 and died September 24, 1930. They are buried at Sacred Heart Cemetery, Owatonna.

Harvesting Grain in Deerfield Township (1930s)

Anna, Emma, and Elizabeth "Ella" (c1905)
(Daughters of Frank & Mary (Benesch) Pirkl)
Anna, born in June 1894 married Bernard John Brickner and died April 11, 1962 in Prescott, Wisconsin.
Emma born August 27, 1904, in Deerfield. married Vincent Adolph Ryshavy on August 16, 1922, in Steele
County, Minnesota. She died on April 27, 1968, at the age of 63.
Ella, was born September 28, 1896 married Anton Schmanski and died August 17, 1970.

John & Rosa (Langer) Pirkl
(Married 1895)
(Photo courtesy of Paul Pirkl)

John & Rosa (Langer) Pirkl Family (c.1917)
(Photo courtesy of Paul Pirkl)

Pirkl/Langer Family Gathering (Early 1940s)

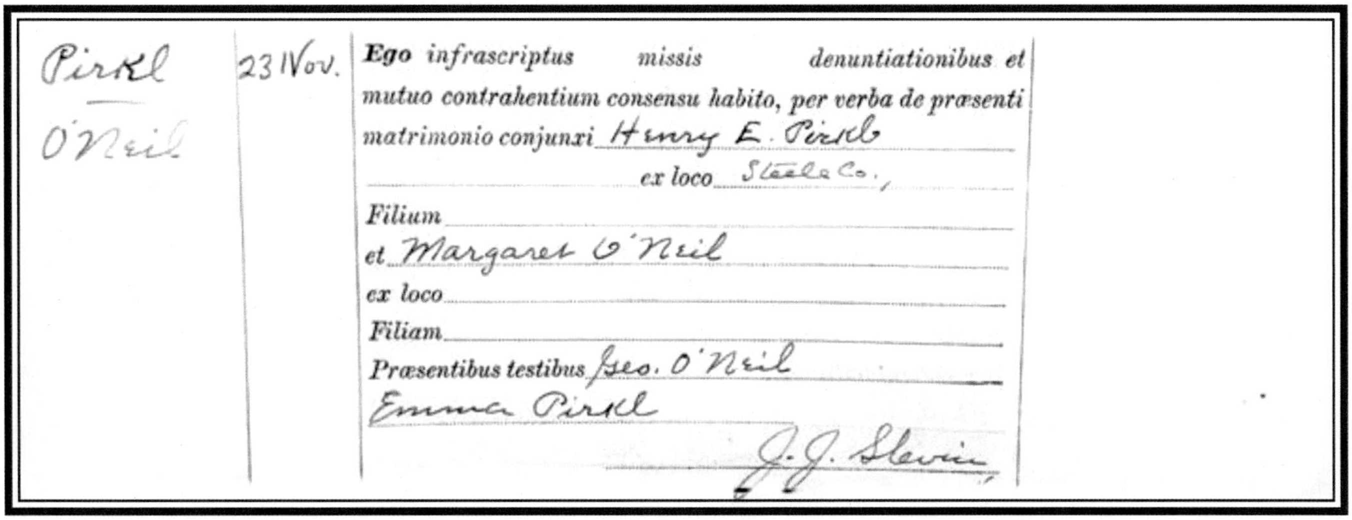

[Marriage record - handwritten Latin text]

Pirkl
O'Neil

23 Nov.

Ego infrascriptus missis denuntiationibus et mutuo contrahentium consensu habito, per verba de præsenti matrimonio conjunxi *Henry E. Pirkl*

ex loco *Steele Co.,*

Filium

et *Margaret O'Neil*

ex loco

Filiam

Præsentibus testibus *Geo. O'Neil*

Emma Pirkl

J. J. Slevin

Marriage of Henry E. Pirkl and Margaret O'Neill at Corpus Christi on November 23, 1920.
Witnesses were George O'Neil and Emma Pirkl
(Recorded at Immaculate Conception Church, Faribault).

Henry Pirkl, the son of Frank and Mary (Benish) Pirkl, was born Jan. 12, 1892, in Deerfield. On Nov. 12, 1920, he was united in marriage to Margaret O'Neil at the Immaculate Conception church in Faribault. Mr. Pirkl, who was 61 at the time of his death, passed away Dec. 14, 1953 after a lingering illness.

He is survived by his wife; one daughter, Mrs. John Robinson (Genevieve), and two granddaughters, Margaret and Betty Robinson of Waseca; and the following brothers and sisters: Albert Pirkl, Dundas, Frank Pirkl, Medford, Mrs. Ben Brickner, Prescott, Wis.; Mrs. Anthony Schmanske and Mrs. Emma Ryshavy, Morristown; Charles Pirkl of Deerfield; Ben Pirkl and Mrs. Henry O'Neil of Faribault.

Funeral services for Henry Edward Pirkl of Morristown, were held Dec. 16, 1953 at the Holy Trinity Catholic church in Waterville. The Rev. Father McCormack officiated. Burial was in the Corpus Christi cemetery at Deerfield.

Margaret A O'Neill was born in 1901 in Minnesota. She was the daughter of John and Anna (Malone) O'Neill. She married Henry Edward Pirkl on November 12, 1920, at Corpus Christi Catholic Church, Deerfield. Following the death of Henry Pirkl in 1953, she married Carl Friedrich Wilhelm Possin on June 2, 1960, in Rice County. She died in 1977 in Deerfield, at age 76 and is buried in Corpus Christi Cemetery..

****

Pallbearers for Henry Pirkl were Clement Brickner, Prescott, Wis.; Donald O'Neil, Faribault; Louis Pirkl, Waseca; William Pirkl, Owatonna; Robert Wesley, Elysian; and Steve Pittman, Morristown. Out-of-town relatives who attended the funeral were Mr. and Mrs. Ben Brickner, and Mr. and Mrs. Clement Brickner, of Prescott, Wis.; Mr. and Mrs. Leo Brickner, Rice Lake, Wis.; Miss Emilee Benish of St. Paul, Mr. and Mrs. Earl Amundson of Minneapolis, Mr. and Mrs. Lloyd Mathis, Mrs. Teana Pirkl, Mr. and Mrs. Joseph Partridge, all of Owatonna, Mr. and Mrs. Louis Pirkl of Waseca, and Mr. and Mrs. Robert Wesley of Elysian. *Faribault Daily News (December 22, 1953)*

PIRKL FAMILY

Peter & Justine (Langer) Pirkl
(Married November 25, 1901)

Peter Pirkl died August 21, 1941, buried Sacred Heart Cemetery, Owatonna. Justine was born in 1883 in Germany and was the daughter of Edward and Johanna (Suz) Langer. Attendants at the marriage were Mary Graff and Frank Pirkl.

Peter William Pirkl
(1869-1941)

Peter William Pirkl was born February 5, 1869 in Steele County to Franz and Rosina (Holub) Pirkl. He grew up on the family farm in Deerfield and attended the local school. He married Justine Langer on November 26, 1901 in Owatonna. They had three children; Leo Wilhelm Pirkl, Agnes Marie Pirkl, and Louis (Aka Aloysius) M. Pirkl

Peter and Justina Pirkl took over the family farm from Peter's parents where they farmed until retirement. Louis Pirkl took over the family farm and he and his wife, Lucille shared their house with Justina after Peter's death on August 21, 1941 in Deerfield Township. The cause of death is listed as Cerebral Arteriosclerosis.

Census Records for Peter Pirkl:
Residence: 14 Jun 1905 in Deerfield, Steele County. Age: 35
Residence: 1920 in Deerfield, Steele, Minnesota; Age: 50; Marital Status:

Justine (Langer) Pirkl
(1883-1970)

Justine Langer, daughter of Edward and Johanna (Suz) Langer was born December 19, 1882 at Rudoltice, East Bohemia, now Czech Republic She married Peter William Pirkl on November 26, 1901, in Owatonna. They had three children during their marriage. She died on November 23, 1970, in Medford, Minnesota, at the age of 87.

Funeral services for Mrs. Justine Pirkl, 87, a longtime resident of Deerfield Township, Steele County, were held on Nov. 23 at Corpus Christi Church in Deerfield. Interment was made in the Sacred Heart Cemetery in Owatonna. Pallbearers were Harlow Pirkl, Raymond Pirkl, Loren Walter, Richard Bruno, Lloyd Matthes, and Donald Matthes.

Justina was a very traditional farm wife who had an excellent work ethic and could cook about anything one could imagine. She brought many of the old Bohemian recipes with her, so it was always a treat to go to Aunt Tina's house for a meal. *Comments by Paul Pirkl.*

Aloysius "Louis" & Lucille (Curran) Pirkl
(Married June 24, 1931 at Sacred Heart Church, Waseca, Minnesota)
(Photo courtesy of Paul Pirkl)

72

Back Row--Jack Pirkl, ?, Martin Pirkl, Ida Pirkl(?), ?, ?
Front Row--?, Louis Pirkl, Lucille (Curran)Pirkl, ?
Aprox 1930

Louis & Lucille (Curran) Pirkl Wedding
(June 24, 1931 in Sacred Heart Catholic Church, Waseca).

LOUIS M. "ALOYSIUS" PIRKL
(1908-1976)

Aloysius Louis Martin Pirkl, son of Peter and Justine (Langer) Pirkl was born November 22, 1908 in Deerfield Township, Steele County. Louis completed eighth grade in the local rural school and then engaged in farming. He married Lucille Curran on June 24, 1931 in Sacred Heart Catholic Church, Waseca.

They lived and farmed in Deerfield Township, Steele County, for many years. Mr. Pirkl died in March 16, 1976 in Deerfield. He was survived by his wife Lucille, a daughter, Mrs. John (RoseMary) Meyer, of Kasson; two sons, Harlow of rural Medford and Raymond of Owatonna. Internment took place in Sacred Heart Catholic Cemetery, Owatonna.

LUCILLE (CURRAN) PIRKL
(1910- 1987)

Lucille Pirkl, 76, of Route 1, Medford, died Jan. 12 at Fairview-Dodge County Care Center, Dodge Center. Funeral services at Christ the King Catholic Church, Medford. The Rev. Edward Mountain was the celebrant. Burial was in Sacred Heart Catholic Cemetery, Owatonna. Lucille Curran was born Feb. 12, 1910 in Steele County to Harry and Emma (Sahler) Curran. She married Louis M. Pirkl on June 24, 1931 in Sacred Heart Catholic Church, Waseca. They lived and farmed in Deerfield Township for many years. Mr. Pirkl died in 1976. She is survived by a daughter, Mrs. John (RoseMary) Meyer, of Kasson; two sons, Harlow of rural Medford and Raymond of Owatonna; and seven grandchildren.

Source: *Faribault Daily News; January 14, 1987*

SOME PIRKL FAMILY OBITUARIES

ALBERT H. PIRKL
(1888-1966)

Albert W. Pirkl was born November 15, 1888 and died October 20, 1966. Buried Corpus Christi with spouse Viola M. Gibson Pirkl Bremer. Parents: Frank & Mary Bemish-Benesch Pirkl. *Source: Dalby Database.*

FRANK H. PIRKL
(1890-1959)

Born July 18, 1890; Died July 12, 1959. Buried Corpus Christi cemetery. Parents; Frank & Mary Bemish-Benesch Pirkl. *Source: Dalby Database.*

CHARLES PIRKL
(1898-1961)

Born April 13, 1898; died January 9, 1961. Buried Corpus Christi Cemetery, Deerfield. -Spouse: Mabel E. O'Neil. Parents. Frank & Mary (Bemish-Benesch) Pirkl. Buried at Corpus Christi Cemetery with Margaret Pirkl Possin. Funeral was held 13/Jan/1961. *Source: Dalby Database.*

BERNARD PIRKL
(1899-1978)

Bernard Pirkl Apr/1978 Bernard (Ben) Pirkl, 78, of 918 Fairview, Faribault, died on Saturday, April 15, 1978 at the Rice County District One Hospital. Mass of Christian Burial will be held on Tuesday, April 18, at 11 a.m. from the Sacred Heart Church, Faribault with the Rev. John T. Brown officiating. Interment will be at Calvary Cemetery, Faribault.

Bernard Martin Pirkl was born in Deerfield Township on May 7, 1899, to Frank and Mary (Benesch) Pirkl. He married Laura Duchene on Oct. 9, 1928, at the Sacred Heart Church in Faribault. Mrs. Pirkl preceded him in death in 1969. They had farmed in Wells Township, Rice County from 1928 until their retirement in 1964. He is survived by four sons: Raymond of Bloomington, Victor of Owatonna, Bernard of Faribault, and Bertram of Minneapolis; one daughter, Mrs. James (Bernice) Dee of Rochester; and eight grandchildren.
Faribault Daily News (April 1978)

MABEL (O'NEILL) PIRKL
(1902-1997)

Mabel E, Pirkl 94, of Owatonna and formerly of Medford, died on Saturday, Dec. 20, 1997 at the Owatonna Health Care Center. Funeral services will be held Tuesday at 2 p.m. at the Church of Christ the King in Medford, with the Rev. Robert Herman officiating. Burial will be in the Corpus Christi Cemetery in Deerfield Township, Steele County. Visitation will be held Tuesday from 12:30 to 1:30 p.m. at the Brick-Postlewaite Funeral Home, Owatonna.

Mabel Elizabeth ONeil, the daughter of John and Annie Malone O'Neil, was born December 31, 1902 in Deerfield Township, Steele County. She married Charles Pirkl on October 4, 1921 in Faribault. He preceded her in death on January 2, 1961. She was a homemaker and a member of the Medford Senior Citizens. She is survived by two nieces, Lorraine (and Joseph) Partridge, Owatonna and Lucille (and Robert) Wesley of Elysian; foster granddaughter Kathleen Rich-Eberly, Fresno, Calif.; a foster great-granddaughter; two special friends and other relatives. She was preceded in death by her husband; foster son Walter Rich; her parents; five brothers, Charles, George, Henry, Daniel and Joseph; and two sisters, Agnes Thomas and Margaret Possin. *Faribault Daily News; December 21, 1997*

SOME PIRKL FAMILY OBITUARIES

Harlow Pirkl as a Medic in Korea (c1953)

HARLOW PIRKL

Harlow Louis Pirkl, 74, lifelong resident of Medford, died Sunday, Oct. 15, 2006. Mass of Christian Burial took place on October 19, at Christ the King Catholic Church in Medford with Fr. Edward Mountain officiating. Interment was at Resurrection Cemetery in Medford, with Military Rites. Harlow Pirkl was born on March 8, 1932 in Deerfield Township to Louis and Lucille (Curran) Pirkl. He attended school in Deerfield Township-District 42. Harlow was drafted in the Army on April 6, 1952 and was a medic. He was involved in the Korean conflict and discharged in June of 1954.

On April 15, 1961, he married Joan Wencl at Holy Trinity Catholic Church at Litomysl. The couple farmed in Deerfield Township raising their two children. Harlow worked at OMC, holding many positions thought out the company, from 1965 until his retirement in 1994. He was an honorary life member of the Medford/Deerfield Knights of Columbus, a life member of VFW-Post 3723 in Owatonna and was also a lifelong member of the Corpus Christi Church and Christ the King Church in Medford. Harlow's interests included fishing, woodworking, playing cards, traveling with friends and spending time with his family.

Harlow was survived by his wife of 45 years, Joan, of Medford, and his children, Debbie (Jeff) Thorpe of Byron and Kristi (Steven) Haedtke of Winona; his grandchildren-Matthew, and Ryan Thorpe and Halle and Nicole Haedtke. His is also survived by his brother, Ray (Marion) Pirkl of Owatonna, and his sister, Rosemary (John) Meyer of Kasson.

RAYMOND H PIRKL
(1933–2018)

Raymond H. Pirkl, age 84, passed away on Tuesday, July 10, 2018, at Field Crest Care Center, Hayfield, MN. Mass of Christian Burial was Saturday, July 14, 2018 at St. Joseph Catholic in Owatonna. Ray was born October 4, 1933, in Deerfield Township, Steele County. He was the son of Louis and Lucille (Curran) Pirkl. He attended country school in Deerfield township. Ray enlisted into the Army in 1954 and serviced for two years and received his GED while in the service.

He was united in marriage to Marion Sammon on October 29, 1953 at Immaculate Conception Church in Faribault and this couple were blessed with two children, Randy and Renae. Ray worked at Pure Oil, then, in April 1957, he started at Owatonna Tool Company as a machinist for the next 38 years. He also farmed while working at OTC. Ray retired from OTC on November 30, 1995.

Ray was a long-time member of St. Joseph Church, Knights of Columbus, the Owatonna Eagles Club, and The American Legion. In Ray and Marions earlier years, the couple did quite a bit of traveling with Hawaii being their favorite destination. Ray always enjoyed watching his grandchildren at their sporting and scholastic events and enjoyed polka dancing and he belonged to the Polka club in the area. Ray also enjoyed being part of a bowling team. Survived by his wife of 64 years Marion, son Randy (Kelly) Pirkl of Owatonna, and daughter Renae (Brian) Humphries of Maple Grove, MN. Grandchildren Zach (Kelsey) Pirkl of Pingree Grove, Illinois, Lindsey (Adam) Traxler of Apple Valley, MN, Logan (Ashley) Pirkl of St. Louis Park, MN, Matt Humphries (Andra Trakalo) of Maple Grove, MN, and Mitchell Humphries of Maple Grove, MN, and great-granddaughter Isabella Pirkl. One sister named Rosemary (John) Meyer of Byron, MN. One sister in law, Joan Pirkl of Medford, MN. and several nieces and nephews. He was preceded in death by his parents Louis and Lucille Pirkl, his brother Harlow Pirkl and niece Kelly Meyer.
Source: Faribault Daily News (12/ July/2018)

SCHMANSKI FAMILY BURIALS AT CORPUS CHRISTI CEMETERY

ELIZABETH (PIRKL) SCHMANSKI (1895-1970)

Funeral services for Mrs. Anton (Ella) Schmanski, 73, of Route 1, Morristown, were held on Aug. 17 at the Corpus Christi Church in Deerfield, with the Rev. Glynn officiating. Pallbearers were Roger Mullenmeister, Bertram Pirkl of Faribault, Don O'Neill of Faribault, Cletus Brickner, Prescott, Wis., Raymond Pirkl, and Burton Brickner of Ellsworth, Wis. The Church Choir provided the music.

Elizabeth H. Pirkl was born on Sept. 28, 1895 to Frank and Mary (Benesch) Pirkl in Deerfield. She attended schools in Steele County and Deerfield. She was united in marriage to Anton Schmanski on June 12, 1917 in Deerfield. The celebrant was a priest from Claremont. Following their marriage they resided in Steele and Rice Counties. She was a member of the Corpus Christi Church and the Rosary Society. A notation in her burial record recognizes her loyal work keeping the church clean. Mrs. Schmanski, who passed away at St. Joseph's Hospital in Mankato on Aug. 12, is survived by her husband, Anton; one son, Edward of Mankato, one foster son, Thomas Swintek of Minneapolis; three grandchildren, one great-grandson and one brother, Ben Pirkl of Faribault. She was preceded in death by her parents, four sisters and four brothers. Friends and relatives attended the funeral from Ellsworth, Prescott, Wis., Minneapolis, St. Paul, Owatonna and Waseca. *Faribault Daily News; (24/Aug/1970)*

ANTON SCHMANSKI (1892-1974)

Anton Schmanski son of Andrew & Mary (Buzalski) Schmanski was born in 1892. He marrried Elizabeth Pirkl on June 12, 1917 in Deerfield. The celebrant was a priest from Claremont. Following their marriage they resided in Steele and Rice Counties. At the annual meeting of the Deerfield Creamery in February 1923, Anthony R. Szymanski was elected a director.

Anton Schmanski died at age 82 on April 29, 1974 and is buried in Corpus Christi Cemetery. *Source: Dalby Database.*

EDWARD SCHMANSKI (1918-1988)

Edward Schmanski 70, Medford, died Saturday, August 18, 1988 at Rice County District One Hospital. Services were Wednesday at Brick Funeral Home, Owatonna. Burial took place in Corpus Christi Cemetery, Deerfield. Edward Schmanski was born January 17, 1918. He married Irene Bruzant.

He is survived by two daughters, Mrs. Giles (Sandi) Christenson, Medford; Gwen Schmanski, Owatonna; and two grandchildren. *Faribault Daily News (22/Aug/1988).*

Edward Schmanski & Irene (Bruzant) Schmanski. Parents Anton & Elizabeth (Pirkl) Schmanski.

IRENE MARIAN (BRUZANT) SCHMANSKI (1918-1985)

Irene Marian Schmanski, 67, Medford, died Thursday, April 11, 1985 in Cedarview Nursing Home, Owatonna. Funeral and visitation arrangements were by Brick Funeral Home, Owatonna. She was survived by her husband, Edward; two daughters, Mrs. Giles (Sandi) Christenson of Medford and Mrs. Bruce (Gwen) Saufferer of Morristown and two sisters, Mrs. Thomas (Margaret) Swintek of Minneapolis and Mrs. Dorothy Saufferer of Owatonna. *Faribault Daily News (April 13, 1985)*

PATRICK MORGAN

Patrick Morgan was born in 1841 in Ireland. As a young man, he came with his mother and siblings to Hastings, Minnesota and later to Warsaw township, Rice County. He purchased an eighty acre farm from Jonas H. Winter which had been purchased ten years earlier from the United States Land Office by Silas Newcombe. Patrick Morgan grubbed and cleared the land by hand which was hard and tedious work. In those days, Indians were plentiful.

Patrick Morgan married Mary Condon, born about 1846 at Faribault, Rice County on 26 Dec 1866. She was a native of County Tipperary, Ireland. They had five daughters; Mary, Nellie, Elizabeth and Ann, and one son, John.

Patrick Morgan died May 30, 1910. The 1920 US census shows Mary Morgan, widowed living in Deerfield Township with her son John and his family.

Mary (Condon) Morgan (1843-1926)

PATRICK MORGAN DEATH

Patrick Morgan, an old and respected resident of West Prairie in the town of Warsaw, died Thursday afternoon, May 26, 1910 at his home, death resulting from heart trouble, after a prolonged illness of general debility. The funeral was held Saturday morning May 29, with a Requiem High Mass. Internment was made in Calvary Cemetery. Patrick Morgan was survived by his wife, one son and two daughters.. *Faribault Daily News.*

MARY MORGAN FUNERAL HELD
Passed Away at Home of Her Son, John Morgan of Deerfield,
Last Tuesday, August 12, 1926.

Funeral services for Mrs. Patrick Morgan, who died August 12, 1926 at the home of her son John Morgan, of Deerfield, were held Tuesday morning at 9:00 o'clock at the Immaculate Conception church at Faribault. Burial was made in Calvary Cemetery. Mrs. Morgan's death followed after five months of serious illness throughout which she suffered complications of her health.

Mary Condon was born in 1843 in the County Tipperary in the Parish of Latin. She came to this country with her parents when she was 12 years of age. In 1868, she was married to Patrick Morgan, six children being born to this union. She was survived by her son John of Deerfield, and four daughters --- Mrs. Mary McCarty of Foxholm, Minnesota, Mrs. Nellie Wobbrock of Medford, Mrs. Katie Alheis of Crookston, Minnesota, and Mrs. Elizabeth Bergeron of Minneapolis. One daughter, Annie, passed away 16 years ago. She is also survived by 16 grandchildren. Her husband, Patrick Morgan passed away 16 years ago.

Pallbearers were Wm. Nusbaum Sr., John O'Conners, Frank Voegel, Joe Sammon, William Sammon, and Ed O'Neill. *Source: Faribault Daily News*

Patrick Morgan & Mary Condon were married December 26, 1866 in Rice County, Minnesota.
Patrick Morgan was born in 1841 in Ireland and died May 30, 1910. Mary Condon was born in 1843 and
died August 12, 1926 at the home of her son, John.

FAMILY OF PATRICK & MARY (CONDON) MORGAN

Kathryn Morgan and Oscar Ahles

Mary Morgan and John McCarthy

Blanche Morgan and Amite Bergeron

Nellie Morgan and Ted Wobbrock

Donald Morgan was confirmed in Waseca through Corpus Christi church on May 22, 1938 at 13 years old.

Helen Morgan Confirmation. (About 1925)

From Morgan Family Records;
Everett Morgan made his first communion in the Corpus Christi Church on June 5, 1938 at age 8 years.

Making Hay in Deerfield Township (1930s)

John Joseph Morgan & Mary Ost
(Married February 16, 1909)

John Joseph Morgan
(1876-1972)

John Morgan died on August 2, 1972, at his home in Deerfield Township, Steele County, at the age of 95. Funeral services were held at Corpus Christi Church, Deerfield with Fr. Francis Glynn officiating. He was buried in Resurrection Cemetery, Medford. Mr. Morgan was survived by four sons, Everett of Faribault, Edward and Donald of Deerfield, and Robert of Austin, and three daughters, Mrs. Harold (Margaret) Meyer of Faribault, Mrs. Anna Ness of Deerfield and Mrs. Ernest (Helen) Krueger of Owatonna.

At the time of his death, John Morgan had 34 grandchildren, and 40 great-grandchildren. *Source: US Census, 1920, 1930, 1940, Rice County History: Their History, Our Heritage (1981) and Dalby Database.*

John Joseph Morgan was born on October 20, 1876, near Morristown in Warsaw Township, Rice County, Minnesota, his father, Patrick, was 35 and his mother, Mary Condon, was 25. He married Mary Ost on February 16, 1909. They had seven children in 19 years. By 1915, John and Mary Morgan were living on a farm in Deerfield Township, Steele County about one-half mile from his mother's farm in Rice County. John Morgan's mother Mary Condon passed away in August 1926. John continued working the farm and eventually bought it. In 1941, they built a new house on his mother's farm and moved the family there. In April 1972, John sold the farm to Jim Southworth. The farm had been in the Morgan family 104 years.

John & Mary (Ost) Family
Seated, L-R: John, Everett, Mary
Standing: Helen, John Edward, Ann, Donald, Robert, and Margaret.

John Morgan and family owned and farmed in Deerfield Township about one-half mile from his mother's farm. He rented the home place from his mother. Mrs. Patrick Morgan made her home for twelve years with her son and family until her death, August 7, 1926. Then John and his wife, Mary Ost Morgan, purchased the farm from the estate. In 1941, John built a new house on his mother's place and moved into it Feb. 7, 1942,

John and Mary (Ost) Morgan had four sons and three daughters. The children were Everett of Faribault, Edward and Donald of Deerfield, and Robert of Austin, and Mrs. Harold (Margaret) Meyer of Faribault, Mrs. Anna Ness of Deerfield and Mrs. Ernest (Helen) Krueger of Owatonna.

The Morgan's belonged to the Corpus Christi Catholic Church in Deerfield, which is located 3 miles south of their farm. In the early days, it was customary to walk to church and many other places,

JOHN & MARY (OST) MORGAN CELEBRATE 50TH WEDDING ANNIVERSARY

John & Mary (Ost) Morgan
Fiftieth Wedding Anniversary Celebration --- February 15, 1959
Corpus Christi Church, Deerfield

Mr. and Mrs. John Morgan celebrated their 50th wedding anniversary on Sunday February 15, 1959 at Corpus Christi Catholic Church, Deerfield. The Reverend Harold Mountain officiated at the 10:30 Mass with relatives and friends attending. A dinner was held in the church basement for 60 relatives of the couple. The tables were decorated with yellow and white pompoms with lighted tapers. On the table cloths were red cupids, and small hearts with golden arrows. The room was decorated with white and gold streamers and gold bells. In the afternoon an open house was held in the church basement for approximately 400 relatives and friends of the couple.

A five-tiered wedding cake, with a miniature bride and groom on top with 50th in gold in the crown and white and gold decorations was made by Mrs. Ben Holmquist of Deerfield. The cake was served by Mrs. Morgan's sister, Rose Van den Driesche. A second cake was made by Mrs. Richard Mensing. Mrs. June Van Orsow, a sister of Mrs. Morgan poured. Betty Manderfeld, Louise and Dorothy Meyer, Marjorie Ness, granddaughters the couple were waitresses. Helen Van den Driesche, niece of Mrs. Morgan also waited on tables. Mrs. Ben Holmquist, Ernest Holmquist and Mr. and Mrs. Henry Hager helped with dinner in the kitchen.

Mrs. Morgan is the former Mary Ost of Walcott. The couple were married February 16, 1909 at the church of St. Lawrence in Faribault. Their attendants were George Woods of Faribault and Lena Loggie of Faribault, both deceased.

The Morgans have seven sons and daughters. They are Mrs. Bernard Ness (Ann) of Morristown, Mrs. Ernest Krueger (Helen) of Owatonna, Mrs. Harold Meyer (Margaret), Ed and Donald Morgan of Morristown, Everett Morgan of Faribault, and Robert Morgan of Austin. John Morgan has three living sisters and Mrs. Morgan has two brothers and three sisters. One sister, Mrs. Patrick Condon is deceased. The couple also has 25 grandchildren.

The couple received many lovely and useful gifts and gifts of money from those attending.
Source: Faribault Daily News

Ann Amelia Morgan & Bernard Ness
Married April 25, 1934
Immaculate Conception Church, Faribault.

Standing, L-R: Ann Amelia (Morgan) Ness, Mary (Ost) Morgan, Seated: Great Grandma Amelia Ost holding Marjorie Ness.

Ann (Morgan) Ness, 82, resident of Deerfield Township, rural Morristown, died Wednesday, Feb. 24, 1993, at Pleasant Manor Nursing Home. Services were held at the Christ the King Church, Medford, with the Rev. Robert Herman officiating. Burial was in Resurrection Cemetery in Medford. Ann Amelia Morgan, daughter of John and Mary (Ost) Morgan, was born July 4, 1910, in Warsaw Township, Rice County. She married Bernard Ness on April 25, 1934, in Immaculate Conception Church, Faribault. He preceded her in death on March 1, 1961. Ann Morgan Ness and her daughter Marjorie were Corpus Christi parishioners for many years. She worked for a number of years at Birds Eye Foods in Waseca and Jerome Foods in Faribault. Survivors included two daughters, Marjorie Ness and Mrs. William (Betty) Manderfeld, both of Faribault; five grandchildren; two sisters, Mrs. Helen Kruger of Owatonna and Mrs. Harold (Margaret) Meyer of Faribault; two brothers, Donald Morgan of Morristown and Everett (Bud) Morgan of Faribault; and other relatives. Besides her husband, she was preceded in death by her parents; and three brothers, Edward, Robert and Joseph in infancy.
FarIbault Daily News (Feb. 26, 1993)

Donald & Dorothy (Bakken) Morgan Family
Front Row, L-R: Daniel, Dorothy, Donald, and Dennis.
Back Row; Darla, Dawn, Douglas, Donna, and Diane.

Donald Stanley Morgan, the son of John and Mary (Ost) Morgan, was born on May 2, 1925, in Deerfield Township, Steele County. Don grew up on his family's farm and started farming at the age of 12. This began a life-long career farming in Deerfield Township. On Aug. 16, 1950, he was united in marriage to Dorothy Bakken at Corpus Christi Catholic Church in Deerfield Township. Together they farmed and raised their family. In 1960, Don started Morgan Farm Service and owned and operated this business until 1987. Don was a founding member of the Medford-Deerfield Knights of Columbus and was also a Past Grand Knight. Don also served as a Past Faithful Navigator of the General Shields Assembly Fourth Degree Knights of Columbus. He was inducted into the Rice County Agriculture Hall of Fame in 2011.

Don enjoyed life and his family. He especially enjoyed family celebrations and time spent together. He also liked playing cards, dancing and snowmobiling. He was a member of the Medford-Deerfield Knights of Columbus, the Fourth Degree General Shields Assembly and the Faribault Aerie 1460 Fraternal Order of Eagles.

Donald S. Morgan, 86, of Morristown, passed away Tuesday, April 17, 2012, at Milestone Assisted Living in Faribault, following a sudden illness. Interment will be held at the Resurrection Cemetery, Medford. He is survived by his wife of 61 years, Dorothy Morgan of Faribault; by seven children, Diane (Aldon) Sammon of Faribault, Donna (Mark) Ihlenfeld of Owatonna, Dennis (Deb) Morgan of Morristown, Dawn (Larry) Conrad of Dundas, Douglas Morgan of Medford, Daniel (Donna) Morgan of Medford and Darla (Jeff) Kosanda of Faribault; by 20 grandchildren, Jason (Brenda) Sammon, Steven Sammon, Seth (Nicole) Ihlenfeld, Eric, Wade and Ethan Ihlenfeld, Jessica Morgan, Dustin (Elizabeth) Morgan, Randi Mae Morgan, Cody (Jessica) Morgan, Adam Conrad and fiance Alyssa Tangen, Angela and Ashley Conrad, Tyler, Chelsea, Nicole and Danielle Morgan, Blake, Allison and Kayce Kosanda; by three great-grandchildren, Jacob and Elizabeth Sammon and Aela Morgan; by his brother, Everett "Bud" (LaVonne) Morgan of Faribault and by nieces, nephews and other relatives and friends. He was preceded in death by his parents, his infant son, great-granddaughter, Josephine Sammon, two brothers, John (Ed) and Robert Morgan and by three sisters, Ann Ness, Helen Krueger and Margaret Meyer.

CONDON FAMILY HISTORY

John Patrick Condon (1830-February 15, 1910), was a native of Townland Latin, County Tipperary, Ireland. He was the son of Patrick Condon (1806-1886) and his wife Catherine. Patrick Condon owned a farm six miles south east of Morristown in Deerfield Township.

John Condon worked for a time for James J. Hill during the construction of the Milwaukee Railroad. In 1861, he bought 160 acres of land from Nancy K. Lockwood. In the family's possession is the United States Land Patent signed by President Abraham Lincoln on April 15 1861. The farm has been owned and operated by the same family for many years.

Originally the farm was covered with timber and meadows. In the early days John Condon raised Indian corn or maize which they would carry on their backs to Hastings to get corn meal ground. For supper there was corn meal mush. The leftovers were fried for breakfast.

John Condon's mother's maiden name was Burns. On their voyage across the Atlantic in a sailing vessel---a voyage which took three months---her father died and was buried at sea. John Condon's father also came from Ireland. He lived on the farm in a log house. He died at the age of 104 years. John and Ann (Burns) Condon had four children, Patrick, Frank, Annie and Katie. Patrick married Alice Ost.

Patrick purchased the land from his father in 1902. Forty acres of the original 160 acres were sold to Mr. Crandall. Patrick, who was 83 years old on Jan. 3rd, 1956, and a 2-year old son resided on the farm. There were 14 children in the Patrick Condon family, 7 boys and 7 girls. Six boys and six girls reached adulthood. Sylvester Condon, son of Patrick and Alice Ost purchased the farm in March 1978. *Source: Diane (Morgan) Sammon.*

OBITUARY
JOHN CONDON
(1830-1902)

One of Deerfield's pioneer settlers passed away at his home Friday morning, April 11, after an illness lasting only a week. Pneumonia was the cause of the death. Mr. Condon was born in County Tipperary, Ireland, seventy-eight years ago. He migrated to this country with his parents, arriving at Deerfield in 1856 and since that time has been a continuous resident. In 1870, he married Miss Anna Burns, of Kilkenny.

The union was blessed with four children, Frank Condon, of Chicago; Mrs. Catherine Teresa Ellingsworth, of Kilkenny and Patrick A., and Miss Anna Condon, who resided at home. Besides the widow and children, three brothers and four sisters survive.

Mr. Condon possessed all the characteristics of a thorough and progressive citizen and a noble husband and father. When he first took up his residence here, he erected a log cabin and log stables, but by constant industry he has replaced the cabin with a new frame home, and at the time of his death, had material on the ground for a large barn.

The funeral which was one of the largest ever seen here was held Monday morning from the Immaculate Conception church. The remains were laid in Calvary cemetery by the side of those of his parents. *Source: Rice County Journal, April 16, 1902.*

OBITUARY
ANNA (BURNS/BYRNES) CONDON
(1830-1902)

Mrs. John Condon died at the home of her daughter, Mrs. C. H. Ellingsworth of Fourth Avenue W. Tuesday, Feb. 15th. The cause of her death was diabetes coma of which she had suffered attacks at intervals for some time. The funeral was held Friday morning from the church of the Immaculate Conception.

*****

Anna was one of at least seven children born to John and Ann (Hand) Burns of Bord Townland, County Monahan, Ireland. Ann Hand was born October 17, 1834 in County Monahan.

The family emigrated to the United States. While at sea, John Burns become seriously ill, and died. The officials on the ship wrapped his body in a canvas and after a brief prayer ceremony his body was lowered into the Atlantic Ocean. The Burns family settled in Shieldsville where Ann (Hand) Burns passed away on February 15, 1910. She is buried in St. Patrick's Cemetery, Shieldsville.

John and Ann (Hand) Burns were the parents of seven children; John, James, Garret, Ann, Mary, and Patrick. *Source: Diane (Morgan) Sammon.*

OBITUARY
PATRICK CONDON
(1873-1967)

Funeral services were held for Patrick John Condon, Route 1, Morristown, July 28 at the Immaculate Conception Church with the Rev. George Kinney officiating. Pallbearers were Robert Jensen, Byron; James Condon, Faribault; Gary Condon, Northfield; Larry Heath, Rochester; Michael Condon, Medford and John Webb, Ely. Interment was in Calvary Cemetery.

Mr. Condon was born in Deerfield on January 3, 1873, He was married to Alice Ost on May 12, 1908 at the Immaculate Conception Church. He passed away July 25 at the Owatonna Hospital.

He is survived by 12 children, Lewis of Owatonna; Philip of Morristown; Daniel of Owatonna; Garrett of Northfield; Sylvester of Morristown; Camille of Medford; Agnes Lueth of Zumbrota; Anna Jensen of Morristown; Frances Webb of Ely; Bernadeen Heath of Rochester; Rita Sprolorich of Eveleth and Eleanor Heyer of Morristown. He was preceded in death by his wife, one daughter, one son, and two grandchildren. Relatives and friends from away attending the funeral were from Northfield, Minneapolis, Rochester, Owatonna, Ely, Eveleth, California, Mississippi, Waseca, Faribault, Medford, Zumbrota, Wisconsin, Elysian and Byron.
Source: Faribault Daily News, Aug. 12, 1967.

OBITUARY
SYLVESTER CONDON
(1932-2004)

Sylvester "Sookie" Condon, 72, of Morristown, died Monday, Feb. 9, 2004, at his home of cancer. A Mass of Christian Burial was held on Monday, Feb. 16, 2004, at Christ The King Catholic Church in Medford, with the Rev. Clayton Haberman officiating. Interment was held at the Resurrection Cemetery in Medford.

Sylvester Charles Condon, the son of Patrick and Alice (Ost) Condon, was born on Jan. 12, 1932, in Deerfield Township, Steele County. On Sept. 2, 1960, he was united in marriage to Ethel Schneider in Owatonna. Sylvester was a life long farmer in Deerfield Township.

Sylvester was better known as "Sookie" to many of his friends. His well-known phrase "Mercy, Mercy," will be remembered by all. He enjoyed spending time with his family and playing cards and checkers.

He is survived by his wife, Ethel Condon of Morristown; by a son, Brian Condon of Medford; by five daughters, Roxanne (and Jim) Thibodeau of St. Paul, Patricia Gribbin of Bedford, Texas, Jacqueline (and Tim) Loxley of Cresson, Pa., Kimberley (and Dave) Cramer of Tallahassee, Fla., and Vickie (and Kevin) Karlstad of Lewisville, Texas; by four grandsons, Nicholas, Timothy and Jonathan Loxley and Alec Cramer; by four granddaughters, Molly Thibodeau, Brooke and Erika Gribbin and Lauren Cramer; by two sisters, Frances (and Edward) Webb of Rochester and Eleanor Heyer of Faribault; by a brother, Camille Condon of Medford. He was preceded in death by his parents; five sisters, Lorraine Condon, Agnes Leuth, Anna Jensen, Bernadeen Heath and Rita Spalarich; and by five brothers, John, Philip, Lewis, Gary and David Condon. *Source: Faribault Daily News, February 12, 2004*

OBITUARY
KATHLEEN (O'NEILL) CONDON
(1925-1999)

Kathleen M. Condon, 74, of Morristown, died Wednesday, Nov. 17, 1999 at Abbott Northwestern Hospital, Minneapolis. Funeral services were held at Sacred Heart Catholic Church, Faribault, on Saturday, Nov. 20, 1999. Interment was at Resurrection Cemetery, Medford Township, in Steele County.

Kathleen ONeill, the daughter of George E. and Mary (Barrett) ONeill, was born Oct. 17, 1925 in Rice County. She married Philip A. Condon on Feb. 14, 1942 at Corpus Christi Church in Deerfield Township. He preceded her in death on Jan. 28, 1993. She was a member of the Golden Agers of Morristown. She is survived by five children, Philip (and Mary) Condon Jr. of Stewartville, James Condon of Morristown, Barbara Condon of Elysian, Mark Condon of Morristown and Leslie Condon of Janesville; six grandchildren; four great-grandchildren; one brother, Richard (and Peggy) O'Neill of Warsaw; and one sister, Mary "Frances" Thraen of Faribault. She was preceded in death by her parents; her husband, Philip; and one brother, Leo O'Neill in infancy.
Faribault Daily News, Nov. 18, 1999.

OBITUARY
PHILIP CONDON
(1920-1993)

Philip A. Condon, 72, of Morristown died on Jan. 28, 1993, at District One Hospital. Services were held at Sacred Heart Catholic Church, Faribault. Burial was in Resurrection Cemetery, Medford.

The son of Patrick and Alice (Ost) Condon, he was born on July 10, 1920, in Deerfield Township. He married Kathleen ONeill on Feb. 14, 1942, at Corpus Christie Church in Deerfield Township. He farmed in the Rice County area, and drove a milk truck for the Morristown Creamery. He also was a yard foreman for Associated Lumber in Waseca for 15 years.

He is survived by his wife; five children, Philip Condon Jr. of Stewartville, James, Barbara and Mark, all of Morristown, and Leslie of Waldorf, Minn.; six grandchildren; two great-grandchildren; five sisters, Mrs. Agnes Leuth of Zumbro Falls, Mrs. Frances (Edward) Webb of Rochester, Mrs. Eleanore Heyer of Morristown, Mrs. Bernadeen (Oren) Heath of Kenyon and Mrs. Rita (Tom) Spolarich of Eveleth; and four brothers, Camille of Medford, Lewis of Owatonna, David of Medford and Sylvester of Deerfield. He was preceded in death by his parents; one brother, Garrett; one sister, Anna Cecilia Jensen; and a sister, Lorraine, and a brother, John, both in infancy.
Source: Faribault Daily News, January 29, 1993.

Patrick & Alice (Ost) Condon Family
(Photo taken on the front steps of Corpus Christi)
Patrick and Alice Condon were the parents of 12 children, Lewis, Philip, Daniel, Garrett, Sylvester, Camille, Agnes, Anna, Frances, Bernadeen, Rita, and Eleanor.

OBITUARY
RUTH (SAMMON) CONDON
(1930-2007)

Ruth (Mrs. Lewis) Condon, age 76, of Owatonna, died May 23, 2007, at the Alterra Sterling House in Owatonna. Mass of Christian Burial was held on May 29, 2007. at the St. Joseph Catholic Church in Owatonna, with Fr. Edward McGrath, pastor, officiating. Interment was at the Calvary Cemetery in Faribault.

Ruth Ann Sammon, the daughter of Leo and Margaret (Fitzpatrick) Sammon, was born on Oct. 23, 1930, in Faribault. On Dec. 4, 1954, she was united in marriage to Lewis Condon at the Corpus Christi Catholic Church, Deerfield, Minn. Mr. Condon preceded her in death on Sept. 28, 1995. After their marriage they lived in Deerfield Township, and worked for some of the area farmers. In 1967 they moved to Owatonna, and Ruth started a home day care that she operated for over 25 years. In 1973, Ruth started cooking at the Monterey Ballroom and worked there for over 20 years. She also worked at the Broaster, a restaurant in Owatonna.

Ruth enjoyed listening to old-time music, baking, especially sweets, collecting cow memorabilia, and spending time with family and friends. She was a member of St. Joseph Catholic Church. She was survived by two children, Mary Jo Davis and fiance Dean Schroeder of Owatonna, and Chuck Condon of Morristown; by four grandchildren, Tyrone, Tasha and Tyler Davis, and Brianna Condon Lawson; by three brothers, Richard (and Betty) Sammon of Morristown, Clarence "Butch" Sammon of Longville, Minn., and Joe (and Kay) Sammon of Waseca; by a sister, Yvonne Kaderlik of Faribault; and other relatives and friends. She was preceded in death by her parents; husband; and two brothers, Bill Sammon and Fr. Lawrence Sammon.
Source: Faribault Daily News, May 25, 2007.

WILLIAM & VERONICA (HRUSKA) KVASNICKA

William & Veronica (Hruska) Kvasnicka with son Lawrence.
The William and Veronica Kvasnicka family were very involved in the re-opening of Corpus Christi parish in 1938.
The first parish picnic was held on their farm in 1938. William Kvasnicka passed away suddenly in 1939.

Henry & Anna (Hollinger) Hager

HENRY HAGER
(1904-1975)

ANNA SARAH HAGER *nee* HOLLINGER
(1906-1996)

Henry Hager was born June 30, 1904 in LeSueur County. He attended a LeSueur County rural school known as Horseshoe Lake School. He farmed his entire life in LeSueur and Waseca Counties. Henry and Anna Hager moved to Blooming Grove in November 1943. He was a member of Corpus Christi Catholic Church, Deerfield for about 35 years, serving as a trustee many years and custodian 25 years. He was a member of the Knights of Columbus and the Farm Bureau. He served on the school board of Districts 42 and 2 and on the Medford School Board.

Henry Hager, age 71, Rural Route # 3, Waseca, passed away at farm home in Blooming Grove Township on Thursday December 18, 1975. He was survived by his wife, Anna (nee Hollinger), six daughters; Mrs. Vernon (Loretta) Schwartz, Waterville, Mrs. Willard (Helen) Karsten of rural Waseca, Mrs. Wayne (Roseanne) Barbknecht of Janesville, Mrs. Donald (Sue) Redman of rural Morristown, Mrs. David (Sandra) Sutlief of Princeton, and Mrs. Gordon (Debra) Johnson of Burnsville. He was also survived by eight sons John and Neil of Medford, Donald and Eugene of Owatonna, David at home, Louis of Mankato, Dennis of rural Waterville, and Paul of Waseca. Also surviving are a brother, Albert of Waterville; three sisters, Mrs. Helen Stangler and Mrs. Marie Hollinger of Waterville, and Mrs. Regina Weaver of Kilkenny, and 40 grandchildren, and two great grandchildren.

Funeral Services were held at Christ The King Catholic Church, Medford with Father Francis Glynn officiating. Burial took place in Corpus Christi Cemetery, Deerfield Township, Steele County.

Anna Sarah Hollinger was born October 27, 1906 to Andrew and Sarah (Liebing) Hollinger in LeSueur County. She married Henry Hager on May 22, 1928 at Holy Trinity Catholic Church, Waterville and they farmed for many years in Blooming Grove, Waseca County. She was a member of the Blooming Grove Extension Group, Catholic Foresters, Senior Citizens, Civic Club, an honorary chapter mother for Future Homemakers of America (FHA), several card clubs, Catholic Daughters of the Americas, Court St. Anne of Medford and also a 4-H club leader. She was a volunteer on the Owatonna Hospital Auxiliary. Anna and her family were parishioners at Corpus Christi, Deerfield beginning in 1943.

Anna Sarah Hager passed away at age 89 on April 18, 1996 at her daughter's home in Medford. She was survived by six daughters; Loretta Schwartz and her husband, Vernon, of Waterville, Helen Karsten of Waseca, Rosanne and her husband Wayne Barbknecht of Janesville, Sue and her husband Don Redman of Medford, Sandra and her husband David Sutlief of Princeton, and Debra Halblieb and her husband Mark of Cross Lake. Five sons and their wives; John and Shirley of Medford, Donald and Betty of Owatonna, Louis and Harriet of Mankato, Dennis and Becky of Andover, and Gene and Tena of Owatonna; two daughters-in-law; Donna Hager of Medford and Loretta (Hager) Ratajczyk of Circle Pines; 51 grandchildren, 43 great grandchildren, and two great-great grandchildren. She was preceded in death by her husband Henry, Dec. 18, 1975; two daughters, Lucille and Mary Jean; three sons; Neil, David and Paul; one son-in-law, Willard Karsten; one grandson William Barbknecht; one great-granddaughter Mary Sue Krippner; and five sisters and two brothers.

The funeral was held Monday April 22, 1996 at Christ The King Catholic Church, Medford with burial in Corpus Christi Cemetery, Deerfield. Pallbearers were Rick Hager, Steve Hager, Tim Hager, Mathew Hager, Andy Hager and Ron Hager.

91

Henry & Anna (Hollinger) Hager Family

Front & Middle Rows, L-R; Dennis, Susan, Paul, Henry, Debra (in Henry's lap), Anna, Sandra, Eugene, Rose-anne. Back Row: Loretta, David, John, Neil, Louis, Donald, Helen.

Henry Hager on far right with eight sons who are all members of the Knights of Columbus.
L-R: Donald, John, Dennis, David, Louis, Neil, Gene, Paul and Henry.
(Minnesota State Knights of Columbus Monthly; June 1, 1965)

STEPHEN & ROSAMOND (ROUSSEAU) O'BRIEN FAMILY

Stephen & Rosamond (Rousseau) O'Brien Family.

Stephen F. O'Brien was born to Thomas and Veronica (Loeffler) O'Brien in Kilkenny, LeSueur County on April 18, 1901. He married Rosemond Rousseau in 1929 in Faribault. She preceded him in death in 1948. On June 4, 1951, he married Margaret Eastman in Faribault. She died in 1975. Later that year he married Nellie Theder in Medford. He farmed for many years in Deerfield and in Merton Townships, Steele County.

Stephen F. OBrien, 84, of 515 S. Main St., Medford, died July 25, 1985 at Owatonna City Hospital. Mass of Christian Burial was at the Church of Christ the King, Medford, with the Rev. Edward C. Mountain officiating. Burial was in Corpus Christi Cemetery, Deerfield Township.

Surviving were his wife; four sons, Leonard and Maurice of Reno, Nev., Albert of Orcus Island, Wash. and Michael of Tucson, Ariz.; seven daughters, Mary Smith and Joan Gowan of St. Paul, Rita Kuntz and Grace Skalicky of Owatonna, Pat Berg of Morristown, Maureen Johnson of Reno, Nev., and Frances Allman of Ft. Leavenworth, Kan.; 38 grandchildren; 20 great-grandchildren; two step-daughters, Bonnie Kern of Medford and Joan Amato of Baltimore, Md.; a step-son, Capt. Jay Theder of Dallas, Texas; seven sisters, Agnes Hagerty and Theresa Hanley of Faribault, Mary Brown of Lonsdale, Bonnie Hagerty of Kilkenny, Anastasia Lank of Los Angeles, Sister Catherine O'Brien of Sinsinawa, Wis., and Sister Alice Veronica of Minneapolis. He was preceded in death by a daughter, three brothers and one sister. Source: *Faribault Daily News; 27/July/1985.*

Stephen F. O'Brien (1901-1985)

Stephen F. O'Brien (1901-1985 & Rosamond (Rousseau) O'Brien (1909-1948). Parents of:
Leonard, Maurice, Albert, Michael, Joan, Rita, Grace, Pat, Maureen, Frances & Baby O'Brien.

Agnes and Margaret Fitzpatrick were baptized at Corpus Christi Church in April 1907.

Agnes Bridget and Margaret Louise Fitzpatrick born April 19, 1907, were twin daughters of Michael and Anna (Novak) Fitzpatrick. They had an older brother Joseph Michael Fitzpatrick (1905-1944).

Agnes and Margaret were baptized at Corpus Christi in April 1907. Agnes did not marry and worked at the Faribault State School and Hospital from 1944 until she retired in 1975. Margaret married Leo Sammon.

Agnes and Margaret Fitzpatrick first Holy Communion (c1917). Margaret Fitzpatrick married Leo Sammon. The Sammons purchased the Fitzpatrick farm and lived in Deerfield until their deaths. Agnes Fitzpatrick did not marry. She passed away May 17, 1984 and is buried at Calvary Cemetery, Faribault.

Threshing Grain in Deerfield Township (1920s).

MICHAEL & ANNA (NOVAK) FITZPATRICK FAMILY

Michael Fitzpatrick
(May 1861-September 7, 1916)

Anna Novak
(January 7, 1881-December 11, 1943)

Married February 6, 1904

Michael Fitzpatrick was born in May 1861 in Wheatland, Rice County, Minnesota. He died on September 7, 1916, in rural Morristown, Warsaw Township, Rice County, Minnesota, at the age of 55. Anna Novak January 7, 1881-December 11, 1943. In 1910, Michael and Anna (Novak) Fitzpatrick were living on a farm in Deerfield Township together with children, Joseph, age 5, Agnes, age 3 and Margaret age 3.

Michael Fitzpatrick, prominent farmer of the town of Morristown, died suddenly on Friday afternoon, September 7. Mr. Fitzpatrick was threshing with his neighbors at the Nels Johnson place, southeast of town, and about 4 o'clock it was noticed that he had stopped pitching. Several men hurried to his wagon and found him lying on his load of grain in an unconscious condition. He had not been feeling well all day and at the noon hour refused to eat dinner telling his friends that he would feel better if he did not eat. Doctors were summoned but he was beyond all aid. The funeral was held Tuesday morning from the church of the Immaculate Conception and interment in Calvary Cemetery.
Source: Rice County Journal; September 13, 1916.
Note: Michael Fitzpatrick was the son of Michael Fitzpatrick Sr. and Bridget McCall.

Anna Novak passed away December 11, 1943 and is buried at Calvary Cemetery, Faribault. She was the daughter of Frank and Catherine (Rhines) Novak.

FITZPATRICK/SAMMON FAMILY

Leo & Margaret (Fitzpatrick) Sammon Family (c1941)
Front Row; L-R: Yvonne, Ruth, Lawrence, Richard, William Sammon.
Back Row: Anna (Novak) FitzPatrick, Clara E. (Frydenlund) Fitzpatrick, Joseph FitzPatrick, Agnes Bridget Fitzpatrick,
Leo Sammon, Margaret FitzPatrick Sammon (holding Joseph). Margaret is pregnant with Clarence "Butch" Sammon).

Leo & Margaret (Fitzpatrick) Sammon Farm.
(Previously owned by Margaret's parents, Michael and Anna (Novak) Fitzpatrick).

LEO & MARGARET (FITZPATRICK) SAMMON FAMILY

Leo & Margaret (Fitzpatrick) Sammon Family (October 13, 1962)

L-R: children: Charles Condon, Mary Jo Condon, Jeanine Sammon, Bradley Sammon, Diane Kaderlik, Melvin Kaderlik, Duane Kaderlik, Bruce Kaderlik. Adults, L-R: Ruth (Sammon) Condon, Phyllis (Dienst) Sammon, William Sammon, Kay (Breck) Sammon, Joseph Sammon, Margaret (FitzPatrick) Sammon, Leo Sammon, Richard Sammon, Betty (Zitzman) Sammon, Ervin Kaderlik, Yvonne (Sammon) Kaderlik holding Laurie Kaderlik.

Leo & Margaret (Fitzpatrick) Sammon Family

Pictured L-R; Front Row: Leo, Ruth (pregnant with Charles), Yvonne, Margaret (Fitzpatrick).
L-R, Back Row: Richard, father Lawrence, Clarence (Butch), Joe, William.

JOSEPH & LUCILLE (WALTER) WEBER FAMILY HISTORY

Mr. & Mrs. Joseph Weber

JOSEPH C. WEBER (1914-2009)

Joseph C. Weber, the son of Peter and Anna (Stadler) Weber, was born on Jan. 23, 1914 in Medford. He attended Medford High School and graduated with the class of 1932. On Sept. 28, 1937 he was united in marriage to Lucille Walter. Mrs. Weber preceded him in death on Nov. 21, 1999. Joe farmed for over 40 years in Deerfield Township, Steele County. While farming he also worked as a heavy equipment operator doing road construction for Underdahl Construction. Joe was a member of the Medford Knights of Columbus and the Corpus Christi Catholic Church in Deerfield Township. Joe was an avid fisherman, enjoyed animals, nature and all sports. He also enjoyed spending time with all of his family.

Joseph C. Weber, age 94, of Deerfield Township, Steele County, died on Saturday, Jan. 3, 2009 at his home. Mass of Christian Burial was held on Wednesday, Jan. 7, at Christ The King Catholic Church in Medford, with the Rev. Joseph Pete, officiating. Interment was at the Resurrection Cemetery, Medford. He was survived by two children, Marge Wadekamper of Faribault and Robert (Bernadette) Weber of Owatonna; by 10 grandchildren; 21 great-grandchildren; four great-great-grandchildren; and nieces, nephews and other relatives and friends.

He was preceded in death by his parents; his wife Lucille; his great granddaughter, Genevieve Jones; his son-in-law, Rudy Wadekamper; by two brothers, Jacob (Frances) Weber and Nicholas (Odessa) Weber; and by six sisters, Alma (Fred) Morrissey, Elizabeth (Aloyius) Simmons, Mary (Art) Voegele, Margaret (James) Johnson, Loretta Weber and Eleanor (Francis) Varley.

LUCILLE (WALTER) WEBER (1911-1999)

Lucille Marie Walter, the daughter of Joseph and Mary (Obertein) Walter, was born Nov. 1, 1911, in Adrian. She married Joseph Weber on Sept. 28, 1937, at the Sacred Heart Church, Owatonna. After their marriage, she stayed at home and raised their children. Later she went to work outside their home at several different jobs, but spent the most time working at the Faribault Regional Center. She also volunteered her time whenever she could and spent many hours at the Faribault Clothes Closet. She was active at her church, Corpus Christi Catholic Church in Deerfield Township. There she spent many hours working with the sewing group.

Mrs. Joseph (Lucille) Weber, 88, of Medford, died Sunday, Nov. 21, 1999, at the Faribault Health and Rehabilitation Center. Services were held at Christ the King Catholic Church, Medford, with the Rev. Joseph Pete and the Rev. Robert Herman officiating. Burial will be at Resurrection Cemetery, Medford. Visitation is scheduled for 4 to 8 p.m. today at the Parker Kohl Funeral Home, Faribault, and for one hour prior to service at the church Wednesday. The rosary will be recited at 7 p.m. tonight. She is survived by her husband, Joseph Weber of Medford; two children, Robert (and Bernadette) Weber of Owatonna and Marge Wadekamper of Farbault; nine grandchildren; 11 great-grandchildren; a brother, Paul Walter of Lubbock, Texas; a sister, Dorothy Loken of Waseca; and other relatives and friends. She was preceded in death by her parents; a son-in-law, Rudy Wadekamper; seven brothers, Leo, Lloyd, Joseph, Eldo, Robert, Clarence and Leonard Walter; a half-sister, Gertrude Grabar; and two half-brothers, Alf and Jack Walters. *Source: Faribault Daily News; November 21, 1999.*

ARTHUR & MARY (WEBER) VOEGELE FAMILY HISTORY

Mr. & Mrs. Arthur Voegele

ARTHUR VOEGELE (1907-1991)

Arthur Gregory Voegele, the son of Peter and Anna (Rother) Voegele, was born in Warsaw Township, Rice County, on Dec. 10, 1907. He married Mary Weber on Oct. 2, 1929, in the St. Lawrence Church, Faribault. Mr. Voegele farmed for more than 50 years in Deerfield Township, Steele County (Route 3, Faribault). He was a longtime member of the Medford Knights of Columbus and the 4th Degree Knights of Columbus.

Arthur G. Voegele, 84, formerly of Route 3, Faribault, died Tuesday, Nov. 26, 1991, in District One Hospital. Services were held at 10:30 a.m. Saturday in the Church of Christ the King, Medford, with the Rev. Milo Ernster officiating. Burial was in Corpus Christi Cemetery in Deerfield Township, Steele County. He was survived by his wife, Mary; three sons, Walter of Medford, Howard of Faribault and John of Long Beach, Calif.; two daughters, Mrs. James (Carol) Brown of Concord, Calif., and Mrs. Al (Peggy) Sellers of Nerstrand; 19 grandchildren; 16 great-grandchildren; three sisters, Mrs. Veronica LaCanne and Mrs. Herbert (Mildred) Cook, both of Faribault, and Mrs. Earl (Donna) Nye of Edina; and other relatives. He was preceded in death by his parents; a son, Dennis in 1963; a grandson; five brothers, Donald, Lawrence, George, Carl, and Peter; three sisters, Susan Heselton, Lucille Brayshaw and Margaret Voegele.
Source: Faribault Daily News; Nov. 27, 1991.

MARY (WEBER) VOEGELE (1906-1995)

Mary Ann Weber, the daughter of Peter and Anna (Stadler) Weber, was born on Dec. 28, 1906 in Walcott Township, Rice County. She married Arthur Voegele on Oct. 2, 1929 at the St. Lawrence Catholic Church in Faribault. He preceded her in death on Nov. 26, 1991. The couple farmed for more than 50 years in Deerfield Township.

Mrs. Arthur (Mary) Voegele, 88, of Faribault, died Saturday, March 11, 1995 at the Faribault Manor Health Care Center. Services were held at Christ The King Catholic Church in Medford with the Rev. Robert Herman officiating. Interment was at Corpus Christi Cemetery in Deerfield Township, Steele County. She was survived by three sons, Walter (and Dorothy) Voegele and Howard (and Donna) Voegele, both of Faribault, and John (and Hisako) Voegele of Long Beach, Calif.; a daughter, Peggy (and Al) Sellers of Nerstrand; 19 grandchildren; 22 great-grandchildren; two brothers, Joseph (and Lucille) Weber of Deerfield Township and Nicholas (and Odessa) Weber of Stroud, Okla.; a sister Eleanor (and Francis) Varley of Faribault and other relatives. She was preceded in death by her parents; husband; daughter Carol Brown; son Dennis Voegele; a brother, Jacob Weber; and four sisters, Elizabeth Simmons, Alma Morrissey, Margaret Weber and Loretta Weber.
Source: Faribault Daily News; March 12, 1995

DENNIS PETER VOEGELE (1948-1963)

Dennis Peter Voegele, the son of Mr. and Mrs. Art Voegele, was born Feb. 23, 1948, at Faribault. He attended Medford High School. He died Sunday, Sept. 8, at his home when the tractor he was driving overturned and pinned him underneath. He was 15 years of age at the time of his death. Funeral services for Dennis Voegele, 15, of Deerfield Township, were held at Corpus Christi Catholic Church of Deerfield with Father Harold Mountain of Medford, pastor, officiating at the Requiem Mass. Interment was in the Corpus Christi Cemetery at Deerfield. Pallbearers were Robert Weber, David O'Neil, David Voegele, Fred Voegele, Delbert Voegele and Jim Simmons. Survivors include his parents, Mr. and Mrs. Arthur Voegele of Deerfield Township and rural Faribault, two sisters, Mrs. James Brown of Casper, Wyo., and Mrs. Alvin (Peggy) Sellers of Northfield, and three brothers, Walter of Medford, John with the Navy and stationed in Japan, and Howard at home. *Source: Owatonna People's Press; September 19, 1963.*

HOLMQUIST HISTORY

Ernest & Ellen Holmquist

Ernest W. Holmquist, 92, of Blooming Grove Township, Waseca County, died Friday, June 20, 2003, at the Waterville Good Samaritan Center. A Mass of Christian Burial was held at 11 a.m. on Tuesday at Christ The King Catholic Church, Medford, with the Rev. Robert Herman officiating. Interment was at the Corpus Christi Cemetery, Deerfield Township.

Ernest William Holmquist was born on July 25, 1910, in McPherson Township, Blue Earth County, the son of Victor and Mary Ann (Danberry) Holmquist. On Feb. 19, 1935, he married Ellen Rose Hofmann at St. Andrews Catholic Church in Elysian. After their marriage, the Holmquists farmed west of Elysian for five years. In 1940, they purchased a farm located in Blooming Grove Township and have lived and farmed there ever since.

Ernie was Trustee of Corpus Christi Cemetery from 1954 until 1992. Ernie and Ellen spent several years of their retirement wintering in the South Texas area. Ernie served on the Blooming Grove Township board for several years and was a member of the Farm Bureau. He was survived by two foster sons Tim (and Holly) Jewison and Terry (and Carol) Jewison, all of Blooming Grove Township; five grandchildren; a brother, Clifford Holmquist of Ellsworth, Wis.; a sister, Elizabeth Miller of Brooklyn Center; a brother-in-law, Norman Dusek of River Falls, Wis.; and by other relatives and friends.

He was preceded in death by his parents; his wife on March 22, 1999; four brothers, Bernard, Leo, Leonard and George Holmquist; four sisters, Mildred Huppert, Grace Ray, Irene Bennet and Marie Dusek; and two brother-in-laws, Sydney Bennet and Robert Miller. *Source: Faribault Daily News   22/Jun/2003*

Ellen R. (Hofmann) Holmquist, 86, of rural Waseca, died Monday, March 22, 1999, at the Lake Shore Inn Nursing Home. Funeral services were held at 10:30 a.m. Friday in Christ the King Catholic Church, Medford, with the Rev. Robert Herman officiating. Burial was in the Corpus Christi Cemetery, Deerfield.

Ellen Rose Holmquist, the daughter of Adolph and Clementine (Stangler) Hofmann, was born on Jan. 16, 1913, in Janesville Township, Waseca County. She grew up in the Elysian area and graduated from Waterville High School in 1930. She obtained her certification as a teacher from the Le Center Normal School and spent a few years teaching at various country schools.

On Feb. 19, 1935, she married Ernest William Holmquist at the St. Andrews Catholic Church in Elysian. The Holmquists purchased their farm located in Blooming Grove Township, Waseca County in 1940, and have lived and farmed there ever since. She was a member of the Waseca County Farm Bureau. She was a very active member of the Corpus Christi parish, and beginning in September 1941 served as an officer of the Council of Catholic Women (CCW) at the Deanery level and a Catholic Daughter of America for over 24 years. She and her husband spent several years of their retirement wintering in the South Texas area.

She was survived by her husband, Ernie; two foster sons, Tim (and Holly) Jewison, and Terry (and Carol) Jewison, all of Blooming Grove Township; five grandchildren; two half-sisters, Agnes David of Ellendale, and Irene (and Harry) Youngquist of Minneapolis. She was preceded in death by her parents; one brother, Adolph; one sister, Evelyn Jewison; and an infant granddaughter, Heather Fay on April 25, 1977. *Source: Faribault Daily News   24/Mar/1999*

HOLMQUIST HISTORY

Loretta Hebl and Bernard Holmquist were married on June 29, 1943, at St. Andrews Catholic Church, Elysian, Minnesota. They moved to a farm in Deerfield from rural Waseca in 1950.

BERNARD HENRY HOLMQUIST

Bernard Holmquist was born May 16, 1912 in McPherson Township, Blue Earth County, the son of Victor and Mary Ann (Danberry) Holmquist. He married Loretta Mary Hebl on June 29, 1943, at St. Andrews Catholic Church, Elysian. The couple worked and lived on a farm in rural Waseca until 1950, when they purchased their own farm in Deerfield Township, Steele County adjacent to Corpus Christi Church.

Bernard Holmquist died suddenly on April 27, 1963 at age 51, and is buried in Corpus Christi Cemetery with Fr. Harold B. Mountain officiating.

Bernard Holmquist was survived by his wife Loretta; two sons, Harlan and Gary Holmquist; two daughters, LeAnn and Linda Holmquist; brothers Ernest of Blooming Grove, George and Leo of River Falls, Wisconsin, Leonard of St. Croix, Wisconsin. He was preceded in death by his parents.

Burial took place May 19, 1963 at Corpus Christi Cemetery, Deerfield.

LORETTA MARY (HEBL) HOLMQUIST

Loretta Mary Hebl, the daughter of Joseph and Albina (Stangler) Hebl, was born Oct. 3, 1916, in Iosco Township, Waseca Country. She graduated from Waterville High School in 1934. She then attended LeCenter Normal School for one year and went on to teach in rural school districts until 1943.

She married Bernard Holmquist on June 29, 1943, at St. Andrews Catholic Church, Elysian. The couple worked and lived on a farm in rural Waseca until 1950, when they purchased their own farm in Deerfield Township, Steele County. After her husband's death in 1963, she began working for the State of Minnesota as a special schools counselor. She began that work at the Owatonna State School and went on to work the majority of her career at the Brainerd State Hospital, retiring in 1983. In 1996, she moved to Waterville. She most recently lived in Waseca. She was a long-time member of Corpus Christi Catholic Church in Deerfield Township and St. Francis Catholic Church, Brainerd, and was active in both churches during her membership. Most recently, she was a member Holy Trinity Catholic Church, Waterville, and Sacred Heart Catholic Church, Waseca. During her retirement, she was very active in the Brainerd community, its senior citizens center activities and as a volunteer.

Loretta Mary Holmquist, 82, of Waseca, died Tuesday, July 6, 1999, at the Waseca Medical Center-Mayo Health System. A Mass of Christian burial was held at Christ the King Catholic Church, Medford, with the Rev. Robert Herman officiating. Burial followed at Corpus Christi Cemetery, Deerfield Township, Steele County. She was survived by two sons, Harlan Holmquist (and his wife, Mary Brekke) of Mendota Heights, and Gary (and Kim) Holmquist of rural Waseca; two daughters, LeAnn Holmquist of Bloomington and Linda (and David) Therrien of Prior Lake; 11 grandchildren; eight great-grandchildren; and one brother, Harold (and Agatha) Hebl of St. Paul. She was preceded in death by her parents, her husband and one brother, Donald Hebl.

Source: Faribault Daily News   08/Jul/1999 (Dalby Database)

Bernard & Loretta Holmquist Marker at Corpus Christi Cemetery, Deerfield.

Clarence & Edith (Kniefel) Hoffman Family
Back Row; L-R: Carol, La Vonne, Patricia.
Front Row: Clarence, Edith & LeRoy.

Clarence Hoffman, the son of Julius and Louise (Janke) Hoffman, was born Nov. 6, 1908, at Clinton Falls. He married Edith Kniefel on March 4, 1935, at Sacred Heart Church, Owatonna. He farmed in Deerfield until he retired in 1961, when he moved to Medford. He served on the Deerfield Town Board, Central Coop Assn. Board, Board of Director Trustee for State Bank of Medford, Rural Telephone Board Secretary Treasurer and a member of the Knights of Columbus, Medford.

Clarence E. Hoffman, 84, of 303 third Ave. S.W., Medford, died Wednesday, Jan. 6, 1993, at Cedarview Nursing Home. Services were held January 9, 1993 at Christ the King, Medford, with the Rev. Robert Herman officiating. Burial was in Resurrection Cemetery, Medford He was survived by his wife, Edith; one son, LeRoy of Brookings, S.D.; three daughters, Mrs. Eugene (and Pat) Keller of Owatonna; Mrs. Vincent (and Carol) Steinbauer of Medford and Mrs. Gary (and LaVonne) King of Prior Lake; one brother, Alvin Hoffman of Fla.; and one sister, Amelia Radel of Owatonna; 19 grandchildren; and 12 great-grandchildren.
Source: Faribault Daily News, January 8, 1993 (Dalby Database).

Edith (Kniefel) Hoffman was born June 3, 1914, in Aurora Township, Steele County to Edward and Ella (Hartle) Kniefel. She married Clarence Hoffman March 4, 1935, at Sacred Heart Church in Owatonna. Edith B. Hoffman, 85, of Medford, died March 28, 2000, at the Owatonna Hospital. Funeral services were held March 31, 2000 at Christ the King Church, Medford, with the Rev. Robert Herman officiating. Burial was in Resurrection Cemetery, Medford. She was survived by one son, LeRoy (and Carolyn) of Brookings, S.D.; daughters, Pat (and Eugene) Keller of Medford, Carol (and Vincent) Steinbauer of Medford, and LaVonne (and Gary) King of Burnsville; 19 grandchildren; and 39 great-grandchildren.
Source: Faribault Daily News, March 31, 2000 (Dalby Database).

MORK FAMILY HISTORY

KENNETH MORK
(1928-1994)

Kenneth Mork was born Dec. 12, 1928, to William and Sophia (Marchwick) Morek in Merton Township, Steele County. He graduated from Owatonna High School in 1946 and married Donna Marie Bolinger on July 5, 1949, at Christ the King Church, Medford. He served in the U.S. Army with the occupational forces in Germany at the end of World War II, and was recalled during the Korean Conflict.

Upon returning to Minnesota, he established the Deerfield store in Deerfield Township in 1949. He and his wife Donna operated the store until January 1990. He was also employed by Corcoran Inc. of Waseca from 1986 to 1993. He was a member of Corpus Christi Church in Deerfield, the Medford-Deerfield Knights of Columbus Council #4909, General Shield 4th Degree of Faribault K.C., and was instrumental in starting K.C. Council #4909 at Deerfield. He served as the financial secretary until 1983, and as a member of the Corpus Christi Church trustees and cemetery board for many years. He was a lifelong member of the VFW and a member of the American Legion and Eagle's Clubs of Owatonna.

Kenneth Mork, 65, of rural Waseca, Deerfield Township, Steele County, died Feb. 10, 1994, at the Owatonna Hospital. Funeral services at Christ the King Catholic Church, Medford, with the Rev. Robert Herman officiating. Burial was in Corpus Christi Church Cemetery, Deerfield Township, Visitation was from 2-8 p.m. Sunday at the Brick-Postlewaite Funeral Home, Owatonna, and at the church for one hour prior to services. The Knights of Columbus recited the Rosary at 7:30 p.m. Sunday.
He was survived by his wife, Donna; one daughter, Megan, of Owatonna; two sons, Josh (and Kathleen) of Baltimore, Md., and Jonas of River Falls, Wis.; two brothers, William of Santiago and Richard of Owatonna; two grandchildren; and five nieces and nephews. He was preceded in death by his parents and one son, Tracy, in infancy. *Faribault Daily News (February 11, 1994.*

Kenneth & Donna Mork Family

DONNA (BOLINGER) MORK
(1930-2011)

Donna Marie (Bolinger) Mork was born February 18, 1930 in Elysian, Minnesota, the daughter of Omer and Alma (Lindenburger) Bolinger. Donna later moved to Merton Township with her parents and graduated from Owatonna High School in 1948.

Donna married Kenneth Mork at Christ The King Catholic Church in Medford on July 5, 1949. Together they owned and operated Mork's Deerfield Store until January of 1990. Donna also worked in retail until her retirement due to health issues. She was a member of Corpus Christi Catholic Church, and active in the Ladies CCW organization.

Donna Marie Mork, age 81, passed away August 21, 2011 at the Owatonna Care Center. She was survived by her children Josh Mork of Warminster, PA, Megan (and Paula Freiheit) Mork of Owatonna, Jonas Mork of River Falls, five grandchildren, Ashley (and fiance Jeff Elton) Mork, Heather, Mikenna, Braden, and Keenan Mork. She was also survived by one great grandson Chandler Elton, two sisters Darlene Munson of Owatonna, and Viola Meitzner of Kasson. She was preceded in death by her parents, step mother Polly, husband Kenneth, infant son Tracy, and brother Galen Bolinger.

Funeral services were held Thursday August 25, 2011 at 10:00 A.M. at Christ the King Catholic Church in Medford with Father Edward Mountain officiating. Visitation was held on Wednesday August 24, 2011 from 4-8 P.M. at Michaelson Funeral Home and one hour prior to the service at the church. Burial was in the Corpus Christi Cemetery in Deerfield Township.
Sources Cited: Dalby Database.

CORLESS & MARION (McDONOUGH) COLE FAMILY

Corless & Marion (McDonough) Cole
(Married August 23, 1939 at Sacred Heart Church, Waseca)

Corless A. Cole was born Dec. 25, 1909, in Blue Earth County and was educated in rural schools near Minnesota Lake. On Aug. 23, 1939, he married Marion McDonough at Sacred Heart Church, Waseca. He spent his entire life farming in southern Minnesota, first near Minnesota Lake and then in 1939, he and Marion moved to a farm in Deerfield Township. In 1975, he and Marion moved to Waseca. He was a member of Sacred Heart Catholic Church, the Knights of Columbus, the Waseca and Owatonna Elks, the Corpus Christi Cemetery Board, and the Deerfield Creamery Board. Corless A. Cole, Waseca, age 70, died October 6, 1980 at Methodist Hospital in Rochester after a lingering illness. Survivors included his wife; two sons, Richard of St. Paul and James of Waseca; two brothers, Ken of Waseca and Bernard (Bud) of Tracy: five sisters, Mrs. Luella Pitcher, Mrs. Lola Wynnemer, Mrs. James (Louise) Osmundson and Mrs. Oscar (Loretta) Storlie, all of Waseca, and Mrs. Lorraine Stolz, Montclair, Calif.; and six grandchildren. Funeral services were at Sacred Heart Church, Waseca, with burial in Corpus Christi Cemetery, Deerfield.

Marion McDonough was born June 2, 1921, in Waseca, daughter of Edward and Mary Ellen (Conway) McDonough. On Aug. 23, 1939, she married Corless A. Cole at Sacred Heart Catholic Church, Waseca. The couple farmed in Deerfield Township from 1939-75. After retiring from farming, Mrs. Cole and her husband moved to Waseca. Mrs. Cole was a cook at Sacred Heart parochial school for 18 years. She was a longtime member of Sacred Heart Catholic Church, Waseca, and prior to that of Corpus Christi Catholic Church, Deerfield Township. She enjoyed traveling and spending time with her grandchildren. She passed away at age 79 on Nov. 20, 2000 at Lake Shore Nursing Home, Waseca. Her funeral was at Sacred Heart Catholic Church, Waseca. Burial was at Corpus Christi Cemetery, Deerfield. Mrs. Cole was survived by two sons, Jim (and Candace) Cole of Waseca, Richard (and Beverly) Cole of Maplewood; a sister, Mildred Harguth of Waseca; seven grandchildren, two great-grandchildren and many nieces and nephews.

JOSEPH & MARGARET (PFEIFFER) LANG FAMILY HISTORY

Joseph & Margaret (Pfeiffer) Lang

Joseph Lang was born Jan. 8, 1908, in Alton Township, Waseca County, to Andrew and Mary Jane (Vaughan) Lang. He was married June 5, 1934, at St. Jarlath Catholic Church, Iosco Township, Waseca County, to Margaret M. Pfeiffer. He farmed all his life.

Joseph A. Lang, 79, rural Medford, died Saturday, Dec. 5, 1987 at St. Marys Hospital in Rochester. Funeral services were at Christ King Catholic Church, Medford, with the Rev. Edward Mountain officiating. Burial was in Corpus Christi Cemetery. Joe Lang was survived by his wife, Margaret; a son, James W. of Austin; three grandchildren; a foster daughter, Lorraine Hegdahl of San Francisco; a foster grandchild; two foster grandchildren; and four sisters, Esther McGonagle of Mankato, Margaret Francis Edmund of Wisconsin, Celia (Mrs. Art) Scholljegerdes of Waseca, and Genevieve (Mrs. Ray) Farley of Janesville. He was preceded in death by three sisters, an infant brother, an infant grandson and an infant foster son. *Source: Faribault Daily News; December 7, 1987*

Margaret Mary Pfeifer, the daughter of Emil and Josephine (Kapaun) Pfeifer, was born Feb. 26, 1911, in Janesville Township, Waseca County. She attended country school in Waseca County. She married Joe Lang on June 5, 1934, at St. Jarlaths Catholic Church, Iosco Township. They farmed for one year in Janesville Township and for 12 years in Iosco Township. In 1947 they moved to a farm in Deerfield Township and lived there for more than 40 years. Following her husband's death on Dec. 5, 1987, she moved to Waseca. In 1994, she moved to Golden Era Board and Care, Waterville, and for the past two years had been a resident of Prairie Manor Nursing Home, Blooming Prairie. She was a longtime member of Corpus Christi Catholic Church, Deerfield Township; and was most recently a member of the Sacred Heart Catholic Church, Waseca. She was also a member of the Catholic Daughters of America-Court of St. Anne. Margaret M. Lang, 88, died Wednesday, Nov. 10, 1999 at the Prairie Manor Nursing Home, Blooming Prairie. Mass of Christian Burial was held at Sacred Heart Catholic Church, Waseca, with burial at Corpus Christi Cemetery, Deerfield. She is survived by one son, James W. (and Mary) Lang of Austin; one sister, Josephine Jewison of Waseca; one brother, James (and Emma) Pfeifer of Tampa, Fla.; three grandchildren; one great-grandson; and a foster daughter, Lorraine Hegdahl of San Francisco. *Source: Dalby Database.*

EDWIN & MARIE (CIFRA) TUVE FAMILY

Edwin & Marie (Cifra) Tuve {1995}

Edwin and Marie Tuve were members of Corpus Christi parish from 1949 until 1975. Edwin Tuve and Marie Ciffra were married April 27,1949 in Christ the King church in Medford. Their first home was a farm in Deerfield Township where they remained until the fall of 1975 when they moved to Owatonna. In 1991 they moved to Elysian.

Edwin Tuve was born September 13, 1924 and raised in the Elysian area. He died June 14, 1995 at age 70. He is buried in Corpus Christi cemetery. Marie (Ciffra) Tuve was born January 15, 1930 and lived in Medford about three years during the late 1940s prior to her marriage and attended Christ the King parish. She currently lives in Mankato.

The Tuves had one child, Catherine, born September 9, 1950. Catherine was baptized in 1950 and received her first communion June 8, 1958 at Corpus Christi. Catherine married Bob Sigafus at Corpus Christi on St. Valentine's Day, February 14, 1975.

ERNEST & RITA (O'BRIEN) KUNTZ FAMILY

Ernest & Rita (O'Brien) Kuntz Family (1969)
Back Row; L-R: Jerry, Thomas, Gene, Carol.
Front Row: Mary, Sharene, Julie, Rita, Carmen, Ernest.
(Rita {O'Brien} Kuntz was the daughter of Steve and Rosamond (Rousseau) O'Brien).

Excerpt from the Corpus Christi Bingo Party- March 20, 1966
Selling tickets at the door- Henry Hager, Ken Mork, Callers for Bingo-James Frederick & George Larson. Taking Money and tickets- Mrs. George Larson, Mrs. James Frederick
Kitchen Workers: Mrs. Sylvester Dulas, Mrs. Louis Pirkl, Mrs. Eugene Phillips, Mrs. Harlow Pirkl, Mrs. Willard Karsten, Mrs. Leo Sammon, Miss Marjorie Ness, Mrs. Ernest Kuntz.

St. Anne's Guild members brought 2 dozen meat sandwiches each and St. Mary's Guild members brought 2 dozen bars each. We were short of food-workers didn't get anything to eat-especially short of bars- suggest that 4 dozen bars and specify two 1 ½ lb. loaves of bread made into sandwiches for next year's bingo party. We sold chances on donated articles and a large electric coffee urn which was purchased by the treasury. This brought in extra funds. Raffle committee – Mrs. Ernest Holmquist and Mrs. Henry Hager.
Respectfully submitted by Me, Rita Kuntz
(This was the first time that a woman used her first name signing the books. Previous to that time, women were always referred to with their husband's first name, i.e Mrs. Ernest Kuntz, not as Rita Kuntz. Rita (O'Brien) Kuntz was not just a "farmer's wife," she had her own business selling Tupperware and was a woman well ahead of the times).

**At the next bingo party in 1967, they had plenty of food, but the crowd was slightly down, so going forward that was the new standard for the bingo party food.

ELDRED & MARY PHILLIPS FAMILY

Eldred & Mary (Trettel) Phillips

Eldred & Mary (Trettel) Phillips Family
L-R: Carol, Rosemary, Mary, Eldred, Cathy, Michael.

ELDRED PHILLIPS (1925-2015)

Eldred Mathew Phillips, age 89, of Owatonna, passed away April 3, 2015, at Koda Living in Owatonna. Mass of Christian Burial was celebrated at St. Joseph Catholic Church, Owatonna, with a one hour visitation prior the funeral. Military honors will be provided by the Steele County Funeral Unit. Interment Corpus Christi Cemetery, Deerfield Township.

Eldred Mathew Phillips was born on August 9, 1925 in Blackhawk Co., Iowa to Theodore and Mary (Schmitz) Phillips. In 1931 his parents moved their four children to a farm in Rapidan Township south of Mankato. Eldred attended the Rapidan consolidated school and graduated in 1943.

Because food was essential to the war effort, he was given a deferment to farm with his father until 1945. When the deferment was given to a younger brother, Eldred's name moved to the top of the draft board list. He managed to get into the Navy by passing a special test. After his honorable discharge from the Navy, he attended Mankato State College for one year before transferring to the University of Minnesota, where he received a Bachelor's degree in Agricultural education. This is where he met his wife Mary Trettel, and the two got married in Little Falls on December 27, 1949. After teaching vocational agriculture and science at Pine Island for three years, he went into farming. In 1955, Mary and Eldred purchased a farm in Deerfield where they lived for 30 years before moving to Owatonna.

Eldred was a life member of the National Farmers Organization. He and his wife Mary were responsible for publishing the Steele County meeting notice and newsletter for 38 years. Eldred was a life member of the Medford/Deerfield Knights of Columbus, was a past Grand Knight serving in 1988-89, the American Legion, Elks, the University of Minnesota Alumni Association and the Rapidan Historical Society. He served on the Medford School Board from 1973 to 1979, he also served on the Steele Co. Public Health Board for 23 years. Eldred was Knight of the year in 1984 and in 2012. In 1984 the Medford/Deerfield Knights shipped a container of ground corn to Tanzania during a drought period. After retirement Eldred enjoyed woodworking, wine-making, reading, gardening, keeping up with the stock market, traveling and most of all spending time with his family.

Eldred is survived by his wife Mary, children Catherine (Larry) Glovka, of Owatonna, Carol (Charles) Anderson of Meriden Township, Michael Phillips of Deerfield Township, and Rosemary (James) York of Lake Wilson, MN; 12 grandchildren and 9 great-grandchildren; two brothers, Norbert (Matilda "Tilly") Phillips of Canby, Joseph (Martha) Phillips of Good Thunder, MN; sisters, Mary Joan Phillips of Denville, NJ, and Marilyn (Donald) Sieberg of Mankato, and one sister-in-law Darlene Phillips, of Owatonna.

MARY (TRETTEL) PHILLIPS (1923-2021)

Mary L. Phillips of Owatonna died January 15, 2021 at Homestead Hospice House in Owatonna. Mass of Christian Burial took place January 21, 2021 at St. Joseph Catholic Church in Owatonna. Interment was at Corpus Christi Cemetery. A Medford/Deerfield Catholic Daughters of America Rosary was recited at the funeral home. Internment took place at Corpus Christi Cemetery.

Mary was born October 8, 1923 in Little Falls, MN the daughter of Otto and Veronica (Mohr) Trettel. Mary attended Little Falls High School and graduated in 1941. After high school, Mary attended business school in St. Cloud, MN, then went to work for the Morrison County Attorney's Office for a few years. Mary then went to Washington DC to work for the Red Cross. She returned to Minneapolis to enroll at the University of Minnesota, St. Paul campus to receive her Associates Degree. Mary worked at the Veteran Service office at the University of Minnesota in the Civil Service Office.

Mary was united in marriage to Eldred on December 27, 1949 in Little Falls, MN. The couple made their home in Deerfield Township to raise their family of four. Mary was a farm wife along side her husband Eldred while raising the children. She worked in all aspects of the farm, helping wherever was needed.

Mary was a member of the Catholic Daughters of America of Medford/Deerfield Court, League of Women Voters, music guild of Owatonna. She volunteered for Contact, played piano for local nursing homes and sang in the choir at Corpus Christi and St. Joseph Churches. Her hobbies included gardening, cooking and canning.

Mary was survived by her children Catherine (Larry) Glovka of Owatonna, Carol (Charlie) Anderson of Meriden Township, Michael Phillips of Deerfield Township, Rosemary (James) York of Lake Wilson, MN; 12 grandchildren and 16 great-grandchildren; and her sister Florence Mayer of Monticello, MN. Mary was preceded in death by her husband Eldred in 2015, two sisters and two brothers.

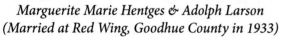

Marguerite Marie Hentges & Adolph Larson
(Married at Red Wing, Goodhue County in 1933)

Marguerite & Adolph Larson

Adolph Larson, son of William (Brynte) Larson and Anna Maria Jansdotter Olsson, was born October 31, 1904 on a family farm in Skelton Township (Cloquet), Carlton County, MN. William Brynte Larson family was from Högen, Gapungebyn, Sweden and immigrating into the United States in November 1889. He married Anna Maria Jansdotter Olsson December 23, 1903 at Duluth (Civil Ceremony), and in January 1904 Superior, WI (religious ceremony).

Adolph Larson married Marguerite Marie Hentges at Red Wing October 31, 1933. They farmed near Red Wing before purchasing a farm in Deerfield Township in 1947.

Marguerite Hentges was born on March 15, 1913, to Frances and Josephine (Uhres) Hentges in Waldbillig, Echternach, Grevenmacher, Luxembourg. In 1933, she married Adolph Larson in Red Wing. The couple farmed near Red Wing before moving to Deerfield Township in 1947. Marguerite and Adolph were members of the Farm Bureau, Farmers Union and Corpus Christi Church in Deerfield. At Corpus Christi, Marguerite was a member of the Corpus Christi Altar Society, Catholic Daughters of America-St. Ann's Court. Her other activitiies included the Card Club and Homemakers Club.

Adolph and Marguerite Larson were the parents of three children; Josephine Matz, George (1937-1992), and Robert (1940-2020).

Adolph Larson, age 76, passed away as a result of a stroke on January 18, 1980 at Owatonna. His funeral was held at Corpus Christi Church with Fr. Cody presiding. Internment was at Resurrection Cemetery, Medford.

Marguerite Marie Larson, age 94, formerly of Owatonna, died Wednesday, April 18, 2007, at Cedarview Care Center, where she was a resident. Marguerite was survived by her daughter, Josephine Matz of Medford, her son, Robert Larson of Owatonna; 12 grandchildren; 27 great-grandchildren; two great-great-grandchildren; along with her sister, Irene Booth of Billings, Mont. A Mass of Christian Burial was celebrated at Christ the King Catholic Church, Medford. Interment was at Resurrection Cemetery in Medford.

LARSON FAMILY HISTORY

Robert & Joyce (Sawyer) Larson

George & Jean (Thiele) Larson with Mathew

Robert Francis Larson, son of Marguerite and Adolph Larson was born on October 9, 1940, in Red Wing, MN. Robert graduated from Medford High School in 1958 and enlisted in the Navy in October of that same year and was stationed at Naval Station Norfolk in Virginia.

Robert came home from the Navy in October of 1961. He was united in marriage to Joyce Sawyer on May 5th, 1962. Robert and Joyce farmed in Steele County for their entire marriage. Many a day was spent cultivating the fields for corn, soybeans, and hay. He also raised various animals: chickens, pigs, sheep, dairy cows, and steers. Robert loved his children more than the farm and would always stop what he was doing that day to be in the house when they got off the school bus. He always took the time to be present for those he loved whether it was his own children or his nieces and nephews.

Robert F. Larson, age 79, of Owatonna, passed away February 29, 2020 at Koda Living Community. He was pre-deceased by his loving wife of 52 years, Joyce; his parents, Marguerite and Adolph; his brother, George; and his brother-in-law, Harlan.

Robert was survived by his sister, Jo Matz; his sister-in-law, Jean Larson; his children and their spouses: Dawn and Mike Beyer (Northfield); Shelly and Chris Marsh (Indianola, IA); Cathy and Brian Mikel (Lonsdale); David and Rose Larson (Owatonna); his loving grandchildren: Jorie Beyer, Bruce Marsh (and Lauren Mallinger), Anna (and Marcus) Tschauner, Emma Marsh (and Garrett Lies), Zach, Carolyn, and Ryan Mikel, Sierra and Savannah Larson; and his great grandson, Emmett Tschauner.

A Mass of Christian Burial was held Saturday, March 7th, at Christ the King Church in Medford. Military Honors were provided by the Steele County Funeral Unit.

George Adolph Larson, son of Marguerite and Adolph Larson was born November 28, 1937 in Red Wing, MN. George was about ten years old when his parents purchased a farm in Deerfield Township. George met Jean Thiele through 4-H club work and were married Dec. 28th 1957. George had one more year in the Navy and was discharged with honor as a 2nd class electrician in late November of 1958. George and Jean purchased a 240 acre farm in Deerfield Township from George's folks. They milked cows, had sheep and hogs and took over the 1000 Hyline parent stock chickens from the family.

George was an original member of the Fr. Carlin Council of the Knights of Columbus. He was also a lector. For several years George also worked nights in maintenance at OTC and also Washington Scientific in Owatonna. George and Jean did all the farm work together from milking to field work. They were also blessed with six children. Tim is married to Joanne (Stene) and they have five children, Katie, Dan, Mariah, Holly and Lynn. Richard is married to Teri (Struck) and they have Will and Maggie. Chuck is married to Diane (Stene) and they have Lauren, Samantha, Cassandra, and Greg. Trina is married to Dean Schmelger and they have Jorge, Julia, John, and Catherine. Mathew is married to Ashly (Pound) and their sons are Tucker and Hunter.

The three oldest sons; Timothy, Richard and Charles, are Ag instructors and FFA advisors. Trina's farm is in the Owen-Withee, Wisconsin area and Matt is a maintenance mechanic for Jerome Foods by Medford and has a motorcycle repair shop at their home. A son, George Jr. was born on the 1st Straight River Days and passed away at three days of age.

George Larson, age 55, passed away unexpectedly April 22, 1992 at the farm. Jean Ann (Thiele) Larson passed away March 10, 2021 at the Emerald of Faribault.

MORE CORPUS CHRISTI FAMILIES
JAMES & ALMA HURT FAMILY

James Francis Hurt (1899-1988)

James Francis Hurt was born Aug. 6, 1899 at Hallock, Kittson County, Minnesota. He was the son of Anton Hurt & Cecelia "Celia" Prybyeszeski. James married Alma, daughter of Leo and Cora (Fonder) Connor on Sept. 2, 1930 at Marysburg, LeSueur County. They were the parents of Cecelia, RoseAnn, Genevieve, Agnes, Pauline, Kathleen, Connie, Paul, and JoAnne.

James and Alma Hurt were living in Blooming Grove Township, Waseca County by 1935 and moved to a farm at Deerfield in 1947.

They were very active members of Corpus Christi Church beginning in the 1930s. James was a member of the Knights of Columbus, and Farmers Union.

James Hurt, age 89, passed away June 25, 1988 at Rochester, Minnesota. Alma Agatha Connor was born Nov. 12, 1903 in South Dakota and died March 6, 1958 at age 55, in Deerfield. James and Alma are buried in Corpus Christi Cemetery, Deerfield.

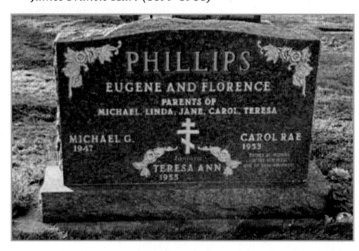

EUGENE & FLORENCE (WENDEL) PHILLIPS FAMILY

Eugene John Phillips, son of Nicholas and Catherine (Kayser) Phillips was born on April 20, 1917 at Jessup, Buchanan County, Iowa. By 1920, the Phillips family was living in Meriden Township. He married Florence Wendell 23 Aug 1946 at Brownsdale, Mower County, Minnesota. Florence Rita Wendel was born Aug.14, 1922 at Rose Creek, Mower County, Minnesota. Eugene and Florence Phillips moved to a farm in Deerfield Township in the late 1940s and remained there until moving to the Cross Lake, Minnesota area in the 1960s.

They had the following children; Michael, (1947), Carol Rae (1953) and Teresa Ann (1955), and Linda.

Eugene John Phillips passed away January 26, 1979 at the Veterans Administration Hospital, Minneapolis. Florence Phillips passed away January 11, 1983 in St Paul, Ramsey County, Minnesota.

Nick Phillips, father of Eugene died February 21, 1956 and is buried in Corpus Christi Cemetery.

Florence (Wendel) Phillips

CHAPTER IV

CORPUS CHRISTI PARISH
RE-ESTABLISHED

Corpus Christi Church as it was located prior to 1939.
The church was closed from 1935 until 1938. In 1938/39, under the supervision of Julius Kohlmeier, a contractor from Owatonna, the church was moved back north and west from the road right of way to higher ground and placed on a foundation. A basement was dug using horses, shovels and scoops. Funds for the project were raised by a series of parish festivals and picnics. The above photo is a keepsake belonging to Margaret (Peggy) Sellers which was saved by her parents, Mary & Art Voegele.

When Father Raymond Snyder was assigned to the parish, he contacted Catholics living in the area, urging them to become involved in the parish.

Through these direct contacts, he was able to learn of a family "down the road" who had lost contact with the Catholic Church or a married couple in which only one partner was Catholic, so the spouse became lax also.

Many people were reluctant to leave their parishes for the uncertain future of Corpus Christi, but Father Snyder's personality and persistence paid off and gradually more and more families began to attend Mass regularly at Corpus Christi.

At the beginning of his tenure, Father Snyder resided with his pastor at Sacred Heart Rectory in Waseca, and came to Corpus Christi only for Sunday Mass. At the time the Rural Electrification Act was passed in 1936, electricity was commonplace in cities but largely unavailable on farms and other rural places. Since there was no electricity, many families did not even have a radio.

Some "Old-timers" tell of Father Snyder, that it was not uncommon to have him show up at your door with no advance notice and accept an invitation to share a meal or at least a cup of coffee. It was through his contacts and zeal that the congregation at Corpus Christi steadily grew.

Once the parish was re-opened and Masses were held regularly, the huge job of renovation began. Father Snyder was a great fund-raiser and his energy and enthusiasm resulted in a thriving parish. By June 1938, there were 43 families registered and regularly attending Sunday Mass at Corpus Christi Parish.

Bishop Francis M. Kelly

Re-Established Catholic Church to Have First Communion Today

Bishop Kelly Confirms Class in Church Having 43 Families

Re-establishment of the Corpus Christi Catholic church, four and one-half miles west of Owatonna on Highway 14, will be observed with a community dinner and picnic Sunday, June 19.

Father Snyder of Waseca is supply pastor of the church, re-established six weeks ago and now having a membership of more than 40 families. Confirmation, a Sacrament, was administered to a class of 18 last Sunday by Rt. Rev. Francis M. Kelly, bishop of the Winona diocese; and First Communion will be received by a group of 14 children today.

CORPUS CHRISTI OBSERVANCE TO BE HELD JUNE 19

1938

The picnic, expected to attract large numbers from Owatonna, Medford, Faribault, Waterville, Morristown and Waseca, will follow an 8:30 o'clock Mass. A dinner will be served and lunch will be available on the grounds throughout the day.

Moving pictures, k-ball and other games and entertainment programs will be provided, with awards to be provided for the numerous winners. Stands of various types will be maintained on the grounds.

The program is expected to benefit the church fund being raised to move the church a short distance back from the highway and to erect a permanent foundation under it. Services were resumed at the church, located one mile south of the Deerfield town hall, a few weeks ago after a three-year period of non-use.

A dance, first planned for the same evening, has been postponed for a few days, with announcement of the date expected to be made June 19.

June 5, 1938

Note: Francis Martin Kelly (November 15, 1886 – June 24, 1950) served as bishop of the Diocese of Winona from 1928 to 1949. He became secretary to Bishop Patrick Richard Heffron in 1914, and taught philosophy at St. Mary's College and St. Teresa's College between 1915 and 1926. He was chancellor of the diocese (1919–26) and vice-rector of St. Mary's College (1918–26).

CORPUS CHRISTI CELEBRATION TO BE HELD SUNDAY

Photo News; Owatonna (June 17, 1938)

Afternoon and Evening Entertainment Will Be Presented

****

Deerfield Catholic Church Program To Be For Public

A chicken dinner, an afternoon program of races, K-ball and other entertainment and an evening of movies will mark the celebration arranged for Sunday by the Deerfield committee of the Corpus Christi church.

The Catholic church picnic and bazaar will be held at the William Kvasnicka farm, five miles west and two· and one half miles north of the Owatonna - Waseca road; or five miles west and two miles south of Medford; in other words, a half mile south of the Deerfield town hall.

Tug-o-war, married men vs. single men; ladies' rooster race, ladies milking contest, men's egg race, boys and girls foot race, under 8 years; boys' weiner race, 8 to 12 years; girls' peanut race, 8 to 12 year; foot, races for both boys and girls, over 12 years of age, a special race for winners of previous races a boys' and girls' peanut scramble and a k-ball game.

Cash prizes of 50 and 25 cents will be given for first and second place . winners. Horse shoe pitching, corn games (Bingo) and other entertainment numbers will be provided throughout the afternoon.

Named as speaker for the day are M. R. Cashman and Edward W. Springer of Owatonna and Peter Donkers of Faribault. An auction will climax the afternoon program while movies will be held at night. The public is invited to the day-long program.

Father Raymond Snyder (1938)

FIRST PARISH PICNICS WERE AT THE WILLIAM & VERONICA KVASNICKA FARM

The William and Veronica Kvasnicka farm was the site of the first Corpus Christi parish picnic in 1938. The Daily People's Press featured a weekly guess the name of the mystery farm contest. The Kvasnicka farm was included in the contest. The farm has a sad history. William died there in 1939. In the 1990s, the then owner, killed his wife in the house and blew it up to hide the evidence. Later owners rebuilt the property, but most of the other out-buildings are gone. Due to William's sudden death in early 1939, that year the Corpus Christi Parish Picnic was held at the William Mullenmaster farm.

Cool woods in the Kvasnicka grove, furnished the background for trapshooting at the Corpus Christi picnic, which kept the committee in charge of this event busy all day. Photo courtesy of Lori (Kaderlik) Hatfield.

THOUSANDS ATTENDED THE FAMOUS CORPUS CHRISTI PICNICS

A corner of the big outdoor dining "hall" which saw more than 200 fed in a single "shift" and new shifts began as fast as places were vacated. Part of the huge crowd attending the Corpus Christi Parish Picnic at the William Kvasnicka Farm in 1938. The photo shows only a small portion of the huge throng served that day.

A part of the committee, too busy through the day for PHOTO NEWS cameraman to get a shot of the complete group. Left to right, Peter Stirens, James Brady, George Brady, Mrs. Henry Theder; Mrs. C. J. Jones, Joseph Pete, the Rev. Father Raymond Snyder, rector of the parish, and Bernard Matz.

The photos of the Corpus Christi parish picnics are from news clippings from the Owatonna Photo News, salvaged from a scrap book assembled by Phyllis Maas and contributed by Evelyn Brady. Lori (Kaderlik) Hatfield also shared an original copy of the Photo News from June 13, 1940.

THE PICNICS RAISED MUCH NEEDED FUNDS & BECAME A SOCIAL EVENT

Children's activities at the Corpus Christi Parish Picnic in June 1938.
The entertainment which attracted the attention of the even the smallest youngsters, included pony rides and goat-drawn transportation. The goat-pulled wagon above has a load of happy youngsters.

The Medford high school band, directed by Principal Orlando Hill, provided live entertainment with a musical program for the picnic.

CORPUS CHRISTI PICNICS

Stories about "The Big Corpus Christi Picnics" of the late thirties and early forties often surfaced when conversation centered around the "good old days."

The June picnics were followed by a Sauerkraut Festival in October. By that time on the farm, the cabbage was mature and made into sauerkraut in readiness for another church benefit.

As one report stated, every man, woman and child was pressed into service at these picnics and outside help was welcomed. We must remember that refrigeration and automatic stoves were not to be found!

The very first picnic was held in the spacious yard of Mr. & Mrs. Wm. Kvasnicka, while the following year it was held on the Wm. Mullenmaster farm.

Tables were set up under the big trees, equipment borrowed from everywhere possible, a bountiful chicken dinner was served, and all manner of games and gadgets were employed to entice spending.

There were games of chance, raffles, trap shooting, even airplane rides and a barn dance with free movies projected to hold the crowd there. Hundreds of people attended and a tidy sum was realized. After it was all over, the exhausted workers put the supplies away and had to return the following day to clean up.

CORPUS CHRISTI CHURCH PICNIC WILL BE JUNE 18

_1939_

ChickenDinner, Program and Bowery Dance to Be Features

—

The annual picnic for the congregation and friends of the Corpus Christi church of Deerfield will be held at the William Mullenmaster farm Sunday, June 18. _1939_

A chicken dinner will be served by ladies of the church, starting at 11:30 o'clock, after which an afternoon entertainment program will be held and music will be furnished by the Melody Kings. A bowery dance will be held and music will be furnished by the Melody Kings. A bowery dance will be t..e evening feature, along with moving pictures.

With an enjoyable program arranged, all are invited to attend.

Source: Scrapbook of Phyllis Maas

The coffee for the Corpus Christi Parish Picnic was made by putting the grounds in a cheese cloth bag and taken to the creamery where 10 gallon cans were filled with boiling water. Today, we couldn't even locate a creamery to carry out this detail, but at that time, the Medford creamery was in full operation and there were two dozen creameries in Steele County.

With reference to a "bountiful" chicken dinner, a reader may ask "Where did all the food come from?" Indeed, it was donated by these 43 families referred to in the reprinted photo news article. A typical list of items each family was expected to donate included:
- 6 chickens, all roasted and ready to serve;
- dressing, made up using 2 loaves of bread;
- 2 quarts of gravy
- 2 large cans of corn
- 2 large cans of cranberries
- 1 pint of jam and l lb of butter
- 1 bunch of celery or carrots
- 5 lbs of tomatoes
- 5 pies
- 1 cake
- 1 quart of pickles

In addition to the food, each family was asked to donate a prize for the bazaar.

Preparation of all this food began at home before packing it all up on Sunday morning must have been a major accomplishment.

The coffee was made by putting the grounds in a cheese cloth bag and taken to the creamery where 10 gallon cans were filled with boiling water. Today, we couldn't even locate a creamery to carry out this detail, but at that time, the Medford creamery was in full operation.

Consider also, that the country was just recovering from the "Great Depression" and moving into World War II with forced food rationing. As a result of rationing, there was the allotment of food stamps to be reckoned with. The fact that these were farm people who raised chickens and hogs, milked cows and had gardens does not lessen the significance of their contribution.

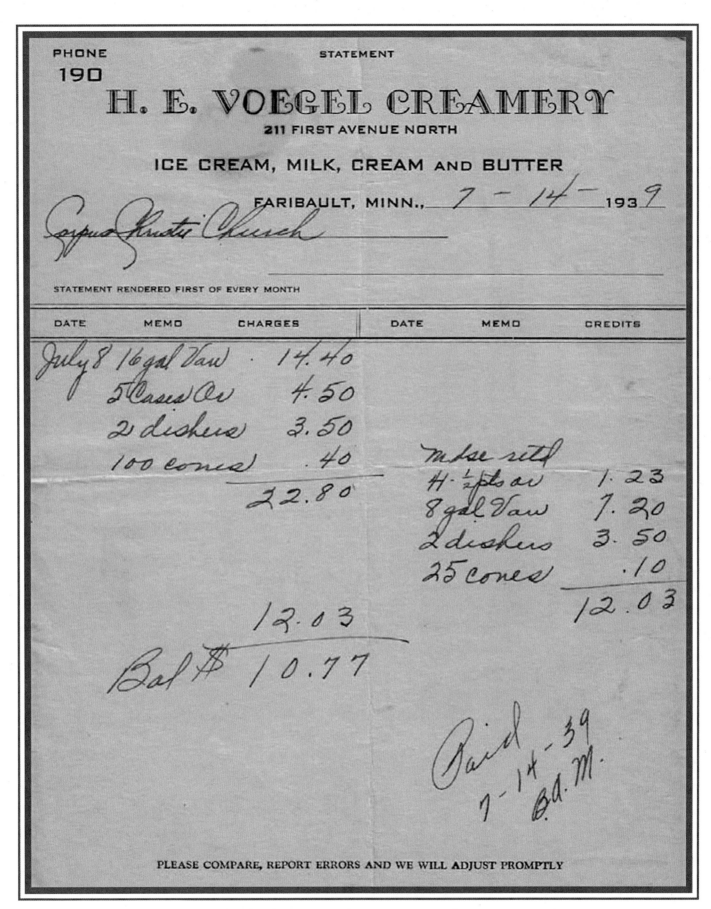

Supplies for the Corpus Christi Picnic in July 1939.

Corpus Christi General Planning Committee (1939)
Pictured, L-R: General Committee members; John Karaus, George Brady & Father Raymond Snyder.

Father Raymond Snyder was gregarious and comfortable in almost any setting.

At left: Father Raymond Snyder relaxes in a parishioner's kitchen. During the late 1930s and 1940s, most farm families did not have telephones and electricity was still a novelty. Fr. Snyder was known to make unannounced visits to families in the re-established Corpus Christi parish. He always was ready to accept an invitation to stay for a cup of coffee and a piece of homemade apple pie.

During 1938/39, and the early 40s, Father Snyder used his out-going personality to encourage Deerfield-area Catholics to return to Corpus Christi for Mass and brought several lapsed Catholic families back to the Church.

CORPUS CHRISTI PICNIC ATTRACTS THOUSANDS

Steele County Photo News (Thursday June 22, 1939)

A view of the big "outdoor dining hall"-not big enough to care for more than a small portion of the throng at the Corpus Christi Parish Picnic on June 19, 1939.

The front end of a long "Army-Style" lunch line at the Second Corpus Christi Parish Picnic on June 19, 1939 at the William Mullenmaster Farm in Deerfield Township. The first picnic was held in June 1938 at the William Kvasnicka farm. William Kvasnicka died suddenly in early 1939 and the Mullenmaster family agreed to host the picnic.

The best attended summer picnic crowd of the season was registered Sunday June 18, 1939 when the Corpus Christi church of Deerfield township held its annual picnic at the grove on the William Mullenmeister farm with between 2,000 and 3,000 attending, many coming long distances for the affair.

The sumptuous chicken dinner served by ladies of the parish was a major attraction for the crowd attending. A small percentage of the diners and prospective diners could be caught within the lens angle of the PHOTO NEWS photographer's Speed Graphic and are shown above.

3,000 at Corpus Christi's Sauerkraut Festival

A small segment of the big crowd which packed the big army hospital tent as the serving of dinner started.
Identification was a challenge but Jacob and Phyllis Maas appear toward the upper right in the above picture.

Approximately 3,000 persons joined members of the Corpus Christi parish of Deerfield township as they held their Second Annual Sauerkraut Festival at the church grounds Sunday.

The affair opened with a sumptuous pork and sauerkraut dinner, with all the trimmings, before the noon hour and lasted well into the evening, including another sumptuous evening meal.

Entertainment made available to those attending was widely varied and included a motion picture presentation in the evening. Approximately 1,000 vehicles were parked in a field next to the Corpus Christi grounds. (See below).

About 1,000 cars were parked in a field near the Corpus Christi grounds.

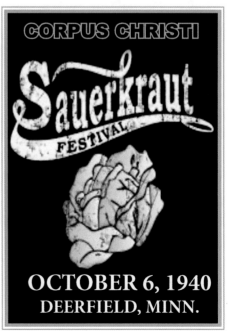

CORPUS CHRISTI
Sauerkraut
FESTIVAL

OCTOBER 6, 1940
DEERFIELD, MINN.

Nº 168

Annual Bazaar

CORPUS CHRISTI PARISH
Deerfield - October 22, 1939
TICKETS, 25 CENTS

$5 Cash .... Walter Diers, Medford
½-ton Coal . H. A. Theder, Medford
$5 Cash, Larson Beverage, Medford
$2 Cash ...... State Bank, Medford
49-lb bag Flour, S. C. Pike, Medford
Kitchen Clock ...... C. J. Larson
  Hardware, Medford
3-lbs Butter .... George Brady
2 Roosters ...... John Reichart
1 Pair Handmade Pillow Slips
  Mrs. Leo Brady
1 Set Embroidered Dish Towels
  and 3 Roosters, Mrs. Geo Brady
1 Calf .... Vic Paquin
1 Pig .... Charles Brady
1 Sheep .... John Morgan
3-gal. Honey .... J. F. Brady
1 Turkey ... W. T. Muellenmeister
2 sacks Potatoes . Mrs. Vanderputte
Pair of Pillow Cases .... Mary Ann
  Vanderputte
1 Brace Ducks .... Ed. Kniefle
6-lbs Butter .... Jim Hurt
2 Chickens .... Joe Betchwars
7 Chickens .... Peter Sterns
1 Pig ....George Boucher
$5 Cash .... Father Snyder

Bring a Friend to Noon Dinner

Nº 424

Annual Picnic

CORPUS CHRISTI PARISH
At Wm. Kvasinscka Farm
Deerfield - June 9, 1940
Tickets 25 Cents

$5 Cash, Larson's Beverage Store
$5 Cash .... George Boucher
Roaster -- Larson's Hdw., Medford
1 Gal. White Paint ...... Alexander
  Lumber Yard, Medford
Sack of Flour .... S. C. Pike
Gal. Ice Cream, Green Lantern Cafe
3 lbs. Chocolate Cr. Coffee, R. H. Lee
2 gal. Transmission, Medford Motors
$2 Cash .... George Brady
1 Pig .... Wm. Neusbaum
$3 Cash .... John Reichert
$2 Cash .... K. C. Jones
3 Chickens .... Vic. Paquin
6-lbs. Butter .... Jim Hurt
$3 Cash .... Wm. Vandeputte
$2 Cash .... Ed. Kniefle
1 Pig ... Leo & Wm. Mullenmeister
$2 Cash .... Anton Kniefle
15-doz. Eggs ...... Charles Brady
2-gal. Honey .... J. F. Brady
1 Card Table .... Brick Fur. Co.
4 Chickens .... Mrs. B. Matz
5-gal. Oil .... H. A. Teders
4 Broilers .... John Karaus
Sack Concentrate ...... Henry Berg
10-lbs. Butter, Mrs. Peter Stirens-
  Peter Stirens, Jr.
1 Sheep .... John Morgan
3-lbs. Butter ...... Anton Schmanski
$1 Cash .... Service Garage
$5 Cash .... Diers Arcade
$5 Cash .... Father Snyder

Bring a Friend to Noon Dinner

Nº 39

Annual Picnic

CORPUS CHRISTI PARISH
Under Big Tent
At Wm. Kvasinscka Farm
Deerfield - June 15th, 1941
Tickets 25 Cents

Geo. Boucher _____ $5.00
John Reichert _____ $2.00
Mrs. Anna Stirens _____ $2.00
Wm. Nusbaum ____ 4-lbs. Butter
Casper Kayser _____ $2.00
James Hurt _____ $5.00
J. F. Brady _____ $2.00
John Karaus _____ 4 Broilers
Mrs. Wm. Kvasnicka and family ...
  1 Pig
Charles Brady ____ 30-doz. Eggs
E. P. Knifel _____ $2.50
John Morgan _____ 3-lbs. Butter
F. H. Pirkl _____ 3-lbs. Butter
Vic Paquin _____ 1 Pig
John Gillen _____ $5.00
Wm. & Leo Mullenmeister ___ $7.00
Geo. Grady _____ $5.00
Ernest Holmquist _____ 1 Pig
Patrick Condon _____ 5-lbs. Butter
Geo. Miller _____ $5.00
Geo. Matejeck _____ 3-lbs. Butter
Wm. Gutting _____ 1 Sack Flour
C. J. Jones _____ $2.00
Peter Stirens Jr. _____ $2.00
Commander's Elevator, Morristown
  1 Sack Flour
Kruger's Furniture, Morristown ...
  9x12 Congoleum Rug
Dr. Francis, Morristown ___ $2.00
Central Lumber Co., Morristown
  1 Quart Paint
Morristown Feed Mill _____
  1 Bag Chick Starter
Anton Kubista _____ 5-lbs. Butter
H. A. Theders _____ $2.00
S. C. Pike - 50-lbs Gold Mine Flour
L. P. Larson _____ $5.00
Ann's Eat Shop . 1-gal. Ice Cream
Alexander Lumber Co. of Medford,
  1 gal. Paint
W. H. Diers _____ $5.00
Medford Service Garage ___ $1.00
National Service Station . 2-gal. Oil
H. G. Lee - $1 worth of Mobile Oil
Medford Motors _____ 2-gal's. Oil
Medford Washed Sand & Gravel
  Co. .. 2 Individual Hog Troughs
Father Snyder _____ $5.00

Bring a Friend to Noon Dinner
Rain or Shine

DEERFIELD
STORE
GOOD FOR 10c
If Returned With Bottle

Deerfield Store Coupon

SECOND ANNUAL CORPUS CHRISTI PARISH SAUERKRAUT FESTIVAL (OCTOBER 6, 1940)

An estimated 1,000 automobiles owned by guests were crowded onto the field adjacent to the church grounds.

This picture with twenty-eight faces, includes Irene (Bruzant) Schmanski, Dorothy (Bruzant) Saufferer, Veronica Vandeputte, Lucille Weber, Lucille Pirkl, Mrs. Kubista, Mary Alice Brady, Mary Ann (Vandeputte) Turner, Mary Grace Kvasniscka, and Clara (Pete) Judd.-Photo News Photos and Flashphoto.

The above photo with twenty-two Corpus Christi ladies posing in their aprons, includes Clara Vandeputte, Mary Brady, Veronica Kvasniscka, Mary Morgan, Amelia Brady, Mrs. Joachim, Irene Paquin, Mrs. Kubista, Veronica Vandeputte, and Dorothy (Bruzant) Saufferer.

PICNICS PAID FOR THE PARISH

(The Courier -- March 1989)

Corpus Christi Church, about ten miles northwest of Owatonna, is a small rural parish served by Christ the King parish in nearby Medford. It is among the oldest Catholic communities in the diocese; the church itself -although remodeled and modernized throughout the years -probably dates to 1869.

In about 1850 Andrew Wertzler moved to Deerfield and homesteaded the land on which the church is located, a site which he donated for the purpose.

Corpus Christi has always been a mission parish, served originally by priests from Claremont, Waseca or Owatonna. Many local Catholics, however, attended the larger churches until the arrival of Father Raymond Snyder in 1938.

Father Snyder, from St. Hyacinth's parish in Owatonna, contacted all the Catholics in the area and encouraged them to attend Corpus Christi. Initially, people were reluctant to leave their parishes for the uncertain future of the smaller one, but gradually Father Snyder's persistence won them over.

Once the congregation was of healthy size, some major renovating of the church was undertaken. First it was moved to a new foundation farther back from the road right-of-way and given a basement. The church interior was redone, the pews refinished and a new stove and electric lights installed.

Almost all the work was accomplished with volunteer labor, and funds were raised by "parish picnics" as Father Snyder called them.

The "picnics" were really full-blown fund raisers which included everything from traps-shoots to airplane rides. For a time these were even held in a huge circus tent and provided the major source of income for the parish until they were discontinued in 1951.

In 1943 the Medford parish of Christ the King was established and many members of the smaller Corpus Christi parish transferred there; nevertheless, both parishes have expanded greatly and a close relationship continues.

In January of 1966 the parish saw one of its own ordained a priest: Father Lawrence Sammon, SYD, who went to work as a Divine Word Missionary in Mexico. Ten years later, another son of the parish was ordained - Father Joseph Pete.

FINDING A RECTORY FOR FATHER SNYDER

By Carla (Maas) Brady

The first Rectory located at 119 1st Street NW, Medford.

The parish of Corpus Christi in Deerfield included Catholic families of Medford who had formerly belonged to parishes in Owatonna and Faribault. In 1943, there were only 12 Catholic families in the village of Medford. As the Deerfield church was located in the country about six miles west of Medford and some lacked the means of transportation, an old school bus was purchased to provide transportation to Sunday Mass. Beginning in 1939, this bus was driven and maintained by C.J. "Casey" Jones. This routine continued for about four years, until the basement of Diers Arcade was rented in 1943, becoming the first "Christ the King Church" per approval by the diocese of Winona.

Parishioners decided that after the assignment of Fr. Raymond Snyder in 1943 to serve both parishes, it would be a good idea to have a parish house for him. He had been living at the Sacred Heart Rectory and driving to Deerfield.

A property at 119-1st Street, Medford was purchased July 27, 1945. Gene Keller, who was in high school then, tells the story that the rectory house above where Father Snyder lived early on, needed new shingles so Gene's dad, Francis (Keller) and Byron F. Brady went to Owatonna to the lumber yard to pick up the shingles that had been decided upon.

As was the expected practice in those days, volunteers from both churches were willing to help get the job done. They organized a date, and the crew was at the rectory eagerly awaiting the return of Francis and Byron. As a joke to those waiting, Francis and Byron asked the lumber yard if they had some old and different colored shingles they could mix in with the bundles of new shingles. That is what the lumber yard did. Boy did the crew give Francis and Byron a time about what kind of purchasing they did when the crew started doing the work.

This was the home of Father Snyder until he was transferred to Our Lady of Mount Carmel, Easton, Minnesota in 1952. Before he was transferred, he began the construction on the detached rectory just south of Christ the King Church. The rectory was completed after Father Harold Mountain arrived. In the 1952 Financial Report of Corpus Christi Church, it was noted that the total cost of the rectory was $30,159.75. Deerfield was responsible for half of that payment or $15,079.75.

It was also noted that Corpus Christi had raised $7,620.89 prior to 1952 for this project. Per the warranty deed #112994 of 5/29/52, the old rectory was sold, signed by Edward A Fitzgerald, President (Bishop) along with Harold B. Mountain (Pastor), Byron Brady (Secretary and Director), Henry Hager (Treasurer and Director) and Joseph F. Hale (Director and Vicar General). Per the Financial report, $9,313.13 was received for the old rectory, and was put towards Corpus Christi's portion of the new rectory, satisfying the remainder $7,458.89, and adding to the Corpus Christi treasury $1,854.17. (See financial report from 1952).

Sources Cited:

1). Christ the King History 2019.

2). Per deed of record dated July 27th, 1945: The Church of Christ the King, Medford Minn., and Corpus Christi Church Deerfield, Minn. as Joint owners purchase the 1 ¾ story wood framed house with .39 acres from a widow, Ella M Bailey in the village of Medford.

RECEIPTS

		(EXPENDITURES)	
Church support.................. $	3,410.43	Pastor's salary............... $	490.00
Transferred from Blu Fund.....	1,854.17	Sacristy and sanctuary........	643.21
Balance hand Jan 1st 1952......	332.98	Board.........................	315.06
Offertory......................	138.82	Housekeeper salary............	235.00
Donation.......................	75.00	Livery........................	228.50
Children.......................	52.44	Misc. gas, tel. water etc....	210.67
Confirmation...................	20.00	Fuel..........................	102.48
(Diocesan)		Church custodian.............	100.00
Prop. of the Faith............	54.00	Insurance.....................	49.25
Charities.....................	39.00	Religion books, office expense	49.10
Winonan.......................	42.00	Extra priests................	35.00
Seminary......................	24.00	(Diocesan)	
Sweden Missions...............	22.00	Diocesan tax..................	250.00
Holy Father...................	26.00	Prop. of the Faith...........	54.00
War Relief....................	9.00	Winonan.......................	42.00
Holy Land.....................	3.00	Charities.....................	39.00
Indian and Negro..............	15.50	Seminary......................	24.00
		Holy Father..................	26.00
Grand Total...$5,118.33		Holy Name.....................	10.00
		Confirmation..................	25.00
Respectfully submitted:		Indian and Negro.............	15.50
Father Mountain..... pastor.		Swedish Missions..............	22.00
Henry Hager......... trustee.		War Relief....................	9.00
Byron Brady......... trustee.		Retreat.......................	10.00
		Holy Land.....................	3.00

Total expense.. $ 2,989.78
Bal. on hand now. 2,128.55
Grand Total.... $ 5,118.33

****

1952　ALTAR AND ROSARY SOCIETY　1952

(Receipts)		(Expenditures)	
Guilds...................... $	138.80	Religious supplies........... $	292.75
Religious articles sold.....	204.63	Religious education..........	125.00
Sister's collection.........	70.50	Deanery dues and welfare.....	66.14
Misc........................	18.71	Misc.........................	17.23
Total income.$	432.64	Total expense.. $	501.12
(1952) Bal. Jan 1st	125.14	Balance now....	56.66
Grand Total..$	557.78	Grand total... $	557.78

Respectfully submitted:
Mrs. Louis Pirkl... President.
Mrs. Ernest Holmquist..Sec..Treas.

CONTRIBUTIONS

Boch, Lloyd................... $	17.00	Hurt, James.................... $	30.50
Brady, Byron..................	82.50	Hurt, James Jr................	2.00
Brady, James F...............	35.00	Kniefel, Mrs. Anton..........	29.45
Brady, James M...............	67.00	Kersten, Mrs. Willand........	65.00
Bryant, Richard..............	24.00	Klukas, William.............	60.00
Cole, Corliss................	51.75	Kvasnicka, Lawrence..........	50.00
Condon, Sylvester............	8.50	Kvasnicka, Mrs. William......	100.00
Dickson, Mrs. Charles........	27.30	Lang, Joseph.................	35.25
Eustice, Donald..............	12.60	Larson, Adolph...............	59.00
Gostarek, Michael...........	23.00	LeMieux, Albert..............	71.25
Hager, Henry.................	95.00	Malecha, Frank...............	2.65
Hager, Raymond...............	7.10	Miller, George..............	108.00
Hoffman, Clarence............	48.50	Mohs, Bert...................	67.00
Holmquist, Bernard..........	71.85	Morgan, Donald...............	23.75
Holmquist, Ernest............	66.00	Morgan, Edward...............	29.00

1952 Corpus Christi Parish Annual Report Published in January 1953 (Page 1).

130

NAME	AMOUNT		NAME	AMOUNT
Morgan, John	$ 33.00		Pirkl, Harlow	$ 7.10
Mork, Kenneth	39.15		Pirkl, Mrs. Justine	13.80
Mullenmaster, Leo	86.70		Pirkl, Raymond	13.75
Ness, Mrs. Bernard	7.00		Rath, Floyd	50.00
Nusbaum, Donald	5.00		Reyant, Peter	55.75
Nusbaum, Richard	51.75		Sanken, Leo	8.00
O'Neil, George	26.50		Sanken, William	18.00
Pete, Joseph Jr.	59.00		Schmanski, Anton	58.00
Paquette, Raymond	4.00		Stirens, Mrs. Peter	44.00
Phillips, Gene	90.50		Tuve, Edwin	14.70
Pirkl, Charles	75.25		Voegele, Arthur	65.00
Pirkl, Frank	31.50		Voegele, Miss Carol	50.25
Pirkl, Louis	60.00		Weber, Joseph	65.50

BUILDING FUND

Total cost of rectory was $ 30,159.75 It was to be shared equally in cost by Corpus Christi and Christ the King. Corpus Christi was also to receive the old rectory, which was sold for $ 9, 313.13.

$ 15,079.75 Deerfield's share of cost.
  7,620.89 raised by Deerfield prior to 1952.
$ 7,458. 96 owed by Deerfield at beginning of year.

$ 9,313.123 price received for old rectory.
  7,458.89 still owed.
$ 1,854.17 placed in the treasury of Corpus Christi as listed above on report.

CHILDREN

NAME	AMOUNT		NAME	AMOUNT
Holmquist, Harlan	$ 6.05		Kvasnicka, William	$ .53
Cole, Richard	5.15		Hager, Roseanne	.46
Pirkl, Rosemary	4.65		Hager, Dennis	.27
LeMieux, Anne Marie	3.53		Reyant, Henry	.23
Mullenmaster, Leo	3.41		Brady, Sharon	.23
Mullenmaster, Colette	3.13		Hurt, Pauline	.26
Miller, Philip	3.07		Weber, Marjorie	.15
Nusbaum, Gerry	2.90		Hoffman, LaVonne	.10
Mullenmaster, Anne	2.58		Hoffman, Carol	.15
Larson, Robert	2.58		Hager, Louis	.10
Dickison, Robert	2.52		Eustice, Ronald	.10
Dickison, Freddie	2.35		Hager, Paul	.10
Dickison, Donald	2.15		Ness, Marjorie	.10
Brady, Carolyn	1.75		Hurt, Kathleen	.10
Hager, David	1.21		Mullenmaster, William	.10
Mullenmaster, Mary	1.20		Hager, Susan	.10
Ness, Betty	.87		Lang, William	.05
Hurt, Joanne	.57		Hager, Gene	.05

CATHOLIC WILLS

Attorneys tell us that no matter how much or how little one may own, it is very wise to have a will. It eliminates many many problems, not only legally.

In making a will one attempts to provide for his loved ones, and for those that are dependent upon him. For that very same reason one should never make a will without mentioning God and the Church of God here on earth. It is truly a sign of our love of God when we remember His works here on earth, and surely no better way could that be done that to remember the parish where one had the privelege of adoring God during our life time.

One should set aside a certain amount for Masses also for the eternal repose of one's soul, rather than depending upon the charity of others.

May God bless you for the sacrifices you have made for religion.

1952 Corpus Christi Parish Annual Report Published in January 1953 (Page 2).

BAZAAR TO MARK FIRST SOCIAL FUNCTION OF MEDFORD CATHOLIC CHURCH
PHOTO NEWS (NOVEMBER 4, 1943)

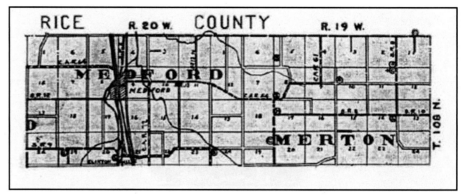

The above section of the Steele County map was allocated in 1943 to the parish of Christ The King by the most Reverend Leo Binz, Bishop of the Diocese of Winona.

Formal establishment of the first Catholic church in Medford will be noted Sunday, November 7th when parishioners hold their first dinner and bazaar,

The Church of Christ The King is served by Father Raymond Snyder along with Corpus Christi parish in northwest Deerfield along with his Waseca parishes. With increasing interest accumulating in the establishment of a parish in Medford, the past three months have been marked by activity in which some 40 families now make up the parish.

Holding Mass in the basement of the Diers Arcade each Sunday morning, parishioners have now purchased the Rafdal Garage building. For the present, social meetings will be held in that location and as quickly as possible, the garage building will be remodeled to serve as a temporary church until Victory permits resumption of building.

The annual bazaar is keyed to the slogan of the parishioners "Help The New Church" and will open at noon at the Rafdal Garage location with dinner followed by bazaar activities in the afternoon. Mass will be said at the Diers Arcade by Rev. Snyder at 10:00 a.m.

Vince Steinbauer Sr. and Steve Majusiak of Medford are trustees of the new church. In charge of the women's work for the annual bazaar are Mrs. Clarence Jones and Mrs. Steve Majusiak while Clarence Jones and Steve Majusiak are directing the men's activities.

His excellency, the Most Rev. Bishop Leo Binz, D. D. in instituting the parish at Medford, declared the following: Whereas it is provided in the canon law of the church that the territory or a diocese should be divided into distinct parts for the spiritual care of souls and since there has been an altogether special increase in the number of Catholic people in and about the town of Medford we do hereby decree the erection of a new parish in honor of Christ The King for the above mentioned town of Medford and we hereby solemnly declare the parish of Christ The King canonically constituted with all rights, privileges, and prerogatives which other parishes have and enjoy under the general law of the church and the particular statutes of the Diocese of Winona.

It is further decreed that the territorial limits of Christ The King, Medford shall be as follows: To the north, the Rice County line; to the west, the Deerfield Township line; to the east, the Dodge County line; and to the south, a line straight east and west from the Clinton Falls creamery.

The Copper Kettle now occupies the former Diers Arcade where the original Masses in Medford were held. The present Knights of Columbus Lodge includes what was the Rafdal Garage where Christ The King parish held social meetings and other activities in the early 1940s.

This clipping is courtesy of Joe and Lucille Weber.

1947 CORPUS CHRISTI PARISH MEMBERSHIP

Herbert Androli
George Boucher Sr.
Byron Brady
James F. Brady
James M. Brady
Richard Bruzant
Donald Caron
Vincent Chavie
Corliss Cole
Patrick Condon
Joe Deml
Donald Eustice
Leo Gostomczik
Henry Hager
Arvid Hanson
Clarence Hoffman
Bernard Holmquist
Ernest Holmquist
James Hurt
Stephen Judd
Mrs. Jirele
John Karaus
Martin Klebel
William Klukas

Anthony Kniefel
Robert Kniefel
Sylvester Krenik
Lawrence Kvasknicka
Mrs. William Kvasnicka
Joseph Lang
Edwin Langworthy
Adolph Larson
Albert LeMieux
Albert Lorenz
Franklin Maas
Charles Miller
George Miller
Bert Mohs
A. Montgomery
John Morgan
Robert Morgan
Leo Mullenmaster
William Mullenmaster
Mrs. Bernard Ness
Richard Nusbaum
William Nusbaum
Floyd O'Connor
George F. O'Niell

Raymond Paquette
Joseph Pete
Nora Petricka
Eugene Phillips
Charles Pirkl
Frank Pirkl
Louis Pirkl
Peter Reyant
Leo Sammon
Anton Schmanski
Charles Schuller
Peter Stirens
Thomas Swintek
Theodore Szmanski
Casper Tiedeken
Mr. Tobin
Arthur Voegele
Joseph Weber
Art Wildon
Joseph Wieczoreak
Felix Wochnik
Mrs. George Yause

There was a 6-month span of time beginning in 1942 and extending into 1943, prior to the establishment of Christ the King, when Father Snyder was appointed to a pastorate at Fountain and Wykoff, and Father Alois Quillian assisted in Waseca and attended to Corpus Christi Parish. After this 6-month period, Bishop Binz announced that the pastor of both congregations would be Father Raymond Snyder and he remained there until 1952.

His successor was Father Harold Mountain, who served until 1968. It was during this time that Bishop Edward Fitzgerald required all cemeteries to be platted, a cemetery association formed and financial records be kept and sent to the Chancery.

In the early years of the cemetery, graves were dug in a haphazard manner; some were unmarked and no records kept. The Articles of Association of Corpus Christi Cemetery were signed in March 1954.

At that time, the original part of the cemetery to the east was set aside and new lots were platted on the west side.

In 1950, an altar and large crucifix was erected, which added much to our beautiful cemetery, nestled against a wooded background, which is also church property. During the 1980s, through the diligent efforts of Kenneth Mork, the brush and excess trees were cleared away to allow platting to the boundary line on the west.

The stained glass windows were installed during the early 1940s.
Note that the name "Mullenmaster" is spelled incorrectly on the bottom window.

Donated by
Mr & Mrs. J. F. Brady Sr.

In Memory of
Mr & Mrs. Thomas Brady

136

Donated by
Mrs. Mrs. Peter Sterens

Donated by Mr. & Mrs.
m. Mullinmaster & Family

137

Note that the name "Sterens" is spelled several different ways in early church records. Regardless of spelling, it is the same family.

CHAPTER V

CORPUS CHRISTI PRIESTS, RELIGIOUS & PARISH STAFF

LIST OF CORPUS CHRIST PASTORS
Pastors/Parochial Vicar/Priest Moderator/Mission Pastor

Father Keller of Faribault exercised pastoral care of the few pioneer families in the Deerfield area from 1865 until he was transferred to another parish in 1869. The Directory lists his successors at Faribault serving Deerfield. They were as follows:

Mission Pastor Father Clement Scheve, 1869 - 1870;

(1870-1923)

Father Arthur Hurley, 1870 - 1874

Father Lawrence Wiesler, 1874 - 1875.

Mission Pastor Rev. James Cotter

Mission Pastor Rev. George Keller

1875-1879: Mission Pastor Rev. Francis Pribyl

1879-1885: Father Walter Raleigh

1885-1889: Father John Solnce

1891-1903: Mission Pastor Mgsr. John Pivo

1894-1896: Mission Pastor Rev. Patrick Kiernan

1903-1909 Rev. John Meyers

1909-1938: The following pastors from Claremont served until 1938; Father John Meyers,1903-1909; Father James Cotter, 1909-1916; Father Thomas McCarthy 1916-1921; Father H. H. Forkenbrock, 1921-1923; Father Frank Schimek, 1923-1929; Father Robert Jennings, 1929-1932; Father John Misiak, 1932-1935; Father Alfred Frisch, 1935-1938.

1935-1937 Church was closed

1938-1942 Rev. Raymond Snyder (He lived in Waseca and traveled to Deerfield).

1942-1943 Rev. Alois Quillin

1943-1952 Rev. Raymond Snyder

1952-1968 Rev. Harold Mountain

1968-1969 Rev. Patrick Russell

1968-1976 Rev. Francis Glynn

1976-1977 Msgr. Warren Ryan

1977-1985 Rev. John Cody

1985-1989 Rev. Edward Mountain

1989-1992 Rev. Milo Ernster

1992-2002 Rev. Robert Herman (pastor)

2002-2007 Rev. Robert Herman (priest moderator)

2007-2016 Rev. Robert Herman continued to celebrate Mass at Corpus Christi. During this time Father Herman was living near the Mississippi River at Buffalo City, Wisconsin and driving to Deerfield and Medford each weekend to celebrate Mass.

2012-2016 Rev. Edward McGrath (Corpus Christi and Christ The King were "clustered" as mission churches under the auspices of St. Joseph parish in Owatonna.

Note: From the 1990s until about 2016, Father Clayton Haberman, who was retired and living on Cannon Lake, Faribault was available for baptisms and spiritual guidance.

Father George Keller (Missionary)

Father Francis Prybil (Missionary)

Father George Keller was the first priest to hold services in Steele County. At the time he was connected to the Archdiocese of St. Paul and lived in Faribault during the late 1850s and 1860s.

Father Keller had charge of the mission from Faribault south to the Iowa-Minnesota state line. Records show that Father George Keller came to Deerfield as early as 1855 to perform marriages. Services were held in private homes until the construction of the Corpus Christi Church. Father Keller traveled throughout Southern Minnesota on horseback. There were no roads, only trails. This was about the time of the 1862 Sioux Uprising and there was still a significant Native American population in the area. During the uprising, many of the residents fled the area.

In 1856, Fr. George Keller organized a Catholic group at St. Mary's in rural Waseca County. The first services were held at the home of John Lynch.

One of the most interesting pastors of the parish was Father Francis Pribyl. He was born November 30, 1852 in Rimov near Budejovice in Bohemia. At the age of 12 he arrived in Winona, Minnesota with his parents on November 12, 1864. In 1868 he became a student at the College of St. John at Collegeville near St. Cloud. He finished his theological studies at St. Francis Seminary, near Milwaukee.

Father Pribyl was ordained in St. Paul in 1875. That same year he was sent as a pastor to Owatonna.

Later he was sent to Montana where he published a weekly newspaper "Czecho American." It became a very widely distributed paper in a short time. In 1888 he started a Czech daily paper, "Union," together with the Sunday paper, "Catholic."

Perhaps he was also the inventor of the first fountain pen ever made which later was manufactured in Brooklyn. A New York concern offered him $5000 for the patent on the pen.

Monsignor Patrick Kiernan

SOME EARLIER CORPUS CHRISTI PASTORS & MISSIONARIES

Monsignor John Pivo (1891)

Monsignor John Pivo was born on May 12, 1865 in Kocin, a small village in the southern part of present day Czech Republic. He was graduated from the high school in Ceski Budcjovice and from college in Jindricho-Hradci.

Early in life he was filled with the great desire of becoming a priest. This ambition was nutured at the Belgian Seminary in Louvain where he completed his course in Philosophy and where he later met Archbishop John Ireland. Archbishop Ireland was then in Europe seeking candidates for his newly organized Seminary in St. Paul. He was deeply impressed by the alert and studious philosophy student, John Pivo.

At the time, the need was great for priests to serve the vast number of immigrants in the newly organized State of Minnesota. John Pivo's knowledge of the Bohemian, German and Polish languages was the answer to Archbishop Ireland's immigrant problem. Because many of John Pivo's relatives and friends had already migrated to America, the Archbishop's invitation was eagerly accepted.

Eleven young men, together with John Pivo, made up the first class of foreign born students in the St. Paul Seminary.

Father Pivo was ordained to the Holy Priesthood on November 15, 1890 by Bishop McGollrick and was appointed to the German-Irish parish in Madison, Minnesota. The difficult pioneer life of his parishioners was shared equally by the eager young priest. He found himself serving about ten far distant settlements in the Madison area. There were no roads, no churches and no conveniences that today we take for granted.

The following year on May 11, 1891, Father Singer, pastor of Sacred Heart parish in Owatonna, died. Due to Father Pivo's knowledge of many languages, he was appointed to take over in the Owatonna area.

His care extended not only to the Catholics in all of Steele County, but also to Catholics in Austin, Albert Lea, Waseca and New Richland. Deerfield was included in Father Pivo's vast territory.

What a work that was, and what a man the youthful Father Pivo had to be. The strong Catholic life of this area is today a living tribute to the struggle, the hardships, the zeal and the ambition of Father Pivo.

As the years passed, Father Pivo won the love and devotion of his people. He was held in the highest esteem by the entire community and for his spiritual service, he was rewarded by his Church with the titled dignity of Monsignor. Neither this praise, this esteem nor this reward was sought after by Father Pivo. He was truly great in his humility and when he retired on September 1, 1936, we all sorrowed. *Source: The Story of Sacred Heart Church of Owatonna, Minnesota.*

CORPUS CHRISTI PASTORS

Father John Meyers (1903-1909)

Father Raymond Snyder
(1938-1942) & (1943-1952)

Father Alois Quillin
(1942-1943)

Father Harold B. Mountain
(1952-1968)

Photos courtesy of Catholic Diocese of Winona & Rochester

Father Francis Glynn
(1968-1976)

Father Warren Ryan
(1976-1977)

Father Warren Ryan succeeded Father Glynn in 1976 for one year and then Father John Cody became the pastor assisted by Father Raymond Snyder until the latter retired the following year.

Father John Cody
(1977-1985)

Father John Cody had a remarkable sense of humor; after all he was Irish. He seldom, if ever, asked for more money from the altar, but his subtle messages in the weekly bulletin, were eagerly awaited each Sunday and encouraged giving and good behavior. On various pages of this book, we have included some of his many comments and words of wisdom which were included in the bulletins between 1977 and 1985. Enjoy!

CORPUS CHRISTI PASTORS FROM 1985 THROUGH 2009

Father Edward Mountain
(1985-1989)

Father Milo Ernster
(1989-1992)

Father Robert Herman
(1992 until closing of Corpus Christi)

Father Clayton Haberman
(Assisting 2004-2009)

FAREWELL PARTY FOR FATHER RAYMOND SNYDER (1942)

Farewell party.

A farewell party was given at the Corpus Christe Church Parlor Monday evening in honor of Rev Father Raymond Snyder of was who was promoted to a future parish at Wykoff Minnesota Rev Father Snyder came to Deerfield Deerfield Community in 1938 and built up Corpus Christe parish. from a few member to a large parish. In cold winter weather when storms were severe and roads blocked Father Snyder would make his parish to say Mass. He not only was an endeared friend to his own parishioners but to every one he came in contact with. His personality was exceptional He was always willing to lend a hand to every one in there trials of life. He will be missed by every one

(Continued on next page)

in this community.

We all wish him the best of success in his new parish.

A purse of silver was presented to Rev. Father Snyder by his parishioners and friends.

Rev. Father Quillan will take charge of Corpus Christi parish at Deerfield.

From a notebook kept by the women of Corpus Christi Parish.

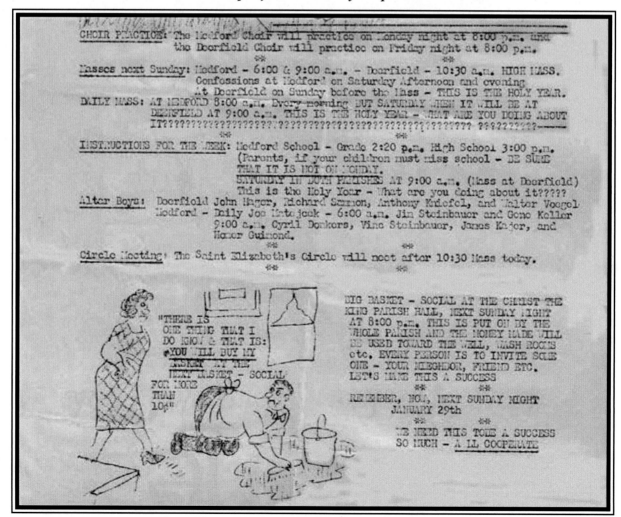

Christ The King /Corpus Christi Parish Bulletin (1950)

FATHER MOUNTAIN RETIRES FROM BEING A PASTOR, BUT WILL ALWAYS BE A PRIEST

By Marcia Gandrud
Staff writer

Father Edward Mountain doesn't like the word "retirement," and prefers to think of himself as being "recycled."

On October 10, his pastoral duties will be drawing to a close at Church of Christ the King in Medford and Corpus Christi Church in Deerfield. He was ordained 42 years ago at the Church of St. John the Baptist, Mankato.

"I will never retire from being a priest. I will always be a priest. but soon I will not be a pastor anymore. However, I will still be doing God's work, in whatever way the Diocese of Winona wants me to serve.

"During all my years as a pastor, I've had a lot of sole responsibility (for my churches and the church-goers). Now, with more free time, I'll be able to concentrate on soul responsibility," he said.

Father Mountain agrees with the Archbishop of London who said anybody over 60 years of age should spend time getting ready to meet their maker. "And that's just what I'm going to do--spend more time in prayer," Father Mountain, 65, said.

He is looking forward to traveling with his brother, Father Harold Mountain, who is a retired priest living in Mankato. An avid football fan, Father Edward Mountain will be blessing the Notre Dame team before its game with Miami in November.

Father Mountain entered the priesthood because of a calling from God and his family's influence.

As he looks back on his work, the thing that made the greatest impression on him is how people's viewpoints change when they are faced with a crisis such as the prospect of death.

For about five years, he was a chaplain at St. Marys Hospital in Rochester, and met many desperate people coming from
all over the world to seek help. "For many of these people, their medical condition really brought them back to the church, he said.

Father Edward Mountain will be retiring from Church of Christ the King in Medford on Oct. 10. A reception will be held for him Sunday from 7 to 9 p.m. at the Knights of Columbus Lodge in Medford. A short program will begin at 7 p.m. (Photo by Marcia Gandrud).

As he thinks back over his many years in the ministry, he remembers some significant changes in the Catholic Church. One major change is Mass being said in English instead of Latin.

Also, many lay people now participate in the services more than they used to, because of the shortage of priests.

Father Mountain plans to live in Owatonna when his pastoral duties cease. His change in lifestyle will leave him more free time for a favorite hobby, golfing.

Many people have fond memories of their association with the Father. Kenny Mork of Waseca, said "Father Mountain is a wonderful man, and he gives the best sermons around. He's just one of the many good priests the people in this area have been blessed with. Father Mountain would do anything for anybody. Even if it was 20 degrees below zero, he would go and help somebody."

Another parishioner, Lillian Arnold, said Father Mountain helped her by renewing some of the forgotten faith she had learned earlier ln her life.

A woman from Faribault, Jean Gillis, said she will always remember how thoughtful and caring Father Mountain is. 'When our son was hurt recently in an accident at work, Father knew just what to say to console us. Even in a crisis, he finds something for us to be thankful for, and it helps put the situation in perspective. He'll be missed by the whole community, but he deserves the relaxation of retirement," she said.

Charles Wencl appreciated the Father's "profound advice. I went to him a couple of times, about different things, and he didn't just say, 'do this or do that.' He gave me options, and helped me make a choice. I'll always remember his devotion to the Virgin Mary. Father Mountain will be greatly missed," he said.

"I think Father Mountain is great. He is easy to get along with, has a good sense of humor, and is very religious. Father is also a good role model for people in the community, showing them how they should live. And another thing-- he's always there when you need. him. I'll be sad to see him leave, but I understand it's necessary," Mary Ann Turner said.

Don Redman said, "It was a pleasure knowing Father Mountain. My son Nick really enjoyed serving mass for him. I will also remember the appreciation and praise he gave for the special effort put into the music at the Deerfield church."

"Father has always been cooperative and supportive of church programs and activities. He's always very compassionate to those in need. He Instituted the practice of saying the rosary before Mass, and I know this will continue even after he's gone. I will always remember his love and devotion for Mary. the mother of Jesus," Pam Kay said.

John Hager said he will always remember Father Mountain's homilies. "He's an excellent speaker. When he's talking, everybody's listening. It's so quiet you could hear a pin drop when he's speaking. And another thing, he is really down to earth and relates well to people," he said.

To show their appreciation for his many years of dedicated service, members of the two parishes will have special music at the 9 and 10:30 a.m. Masses this Sunday, featuring the adult choirs and the student handbell choir. The recently erected Marian Shrine will be dedicated at Church of Christ The King following the 10:30 Mass.

In addition to the two churches he will be serving for a couple more days, Father Mountain is currently serving, he has also served St. Peter and Paul's Catholic Church at Blue Earth; St. Augustine's Catholic Church at Austin; Cathedral of the Sacred Heart at Winona; St. Marys Hospital at Rochester; St. Joseph's Catholic Church at Lakefield; and St. John the Baptist, Minneota; and Sacred Heart Catholic Church in Owatonna.

There will be a retirement and farewell reception for Father Mountain Sunday from 7-9 p.m. at the Knights of Columbus Lodge in Medford. A short program will begin at 7 p.m.

Even though Father Mountain will no longer be a pastor, he has a lot of fond memories of his parishioners. "I will always remember the people I have worked with. People are basically good, supportive. and cooperative," the Father said.

DUST THOU ART

FATHER EDWARD MOUNTAIN STANDS IN THE SHADOW OF DEATH

By Jeffrey Jackson, Press Managing Editor

Owatonna People's Press (February 21, 2007)

OWATONNA- Edward Mountain used to tell the members of his parish that God wouldn't let him die until Notre Dame won another championship.

"Since that time, the girls have won a soccer championship and a basketball championship," Father Mountain said from his Owatonna home. Then he paused just long enough to allow a big smile to break naturally across his face. "I think God got mixed up," he said.

For the 82-year-old Catholic priest - whose living room is adorned with at least as much Notre Dame football memorabilia as it is religious iconography - it may indeed seem as if the divine had forgotten that promised championship.

Notre Dame hasn't won a national football crown since 1988. And Father Edward Mountain is dying.

"This could very well be my last Lent on earth," Mountain said about the 40-day liturgical season that begins today and ends on Easter.

For years, Mountain has battled what he calls "the Irish affliction" - little patches of cancer that grow on his light, almost translucent Irish skin. And for years, he would have them removed. He would even joke with his parishioners that he would never look old because the doctors kept cutting out the wrinkles. But last summer, the doctors discovered that a few patches on his scalp were something more. He had melanoma and the prognosis was not good.

Father Edward Mountain on the eve of Ash Wednesday in 2007 at Sacred Heart Catholic Church in Owatonna.

He underwent surgery, which, at first, the doctors thought had been successful. They were wrong. "They thought they had it, but they didn't," he said matter-of-factly. In the intervening months, he is part of a special study at Mayo Clinic in Rochester using new treatments - treatments that have helped him some. Yet, he is also very realistic about the prognosis.

Indeed, the doctors told him last summer that if he did nothing, he might last nine months.

With the treatment, it should be longer, though how much longer he doesn't know. "They tell me they can't do much for it," he said.

Father Edward Mountain (left) and his brother Father Harold Mountain, met with Pope John Paul II.

Even after nearly 60 years in the priesthood, coming face to face with his own mortality has led Father Mountain to look at the church and its liturgy through new eyes. He paused and recalled the words of the liturgy spoken on Ash Wednesday - "Remember, man, thou art dust and unto dust thou shall return. That has particular significance for me this year," he said.

Still, in the weeks leading up to Lent, as he has undergone chemotherapy, Father Edward Mountain has continued to live his life as he always has - seeking God's will and not his own.

"Your prayer life deepens when you realize that you're going to be seeing God ·pretty soon," he said.

Life among Lutherans
Not even the frigid fury of a Minnesota winter would keep the Mountain family of rural Blue Earth County from their life of religious devotion.

When the roads were blocked with snow, preventing Edward Mountain's father - also named Edward - from driving the family to St. Joseph's Catholic Church in Good Thunder, the family patriarch would find alternative means of transportation.

"Dad would hitch up the sleigh," Father Mountain said, "and the family would pile in and allow the horses to pull them the 4 to 5 mile trek into the city. The road to the priesthood it seems, was paved with snow and ice.

Good Thunder, a small community about 12 miles south of Mankato, remains today predominantly Lutheran, just as it was during Edward Mountain's youth.

With a population of about 500, the town always managed to support two Lutheran churches and a Lutheran school. That sort of atmosphere would seem to be overwhelming to a Irish-Catholic boy in those pre-Vatican II days.

Edward Mountain took it all in stride and managed to reach across the theological divide. "All my friends were Lutheran," he said.

He said, "In fact," he added "my best friends were the children --- a son and a daughter of the Lutheran pastor in town. In fact, during high school for a time, I dated the daughter, making the pastor curious about my intentions." "He asked me what I was going to do with my life," Mountain said. "I told him I was thinking about becoming a priest and he said, Thank God!"

That decision to become a priest was affected at least in part by his older brother Harold who was in the seminary while Edward was in high school. But at least according to one story his brother used to tell, Edward Mountain's decision to become a priest came much earlier in life than that.

"My brother told a story about when we were little kids on the farm, stacking wood in the basement and the parish priest came by to visit us," said Father Mountain.

Harold Mountain would say that it was then that young Edward Mountain decided to become a priest. When Harold asked his brother why he wanted to become a priest, Edward had an answer. "I said because priests always dressed up and never have to work," Father Mountain said. smiling, then adding quickly that he didn't remember the incident.

From chaplain to patient
Every night when patients would come into St. Marys Hospital in Rochester, Father Mountain, then working as a chaplain at the hospital, would go to visit them. Heart surgeries and brain surgeries that are today much more commonplace. In the mid-1950s, still new even at institution like the renown Mayo Clinic. And every night, Mountain did not know what he was going to find as he tried, as best he could, to prepare the frightened patients for what lay ahead.

He would console them and tell them that God loved them. If they were Catholic, he would hear their confessions or administer the anointing of the sick.

"We did more miracles than the doctors did at Mayo - spiritual miracles," he said. "Those were the things they never saw. People turned back to God."

Father Mountain became a chaplain at the hospital in 1955, a scant eight years after he was ordained. He had been serving as a parish priest for a small congregation where he felt he wasn't doing enough. So when the chaplaincy came open at the Rochester hospital, he applied for it. It was not always easy work. At times, patients would die on the operating table and Father Mountain would accompany the doctors to break news to the families. On occasion, it was Father Mountain himself who would try to explain to the families what had happened and try to comfort them.

"Sometimes they just wouldn't be consoled," he said. He remembered a time when a couple lost their son - a 13-year-old boy who died as he was undergoing heart surgery. The doctor tried to talk to the couple, but they wouldn't listen. Instead, they cursed the doctor and cursed Mayo Clinic. That is when Father Mountain went to visit them. But no matter how he tried to comfort them, they wouldn't listen.

"They cursed me, they cursed the church, they almost cursed God," he said. Fifty years later, the memory still haunts him. "Some things you carry with you the rest of your life," he said.

As he paused to think about those parents and the death of their son, he recalled a central theme of his ministry and the homilies he preached.

"In my sermons I've talked about the importance of faith when your back is against the wall," he said. "It's the only thing you've got."

It is that faith, he said, that is sustaining him as he faces his own mortality and the very real possibility of his own impending death.

"I've been preaching for 60 years that death is not the end, but a beginning," he said. "I'm happy to go to heaven, but I am human enough not to want to go through with dying."

Having worked as a chaplain at St. Marys Hospital, along 1 with his many years as a pastor, Father Mountain has seen the toll that cancer can have on the body. "Cancer death can be not very pretty," he said.

Later, he speaks with hope, not necessarily that his cancer will be cured -though he has not given up on that -but with hope that no matter what happens to him that God will carry him through.

"The Lord has blessed me," he said. "If l am suffering now before I go out, he will be with me."

It is not-the first time he has talked to people about this passage of life he is going through. Kay Krumholz of Owatonna said that on more than one occasion, she has spoken with Father Mountain about his cancer and his prognosis.

"He said he wasn't afraid to die, but he wasn't looking forward to the process," she said.

Then again, she said, at other times - particularly lately - his perspective on death and dying were different.

"He would say to me, 'When it's 30 below, heaven doesn't look so bad,' " she said, adding, "He hates cold weather."

Priest and friend
Krumholz met Father Mountain back in the 1940s when he was serving as the assistant pastor the parish of Blue Earth, her hometown.

She was in college at the time, but came home at Christmas and had the opportunity to play the organ at the Christmas Eve Mass. The occasion also marked Father Mountain's first Christmas Eve sermon.

Thirty years later, when Father Mountain became the pastor of Sacred Heart in Owatonna, Krumholz, who was then playing organ for the Owatonna congregation, renewed her friendship with the priest. It is a friendship that has lasted for 30 years.

Recently, when Krumholz went through hip-replacement surgery, Father slipped on his clerical collar - wearing it atop of Notre Dame sweater, of course - and drove to the hospital to visit his friend.

"We're blessed to have him in our midst," she said.
That is how people who have known him, worshiped with him and prayed with him describe Father Mountain - as a blessing.

"He's a wonderful man - kind, gentle, with a great sense of humor," said Mary Tellijohn, who also has been a friend of the priest since he first came to Owatonna.

He performed the weddings of many of Tellijohn's children and was there with her at the funerals of her parents, traveling to LeSueur to support her. He was, she said, always right there. "How do you begin to talk about him? He's been such a friend, so much a part of the family," she said.

Except for a few times every autumn. Then, when the air grew crisp, Father Mountain would journey with his brother. the older Father Mountain to South Bend, Indian to watch his beloved "Fighting Irish" football team.
We always said he was going on religious retreat to Notre Dame," Krumholz said echoed by Tellijohn.

"We knew he was going to the football game," Tellijohn said.

The sort of openness with which Mountain has lived is evident even now as he faces the disease that may claim his life. He will speak frankly about his cancer, how it has progressed and what the doctors are doing, as well as speaking about his faith and how it has helped him at this juncture of his life. And that, Tellijohn said, is comforting to other cancer patients who are fearful of what lies ahead.

"So many have fought cancer," Tellijohn said, "and they are open to visiting with him because they know that what they went through he is going through. A lot of the time they think they are the only one going through it. He is open to sharing how it is affecting him. "

A struggle for the soul

Night is the hardest time for the priest. When he awakens in the early morning hours, long before the sun has risen, and tries to fall back to sleep, thoughts of his own future and his own fate begin to crowd in. It is then, he said, that his thoughts turn to the devil.

Recently, in preparation for Lent, Father Mountain has been re-reading The Screwtape Letters, an imaginary series of letters from a senior demon, known as Screwtape, to his subordinate, Wormwood. The fictional work, penned by scholar and Anglican apologist C.S. Lewis, talks about how the forces of evil work to win the souls of humanity.

"The battle for the soul. That's what Lent should be about - a struggle for the soul,"· Father Mountain said.

And it is a night when he feels those demons, led by the Prince of Darkness, fighting most for his soul.
"The devil works extra hard for you when you're dying," he said.

It is not the first time that the priest has faced death recently. In November, his brother, who was living in a nursing facility in Mankato, died unexpectedly.

"I talked to him Saturday evening," he said, "and the only thing he was mad at that day was that they didn't carry the Notre Dame-Air Force football game on TV."

The next morning, Father Mountain received a telephone call from the nursing home telling him that his brother, whom he loved and admired, had died during the night.

The two brothers had traveled together, played golf together, worked side-by-side and cheered in unison for their beloved Fighting Irish. And they were looking forward to a celebration in June. Had his brother lived, he would have celebrated a milestone in his career- 65 years as an ordained Catholic priest. At the same time, Father Mountain will celebrate his 60 anniversary in the priesthood.

After his brother's death, Father Mountain spoke to a family friend who told him that his brother would've wanted to die the way he did.

"The friend said that my brother always prayed every night that he would not die of cancer," Father Mountain, then smiled. "And I said, 'Well, why didn't he tell me that?"

Though still he has dark nights of the soul where that struggle becomes intense, his humor and his faith keep him strong.

"God is wise," he said. "We don't know when we're going to die." Then he paused. "I've had a great life," he said. "God has carried me through."

CHRIST THE KING CATECHETICAL SCHOOL, (1958-1983)

The families at Corpus Christi began pledging money for the construction of the Convent in 1957 which was noted in the report of giving.

In the1958 report shown below, there is a line item of a donation of $1,275.00 from Corpus Christi which was paid towards the construction of the building. Further down in the report (not shown), the Altar and Rosary Society paid $200.00 towards the Sisters of Notre Dame and paid $75.00 for the Dominican Sisters. In 1959 the Corpus Christi families donated $448.60 towards equipment for the convent. The Deerfield Altar and Rosary Society ladies paid $500 towards the sister's salaries. This was an exciting time for the church to have a place to house the sisters who were educating our children as well as a place to hold the religion classes.

Catechetical School under construction during 1958.
(Source: Christ The King History)

CORPUS CHRISTI CHURCH REPORT

1958

EXPENDITURES

Pastor's salary.....$	420.00
Extra clergy........	92.00
Custodian...........	260.00
Convent contribution	1,275.00
Transportation......	426.00
Housekeeper.........	181.00
Office..............	124.70
Fuel...............	140.00
Investments........	500.00
Catechetical expense	196.94
Church expenses.....	153.95
Sanctuary & sacristy	198.83
Household expense...	505.66
Insurance..........	98.50
Elec. Tel, water etc.	310.36
Diocesan expense....	717.45
Total expense $5,594.39	

Ida Arnold, Grandparents and Great Grandparents of the Arnold & Skalicky parishioners, donated the lot for the school which is located directly south of the Christ The King rectory at 212, 2nd Avenue N.W., Medford. Digging for the foundation began March 25, 1958. The building was erected by local contractor Theodore Thom.

On August 22, 1958, Father Harold Mountain brought Sisters M. Aquin Svoboda, M. Roberta Rother, and M. Willene Murphy to open the fourth catechetical school of the Mankato Province of the School Sisters of Notre Dame in Medford, Minnesota. The convent was a two and a half-story brick and wood structure which was comfortably arranged. The lower level served as the school and the upper levels as the convent. Everything was ready for the sisters.

Permission has been secured from the Medford High School Board to release all pupils for Religious instruction. Release-time religion classes began September 3, 1958, for the first six grades and September 9 for the junior and senior high school students.

Instruction for grades 1-4, was 4 times per week, grades 5 & 6 for 3 times per week, and the remainder of grades for 2 full hours per week. Father Mountain served the first Mass at the convent on August 22, 1958. The enrollment in 1958 was 170 students and reached 221 four years later. Since the public school was five blocks from the convent, the sisters accompanied the lower classes to and from the schools.

In the 1970s the school became the Regional Christian Education Center and the coordinators/coordinator taught and supervised teachers for the catechetical classes for three parishes: Christ the King at Medford, St. Ann in Janesville and St. Vincent de Paul in West Concord. The coordinators, who had their headquarters in Medford, had under their supervision at various times from 30 to 95 lay teachers.

When Sister Dolores Schmitz, coordinator at the Regional Center from 1971-1983, left to take up another assignment, the convent was closed.

Sister Dolores Schmitz, SSND

Sister Dolores Schmitz SSND

Sister Dolores served Christ the King and Corpus Christi parishes as Director of Religious Education from 1971 until 1982.

Sister Dolores was born August 7, 1923, near Raymond, Iowa, and baptized Dolores Frances three days later at Immaculate Conception Church, Gilbertville. She was the fifth of the family's thirteen children. She wrote of her family, "My parents, Leo and Martha Schmitz, were devout Catholics and gave to their children a deep love for the Church.

Their faith, which they shared, helped me throughout my life's journey. It was in my family life with Mother, Dad, my brothers and sisters, that I learned the meaning of love, respect, and affirmation. It was in my home also that the foundations were laid for a life of deep faith and prayer.

We were a close family, always ready to help each other." (The family was known as a "Deere" family because eight boys worked at the John Deere plant in Waterloo at some time in their life, while three bought only John Deere machinery for their farms.)

Sr. Dolores attended Immaculate Conception School in Gilbertville, Iowa where she graduated from eighth grade in 1937. That year, she enrolled at Good Counsel Academy in Mankato as a freshman. Following high school graduation in May 1941, Dolores entered the School Sisters of Notre Dame (SSND) candidature on August 28. 1945. She took college classes during her first year in the candidature and, as a second-year candidate, taught third grade at SS. Peter & Paul School, Mankato. She was received into the novitiate in July 1943, and given the name of one of her brothers, Sister Mary Kenneth. She later returned to her baptismal name.

She professed first vows in 1944, and began the first of three SSND ministries – teacher, mainly of junior high students. For the next nineteen years she taught in the following schools: St. Felix, Wabasha; St. Francis de Sales, St. Paul; Holy Rosary, North Mankato; Assumption, Cresco, Iowa; SS. Peter & Paul, Mankato; SS. Peter & Paul, Loretto; St. Mary, New England, North Dakota; Blessed Sacrament, Waterloo, Iowa; St. Gertrude, Raleigh, North Dakota; and St. Stanislaus, Winona. She earned a bachelor's degree from the College of St. Catherine in 1952.

Sister Dolores' second ministry, Director of Religious Education (DRE), began in 1965, when she helped staff the Fitzgerald Religious Education Center in La Crescent. She had prepared for this ministry by earning a Certificate in Theology from Mount Mary College, Milwaukee, in 1959 and a Confraternity of Christian Doctrine (CCD) certificate in 1965 from the College of St. Mary, Omaha. In 1966, Sister Dolores became the DRE at St. John Catechetical School, Minnesota Lake, where she stayed for four years. Her final DRE position was at Corpus Christi/Christ the King Catechetical Center, Medford (1971-1983).

In her time at Corpus Christi and Christ the King, she was appointed Director of Religious Education for Preschool through Senior Year of High School.

She worked with the parishes to establish lay people as religious education teachers. She is remembered for instituting the Annual Christmas Pageant with the children of the parish, preparing students for the Sacraments, and bringing the Good News of Jesus into every human. She also would take youth for visits to the Mother House in Mankato. Going out for dinner would also be part of the day, which all the students always looked forward to. She also facilitated retreats for youth and adults through her years.

St. Mary Parish, Waverly, Iowa, was the setting for Sister Dolores' third ministry: pastoral outreach with special attention to the elderly, homebound, infirm, those with special needs, and the dying. Beginning in 1983, she immersed herself into parish life. One of the pastors with whom she served wrote in 2002, "I want to congratulate Sister Dolores for almost one-third of her years of ministry, she has served St. Mary's Parish in a magnificent way. She has been in homes, hospitals and care centers, ministering to many people – Catholic and non-Catholic – in their times of need. She has also touched lives of our people with special needs and reaches out to many of our poor and elderly. She truly lives the vows of religious life."

Sister Dolores (Mary Kenneth) Schmitz, 92, died unexpectedly, yet peacefully at 8:55 a.m. on Saturday, February 27, 2016, in Notre Dame Healthcare, Mankato, Minnesota. She had participated in a retreat which concluded Thursday. On Friday, she excitedly told pastoral minister Sydelle McCabe, "I'm going home!" and on Saturday morning she fulfilled that statement.

Sources: Martha Pete's personal records. See more about Sister Dolores in the Memories Section. Obituary provided by Sister Mary Kay Ash.

Sister Luella

Sister Luella Zollar, the oldest of eight children, was born June 21, 1925, in Wilton, North Dakota. Her father, Louis, was from northern Minnesota and was a Soo Line depot agent. Her mother came with her family from Ukraine and settled in Wilton, North Dakota. She was received into the novitiate in 1945 and given the name Sister M. Luella. After she professed first vows in 1946, she was assigned to Wilno, Minnesota.

In 1947, she and three other sisters traveled by truck from Wilno to Eden, South Dakota, to reopen Sacred Heart School, which had been closed for 15 years. In 1960, Sister Luella and Sister Rose Franzwa began working first at Christ the King Catechetical School in Medford, Minnesota, where they stayed until 1966, and then at St. Theresa Catechetical School in Mapleton.

In 1969, Immaculate Conception Catholic School in Forsyth, Montana, closed and became a catechetical center. Sisters Luella and Esther Boor responded to the invitation to staff the center, sight unseen. In addition to conducting classes at Forsyth, they traveled to five other Montana communities, and met with students after the regular school day.

Sister Luella Zollar, SSND, 96, died January 10, 2022, in Notre Dame Health Care Center.

Sister Aquin

Sister Aquin (Elizabeth Svoboda) was born November 8, 1915, on the family farm northwest of Silver Lake. During the spring of her junior year she and six other aspirants asked to enter the SSND candidature the next fall. She and three others returned to Good Counsel that summer, finished their high school course work, and entered the candidature on August 27, 1933. She took college classes during her first year in the candidature and taught second grade at St. Matthew School, St. Paul, during her second year. She was received into the novitiate on July 16, 1935, and given the name Sister Mary Aquin. Following profession in 1936, she spent one year studying at the Dubuque Franciscan motherhouse and then began her teaching ministry.

In 1958, Sister Aquin was one of the first sisters in the Mankato Province to become involved full-time in Religious Education (CCD). She was one of three to open Christ the King Catechetical Center in Medford, and remained there until 1960. She had previously taught two-week summer catechetical school at Corpus Christi as early as 1953.

Sister M. Aquin Svoboda, 97, died peacefully October 3, 2013, in Notre Dame Health Care Center.

SCHOOL SISTERS OF NOTRE DAME ASSIGNED TO CORPUS CHRISTI & CHRIST THE KING			
All those listed below are deceased			
Sister Name	Start Date	End Date	Title
M. Roberta Rother	8/1/1958	8/1/1959	Teacher-Primary
M. Aquin Svoboda	8/1/1958	8/1/1960	Teacher, Religious Education
Grace Spiess	8/1/1959	8/31/1960	Teacher in Catechetics
Adelpha Sobek	9/1/1959	7/31/1961	Teacher in Catechetical School
M. Luella Zollar	8/1/1960	8/1/1966	DRE-Director of Religious Education
M. Rose Franzwa	8/1/1960	8/31/1966	Catechetical Teacher
Maria Gergen (Gonzales)	8/1/1961	8/31/1962	Catechetical Teacher
La Salle Hamm	8/1/1962	8/31/1967	Aide
Robertine Lamm	8/1/1966	1/31/1967	Catechetics Teacher
Susanna Kropf	8/1/1966	8/1/1967	Teacher Religious Instruction
Rita Studer	8/1/1969	8/1/1971	Teacher Religious Instruction
Dolores Schmitz	8/1/1971	8/1/1983	DRE-Director of Religious Education
Former SSND Sisters (May or may not be deceased)			
Eucharista Dalle	8/1/1970	8/1/1971	Help at Medford
Herbert Goerger	11/1/1969	8/1/1971	Religious Educator
Maurice Schimek	1/1/1967	8/1/1967	CCD & Music
Willene Murphy	8/1/1958	8/1/1959	Elementary School Teacher, Grades 1,4 & 5.

AMY HELLEVIK- PARISH DIRECTOR 1992-2012

Amy (Pete) Hellevik

I am the youngest of the 9 children of Joe and Martha Pete and a life-long Corpus Christi parishioner. When I was 11or 12, my parents bought an organ and because our church organist had retired, they put my sister, Janice, and me to work, taking lessons and preparing to accompany Sunday services. My sister started out and played for about 3-years, and then went to college. I inherited the job. During the early years I was accompanied by Jonas Mork. We were up in the choir loft. When Jonas left the area, I continued to play nearly every Sunday morning for the next 35 years at Corpus Christi and 20 years for Christ the King.

In June of 1992, after graduating from Minnesota State, Mankato, I was preparing myself for a career. Being married with a 1-year-old and another on the way, my husband Brian and I decided that I would try for a part-time position while our children were small. At this time, there was a position posted for Religious Education Director for Christ the King and Corpus Christi. I applied, was interviewed, and received the job which I held for the next 10 years.

I brought back the Christmas program in both churches. In addition to weekly classes (Preschool to grade 10) for students from October through April, some of the other Religious Education program highlights

that took place when I was in charge were student retreats, youth choir, creating learning centers for all grades, teacher retreats, attending Diocesan youth events, and fun trips for the servers and youth choir. We prepared students for the Sacraments of 1st Communion, Penance and Confirmation. This was followed by the 1st Communion children leading us at May Crowning on Mother's Day.

In the spring of 2002, I was approached by Fr. Robert Herman, informing me that he was looking to retire in the summer. There was an opportunity for him to stay on for Sacramental needs while hiring a lay person for all other administrative responsibilities for both parishes. I had graduated with a business degree from Mankato State University, and I had the qualifications needed to Be "Parish Director." I met with Bishop Bernard Harrington and Fr. Robert Herman and was offered the position and accepted. I was up for this new opportunity and challenge which I held for the next 10 years.

During my time as Parish Director, a Financial Council was started to join the Pastoral Council in the leadership of the parishes. Under their guidance and advice, I managed the physical, financial, sacramental preparation, and support needs in the parishes while Fr. Herman was able to focus on sacramental and liturgy celebrations. While in this position, I was very focused and dedicated on being transparent and fiscally responsible with a balanced budget in all the directives in the parishes. With the help of skilled and experienced parishioners from both parishes, we merged together and completed many parish and building projects at Christ the King and Corpus Christi. The largest was the addition (which included restrooms and elevator) at Christ the King, being fully paid for before completion. The members of both parishes truly took ownership and responsibility in the planning and building phases of this project. This was the largest of many physical projects that took place in my tenure. We also had many celebrations and guest performers during this time. In the spring of 2012, I resigned from the position of Parish Director, but still remained an active member of Corpus Christi Parish, continuing to play piano for Sunday morning Mass.

In summing up my 20 years, I wish to express my appreciation and joy for the opportunity to work for Corpus Christi and Christ the King for 20 years. The connections I have made, and friendships that I still maintain are invaluable and I am most grateful.

**Amy's leadership allowed us to grow stronger over her years of service. She did a wonderful job pulling our parishes together and leading us forward. Under her leadership we were able to grow our treasuries so that we have the reserves to remain viable even now as an Oratory. Thank you, Amy!!!

Corpus Christi Church
(Photo compliments of Judy {Spinler} Brady).

CHAPTER VI

CORPUS CHRISTI PARISH ACTIVITIES

USO
Nation Defenders drive.
1943

1.00	John Morgan	Morriston Min
1.00	Sam Jones	"
1.00	Agnes Fitzpatrick	" "
.50	Maylen Hanson	Medford Min
1.00	Peter Pirkl	" "
1.00	Louis Pirkl	" "
1.00	Elmer Minske	Waseca Min
1.00	Mrs Peter Stirens Sr	" "
1.00	Peter Stirens	" "
2.00	Streling Deming	" "
.50	Walter Schmistke	Morriston Min
.50	Ed Whitich	" "
1.00	Jess Saufferer	" "
.25	Walter Villwock	" "
1.00	Wyatt Deming	" "
1.00	Henry Eisert	" "
	Chas Pirkl	
	Ernest Rosendall	
	Pat Condon	
	Chas Wendt	
	Harold Karsten	
	A Sharp	
	Eric Hein said he gave some	
	Cliffer Thompson 3 Grant Thompson	

During World War II a collection was taken to support the United Service Organization (USO). The above list shows that both Corpus Christi parishioners and non-parishioners contributed to support our troops.

Corpus Christi Sanctuary (Before Vatican II --- 1940s; Priest not identified)

Procession and outdoor evening Mass in the Corpus Christi Cemetery.
(The church bulletin for May 27, 1945 on the facing page describes a Corpus Christi evening procession)
The same bulletin reminds us that America was still at War in Europe and Japan. Parishioners were encouraged to purchase War Bonds to fund the war effort as well as to build the new church at Medford. The names of parishioners purchasing War Bonds would be published in the next church bulletin.

Corpus Christi Procession Group (1940s)
This appears to be the order of procession described on the next page; Cross Bearer, Altar Boys, boys and girls, Priests, etc. William Sammon (front row, with bow tie second from left); Joseph Sammon (front row, far right). Hilary Sammon is the blonde-haired boy in the back row on the left side looking directly the camera. The feast of Corpus Christi is liturgically celebrated on the Thursday after Trinity Sunday and this celebration may have coincided with those events.

BUY A WAR BOND

FOR YOUR NEW CHURCH

May 27, 1945

Trinity Sunday

IS YOUR NAME ON THE 1945 THERMOMETER?

Your V-E Bond will help win the war!
Your V-E Bond will help build your Church!

Corpus Christi   Christ the King

Deerfield   Medford

NEXT SUNDAY THE THERMOMETER WITH THE NAMES OF THE BOND GIVERS
WILL BE IN THE BULLETIN. WILL YOUR NAME BE ON IT??????

* *

Trinity Sunday

The Mystery of the Trinity is the principal and fundamental doctrine
of Christianity; to reject it would be to deny the Christian Faith. In the Name of
the Blessed Trinity the Church administers all the Sacraments; in the Name of the
Blessed Trinity she consecrates and blesses persons, places, and things; in the Name
of the Blessed Trinity she begins and ends all her prayers. In the Name of the
Blessed Trinity we were received into the Church by Baptism. When our last hour
draws near, the priest accompanies our departing soul with the words, "Depart, O
Christian soul. . . . in the Name of the Father, and of the Son, and of the Holy Ghost.

As often as we make the Sign of the Cross we profess our faith in
this most fundamental Mystery--make it often--make it well.

*** *** *** *** *** *** *** *** *** *** *** *** *** *** *

MASSES NEXT SUNDAY, June 3, 1945

Corpus Christi

Thirteen Hours Devotion
Mass........................8:30 a.m.
Confessions......Sat. 5:00-6:00 p.m.
.....Sun. 7:30-8:15 a.m.

Christ the King

Mass....................10:00 a.m.
Confessions............. 9:45 a.m.
Saturday Mass......... 8:30 a.m.

Hours of devotion are posted in the Vesti-
bule.   Sermon and
CORPUS CHRISTI PROCESSION.....7:30 p.m.   The ORDER OF THE PROCESSION is as
follows:

Cross Bearer, Alter Boys, Boys and Girls, Priests, Flower Girls, Censor
Bearer, Priest with the Holy Eucharist, Members of the Circles with their
husbands, and all others.

The Deerfield Ladies will serve lunch afterward in the Corpus Christi Church
Parlors.

Let us all show our love to Christ by bringing a friend with us.

- -

CONGRADULATIONS to the following boys and girls of Deerfield who made their First
Holy Communion last week:

Paul Gillis   Lawrence Sammon
Gerald Kerrans   Roger Sammon
Marlys Kerrans   Patrick Vogele
Eileen Sammon   Donald Hager
Mass EVERY Sunday!   Holy Communion every two weeks!
* *

BANNS OF MARRIAGE: For the third time between Myron Turner and Mary Ann Vandeputte,
both of Christ the King Parish.
For the second time between Orville Young and Marguerite Majusiak,
both of Christ the King Parish.

- -

Corpus Christi/Christ The King Parish Bulletin (May 27, 1945)

163

CORPUS CHRISTI ALTAR & ROSARY SOCIETY ACTIVITIES (1961/62)

1962   CORPUS CHRISTI ALTAR AND ROSARY SOCIETY   1962

PRESIDENT....MRS. HENRY HAGER.   SEC. & TREAS...MRS. JOSEPH LANG

ST. ANNE'S GUILD

Mrs. Byron Brady
Mrs. James F. Brady
Mrs. James M. Brady
Mrs. John Bruender
Mrs. Corliss Cole
Mrs. J. Dulas
Mrs. Lewis Condon..Ass't Chairlady.
Mrs. Donald Eustice
Mrs. Geneivieve Francl
Mrs. Marvin Kavitz
Mrs. Anthony Kniefel
Mrs. Lawrence Kvasnicka
Mrs. Joseph Lang
Mrs. Adolph Larson
Mrs. George Larson
Mrs. Lawrence Meisinger
Mrs. Bert Mohs
Mrs. Leo Mullenmaster
Miss. AnnMarie Mullenmaster
Mrs. Eugene Phillips
Mrs. Eldred Phillips
Mrs. Joseph Pete
Mrs. Edwin Tuve
Mrs. Frank Reyant
Mrs. Peter Reyant Chairlady.
Mrs. Arthur Voegele
Miss. Margaret Voegele
Mrs. Wally Voegele
Mrs. Joseph Weber
Miss. Marjorie Weber
Mrs. Clifford Fisher

ST. MARY'S GUILD

Mrs. Phillip Condon
Mrs. Kenneth Dahle
Mrs. Charles Dickison
Miss. Lois Dickison
Miss. Mary Lou. Dickison
Mrs. Henry Hager
Mrs. Neil Hager
Mrs. Raymond Hager
Mrs. Bernard Heim
Mrs. Bernard Holmquist
Mrs. Ernest Holmquist.Chairlady
Mrs. Paul Hurt
Mrs. William Klukas
Mrs. Bernard Ness
Miss. Marjorie Ness
Mrs. George Miller
Mrs. Roland Miller
Mrs. Donald Morgan
Mrs. John Morgan
Mrs. Kenneth Mork
Mrs. John Pelant Ass't Chairla
Mrs. Bernard Pfrerer
Mrs. Charles Pirkl
Mrs. Harlow Pirkl
Mrs. Justine Pirkl
Mrs. Louis Pirkl
Mrs. Leo Sammon
Mrs. Anton Schmanski
Miss. Geneivieve Hurt
Miss. Agnes Hurt
Miss. Joan Hurt
Miss. Pauline Hurt

COMMITTEE CHAIRLADIES

Catholic Relief Services...........Mrs. Frank Reyant
Bishop's Committee.................Mrs. George Larson
Apostolate to the Aged............Mrs. Bernard Ness
N.O.D.L...........................Mrs. Harlow Pirkl
Parish reporter...................Mrs. Kenneth Mork
Libraries and Literature..........Mrs. Geneivieve Francl.
Rural Life........................Mrs. Bert Mohs
Vocations.........................Mrs. Leo Sammon
Discussion Clubs..................Mrs. Eldred Phillips.

1961...FINANCIAL REPORT FOR THE ALTAR AND ROSARY SOCIETY

Bal..Jan. 1st 1961......$ 148.51	Sister's salaries.....$ 513.00
Bingo profit.............. 478.15	W.C.C.W. dues......... 12.00
Food sales at Auction... 109.41	Shoe Fund............. 12.00
E.C.C.W Dues collected.. 12.25	W.C.C.W Convention.... 11.00
Shoe Fund collection.... 12.00	Misc. expenses........ 51.56
Lunch money.............. 9.96	TOTAL EXPENSES.... $599.56
TOTAL RECEIPTS....$780.25	Respectfully submitted:
TOTAL EXPENSES.... 599.56	Mrs. Corliss Cole...President.
Bal. Dec.4th'61...$180.72****	Mrs. Geneivieve Francl..Se.Tre

PRESIDENT....Mrs. James M. Brady   SEC. & TREAS...Mrs. Donald Morgan

ST. ANNE'S GUILD   *1963*   ST. MARY'S GUILD

Mrs. Byron Brady	Mrs. Wayne Barbknecht
Mrs. James F. Brady	Mrs. Phillip Condon
Mrs. James M. Brady	Mrs. Kenneth Dahle
Miss Sharon Brady	Mrs. Henry Hager
Mrs. John Bruender	Mrs. Donald Hager
Mrs. Corliss Cole	Mrs. Neil Hager..Ass't ChairLady.
Mrs. Sylvester Dulas	Mrs. Raymond Hager
Mrs. Louis Condon	Mrs. Bernard Heim
Mrs. Donald Eustice	Mrs. Bernard Holmquist
Mrs. Charles Filan	Mrs. Ernest Holmquist
Mrs. Aharon Fisher	Mrs. Paul Hurt
Mrs. Marvin Kavitz	Mrs. William Klukas
Mrs. Anthony Kniefel	Mrs. Bernard Ness...Chair Lady.
Mrs. Lawrence Kvasnicka	Miss. Marjorie Ness
Mrs. Joseph Lang	Mrs. George Miller
Mrs. Adolph Larson	Mrs. Roland Miller
Mrs. George Larson	Mrs. Donald Morgan
Mrs. Robert Larson	Mrs. John Morgan
Mrs. Lawrence Meisinger	Mrs. Kenneth Mork
Mrs. Bert Mohs	Mrs. John Belant
Mrs. Leo Mullenmaster	Mrs. Bernard Pfiefer
Miss. AnnM. Mullenmaster	Mrs. Charles Pirkl
Miss. Mary Mullenmaster	Miss. Rosemarie Pirkl
Mrs. Eldred Phillips..ChairLady.	Mrs. Justine Pirkl
Mrs. Eugene Phillips	Mrs. Louis Pirkl
Mrs. Joseph Pete	Mrs. Harlow Pirkl
Mrs. Edwin Tuve	Mrs. Leo Sammon
Mrs. Mrs. Peter Reyant	Mrs. Anton Schmanski
Mrs. Arthur Voegele	
Mrs. Walter Voegele Ass't Ch.L.	
Miss. Margaret Voegele	
Mrs. Joseph Weber	
Mrs. Clifford Fisher	

COMMITTEE CHAIRLADIES

Parish Reporter..........Mrs. Bert Mohs.
Bishop's Committee.......Mrs. Bernard Heim.
NODL....................Mrs. Rolland Miller
Libraries and Literature.Mrs. Eugene Phillips.
Discussion Clubs........Mrs. Eldred Phillips.
Rural Life..............Mrs. Anthony Kniefel.
Vocations...............Mrs. William Klukas
Apostolate to the Aged...Mrs. Joseph Lang
Catholic Relief Services.Mrs. Henry Hager.

1962......FINANCIAL REPORT FOR THE ALTAR AND ROSARY SOCIETY

RECEIPTS		EXPENSES	
March parish party profit......$490.00		Sister's Salaries..$570.00	
Dec. party and raffle " 335.13		W.C.C.W. Dues...... 9.50	
Religious goods profit 25.27		Shoe Fund.......... 8.10	
K. of C. breakfast " 26.00		Misc. 61.77	
Interest 12.00		TOTAL..... 649.37**	
W.C.C.W. Dues................. 9.50			
Shoe Fund..................... 8.10		Respectfully submitted:	
Lunches at meetings.......... 7.25		Mrs. Henry Hager..President.	
TOTAL.....$ 913.25		Mrs. Joseph Lang..Treasurer.	

Bal. Jan. 1st 1962............. 128.92
    GRAND TOTAL.....$1,042.17
        Expenses........$ 649.37
Bal. Dec. 8th, 1962..........$ 392.80

COUNCIL OF CATHOLIC WOMEN (CCW)

With the organization of the Council of Catholic Women within the Winona Diocese in 1941, one of the first information/organization meeting was held in the area at Sacred Heart Church in Waseca, Ellen Holmquist of Corpus Christi Parish was noted as being present in a news clipping.

In 1945 under the direction of Fr. Harold Mountain, and along with a big push from the diocese of Winona the Council of Catholic Women (CCW) was formed. It was the life blood of the church and was used for outreach to carry on the mission of the church to help the less fortunate. The CCW replaced the Altar and Rosary Society formally. Fr Mountain assigned the ladies to office at the beginning of each calendar year. Fr. Mountain also audited the books before assigning the new officers the next year. He presented gifts to the officers on completion of their terms. Meetings were held quarterly at the church, with Fr. Mountain attending all meetings and opening with the prayer of "Our Lady of Good Counsel." It was common for a speaker to come in and talk about activities or concerns that may have needed addressing.

Corpus Christi was part of the Waseca Deanery which included Janesville, Waldorf, New Richland, Waseca, Medford, Owatonna, Litomysl and Deerfield. Deanery Meetings were held with other area churches in the deanery quarterly beginning with a Mass.

PRAYER TO OUR LADY OF GOOD COUNSEL

0 Lord of heavenly wisdom+ who has given us your own Mary Mother to be our guide and counselor in this life+ grant that in all things we may have the grace to seek her maternal instruction and to profit by it in humility and love.

0 Mother of Good Counsel + Patroness of the National Counsel of Catholic Women + help us to understand and fulfill the mind and will of your Divine Son+ Jesus Christ. Under the blessing of the Father+ and by the power of the Holy Spirit + may we be responsible and intelligent daughters of the Church + May we labor in the spirit of renewal to realize more perfectly the Kingdom of God here below as the only true preparation for our share in the Kingdom of Heaven.+ And may we+ in all we think or do or say+ be filled with the same love of God and neighbor that overflows from your own Immaculate Heart.

Corpus Christi hosts Deanery Meeting July 26th, 1967. Served 150-170. Dessert was Angel food cake frosted with Jello & strawberries, mints & nuts-coffee. Used 10 angel food cakes, 2 bags of mints 1 small can mixed nuts & poly bag of salted peanuts. (should have had more nuts), 1 pt half & half (should have had 2). Used nearly 3-2# cans of coffee. Coffee depends on how you make it. Kitchen crew: Rita Kuntz, Dorothy Voegele, Joan Pirkl, Helen Karsten, Mrs. Adolph Larson, Ernie Holmquist & Henry Hager served coffee and helped clean up. Also helping with clean up and dishes 7 serving: Dolly Kniefel, Mrs. Art (Mary) Voegele, Mary Fredericks and Donna Mork. Mrs. Reyant took care of the nice flower arrangements. The basement was packed, and we were short of chairs. (excerpt from CCW minutes)

Corpus Christi women were divided into two guilds (St. Mary's and St. Anne's) with a chairperson named for each guild. The guilds were called upon at different times for cleaning church, funeral assignments, bingo parties, bridal showers, sacramental luncheons, lawn raking and the like. It took the whole church being involved to make it successful. As a member, you accepted the fact that you were a vital part, you would be involved and do your part. That was true until the day our church doors were closed. Because of this, we were a family with a strong sense of duty, and we took pride in the fact that we worked together and made things happen.

In December of 1966, Father Mountain asked that all officers keep their offices until June in keeping with the bishops request that the new officers attend the convention in the fall after they take office. This started the practice of holding office from July 1 through June 30 the following year. After this, that was how the officer terms ran.

June 2, 1967, the last meeting of the year, new officers were announced by Father Harold Mountain. Father Cody of Ellendale was our guest speaker, his topic was his work with the Mexican migrants, and he showed us some interesting slides. Lunch committee Mrs. Byron Brady, Mrs. James M Brady, Mrs. James F Brady, Mrs. Leroy Hoffman and Miss Edith Brady.

Sunday August 4, 1968 was our farewell party to Fr. Harold Mountain in the church parlors from 7:00-9:00 pm. Party was held jointly Christ the King and Corpus Christi with CC paying 1/3 of the expenses.

Creta Mullenmaster, Jane Brady, Edith Hoffman, & Marian Cole.

Everything went very smoothly. It was a very hot humid evening. About half of the people didn't stay to eat after talking with Father because of the heat. We served only 500. Menu: cake, nuts, mints and coffee. Fifteen sheet cakes were ordered from the Faribo Bake Shop, only 5 used, 10 cans nuts- 2 used, 6 bags of mints-4 used, 5lbs of coffee-3 used 1500 paper plates- 500 used, 500 paper cups-100 used. Decorations were a green shamrock on the white tablecloths and a small vase of flowers on each table. The cake was white with a green leaf on each piece.

Wednesday, August 7th 1968, was the installation of Father Francis Glenn held at Christ the King Church with Monsignor Henry Speck installing Father. Reception was held jointly in the basement parlors. The left-over cake from Father Mountain's farewell was used at this event with coffee, nuts and mints. We served an estimated 200 people using 3 sheet cakes. The weather was very hot and humid. We sold some of the cake that was still left over.

December 5, 1976 a confirmation reception for Bishop Waters, parishioners and confirmation students was held in the church basement of Corpus Christi after the Confirmation Mass on Sunday afternoon. Ladies of the parish were asked to bring finger foods- cookies, bars etc., while coffee and orange drink were served as beverages. Flowers provided by Agnes Reyant and table centerpieces by Luella Heim.

Church cleaning October 19, 1978 in preparation for confirmation, the boys and girls jointly with St. Anne's circle washed and waxed the church floors upstairs with "Future," a heavy wax and used "Mop and Glo," down in basement. The confirmation boys cleaned brush behind the church. The confirmation girls scraped paint off windows and cleaned all the cupboards in the basement kitchen. The ladies who helped: Lucille Weber, Mary Voegele, Dorothy Voegele, Mary Phillips, Evelyn Brady and Martha Pete. The boys and girls who were there: Carmen Kuntz, Missy Fredericks, Dan Morgan, John Kniefel, Brian Condon, Penny Frederick, Dan Hurst, Kimberly Peterson, Jeff VonRuden, Trent Sehnert and Janice Pete.

Confirmation was held on November 19, 1978 at a 3:00pm mass with Bishop Watters, and Fr. Cody presiding. Reception followed in the church basement."

Area deanery meeting hosted by Christ the King on Jan 31, 1979. Corpus Christi had the largest attendance after Christ the King. They will have the Mass said for us for having the largest attendance. Those present: Marjorie Ness, Ann Ness, Marguerite Larson, Luella Heim, Martha Pete, Mary Phillips, Diane Sammon, Dorothy Morgan, Evelyn Brady and Anna Hager. Mass started at 1:00pm with Father Cody as celebrant. International Affairs report was by Luella Heim. The year 1979 was the *"Year of the Child,"* and 1980 was the *"Year of the Family."*

Presidents of our CCW Organization- that provided the leadership for our organization through the years.

PRIOR TO 1960:
Jane Brady
Margaret Lang
Bertha Mohs
Lucille Pirkl
Margaret Miller
Mary Voegele
Ellen Holmquist
1960 -Donna Mork
1961 -Marian Cole
1962 -Anna Hager
1963 -Evelyn Brady
1964 -Dorothy Morgan
1965 -Dolly Kneifel
1966 -Mary Frederick
1967 -Jean Larson
1968 -Joan Pirkl
1969 -Dorothy Voegele
1970 -Ethel Condon
1971 -Marie Tuve
1972 -Lois Nelson
1973 -Jacqueline Dulas
1974 -Kay Von Ruden
1975 -Rita Kuntz
1976 -Mary Phillips
1977 -Diane Sammon
1978 -Martha Pete
1979 -Evelyn Brady
1980 -Susie Redman
1981 -Carla Brady
1982 -Lois Nelson
1983 -Mary Frederick
1984 -Deb Morgan
1985 -Terri Brady
1986 -Connie Brady
1987 -Jean Larson
1988 -Donna Hager
1989 -Judy Brady
1990 -Carla Brady
1991 -Dorothy Morgan
1992 -Cathy Hackett
1993 -Linda O'Connor
1994 -Joan Kuhlman
1995 -Luella Heim
1996 -Jacqueline Dulas
1997-Amy Hellevik
1998-Diane Sammon
1999-Amy Hellevik
2000-Judy Brady
2001-2016 Carla Brady
* Jean Larson; Sec/Treas. 2006-2016

After Sister Delores left for another assignment, the lay people had to step up to run the religious education program. Due to the changes that took place, the Christmas pageant went by the wayside.

During Amy Hellevik's tenure as Religious Education Coordinator, one of the highlights in both parishes was bringing back the Annual Nativity Pageant (once done under Sister Delores) with getting as many children as possible involved.

The church sewing ladies from both parishes made enough costumes for all the children, with plenty extra animal costumes for the little ones. Every year, the traditional nativity story would be acted out for the parishioners and visitors. Both churches, Christ the King and Corpus Christi were always packed.

We found a live baby in one of our parish families to take the role of Jesus. They were gifted a Christmas ornament as a keepsake for preforming the role of baby Jesus.

In addition to Mary & Joseph, many angels, kings, shepherds, animals and the drummer boys were required to complete the Christmas scene.

We always practiced the Saturday before the presentation with the pageant being held at the beginning of the Mass. The children were expected to memorize their lines. We always had plenty of help from the parents, and the children took their parts very seriously. We incorporated as many animals as possible in the manger scene so the smaller children could be included. The children looked forward to this tradition.

It was during the offertory of the same Sunday that the children were asked to come forward to decorate the Christmas tree with homemade ornaments that were made in their religion classes. We always made sure that extra ornaments were available for all the children. Then after Mass, we held a finger food brunch in the church basement.

We had a wonderful assortment of hand-held treats. Santa would appear with gift bags for each of the children, and the extra bags were given to some of the older members of the church. The bags were provided by the CCW ladies, and included peanuts, candy and a religious Christmas ornament.

Donald Morgan would give out apples to everyone present. This day always kicked off the Christmas spirit in our church. As some of our youth grew up and moved away and started having children of their own, they too, were allowed and encouraged to participate in the Corpus Christi Christmas pageant.

On the next page, lower left, Fr. Robert Herman is singing a duet with Brian Hellevik as part of the Corpus Christi traditional Christmas celebration. Photo c2007).

168

AFTER MASS PRE-SCHOOL

WORLD DAY OF PRAYER

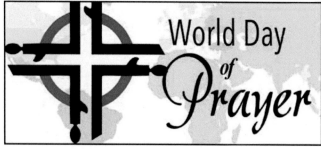

The year 1991, was the first year that neighboring churches began praying for world peace. We clustered with the Blooming Grove Methodist Church in Deerfield and the Peace Methodist Church from Morristown which became known as the "World Day of Prayer." Printed materials were provided for the event. The 3 churches would send representatives to a planning meeting prior to the event to decide on how the material for the service would be divided. We took turns hosting the service. The host church would provide a speaker as well as refreshments after the service. 1993 was the first year that Corpus Christi hosted the event. This continued until 2003 when it was decided that attendance was wanning and so the effort was abandoned. We worked well with our neighboring church communities as we knew many of the families through other social gatherings.

INTERNATIONAL DINNERS
WITH FATHER ROBERT HERMAN

During his pastorate, Father Robert Herman held many international dinners over the years with ethnic themes including Polish, Italian, Greek, Czech, German, French and Viennese Empire. Music to correspond with the these themes was played during the meal. The meals were prepared by members from both parishes, with the idea that it was not going to be a big money maker, but rather a great social event. Seating was limited to a crowd that could fit in the church basement comfortably. Libations were served and the events were always festive.

The final International Dinner, held in November 2011, was prepared by the Men's Choir. This dinner was a combination of several cultures, and the meal showcased Fr. Robert Herman's mother's Bohemian Rye bread prepared by Martha Arnold, French Onion soup prepared by Gary Wiersma, Loin of Pork (*Schab Pieczony*) with applesauce, minted peas, mashed potatoes/gravy, and for dessert Black Forest Cake with brandied cherries and whipped cream frosting (made by Carla Brady with Jean Gillis assisting with assembling the cakes)

Bishop Quinn joined for liturgies that weekend, then joining us for dinner in the church parlor afterwards. We were able to acquire dinnerware from Jerry's restaurant in Owatonna (provided by Greg Wencl) which dressed up the tables to mirror a fine dining experience. Entertainment was provided by the Men's Choir and the choir members prepared and plated the meal. The Confirmation students were the waiters and waitresses for the evening.

The Bishop was very complimentary on the parish community working together to make this event enjoyable and successful. The church basement was full and a great time was enjoyed by all.

Amy Hellevik with the 2005 Corpus Christi Choir

Quality music has been a long-standing tradition at Corpus Christi. Early music was provided by Rosmund O'Brien, Merle Gostomczik, Loretta Holmquist followed by Mary Phillips with youth as well as adult choirs participating. When Mary Phillips retired from the organist's position in the early 1980s, Joe Pete decided that his girls would take organ lessons and carry on the music at the church. Jancie Pete Mertz was going to play the organ in the choir loft on her first Sunday and she froze, unable to perform, her younger sister Amy Pete (Hellevik) stepped in. Amy had memorized one song "Sing Praises to the living God." That Sunday, we heard the song during 3 different sections of the mass. This began Amy's long career in the music ministry for Corpus Christi. Janice continued to play until she graduated from high school.

In her high school days, Amy Pete, later Hellevik, was assisted by Jonas Mork on the guitar, working well together. Choir practice was held on Saturdays at 1:00 pm. Carla Brady would pick the kids up in her blue 4-door Ford Maverick, bringing them to practice.

It was during this time that the choir also did outreach. We would pile in the car (no seatbelts), several layers deep, arriving at the homes of some of our older parishioners, ready to sing Christmas carols. We were rewarded with treats for our efforts.

The music was inclusive, providing songs that the congregation could sing along with. The choir moved from the loft to the left front of the church where the electric piano was placed, removing the organ from the loft.

The music program grew over the years. Bells were added at Christmas time, to make the Mass special along with violins played by Justin Hellevik and Alvin Miller. Jenelle Hinchley was so very kind to direct the Christmas bell choir. Trumpets were added for the Easter Mass. Amy continued to play for our church until 2015. Brenda Manderfeld and Deb Sontheimer were gracious in helping us with the music at Mass for the final year until our closing in 2016. Now, when we have our special Oratory Masses, Amy comes back to play, we get some of the old choir members to sing, and the music fills the church once again.

1978 CORPUS CHRISTI PARISH MEMBERSHIP

BRADY, Mrs. Amelia
(Deceased)
BRADY, Byron & Jane
Route # 1, Medford
BRADY, Byron P. & Carla
Route # 1, Medford
BRADY, James & Evelyn
Route # 1, Medford
BRADY, Patrick
Route # 1, Medford
CONDON, Donald & Caroline
Route # 1, Box 187A, Medford
CONDON, Sylvester & Ethel
Route # 1, Morristown
DULAS, Sylvester & Jacqueline
Route # 2, Medford
EUSTICE, Donald & Alice
Route # 3, Waseca
FREDERICK, Clare Jr.
Route # 1, Morristown
FREDERICK, James & Mary
Route # 3, Faribault
GOETTL, James
Morristown
HAGER, David
Route #3, Waseca
HAGER, Henry (Dec.) & Ann
Route # 3, Waseca
HAGER, Neil & Donna
Route # 1, Medford
HEIM, Bernard & Luella
Route # 1, Morristown
HOLMQUIST, Ernest & Ellen
Route # 4, Waseca
HURT, James
Route #3, Waseca
HURST, Jerry & Nancy
Route #3, Waseca

JEWISON, Terrance & Carol
Route #3, Waseca
JEWISON, Timothy & Holly
Route # 4, Waseca
KARSTEN, Willard & Helen
Route #3, Waseca
KNIEFEL, Anthony & Dolly
Route #5, Owatonna
KUNTZ, Ernest & Rita
Route #1, Owatonna
LANG, Joseph & Margaret
Route # 1, Medford
LARSON, Adolph & Marguerite
Route # 1, Owatonna
LARSON, George & Jean
Route #5, Owatonna
LARSON, Robert & Joyce
Route # 1, Owatonna
MLENEK, Lyle
Route #4, Waseca
MILLER, Roland & Lillian
Route #1, Morristown
MILLER, Ronald
Morristown
MORGAN, Dennis & Debra
Route #1, Morristown
MORGAN, Donald & Dorothy
Route #1, Morristown
MORGAN, John E. & Charlotte
Route #1, Morristown
MORK, Ken & Donna
Route # 3, Waseca
NELSON, Lois (HEIM) & David
408 3rd St. NE., Medford
NESS, Ann & Marjorie
Route # 1, Morristown
PETE, Joseph & Martha
Route # 2, Medford

PETERSON, DueLloyd & Betty
Route # 3, Waseca
PFIEFER, Bernard & Hazel (Deceased)
Route # 1, Morristown
PHILLIPS, Eldred & Mary
Route # 3, Waseca
PIRKL, Mrs. Lucille
Route # 1, Medford
REDMAN, Donald & Susan
Route # 1, Morristown
REYANT, Peter (Dec.) & Agnes
617 S Walnut Owatonna
SAMMON, Aldon & Diane
Route # 1, Morristown
SAMMON, Leo (Dec.) & Margaret
Route # 1, Morristown
SEHNERT, Marge
Route # 1, Owatonna
SUTLIEF, David & Sandra
Morristown
THOM, Michael & Sandra
Route # 3, Faribault
VON RUDEN, Eugene & Katherine
Route # 1, Morristown
VOEGELE, Arthur & Mary
Route # 3, Faribault
VOEGELE, Robert
Route # 3, Faribault
VOEGEL, Walter & Dorothy
Route # 1, Medford
WEBER, Joseph & Lucille
Route # 1, Medford
WIECZOREAK,
George & Sharon
Route # 3, Waseca

CORPUS CHRISTI PARISHIONERS (1978)

Mrs. Amelia Brady

Byron Brady Family

Byron & Carla Brady

James Brady Family

Patrick Brady

Donald Condon Family

CORPUS CHRISTI PARISHIONERS (1978)

Sylvester Condon Family

Sylvester & Jackie Dulas Family

Donald & Alice Mae Eustice

James Frederick Family

James Goetl & Amy

David Hager

CORPUS CHRISTI PARISHIONERS (1978)

Mr. & Mrs. Henry Hager

Neil Hager Family

Bernard Heim Family

Mr. & Mrs. Ernest Holmquist & Terry Jewison

James Hurt Family

Jerry Hurst Family

Mr. & Mrs. Tim Jewison

Willard Karsten Family

Anthony Kniefel Family

Ernest Kuntz Family

Joe & Margaret Lang Family

Mr. & Mrs. Adolph Larson

CORPUS CHRISTI PARISHIONERS (1978)

George Larson Family

Robert Larson Family

Lyle Mlenek Family

Roland Miller Family

Ronald Miller Family

Mr. & Mrs. Dennis Morgan

CORPUS CHRISTI PARISHIONERS (1978)

Donald Morgan Family

John E. Morgan Family

Kenneth & Donna Mork Family

David & Lois Nelson

Ann & Marjorie Ness

Joseph Pete Family

CORPUS CHRISTI PARISHIONERS (1978)

DueLloyd Peterson Family

Mr. & Mrs. Bernard Pfeiffer

Eldred & Mary Philips Family

Mrs. Louis Pirkl

Donald & Susan Redman Family

Mr. & Mrs. Peter Reyant

CORPUS CHRISTI PARISHIONERS (1978)

Aldon Sammon Family

Leo Sammon Family

Marge Sehnert Family

David Sutlief Family

Michael Thom Family

Gene Von Ruden Family

CORPUS CHRISTI PARISHIONERS (1978)

Mr. & Mrs. Arthur Voegele

Robert Voegele Family

Walter Voegele Family

Mr. & Mrs. Joseph Weber

Geoege Wieczoreak Family

CORPUS CHRISTI (1978)

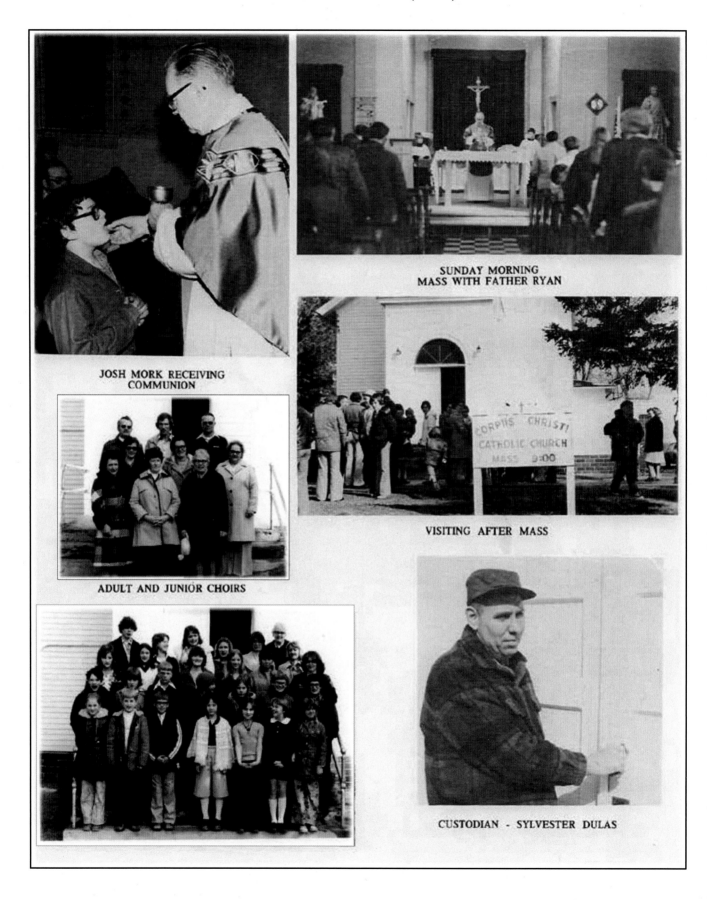

JOSH MORK RECEIVING COMMUNION

SUNDAY MORNING MASS WITH FATHER RYAN

VISITING AFTER MASS

ADULT AND JUNIOR CHOIRS

CUSTODIAN - SYLVESTER DULAS

Mrs. Peter (Agnes) Reyant

NOTICE.— 1711

NOTICE. Floyd O'Connor who lives next to Byron Brady has a very sick baby (Kathleen) at Saint Mary's Hospital in Rochester. The Drs. have asked him and his wife to remain close to her. WILL A GROUP OF THE MEN IN TH PARISH HELP HARVEST HIS CROP. COME MEN LET US GET TOGETHER AND DO IT FOR A FRIEND.
****
May God Bless you.

Corpus Christi Church Bulletin (August 10, 1947).

Sharon Brady at May Crowning (May 1953).

Statues of the Blessed Virgin Mary and St. Joseph in the front of Corpus Christi Church.
In 1999, Evely Brady was commissioned by the CCW ladies of Corpus Christi to restore and repaint the statues which had lost their luster over many years.

In June of 1995, under the direction of Fr. Herman, an electric piano was purchased for Corpus Christi. This was the first time that the choir moved from the upstairs balcony to the downstairs location at the front of church. The cost was over $3,000 and CCW ladies made an initial contribution of $1,000. Parishioners were asked to donate to the project. After collection of over $2,000 from the parish, one Sunday after Mass, Dorothy Morgan approached Amy Hellevik (Administrative Director) and said, "How much do you need yet for the piano?" Amy checked the bulletin gave her the amount. Dorothy said: "Donald, give me the checkbook!" So the final payment on the piano was received that day.

CORPUS CHRISTI FUNFEST (1986-2010)

By Carla (Maas) Brady
(Information taken from officer minutes)

As Bingo Parties were discontinued around the mid 1980s, we (Who is we? Council of Catholic Women?) followed with Corpus Christi and Christ the King working on a joint fundraiser with each parish sharing profits 50/50. This profit was used to support the Religious Education Program. In 1986, Christ the King decided not to participate in a joint fund raiser so the decision was made that we would attempt to have a fundraiser on our own. We started with a chili feed fun day that eventually became known as the Corpus Christi Funfest being held each spring and running for 25 years.

About 25 women were in attendance for the planning meeting on February 25th, 1986, to work out the details for our first fun day. We set the date of the first event for April 6, 1986 as a chili feed/bingo party fun day. Chili was served from 11 am-2 pm with bingo, potluck raffle, quilt raffle and kid's games taking place during the event. Chairpersons were as follows: Food- Dorothy Morgan/Carla Brady, Kid's Games- Diane Sammon/Donna Hager, Publicity- Jean Larson, Raffle-Luella Heim/Sharon Wieczoreak, Dining Room- Susie Redman/Lois Nelson; Tickets-Terri Brady; Bingo-Don Morgan.

Each chair took their job seriously and worked out the details for her area. Each family was asked to bring 12 prizes for the kid's games or donate $5 toward prizes. A collection box was placed in the back of church to gather the items prior to the event. We decided on two raffles - a potluck raffle and a quilt raffle. For the Potluck raffle, each family was to donate one item with chances at $.10 each, 3/$.25, or 12/ $1.00. Items were to be deposited in front entrance of church with donor's names on it. Any perishable items brought the day of the event were checked in by Luella Heim. The sewing group donated a beautiful quilt with chances selling for $.50 each or 3/$1.00. The menu consisted of: chili, crackers, bread, cheese slices, carrots and celery sticks, milk, coffee, pickles. Cakes and bars were provided by each family. Eight women donated hamburger (65 pounds) browned with onions. Dorothy Morgan and Carla Brady prepared the chili early on Sunday morning. Members of the Knights of Columbus manned the bars selling adult beverages with the profit used to support the KC Hall. Don Morgan did a great job at calling the Bingo. He used some of the raffle prizes as bingo prizes. Prior to the event, we held a bake sale at Faribault West Mall to cover cost of food. It was also a chance to sell raffle tickets on the quilt. Also, we set quilt up at Mork's Deerfield Store so people could buy chances there.

In 1988, a second soup was added: vegetable beef. In 1989 this event became the Corpus Christi Funfest. Many months in those early years were spent on planning and working out the details. Going forward, we tried to be consistent and host the event at the Medford KC Lodge, usually the first or second week of March. We advertised in the local papers, promoted the event through church bulletins, and expected everyone to sell tickets to the event. Our parish was up to the task and each year we tried to make it bigger and better.

Recipe for the Chili:
Made 4 batches that first year

10# Hamburger (browned with onions and well-seasoned)
2 gallons of red kidney beans
¾ gallon of tomato paste
½ cup brown sugar
2 Tbsp of Chili powder
2 Stalks of celery 0
2 cups of onions (chopped and sautéed in butter)
2 qt tomato juice donated
1 qt whole tomatoes donated
1Qt spaghetti sauce (Carla's Homemade)
Add water the next day as needed depending on the thickness makes 1 -18qt roaster

Also, in 1989, we added some new kid's games and a cake walk. We set the games up on the stage, and the east end of the dance floor on the larger side of the KC hall. In 1992, Dennis and Deb Morgan, Morgan's Ag Service, donated all the paper products to provide less work washing dishes and cleanup. This was a very welcome change for this huge undertaking. We continued to expand our salad bar, increase donations of homemade baked goods for dessert, and we added Jello "jigglers" for the kids. If a family provided the jigglers, they were not required to make bars. Around that time, we also added hot dogs to accommodate the children.

At the end of the event, leftovers were sold to capture as much income as possible. The event continued to pick up popularity. Don Morgan and son Doug offered Bingo after the big lunch crowd was through and we were able to clear a few tables on the small side of the lodge. They took care of calling and collecting of money and used the bingo game and cards from church for the event. There were several people that hung around just for the bingo.

Funfest Meal Ticket

Funfest Quilt Raffle Ticket

Depending on what was happening at the KC Lodge determined how our preparations for the event transpired. If the hall was booked for an event on Saturday evening, we would gather in the church basement at Christ the King to prepare our soup and offerings for the next day. That also meant that the Sunday crowd at the Deerfield church would be reduced due to setting up of the hall the day of the event. Sometimes we were fortunate to get in the hall the day before, making setup and preparations much more efficient.

In 1994, we replaced the vegetable beef soup with wild rice soup. We purchased the soup from a company in Iowa for the next two years. Due to their soup being discontinued, in 1996, we were making our own wild rice soup. The soup was well received. We made two electric roasters full. That year, we ran out of wild rice soup before 1:00 pm and made notes to increase amount for the next year and reduce the chili a little. Tammy Hager was able to get turkey for the soup donated by Jerome's Food reducing the cost of making the new soup. Jan and Dean Herda donated crackers for our event. We always appreciated the support from area companies to help us succeed.

We had a good run with our event. The KC Hall was sold in fall of 2008, so during the last two years of our Funfest, the food was prepared by Celebrations (the new owners of the KC Hall). We provided them with our recipes to follow. It was very good but wasn't the same as it was when we prepared our own food. During that time, we surveyed our church members and found that most felt that the event had run its course. We voted to discontinue the event, making 2010 our last year to host the Annual Corpus Christi Funfest. While searching through the records of the CCW ladies books, I was able to piece together the financial summary of our Funfest activities from 1986 through 2010 (See following page).

Recipe Wild Rice Soup:
2 batches listed below equals one electric roaster
22 cups of water
6 Tbsp Chicken Soup Base
1 ½ cups Onion (chopped and sautéed in butter)
1 Stalk of Celery (chopped and sautéed in butter)
2 Tbsp pepper
¾--36 oz pkg Kraft Long Grain & Wild Rice mix (seasoned)
1 -Kraft Coffee Swirl coffee creamer (non-dairy) 19.2 oz
1 cup additional un-cooked wild rice
5 lbs of cooked chopped turkey (larger chunks)
2 Tbsp of soy sauce
Thicken with corn starch. When adding water, have boiling and add a little soup base so that soup does not get too watered down

CORPUS CHRISTI FUNFEST DATA (1986-2010)

	Income	Expenses	Profit	Tickets sold	Adults	"Children; 5-12"
1986	1,681.45	149.62	1,531.83	Adults-191, Kids-50	$2.50	$1.50
1987	1,817.90	181.11	1,636.79	Adults-170, Kids-60	$2.50	$1.50
1988	1,927.20	168.54	1,758.66		$2.50	$1.50
1989	2,275.27	353.05	1,922.22		$2.50	$1.50
1990	2,208.25	395.45	1,812.80	Adults-244, Kids-92	$3.00	$1.50
1991	3,113.58	249.05	2,864.53	Adults -290, Kids-86	$3.50	$2.00
1992	3,657.35	330.09	3,327.26	Adults-349 Kids-94	$4.00	$2.00
1993	3,296.38	487.01	2,809.37		$4.00	$2.00
1994	3,702.25	556.64	3,145.61		$4.00	$2.00
1995	4,385.15	639.59	3,745.56	Adults-420, Kids -121	$5.00	$2.00
1996	4,302.88	786.34	3,516.54		$5.00	$2.00
1997	4,042.22	1,201.85	2,840.37		$5.00	$2.00
1998	4,074.21	1,067.16	3,007.05		$5.00	$2.00
1999	4,042.22	1,102.49	2,939.73		$5.50	$2.00
2000	4,150.61	1,392.30	2,758.31		$5.50	$2.50
2001	4,613.30	1,043.75	3,569.55		$6.00	$2.50
2002	3,704.02	835.87	2,868.15		$6.00	$2.50
2003	4,085.63	1,000.70	3,084.93		$6.00	$2.50
2004	4,340.05	1,386.30	2,953.75	Adults-275, Kids-41	$6.50	$3.00
2005	4,356.75	1,122.23	3,234.52	Adults-210, Kids-27	$6.50	$3.50
2006	4,865.79	1,163.40	3,702.39		$7.00	$3.00
2007	5,244.40	1,192.55	4,051.85		$7.00	$3.00
2008	5,579.75	1,092.12	4,487.63		$7.50	$3.00
2009	4,900.06	1,864.94	3,035.12	Adults-216, Kids-33	$7.50	$3.00
2010	5,031.60	1,968.97	3,062.63		$8.00	$3.50

Notes:
1986   Fun Day Chili Feed, Bingo , Kids Games & Raffle.
          We had homemade chili, vegetble soup, with salad and dessert
1989   *The income includes $242 from February 11th bake sale in Faribo West Mall
1992   *We began using paper plates and cups to reduce cleanup
1994   *We added Wild Rice Soup to menu
1998   *We started silent auction baskets
2002   *There was poor weather, snow storm
2005   *We changed child tickets to 5-10 age
2005   *We paid rent/hall use for this and following years
2006   *We purchased hamburger this year
2007   *The Knights of Columbus gave back the KC Hall rental fee/ hamburger donated
2009-2010   *The meal was prepared by Celebrations (new owners of KC Hall)

CORPUS CHRISTI--DEERFIELD FUNFEST

MARCH 10, 1996
KNIGHTS OF COLUMBUS HALL, MEDFORD, MN.
**HOMEMADE CHILI, WILD RICE SOUP
HOTDOGS-OUR FAMOUS SALAD BAR
GAMES-PRIZES-BINGO-DOOR PRIZES
FUN! FUN! FUN!**

THE CORPUS CHRISTI LADIES PARISH COUNCIL HAS SET THE DATE FOR THIS YEAR'S RELIGIOUS EDUCATION FUND RAISER FOR MARCH 10, 1996. WE WILL BE HAVING OUR FAMOUS CHILI, HOTDOGS, WILD RICE SOUP, AND A SCRUMPTIOUS SALAD BAR. SET UP WILL BE ANNOUNCED AT A LATER DATE. ALL ARE ENCOURAGED TO HELP. THE MORE HELPERS, THE FASTER WE CAN BE DONE.

THE FUNDS RAISED AT THIS FEST, ON MARCH 10, ARE USED TO HELP FUND THE RELIGIOUS EDUCATION OF OUR CHILDREN AT THE RELIGIOUS EDUCATION CENTER. WE HAVE ONLY THIS ONE EVENT EACH YEAR. WITH THE HELP AND SUPPORT OF <u>ALL</u> CHURCH MEMBERS WE WILL HAVE ANOTHER SUCCESSFUL YEAR. PLEASE VOLUNTEER WHEREVER YOU CAN. <u>**THANK YOU**</u>!

<u>MEAL TICKETS</u>: ENCLOSED YOU WILL FIND SOME MEAL TICKETS. THESE ARE FOR THE MEAL ONLY. IT DOES NOT INCLUDE THE GAMES, ETC. THE PRICE FOR THE MEAL TICKETS ARE $5.00 FOR ADULTS AND $2.00 FOR CHILDREN (5-12 yrs). CHILDREN UNDER 5 ARE FREE. PLEASE TRY TO PURCHASE OR SELL ALL THE TICKETS YOU RECEIVE, AND IF YOU NEED MORE, LUELLA HEIM AND JACKIE DULAS WILL HAVE THEM. THE SALE OF THESE TICKETS FOR THE MEAL, WILL GUARANTEE OUR SUCCESS. TICKETS WILL BE FOR SALE AT THE DOOR, ALSO.

FARIBAULT FEDERAL HAS AGAIN GENEROUSLY DONATED SAVINGS BONDS FOR DOOR PRIZES. THERE WILL BE <u>TWO</u> $50 BONDS GIVEN AWAY. PLEASE HAVE THE PEOPLE WHO BUY THE TICKETS WRITE THEIR <u>NAME</u> AND <u>PHONE NUMBER</u> ON THE BACK. ONE WILL BE DRAWN FOR AN ADULT AND ONE FOR A CHILD. MENTION THE DOOR PRIZES WHEN YOU ARE SELLING THE TICKETS, AS IT IS A NICE BONUS TO THE MEAL. *<u>**NEW THIS YEAR**</u>* PRE-SCHOOLERS WILL BE GIVEN A COMPLIMENTARY TICKET AT THE DOOR TO QUALIFY FOR THEIR OWN PRIZE DRAWING.

<u>POTLUCK RAFFLE</u>: PAT O'BRIEN, RITA KUNTZ, AND MARK & MARLENE STADLER WILL BE CHAIRING THIS AREA. EACH FAMILY OF THE PARISH IS ASKED TO DONATE ONE ITEM FOR THE RAFFLE. SUGGESTIONS ARE TOWELS, GAMES, CRAFTS, CASH, SMALL APPLIANCES OR IT CAN BE FOOD. IF THE ITEM IS PERISHABLE, PLEASE CONTACT ONE OF THE CHAIRPERSONS TO MAKE ARRANGEMENTS. PLEASE LABEL YOUR ITEMS WITH YOUR NAME. YOU CAN LEAVE THEM IN A BOX AT THE BACK OF THE CHURCH.
MAKE YOUR OWN RAFFLE TICKETS BY CUTTING 2" BY 4" PIECES OF <u>WHITE</u> PAPER. SELL THEM AT 1/.25 OR 5/$1.00. HAVE THE INDIVIDUAL SIGN THEIR NAME AND PHONE NUMBER ON ALL RAFFLE TICKETS AND TURN IN THE DAY OF THE FUNFEST FOR THE DRAWING. SELL! SELL! SELL!

*******PLEASE KEEP <u>ALL</u> MONEY TOTALS SEPARATE FOR THE MEAL TICKETS, THE RAFFLE TICKETS, AND THE QUILT TICKETS. ALL MONIES ARE TO BE TURNED IN AT THE FUNFEST. THOSE OF YOU WHO WORK ON SATURDAY--PLEASE TURN IN YOUR MONEY TO LUELLA HEIM OR JACKIE DULAS TO EASE THE RUSH ON SUNDAY.

<u>ADVERTISING</u>: LOIS NELSON HAS VOLUNTEERED TO HANDLE THE PUBLICITY OF OUR EVENT. DIANE SAMMON WILL ADVERTISE IN MORRISTOWN. <u>THANK YOU</u>.

<u>QUILT RAFFLE</u>: WE HAVE 12 ITEMS ON THE RAFFLE THIS YEAR. EACH ITEM IS A TREASURE AND WELL WORTH WINNING. CHANCES ARE 1/$1.00 OR 3/$2.00. EACH YEAR OUR RAFFLE BRINGS IN A LARGE AMOUNT, SO EVERYONE MUST <u>SELL MANY</u> CHANCES. LUCILLE WEBER, ELLEN HOLMQUIST, MARGUERITE LARSON, AND ALICE EUSTICE ARE IN CHARGE OF THE DISPLAY AND TICKET SALES.

<u>MINNOW RACES</u>: THE MINNOWS WILL BE SWIMMING AGAIN, UNDER THE DIRECTION OF TIM KUHLMAN AND DENNIS MORGAN. COME AND CHEER YOUR MINNOW ON TO VICTORY. YOU COULD PICK A WINNER!

CORPUS CHRISTI---DEERFIELD FUNFEST
March 10, 1996

KIDS GAMES: THE KID'S GAMES WILL BE CHAIRED BY LORI HAGER, KATHY GILLIS AND JACKIE BERG, WITH THE HELP OF THEIR FAMILIES AND THE 9TH & 10TH GRADES. EACH FAMILY IS TO DONATE 20 ITEMS FOR PRIZES FOR THE GAMES. SOME SUGGESTIONS: STICKERS, CANDY, LITTLE NOTE PADS, ERASERS, PENCILS, CRAYONS, CARS, COMBS, BOOKS, PUZZLES, OR ANYTHING THAT KIDS WOULD LIKE. IF YOU PREFER, YOU MAY MAKE A CASH DONATION TO LUELLA HEIM, **4 WEEKS BEFORE THE FUNFEST**, OF AT LEAST $7.00 AND ITEMS WILL BE PURCHASED FROM A WHOLESALE CATALOG. WE WOULD LIKE THESE ITEMS NO LATER THAN 2 WEEKS BEFORE THE FUNFEST. WE WILL HAVE A BOX IN THE BACK OF CHURCH OR GIVE THEM TO ONE OF THE PEOPLE IN CHARGE OF THIS AREA. THE TICKETS FOR THE KID'S GAMES WILL SELL 3/$1.00 AT THE KC HALL THE DAY OF THE FUNFEST. GEORGE AND CATHY HACKETT WILL BE IN CHARGE OF THE TICKETS.

KITCHEN & FOOD: CARLA & BYRON BRADY AND JUDY & JAMIE BRADY WILL CO-CHAIR. WE NEED MANY VOLUNTEERS TO HELP WITH THE PREPARATION AND SERVING OF THE FOOD, AS WELL AS WASHING DISHES. IF YOU HAVEN'T VOLUNTEERED TO HELP, YOU WILL HELP IN THE KITCHEN OR DINING AREA.

SALAD BAR: DOROTHY MORGAN AND JOYCE LARSON HAVE VOLUNTEERED TO OVERSEE THE SALAD BAR, KEEPING THE TABLE FULL AND FRESH LOOKING.

BARS: AMY HELLIVIK AND DIANE SAMMON WILL KEEP THE BARS LOOKING APPETIZING AND ASSIST AT THE SALAD BAR. EACH FAMILY IS ASKED TO BRING TWO (2) 9X13 PANS OF BARS, EXCEPT THOSE THAT ARE DONATING MEAT FOR THE CHILI. PLEASE BRING THE BARS ALREADY CUT.

JELLO JIGGLERS: WE HAVE SEVERAL VOLUNTEERS BRINGING JIGGLERS. THE RECIPE IS ON THE BOX.

DINING ROOM: TERRI & DENNIS BRADY, JANE & RANDY ROWE, DEB MORGAN, JEAN LARSON WILL BE HOSTING THE DINING ROOM. TABLES NEED TO BE SET AND CLEARED AS THE PEOPLE FINISH EATING, AS WELL AS SEATING PEOPLE. MORE HELP IS DEFINITELY NEEDED HERE. LOIS NELSON WILL SERVE AS HOSTESS AND DIRECT PEOPLE TO FILL IN AND CONSERVE SPACE.

CLEAN-UP CREW: THIS INCLUDES **YOU** AND **YOU** AND **YOU**. ALL HANDS ARE NEEDED TO STAY LONGER AND HELP CLEAN UP. SO OFTEN TOO MANY LEAVE EARLY AND THE CLEAN UP IS LEFT TO A FEW. PLEASE HELP OUT WHEREVER YOU ARE NEEDED.

REMEMBER	MEAL TICKETS
	PRIZES FOR THE KID'S GAMES
	BARS AND JELLO JIGGLERS
	POTLUCK RAFFLE DONATION
	VOLUNTEER AND HAVE FUN
	SELL MEAL TICKETS--**SELL** QUILT CHANCES--**SELL** RAFFLE TICKETS

THANKS TO EVERYONE. MANY HANDS MAKE LIGHT WORK!

By 1998, we decided that we would try what they called silent auction baskets, and discontinued the quilt raffle. We asked Deerfield families to make themed baskets and printed a flyer with the basket theme and by whom it was donated. The generosity of our church families was greatly appreciated for this endeavor. By 2002, we had 23 baskets that generated $887 with no expense to the church.

Corpus Christi 5th Annual Fun Fest Basket Auction 2002

	Theme Basket	Donated by:
39.⁰⁰	1. "Nest Egg"	Americana Bank
41.⁰⁰	2. "Birthday Basket"	Jean Larson
34.⁰⁰	3. "Red Riding Hood's Basket"	Diane Sammon & Dorothy Morgan
30.⁰⁰	4. "Spring Time"	Anonymous
60.⁰⁰	5. "Angels Galore"	Paul & Jean Gillis
22.⁰⁰	6. "Celebrate America"	Dave & Lois Nelson
39.⁰⁰	7. "Touch of Spring"	George & Cathy Hackett
63.⁰⁰	8. "Hand Stamped for You"	Tim & Joanne Larson & Family
20.⁰⁰	9. "On the Go"	Anna Brady
20.⁰⁰	10. "Crayola Fun"	Randy & Tracie Schimek & Family
46.⁰⁰	11. "Everything Precious for Your Baby"	Byron & Carla Brady
47.⁰⁰	12. "Jr. Slugger"	Jay & Jackie Reuvers
27.⁰⁰	13. "Glamour with Mary Kay"	Randy & Tracie Schimek & Family
41.⁰⁰	14. "Precious Moments Memory Box"	Alyse & Laurie Hager
25.⁰⁰	15. "Kitchen Ideas"	Joe & Martha Pete
30.⁰⁰	16. "Campfire Fun"	Sammon Trucking & Steve Sammon
27.⁰⁰	17. "Easter Basket"	Jackie Dulas
55.⁰⁰	18. "Ready for Spring"	Paul & Jean Gillis
65.⁰⁰	19. "Tonka Time"	Justin, Emma & Jacob Hellevik
42.⁰⁰	20. "Who's Going to Fill Your Shoes?"	Alyse & Laurie Hager
40.⁰⁰	21. "Enjoying Memories While Relaxing"	Jane Brady
50.⁰⁰	22. "Good Morning"	Byron & Carla Brady
26.⁰⁰	23. "Pooh and You"	Byron & Linda O'Connor & Family
		Tim & Joan Kuhlman & Family

$887 Total

In order to place a bid, write your personal bid number on the bid sheet next to the basket. All bidding starts at 11:00 a.m. and will close at 1:00 p.m. The winners will be announced at 1:15 p.m.

We would like to thank you for participating in the 5th Annual Fun Fest Basket Auction. Please feel free to bid on any basket as many times as you wish. Please remember that all proceeds benefit the children and young adults in the Religious Education Program in our community.

Special thanks to all those who made donations to this Annual Fun Fest and also to those who helped with planning, preparation and serving of the food, ticket sales, games and clean-up. This day would not be possible without your sharing and kind hearts.

The baskets continued to pick up speed and by 2005 we had 35 baskets generating $1,118. At this time, we were paying $300 rent for use of the KC lodge.

Shopping List 2007 Funfest

Mustard-1 (picnic pack with Relish)
Catsup-2
Corn Starch-1 (have enough)
Dried Onions-large container
Chicken Soup Base – 4
Bay leaves – large container (have enough)
Soy Sauce – 1 bottle
Crackers- 5 boxes
1 gal French Dressing
1 gal Thousand Island
1 gal Ranch Dressing
2-32oz. Bottles Blue Cheese Dr.
4 loaves wheat & white Bread
12 stalks Celery
20lbs of Carrots (10 lbs cooking,10lbs for salad bar)
10 lbs of Tomatoes
5 lbs sweet onions
20 bell peppers
2 bags seasoned Croutons
8 lbs frozen peas
6 doz eggs for salad bar
4 Lbs Wild Rice
2 yellow sliced cheese
1 white sliced cheese
2-5lb grated cheddar cheese
Diane – will Purchase —260 hot dogs – 10 doz buns
6 lbs of butter
 Raisins – 1 bag
1 lb sunflower seeds
zip lock bags-gal & ½ gal
4 gal Dark Kidney Beans
4 gal stewed spicy tomatoes
chili powder (have enough)
Mushrooms (4 lb can)
Pickles
Coffee 6 lbs decaffeinated
 4 gal orange drink at MC Donalds -
6 ½ gallons of Milk

Potato Salad-Dorothy *Morgan*
30 lbs potatoes
3 doz eggs-onions
1 gal Miracle whip
16 oz sour cream

Snicker Salad-Deb *Morgan*
1 box snickers
8 Lg. Cool Whip
5 lbs Gr Smith Apples

Marinated Veg.-Joan *Kuhlman*
 5 bunches Broccoli
 5 bunches Cauliflower
Carrots
48oz of Zesty Itl.

Spam Salad-Lois *Nelson*
3-1lb. Boxes S noodles
6 cans spam
1 gal Mircle Whip
Shredded Cheese-24oz

Pistacho Salad-Carla *Brady*
10 boxes pudding
3-1 lb bags marshmallows
1 gal pineapple tidbits
5 tubs cool whip

Ham Salad - Amy *Hellevik*
3 –4 lbs Ham - miracle whip *2gts*
5# peas, cheese 2 lb cheddar
elbow macaroni (big box)
Ranch Dressing

Cole Slaw *Jean Larson*
3 - 2lb bags cabbage
2 – jars cole slaw dressing
2 - peppers
1 - sweet onion
4- carrots shredded

Eventually we perfected our offering on our salad bar. Some ladies were gracious enough to prepare the salads at home reducing the amount of time we worked in the kitchen to get food stuff ready. By 2005 and after we had perfected our shopping list, and the officers of the CCW went shopping for the groceries. We included the products that were needed for each of the salads. Due to people donating to the silent auction, prizes for the kid's games, and expending a large amount of effort on event day, we decided that the church would pay for all salad supplies as well.

B

BRADY, Byron & Jane
Route # 1, Box 185, Medford
BRADY, Byron P. & Carla
Erin, Byron, Maggie, Emerson & Anna
Route # 1, Box 185, Medford
BRADY, Dennis &Theresa
Charisse
Route # 1, Box 209, Medford
BRADY, James & Judy
Janine, Jennifer, & Jessica
Route # 1, Box 210, Medford
BRADY, Patrick & Connie
Brent, Marissa, Kristin, &
Brandon
Route # 1, Medford
BRANDT, Larry & Rose
P.O. Box 713,, Medford

C

CONDON, Sylvester & Ethel
Route # 1, Box 177, Morristown

D

DULAS, Sylvester & Jacqueline
Judy, Jay & Joel
Route # 1, Box 197, Medford

E

EUSTICE, Donald & Alice
Route # 3, Box 128, Waseca

F

FREDERICK, James & Mary
Route # 3, Faribault

H

HACKETT, George & Kathy
28189 Garfield Avenue
Morristown
HEIM, Bernard & Luella
216 East 1st Street, Medford,
HEIN Daniel & Kathy
26159 Appleton Ave.,
Faribault
HELLEVIK, Brian & Amy
Rt. # 1, Box 188 A, Medford

HOLMQUIST, Ernest & Ellen-
Route # 4, Box 89, Waseca
HOLMQUIST, Gary & Kim
Jennifwer, Jeff & John
Route # 3, Boc 156, Waseca

J

JEWISON, Timothy & Holly
Preston, Garrett
Route #1, Box 177, Morristown
JILEK, Gary & Vivian
Cassidy, Jonathan, Tiffany
Route # 1, Box 175, Morristown

K

KARSTEN, Helen
Route #3, Box 147, Waseca
KUHLMAN, Timothy & Joan
Blaine & Mitch
Route # 1, Box 184, Medford
KUNTZ, Ernest & Rita
Route #5, Box &, Owatonna

L

LARSON, Marguerite
Matt
Route # 5, Box 46, Owatonna
LARSON, George & Jean
Route #5, Box 48, Owatonna
LARSON, Robert & Joyce
Route # 5, Box 48, Owatonna

M

MORGAN, Daniel & Donna
Tyler
Route # 1, Box 232, Medford
MORGAN, Dennis & Debra
Jessie, Dustin, Randi Mae & Cody
Route #1, Box 167, Morristown
MORGAN, Donald & Dorothy
Route #1, Morristown
MORGAN, Douglas
Route #1, Box 199, Medford
MORK, Kenneth & Donna
Route # 3, Waseca

N

NAGEL, Owen & Helen
Amy
Route # 1, Box 218-A, Medford
NELSON, Lois (HEIM) & David
408 3rd St. NE., Medford
NESS, Ann
Route # 1, Morristown

O

OCONNOR, Byron & Linda
Shaun, Tara, Neill, Kate, Cailin &
Orion
Route # 1, Box 196, Medford

P

PETE, Francis & Vickie
Frank & Cassie
302 West Central Avenue,
Medfrod
PETE, Joseph & Martha
Route # 1, Box 188, Medford
PETERSON, DueLloyd & Betty
Route # 3, Box 122, Waseca
PHILLIPS, Michael
Route # 3, Box 153, Waseca

R

ROWE, Randy & Jane
Gary & Carrie
R.R. # 5, Box 54, Owatonna

S

SAMMON, Aldon & Diane
Jason & Steven
5895 W, 270th St, Morristown
STADLER, Mark & Marlene
Marissa, Mary & Mindy
309 W. Central Ave. Medford

V

VOEGELE, Arthur & Mary
Route # 3, Faribault

W

WEBER, Joseph & Lucille
Route # 1, Box 218, Medford
WIECZOREAK, George & Sharon
Route # 3, Box 128, Waseca

Mass with Bishop John George Vlazny

Most Reverend John George Vlazny

CORPUS CHRISTI SPECIAL VOLUNTEERS

Sylvester Dulas, Custodian

Sylvester Dulas became the janitor/custodian at Corpus Christi in early 1976, following the death of Henry Hager. Sylvester continued to watch over the church and perform janitorial duties until 2006 when his health failed. His wife Jackie, continued to care for the church for the next few years.

Sylvester Dulas was born on July 15, 1931 in rural Faribault County. As a boy, Sylvester attended country school at the Pink School House in Faribault County.

He was united in marriage to Jacqueline (Jackie) Beckel on January 31, 1956, at St. John's Catholic Church in Mankato. They lived in Mapleton for a short time and in 1962 moved to Deerfield to start farming where they continued to live. While farming, Sylvester worked at Farmer's Seed and Nursery in Faribault for 12 years, and then at General Equipment in Owatonna for 28 years. His memberships included Deerfield/Medford Knights of Columbus, and Le-Sueur Pioneer Power. Sylvester was the caretaker of Corpus Christi Church for more then 30 years. His life interests included attending auctions, farming, socializing and spending time with his family.

Sylvester E. Dulas, 76, of Deerfield Township, rural Steele County, died September 4, 2007, in Owatonna. Sylvester was survived by his wife of 51 years Jackie; daughters Joyceann Kroger of Sioux Falls, SD and Judy Platz of Hutchinson, MN; sons John Dulas of Hewitt, MN, Jay Dulas of Waseca, MN, Joel Dulas of Owatonna, MN.

Luella Heim, Flower Arranger Extraordinary

Luella (Gillen) Heim was one of Corpus Christi's most faithful volunteers. She is remembered as always being there to help when needed. Luella and her husband Bernard were long-time members of Corpus Christi and raised a family of ten children. Luella passed away during the Covid pandemic on September 28, 2021, two days before her 100th birthday and joined Bernard in her final resting place at Corpus Christi Cemetery.

Paul & Debra Sontheimer with son Brian

Deb Sontheimer served as sacristan and caretaker beginning in 2009, following the Dulas family. She served as caretaker until 2016 when Corpus Christi became an Oratory. Deb also played the piano at Mass in 2016.

CORPUS CHRISTI PARISH ACTIVITIES (1990)

Deerfield Choir:
Front - Amy Hellevik, Melissa Hellevik Judy Dulas . Middle Row: Carrie Redman, Erin Brady, Carla Brady.
Back Row - Brian Hellevik, Mike Phillips. Missing Vicki Condon

Corpus Christi Choir
L-R: Brian Hellevik, Wayne Maas, Carla Brady and Amy Hellevik at the piano.

SEWING LADIES OF CORPUS CHRISTI
By Carla Brady

Front Row, L-R: Luella Heim, Ann Ness, Ellen Holmquist. Back Row: Lucille Weber, Jackie Dulas, Dorothy Morgan, Martha Pete, Marjorie Ness, Diane Sammon, Cathy Hackett Missing Marguerite Larson, Jane Brady

I had the privilege to interview Dorothy Morgan in 2021 and visit with her regarding the sewing ladies at Corpus Christi. The names that came to mind over the years were Evelyn Brady, Jane Brady, Lucille Weber, Luella Heim, Jackie Dulas, Martha Pete, Lucille Pirkl, Cathy Hackett, Diane Sammon, Ellen Holmquist, Marge Lang, Marion Cole, Dorothy Morgan, Ann and Marjorie Ness. We hope we are not missing anyone.

The ladies worked on items such as baby gowns, diapers, sundresses made from old pillowcases in their own homes. They would receive patterns at the area meetings for items needed at the Pope's Store House. They also prepared friendship bags that contained hygiene items, a towel and a washcloth. A list of items to donate was distributed to Corpus Christi parishioners to complete the bags.

The sewing ladies would also gather in each other's homes once a month to work on quilts, putting them together and tying them with yarn. When making the quilts, they used donated materials and raised funds to purchase material as well. The insides of the quilts were old blankets, sheets and mattress pads. During the gatherings, a great comradery along with coffee and snacks were shared. Deerfield parish leaders always worked hard to make sure that the ladies' efforts were noticed in the reports at the annual meetings. The number of items were nothing short of amazing.

Annually, the ladies would display their hard work in the basement at Corpus Christi, sometime in August, prior to being packed up and shipped out to the Winona Council of Catholic Women (WCCW) convention or workshop. This was always an exciting day at the church celebrating the accomplishments of the sewing group.

Following Sunday Mass, a brunch was held in the church basement of finger foods brought by the church members as well as coffee and juice. Parishioners were invited to look at the handiwork of our ladies. It was also a day to buy $1 chances with the lucky winner picking the quilt of their choice from the display. It was no easy task for the lucky winner to chose from all the beautiful quilts. The money raised from the quilt raffle was used to buy supplies and thread for the sewing ladies.

The Pope's Store House, located in Rome, stored the WCCW items for future disasters. The quilts were put on semi-trailer trucks and shipped out from the convention or workshop held in the dioceses. By 1990 the cost to ship the items overseas had become overwhelming, and so a new site was chosen to receive the fruits of the WCCW sewing items. Brother Regis in New Holstein, Wisconsin worked with the Salvadorian Missions. Aldon and Diane Sammon of Corpus Christi transported the items on semis from 1990 through 2010 for the WCCW.

2003
WINONA DIOCESAN COUNCIL OF CATHOLIC WOMEN
INTERNATIONAL CONCERNS COMMISSION
WORKS OF PEACE ANNUAL PARISH REPORT
(One copy for your record, one copy return to Luella Heim)

DIOCESAN ICC CHAIRMAN

DIOCESE _WINONA_

AREA _Waseca – Owatonna_

PARISH NAME _Corpus Christi_

CITY _Deerfield, MN_

NAME _Luella Heim_
ADDRESS _216 SE 1st St #203_
Medford, MN 55049
PHONE _1-507-451-6634_

PARISH ICC CHAIRMAN _Carla Brady_

ADDRESS _6276 NW 76th St._
Medford MN 55049

PHONE _507-451-6227_

WDCCW TREASURER

NAME _Diane Sammon_
ADDRESS _2375 W. 230th St._
Faribault, MN 55021
PHONE _507-334-6832_

ALL CASH DONATIONS ARE TO BE SENT TO TREASURER

BROTHER REGIS SALVATORIAN MISSION WAREHOUSE
(We want numbers only)

Please do not cross out or write in anything

1. Quilts _74_
2. Baby Quilts _16_
3. Baby Clothes _23_
4. Children's Clothes 2-12 yrs. _14_
5. Misc. _27_
6. Sewing Supplies _—_
7. Material _—_
8. Ditty Bags – Full _145_
9. Ditty Bags – Empty _—_
10. Soap, pounds
    Bars _30_
    Bags _—_

CASH DONATIONS
(Only those listed below will be counted)

Please do not cross out or add any other cash.

1. MADONNA PLAN (Bread of Life) Sister Immaculata Guatemala _25.00_
2. FR. LUIS RUIZ MINISTRIES (Boat people, help family) _25.00_
3. MOTHER TERESA _25.00_
4. HELP A CHILD _25.00_
5. WORKS OF RECONCILIATION _25.00_
6. SHIPPING FEES (Ea. Parish is asked to donate @ least $25) _100.00_
7. VANUATA PROJECT (Sister Diocese of Winona) _25.00_

PLEASE TOTAL _$250.00_
(PLEASE DO NOT SEND CASH TO ANYONE BUT TREASURER.)

Above: Commission Report sent to Luella Heim, Diocesan Chair (2003). These reports were filed each year recording sewing groups' activities for each year.

At Right:
Corpus Christi Sewing Group @ 1975
Seated, L-R: Marguerite Larson, Luella Heim, Ann Ness. Second Row: Alice Mae Eustice, Cathy Hackett, Margie Ness.
Back Row: Mary Voegele, Lucille Pirkl, and Lucille Weber.

199

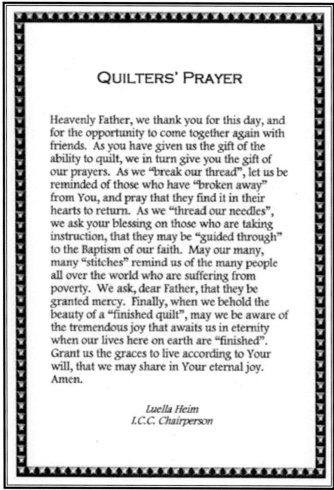

QUILTERS' PRAYER

Heavenly Father, we thank you for this day, and for the opportunity to come together again with friends. As you have given us the gift of the ability to quilt, we in turn give you the gift of our prayers. As we "break our thread", let us be reminded of those who have "broken away" from You, and pray that they find it in their hearts to return. As we "thread our needles", we ask your blessing on those who are taking instruction, that they may be "guided through" to the Baptism of our faith. May our many, many "stitches" remind us of the many people all over the world who are suffering from poverty. We ask, dear Father, that they be granted mercy. Finally, when we behold the beauty of a "finished quilt", may we be aware of the tremendous joy that awaits us in eternity when our lives here on earth are "finished". Grant us the graces to live according to Your will, that we may share in Your eternal joy. Amen.

Luella Heim
I.C.C. Chairperson

Luella Heim served as International Concerns Commission (ICC) for the Winona Diocese. Luella wrote the above prayer to be shared with all quilters throughout the Winona Diocese.

Corpus Christi Church women sew for missions

They are at it again!

The ladies of Corpus Christi Catholic Church of rural route three out of Waseca are busily sewing for the Pope's Storeroom mission project -- much the same as they have done every year.

The picture was taken in the church basement as they packed the results of their 1986 efforts. With a total of well over 200 quilts, 20 layettes and numerous childrens garments as well as 50 ditty bags containing personal hygiene items such as soap, towel, washcloth, and dental supplies, there was need for a good supply of packing boxes. It is proof that "many hands make light work, especially when the work in question is really an act of love.

Mission Projects

The women of Corpus Christi Catholic Church have been busy sewing quilts for the Pope's mission project. The woman in the foreground is Diane Sammon. With an armful of quilts is Ellen Holmquist, and the man in the center is Byron O'Connor.

Sewing Group Article (Photo News; August 1986)

Parishes	Quilts	Baby Qlts	Baby Clths	Child Clths 2-12 yrs.	Misc.	Sew Kits & Mat	Ditty Bags	Soap Bars & #'s	Cash
Deerfield									
Corpus Christi	130	73	121		10		108 F		$300.00
Ellendale									
St. Alden									$100.00
Janesville									
St. Anns	300	13	224	111	308		99 F		$125.00
Litomysl									
Holy Trinity	210	50	53	11		41 K			$200.00
Medford									
Christ the King	218	154	14	103		67 K	108 F 25 E		$200.00
New Richland									
All Saints	17	47	144				40 F		$25.00
Owatonna									
Sacred Heart	193	57	109	48	195		12 F 525 E	35 B	$650.00
Owatonna									
St. Joseph	204	34	83		4				$525.00
Waldorf									
St. Joseph	108	68		91	120	26 K	11 E		$300.00
Waseca									
Sacred Heart	38	29	100						
Total	1418	525	848	365	537	134 K	367 F 561 E	35 B	$2,425.00
						K-kits Y-yards	F-full E-empty	B-bar #-lbs.	

Owatonna/Waseca Area Works of Peace Report for 2000-2001.

Sewing Group
Cathy Hackett, Alice Eustice, Jane Brady, Jackie Dulas, Luella Heim, Dorothy Morgan

Corpus Christi Sewing Group
Jackie Dulas, Luella Heim, Dorothy Morgan & Cathy Hackett.

Byron & Carla Brady Family

Dennis & Theresa Brady with Cherisse

Jamie & Judy Brady with Janine, Jennifer & Jessica

Patrick & Connie Brady with Brent, Brandon, Kristin & Marissa

Larry& Rose Brandt

Sylvester & Jackie Dulas with Judy, Jay & Joel

CORPUS CHRISTI PARISHIONERS (1990)

Donald & Alice Eustice

George & Catherine Hackett

Bernard & Luella Heim

Dan & Kelly Hein

Brian & Amy Hellevik

Ernest & Ellen Holmquist

CORPUS CHRISTI PARISHIONERS (1990)

Gary & Kim Holmquist
Jennifer, Jeff & John

Timothy & Joan Kuhlman
Blaine & Mitch

Ernest & Rita Kuntz

Bob & Joyce Larson

George & Jean Larson with Mathew

Marguerite Larson

CORPUS CHRISTI PARISHIONERS (1990)

Daniel & Donna Morgan with Tyler

Dennis & Deb Morgan
with Jessica, Dustin, Randi & Cody

Donald & Dorothy Morgan

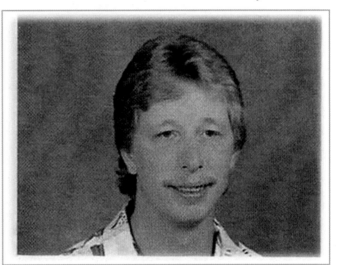

Douglas Morgan

David & Lois (Heim) Nelson with Matt & Sara

Ann & Marjorie Ness

CORPUS CHRISTI PARISHIONERS (1990

Byron & Linda O'Connor with Family

Francis & Vicky Pete with Frankie & Cassie

Joe & Martha Pete

Lloyd & Betty Peterson

Michael Philips

Randy & Jane Rowe

CORPUS CHRISTI PARISHIONERS (1990)

Aldon & Diane Sammon Family with Jason & Steven

Mark & Marlene Stadler with Melisa, Mary, Mindy & Meghan

Jeff & Dena Voegele with Nicholas

Joe & Lucille Weber

Sharon & Joe Wieczoreak

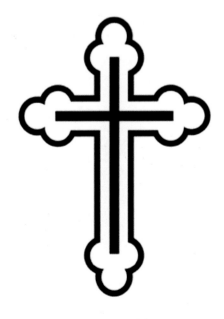

B

BERG, Cary & Jackie
(Mariah)
408 3rd Avenue, Medford
BRADY, Byron & Carla
(Erin, Byron, Maggie, Emerson, & Anna)
Route # 1, Box 185, Medford
BRADY, Byron P. & Carla
Erin, Byron, Maggie, Emerson & Anna
6276 NW 76th Street, Medford
BRADY, Dennis &Theresa
(Charisse)
6924 NW 72nd Ave., Medford
BRADY, James & Judy
(Janine, Jennifer, Jessica & Jordan)
6870 NW 72nd Ave. Medford
BRADY, Jane
7828 NW 665th Ave, Medford

D

DULAS, Sylvester & Jacqueline
(Judy, Jay & Joel)
7225 NW 85th Ave,, Medford

E

EUSTICE, Donald & Alice
2374 97th Ave., Waseca

F

FREDERICK, James & Mary
26541 Dalton Ave., Faribault

G

GILLIS, Richard & Dee Maas
(John, Monica, Nicole)
5280 NW 76th Ave., Medford

H

HACKETT, George & Cathy
26189 Garfield Ave.
Morristown

HAGER, Richard & Laurie
(Brad, Alyse, Wesley)
HANSON, Thomas & Brenda
(Brandon)
8555 NW 85th Ave.,
Morristown
HEIM, Luella
216 SE 1st Street, Medford,
HELLEVIK, Brian & Amy
(Justin, Emma, Jacob)
7698 NW 70th Ave,, Medford
HOLMQUIST, Ernest
14956 410th St., Waseca

J

JEWISON, Timothy & Holly
(Preston, Garrett, Shawn)
42623 180th St.,, Morristown

K

KUHLMAN, Timothy & Joan
(Blaine & Mitch)
P.O. Box 62, Medford
KUNTZ, Ernest & Rita
6350 NW 50th St., Owatonna

L

LARSON, Jean
(Matthew)
4974 NW 62nd Ave. Owatonna
LARSON, Marguerite
2211 Hartle Ave., Owatonna
LARSON, Robert & Joyce
6511 NW 56th St., Owatonna

M

MORGAN, Daniel & Donna
(Tyler, Chelsea, Nicole, Danielle)
5000 NW 60th St.,, Medford
MORGAN, Dennis & Debra
(Jessie, Dustin, Randi Mae & Cody)
8923 NW 86th St., Morristown

MORGAN, Donald & Dorothy
26750 Elmore Ave., Morristown
MORGAN, Douglas
8309 NW 66th St., Medford
MORK, Donna
6597 NW 102nd Ave., Waseca

N

NELSON, Lois (HEIM) & David
P.O. Box 161, Medford

O

O'BRIEN, Patrick
24631 Halland Ave., Morristoen

O'CONNOR, Byron & Linda
(Shaun, Tara, Neill, Kate, Cailin, Orion, Alyssa,Sara, Quinn)
6593 NW 76th Street, Medford

P

PETE, Francis & Vickie
(Francis & Cassandra)
302 Central Avenue, Medford
PETE, Joseph & Martha
7698 NW 70th Ave.,, Medford
PETERSON, DueLloyd & Betty
41209 170th Street, Waseca
PHILLIPS, Michael
9089 NW 56th Street, Waseca

S

SAMMON, Aldon & Diane
(Jason & Steven)
2375 230th Street, Faribault
SCHIMEK, Randy & Traci
(Courtney & Miranda)
7122 NW 76th Street, Medford

W

WEBER, Joseph & Lucille
6927 NW 52nd Ave. Medford

CORPUS CHRISTI PARISHIONERS (1999)

Cary & Jackie Berg with Mariah

Dennis & Terri Brady
with Cherisse

James & Judy Brady with
Janine, Jennifer, Jessica & Jordan

Jane Brady

Pat Brady with Brent, Marissa,
Kristin & Brandon

Sylvester & Jacqueline (Beckel) Dulas

Donald F. & Alice M. (Perron) Eustice

Jim & Mary Frederick

Richard & Dee Gillis with Monica,
John & Nikki

CORPUS CHRISTI PARISHIONERS (1999)

George & Cathy Hackett

Rick & Laurie Hager
Brad, Alysse, Wesley

Thomas & Brenda Hanson
with Brandon

Luella Heim

Brian & Amy Hellevik with
Justin, Emma & Jacob

Timothy & Holly Jewison
Preston, Garret, Shawn

Timothy & Joan Kuhlman
with Blaine, & Mitch

Ernest & Rita Kuntz

Marguerite Larson

Robert & Joyce Larson

*Dennis & Donna Morgan with
Tyler, Chelsea, Nicole & Danielle*

*Dennis & Deb Morgan with
Jessica, Dustin, Randi, & Cody*

Donald & Dorothy Morgan

Douglas Morgan

Donna Mork

Dave & Lois Nelson

Pat O'Brien

*Byron & Linda O'Connor with
Shaun, Tara, Neil, Kate, Catlyn,
Alyssa, Sara & Quinn*

CORPUS CHRISTI PARISHIONERS (1999)

*Frank & Vicky Pete with
Frank Jr. & Cassandra*

Joe & Martha Pete

DueLloyd & Betty Peterson

Michael Philips

*Alden & Diane Sammon
with Steven*

Randy & Tracy Schimek
Courtney & Miranda

Jean & Matthew Larson

Ernest & Ellen Holmquist

Joe & Lucille Weber

CORPUS CHRISTI PARISHIONERS (1999)

John & Shirley Hager

Teresa Reyant

Charlotte Morgan

Harlow & Joan Pirkl

Marjorie Ness

Byron & Carla Brady with Erin, Byron, Moggie, Emerson & Anna

SERVICE TO CORPUS CHRISTI PARISH -- 1999

Corpus Christi Choir

Corpus Christi Ushers

Corpus Christi Lectors

Corpus Christi Religious Education Instructors

EXAMPLES OF FATHER JOHN CODY'S CHURCH BULLETIN HUMOR

```
Our Gifts to God last week:
Christ the King
    plate.....$ 51.00
    adults....  681.00
    kids......   48.00
              $ 780.00

Corpus Christi
    plate.....$ 3.00
    adults....125.00
    kids......  50.00
              $178.00
```

Kids I notice the childrens gift to God for June at Corpus Christi was more than Ct. the King? Ct the has 4 times more children.

From The July 5, 1981 Church Bulletin

SERVICE TO CORPUS CHRISTI PARISH -- 2005

High School-Age Mass Servers; Back: Jordon Brady, Monica Taddei. Front: Justin Hellevik, Alyssa O'Connor.

Corpus Christi Greeters
Mike Philips, Luella Heim & Lois Heim Nelson.

Elementary School Mass Servers; Back: Nicole Morgan, Emma Hellevik, Katie Larson., Nikki Taddei, Chelsea Morgan. Front; Daniel Larson, Sara O'Connor, Brandon Hanson.

Ushers; Back: Orion O'Connor, Tyler Morgan, Cody Morgan, Mike Phillips. Front; Jordon Brady Monica Taddei.

Deerfield Cemetery Board
Dick Gillis & Byron Brady Jr.

CORPUS CHRISTI LITURGICAL ROLES (2005)

Lectors: Cathy Hackett, Diane Sammon, Judy Brady, Carla Brady & Tim Kuhlman.

Lectors: Lois Heim Nelson & Jean Larson

Mass Servers: Wesley Hager, Cailin O'Connor, Cassie Pete with Fr. Herman.

L-R: Neil O'Connor, Mitch Kuhlman, Brad Hager, Frank Pete Jr., Anna Brady, Alyse Hager, Cailin O'Connor, Jessica Brady.

Servers: Dan Larson, Emma Hellevik, Nikki Taddei, Chelsea Morgan, Sarah O'Connor, Nicole Morgan, Brandon Hanson.

Sylvester Dulas, Corpus Christi Custodian

B

BERG, Cary & Jackie
(Mariah, Brody, Janna)
4544 NW 76th Ave. Medford
BRADY, Byron & Carla
6276 NW 76th St., Medford
BRADY, Byron P. & Laura
Isabel, Carsyn, Jules, Taylor
6404 NW 85th Street, Waseca
BRADY, Dennis &Theresa
6924 NW 72nd Ave., Medford
BRADY, James & Judy
(Janine, Jennifer, Jessica &
Jordan)
6870 NW 72nd Ave. Medford
BRADY,Pat
7828 NW 66th Str, Medford

D

DAHLE, Chris & Teya
(Josiah and Noah)
41940 160th Street, Waseca
DULAS, Jacqueline
7225 NW 85th Ave,, Medford
DULAS, Jay & Robin
(Madison, Keegan)
1215 8th St., St, Waseca

G

GILLIS, Richard & Dee
(John, Monica, Nicole, Ian,
Meredith)
5280 NW 76th Ave., Medford
GILLIS, Jason & Amy
(Madison, Emma)
5784 NW 76th St., Medford

H

HACKETT, Cathy
500 Third Ave., NW. #215,
Faribault
HAGER, Richard & Laurie
2322 270th St., East, Medford
HANSON, Thomas & Brenda
(Brandon, BethAnn)
8555-85th Ave., Morristown

HEIM, Luella
216 SE 1st Street, Medford,
HELLEVIK, Brian & Amy
(Justin, Emma, Jacob)
7698 NW 70th Ave,, Medford
HUXFORD, Kim & Lisa
(Logan)
9417 NW 66th St., Waseca
14956 410th St., Waseca

J

JEWISON, Timothy & Holly
(Preston, Garrett, Shawn)
42623 180th St.,, Morristown
JONES, Richard
(Dakota)
6027 NW 62nd Ave., Medford

K

KUHLMAN, Timothy & Joan
7741 NW 62nd Ave., Medford

L

LARSON, Jean
4100 60th St., Lot 124, Medford
LARSON, Robert & Joyce
6511 NW 56th St., Owatonna
LARSON, Tim & Joanne
(Daniel, Katie, Holly, Mariah, Lynn)
List, Daved & Janie
(Devan, Reilly, Adalia
7637 NW 66th St., Medford
Lopez, Concepcion (Janie's mother)
7637 NW 66th St., Medford

M

McGraw, Larry
P.O. Box 303, Owatonna
MORGAN, Daniel & Donna
(Tyler, Chelsea, Nicole, Danielle)
5000 NW 60th St., Medford
MORGAN, Dennis & Debra
8923 NW 86th St., Morristown
MORGAN, Donald & Dorothy
2500 14th St., Faribault

MORGAN, Douglas
8309 NW 66th St., Medford
MORK, Donna
Owatonna Commons, Owatonna

N

NAGEL, Owen & Helen Mary
6119 NW 66th St., Medford
NELSON, Lois (HEIM) & David
P.O. Box 161, Medford

O

O'BRIEN, Patricia
24631 Halland Ave., Morristown

O'CONNOR, Byron & Linda
(Shaun, Tara, Neill, Kate, Cailin, Orion, Alyssa,Sara, Quinn, Brianna)
6593 NW 76th Street, Medford

P

PHILLIPS, Michael
9089 NW 56th Street, Waseca
PITTMAN, Gregory & Jolaine
133390 420th Ave., Waseca

S

SAMMON, Aldon & Diane
(Steven)
2375 230th Street, Faribault
SONTHEIMER, Paul & Debbie
41330 160th St., Waseca
SCHIMEK, Randy & Traci
(Courtney & Miranda, Hannah,
Isaiah, Zachary)
38885 180th St., Waseca

V

VALEK, Leonard & Geraldine
17895 Ames Ct., Faribault
Wadekamper, Marge
7501 West 180th St., Faribault

W

WIEST, Raymond & Nicole
3619 52nd Ave. NW, Owatonna

Cary & Jackie Berg
(Mariah, Brody & Jenna)

Byron & Carla Brady

Byron & Laura Brady
(Isabel, Carsyn, Jules & Taylor

Dennis & Terri Brady

James & Judy Brady
(Janine, Jennifer, Jessica & Jordan)

Patrick Brady

Jackie Dulas

Fr. Clayton Haberman

Cathy Hackett

Thomas & Brenda Hanson
(Brandon & Beth Ann)

Luella Heim

Brian & Amy Hellevik
(Justin, Emma & Jacob)

Kim & Lisa Huxford

Tim & Holly Jewison

Tim & Joan Kuhlman

Bob & Joyce Larson

Jean Larson

Tim & Joanne Larson
(Katelyn, Dan, Mariah, Holly & Lynn)

CORPUS CHRISTI PARISHIONERS (2011)

*Daved & Janie List
(Devan, Reilly, Adalia, Connie Lopez)*

*Dan & Donna Morgan
(Tyler, Chelsea, Nicole & Danielle)*

Dennis & Deb Morgan

Donald & Dorothy Morgan

Douglas Morgan

Donna Mork

David & Lois (Heim) Nelson

Pat O'Brien

Byron & Linda O'Connor Family

CORPUS CHRISTI PARISHIONERS (2011)

Michael Phillips

Greg & Jolaine Pittman

Aldon & Diane Sammon

Steven Sammon

*Randy & Traci Schimek
(Courtney, Miranda, Hannah, Isaiah
& Zaxhary)*

*Paul & Debbie Sontheimer
(Brian)*

Leonard & Gerry Valek

*Marge Wadekamper with
Richard Jones & Dakota Jones*

CHAPTER VII

GLEANINGS FROM THE CORPUS CHRISTI PARISH REGISTERS

CORPUS CHRIST BAPTISMS

April 1907	
Margaret FitzPatrick (Mrs. Leo Sammon)	
Agnes FitzPatrick	
1944	
Brady, Melvin James	James & Evelyn (Maas) Brady
Meyer, Walter Harold	Harold & Margaret (Morgan) Meyer
Mullenmaster, Mary Eileen	Leo & Creta (Lonergan) Mullenmaster
Hager, Paul Albert	Henry & Anna (Hollinger) Hager
Brady, Sharon Ruth	Byron & Jane (Ellingson) Brady
Pirkl, RoseMary	Louis & Lucille (Curran) Pirkl
Holmquist, Harlan Bernard	Bernard & Loretta (Hebl) Holmquist
Morgan, Virginia Lee	Robert & Dorthy (Gasner) Morgan
Nusbaum, Jerome Thomas	Richard & Shirley (Sitte) Nusbaum
1945	
Stirens, Catherine Mary	Peter & Mildred (Pitzner) Stirens
Hoffman, Leroy Allan	Clarence & Edith (Kniefel) Hoffman
Brady, Carolyn Marie	James & Evelyn (Maas) Brady
Gillis, Kathleen Ann	Michael & Gertrude (Blais) Gillis
Mullenmaster, William Paul	Leo & Creta (Lonergan) Mullenmaster
Webb, John Rudolph	Rudolph & Frances (Condon) Webb
Jensen, Jeanne Harriet *(Convert, age 22)*	Harry & Mary Jane (Brynildson) Jensen
Meyer, William Donald	Harold & Margaret (Morgan) Meyer
1946	
Langworthy, Thomas Dale	Edwin & Mary (Denn) Langworthy
Williamson, Richard Eugene	Veronon E & Darlene (Nusbaum) Williamson
Morgan, Patricia Lynn	Robert & Dorthy (Gasner) Morgan
Klebel, Kathleen Wanda	Martin & Margaret (Bruender) Klebel
Lorenze, DeWayne Edward *(Age 7)*	Albert & Dorothy (Baton) Lorenze
Lorenze, Sandra Jean *(Age 2)*	Albert & Dorothy (Baton) Lorenze
Hager, Eugene Michael	Henry & Anna (Hollinger) Hager
Lorenz, Albert	Albert & Arilla (Walkins) Lorenz
Nusbaum, Diane Marie	Richard I& Shirley (Sitte) Nusbaum
Mohs, Janet Louise	Berthald & Bertha (Maki) Mohs
Arndt, Nancy Carolyn	Richard E & Mary (Kvasnicka) Arndt
Miller, Philip George	George & Margaret (Kahnke) Miller
Swintek, Kathleen Mary	Thomas & Margaret (Bruzant) Swintek
Brunkon, Myrtle Emma *(Convert Age 25)*	Benjamin & Lila (Hicks) Brunkon

CORPUS CHRIST BAPTISMS

1947	
O'Neal, David George	George & Ellinore (Knowlton) O'Neal
O'Connor, Darlene Ann	Floyd & Mary Alice (McFadden) O'Connor
Webber, Robert Joseph	Joseph & Lucille (Walters) Webber
Langworthy, Edward Paul	Edwin & Mary (Duin) Langworthy
Hager, Susan Andrea	Henry & Anna (Hollinger) Hager
Mullenmaster, Lawrence Joseph	Leo & Creta (Lonergan) Mullenmaster
Cole, Bonita Jean	Corless & Marian (McDonough) Cole
Brady, Patrick Jacob	James & Evelyn (Maas) Brady
Judd, Alice Marie	David & Clara (Pete) Judd
1948	
Schuller, Linda Marie	Chas & Olive (Bosacker) Schuller
Voegele, Dennis Peter	Arthur & Mary Ann (Webber) Voegele
Klukas, Robert William	William & Mary (Harguth) Klukas
Androli, Lila Mae	Herbert & Myrtle Emma (Brunkon) Androli
Hanson, Charlotte Mary	Arvid & Dorothy (Bruzant) Hanson
Holmquist, LeAnn Loretta	Bernard & Loretta (Hebl) Holmquist
Stirens, Leo Peter	Peter & Mildred (Pitzner) Stirens
Hurt, Constance Jean	James & Alma (Connor) Hurt
Wochnick, Shirley Jeanne	Felix & Bonnette (Braughten) Wochnick
Phillips, Linda Louise	Eugene & Florence (Wendel) Phillips
Morgan, John Chris	Robert & Dorothy (Gasner) Morgan
Cole, James Albert	Corless & Marian (McDonough) Cole
1949	
O'Connor, Eugene Joseph	Floyd & Mary Alice (McFadden) O'Connor
Bruee, Adema	Sheridan & Amanda (Lee) Bruee
Langworthy, Linda Rae	Edwin & Mary (Duin) Langworthy
Mullenmaster, Candace Sue	Leo & Creta (Lonergan) Mullenmaster
Pribyl, Paul Eugene	Silvan & Joyce Marie (Byrne) Pribyl
Pete, Mary Martha	Joseph & Martha (Klecker) Pete
Feller, Stephen Douglas	Bernard & Bernadine (Kniefel) Feller
Hager, Sandra Theresa	Henry & Anna (Hollinger) Hager
Brady, Edith Anne	Byron & Jane (Ellingson)Brady

* Convert, age 52

CORPUS CHRIST BAPTISMS

1950	
Phillips, Jane Elizabeth	Eugene & Florence (Wendel) Phillips
Klukas, James John	William & Mary (Harguth) Klukas
Nusbaum, Sandra Katherine	Richard & Shirley (Sitte) Nusbaum
Brady, Kathleen Mae	James & Evelyn (Maas) Brady
Mullenmaster, Colleen Myrtle	Leo & Creta (Lonergan) Mullenmaster
Pete, Joseph Phillip *	Joseph & Martha (Klecker) Pete
Bakken, Dorothy Ann	Alfred & Mable (Haustal) Bakken
Merckling, Theresa Ann	Ray & Marian (Mohs) Merckling
Merckling, Mararite Marie	Ray & Marian (Mohs) Merckling
Tuve, Catherine Marie	Edwin & Marie (Ciffra) Tuve
Eustice, Marjorie Ann	Donald & Alice Mae (Perron) Eustice
Feller, Marcia Kathrine	Bernard & Bernadine (Kniefel) Feller
1951	
Springer, Richard Robert	Rudolph & Deloris (Soukup) Springer
Morgan, Diane Marie	Donald & Dorothy (Bakken) Morgan
Iverson, Elizabeth Ann Marie	Fred & Margaret (Otteson) Iverson
Kilmer, Arline	Albert & Sophia (Malokavik) Kilmer
Hager, Dayle Ann	Raymond & Shirley Ann (Dahle) Hager
Holmquist, Linda Joan	Bernard & Loretta (Hebl) Holmquist
Mullenmaster, Elaine Ranae	Leo & Creta (Lonergan) Mullenmaster
1952	
Busho, Charlotte Rae **	Harold & Lois (Knauss) Buscho
Brady, Byron Paul	Byron & Jane (Ellingson) Brady
Mullenmaster, Gregory Cyril	Leo & Creta (Lonergan) Mullenmaster
Morgan, Kay Lynn Elizabeth	John & Charlotte (Buscho) Morgan
1953	
Hager, Raymond Craig	Raymond & Shirley Ann (Dahle) Hager
Phillips, Carol Rae	Eugene & Florence (Wendel) Phillips
Byrne, Constance Jane	Arthur & Leone (Heim) Byrne
Morgan, Donna LeAnn	Donald & Dorothy (Bakken) Morgan
Sammon, Bradley Richard	Richard & Betty (Zitzmann) Sammon
Carmichael, Mary Josephine	Carl & Joyce (Sneed) Carmichael
Kavitz, Dale	Marvin & Donna (Zacharska) Kavitz
Kavitz, Marvin Herman ***	Joseph & Golda (Matz) Kavitz
Carmichael, Carl ****	Daniel & Ada (Clark) Carmichael

Ordained to Diacanate 5/23/1975 Ordained Priesthood 5/21/1976
*** Convert, age 28 *** Convert, age 43 **** Convert, age 36*

CORPUS CHRIST BAPTISMS

1954	
Brady, Mary Jane	Byron & Jane (Ellingson)Brady
Pete, Robert Pius	Joseph & Martha (Klecker) Pete
Mullenmaster, Monica Louise	Leo & Creta (Lonergan) Mullenmaster
Holmquist, Gary Victor	Bernard & Loretta (Hebl) Holmquist
Dahle, Barbara Jean	Kenneth & Elizabeth (Pelant) Dahle
Hager, Debra Jane	Henry & Anna (Hollinger) Hager
1955	
Morgan, Mary Lou	John & Charlotte (Buscho) Morgan
Phillips, Theresa Ann	Eugene & Florence (Wendel) Phillips
Meisinger, Joseph Laurence	Lawrence & Esther (Hiniker) Meisinger
Mullenmaster, Thomas Kenneth	Leo & Creta (Lonergan) Mullenmaster
Tierney, Colleen Beatrice	James & Marjorie (Fiereck) Tierney
Springer, Randolph James	Rudolph & Deloris (Soukup) Springer
Kavitz, Robin Elaine	Marvin & Donna (Zacharska) Kavitz
1956	
Dahle, Susan Kay	Kenneth & Elizabeth (Pelant) Dahle
Boch, Randall John	Lloyd & Lucille (Kvasnicka) Boch
Pete, Michael Paul	Joseph & Martha (Klecker) Pete
Mullenmaster, Brian Michael	Leo & Creta (Lonergan) Mullenmaster
Kratt, Donna Rose	Ray & Irene (Geisler) Kratt
Springer, Donna Jean	Rudolph & Deloris (Soukup) Springer
1957	
Walters, Michael Duane	Lowell & Rita (Pumper) Walters
Kniefel, Roxanne Marie	Anthony & Darlene (Rysavy) Kniefel
Hager, Sydney Albert	Raymond & Shirley Ann (Dahle) Hager
Meisinger, Thomas Mathew	Lawrence & Esther (Hiniker) Meisinger
Brady, Dennis James	James & Evelyn (Maas) Brady
Hager, Timothy Neil	Neil & Donna (Kratt) Hager
Pete,Monica Ann	Joseph & Martha (Klecker) Pete
Mullenmaster, Mark Gerard	Leo & Creta (Lonergan) Mullenmaster
Morgan, Dennis Joseph	Donald & Dorothy (Bakken) Morgan
Morgan, Marilyn Ruth	John Edward & Charlotte (Buscho) Morgan
Convert, age 18	

CORPUS CHRIST BAPTISMS (1958-1960)

1958	
Heim, Christine Florence	Bernard & Luella (Gillen) Heim
Bergee, Brian Patrick	Almont & Agnes (Callanan) Bergee
Hager, Dawn Marie	Raymond & Shirley Ann (Dahle) Hager
Brady, Kevin Mark	Byron & Jane (Ellingson)Brady
Kniefel, Mark Anthony	Anthony & Darlene (Rysavy) Kniefel
Morgan, Moira Dawn Renee	Donald & Dorothy (Bakken) Morgan
Kavitz, Dolly Joan	Marvin & Donna (Zacharska) Kavitz
Dickison, Susan Ann	Richard & Miyoko (Shinozaki) Dickison
Springer, Robert Rudalph	Rudolph & Deloris (Soukup) Springer
Dahle, Nancy Ann	Kenneth & Elizabeth (Pelant) Dahle
Mullenmaster, Maurice James	Leo & Creta (Lonergan) Mullenmaster
1959	
Heim, Patrick Joseph	Bernard & Luella (Gillen) Heim
Phillips, Rosemary Alice	Eldred & Mary (Trettel) Phillips
Janes, James Howard	Lloyd & Glendine (Stires) Janes
Condon, Leslie Scott	Phillip & Kathleen (O'Neil) Condon
Miller, Marlys Mary	Roland & Lillian (Dremdie) Miller
Meisinger, Mary Ellen	Lawrence & Esther (Hiniker) Meisinger
Hager, Charles Joseph	Raymond & Shirley Ann (Dahle) Hager
Pete, Francis Luke	Joseph & Martha (Klecker) Pete
Reyant, John Mark	Frank & Theresa (Steinbauer) Reyant
1960	
Hurt, Paul Joseph	Paul & Sharon (Josephia) Hurt
Springer, Debra Ann	Rudolph & Deloris (Soukup) Springer
Mullenmaster, Peter Scott	Leo & Creta (Lonergan) Mullenmaster
Thielbar, ThomasWallace	Lyle & Ruth(Quigley) Thielbar
Heim, Cynthia Jeanne	Bernard & Luella (Gillen) Heim
Reyant, Carol Ann	Frank & Theresa (Steinbauer) Reyant

At left: Baptism of James Allen Brady (1962); sponsors Carolyn and Patrick Brady. Fr. Harold Mountain.

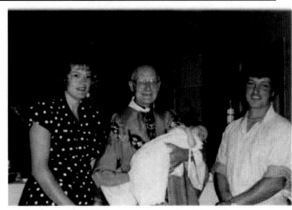

Baptism of Jordan Evelyn Brady (June 30, 1991)
Judy Brady, Fr. Ernster with Baby Jordon, Jamie Allen Brady

CORPUS CHRIST BAPTISMS (1961-1963)

1961	
Hurt, Rachelle Marie	Paul & Sharon (Josephs) Hurt
Hager, Mark Lynn	Raymond & Shirley Ann (Dahle) Hager
Larson, Timothy George	George & Jean (Thiele) Larson
Brady, Charles Curt	Byron & Jane (Ellingson)Brady
Springer, Raymond Joseph	Rudolph & Deloris (Soukup) Springer
Hager, Teresa Ann	Neil & Donna (Kratt) Hager
Bruender, Tammy Jean	John & Betty (Schroeder) Bruender
Morgan, Douglas Donald	Donald & Dorothy (Bakken) Morgan
Meisinger, Susanne Barbara	Lawrence & Esther (Hiniker) Meisinger
Barbknecht, Wayne *	Helmuth & Clara (Klinger) Barbknecht
Kavitz, Todd Anthony	Marvin & Donna (Zacharska) Kavitz
Dahle, Mary Jane	Kenneth & Elizabeth (Pelant) Dahle
Hager, Steven Donald	Donald & Elizabeth (Beckman) Hager
1962	
Larson, Richard Leonard	George & Jean (Thiele) Larson
Brady, James Allen	James & Evelyn (Maas) Brady
Pirkl, Debra Marie	Harlow & Joan (Wencl) Pirkl
Hurt, Kelly Ann	Paul & Sharon (Joseph) Hurt
Bruender, Deborah Kay	John & Betty (Schroeder) Bruender
Barbknecht, Lisa Marie	Wayne & Rosanne (Hager) Barbknecht
Peter, Lawrence Thomas	Joseph & Martha (Klecker) Pete
Voegele, Jeffrey John	Walter & Dorothy (Rese) Voegele
Hager, Michael Jonathan	Raymond & Shirley Ann (Dahle) Hager
Dickison, Cynthia Jo	Frederick & Carol (Zimmerman) Dickison
Kniefel, Dawn Marie	Anthony & Darlene (Rysavy) Kniefel
1963	
Larson, Dawn Rene	Robert & Joyce (Sawyer) Larson
Hager, Samuel Francis	Donald & Elizabeth (Beckman) Hager
Heim, Jeannette Luella	Bernard & Luella (Gillen) Heim
Sammon, Jodie Lynn	Joseph & Kay (Breck) Sammon
Jones, William Joseph **	William & Margie (Weber) Jones
Bruender, Lisa Marie	John & Betty (Schroeder) Bruender
Barbknecht, William John ***	Wayne & Rosanne (Hager) Barbknecht
Janes, Mark Allan	Jemes & Patricia (Mohs) Janes
Springer, Dorothy Ann	Rudolph & Deloris (Soukup) Springer
Voegele, Mark Dennis	Walter & Dorothy (Rese) Voegele
Kniefel, John Scott	Anthony & Darlene (Rysavy) Kniefel
Hager, Robert Edward	Raymond & Shirley Ann (Dahle) Hager
*Convert, age 21 ** Baptised at FBO hospital (Mountain) *** Lived one day.*	

CORPUS CHRIST BAPTISMS

1964	
Hurt, Kathleen Cheryl	Paul & Sharon (Josephia) Hurt
Peterson, Kimberly Joan	DuLloyd & Elizabeth (Kubat) Peterson
Bruender, Christine Ann	John & Betty (Schroeder) Bruender
Pete, Janice Marie	Joseph & Martha (Klecker) Pete
Barbknecht, James Edward	Wayne & Rosanne (Hager) Barbknecht
Morgan, Daniel Thomas	Donald & Dorothy (Bakken) Morgan
Larson, Charles Adolph	George & Jean (Thiele) Larson
1965	
Jones, Carol Marie	William & Margie (Weber) Jones
Larson, Michelle Anne	Robert & Joyce (Sawyer) Larson
Mork, Joshua Kenneth	Kenneth & Donna (Bokinger) Mork
Frederick, Melissa Marie	James & Mary (Cassen) Frederick
Morgan, Darla Mary	Donald & Dorothy (Bakken) Morgan
1966	
Hoffman, Troy Alan	LeRoy & Carolyn (Brady) Hoffman
Kuntz, Mary Diane	Ernest & Rita (O'Brien) Kuntz
Hager, Tonette Marie	Neil & Donna (Kratt) Hager
Redman, Lavonne Katherine	Donald & Susan (Hager) Redman
Pelant, James John	John & Judith (Wesby) Pelant
Dulas, John Jacob	Sylvester & Jacqueline (Beckel) Dulas
Pirkl, Kristine Ann	Harlow & Joanne (Wencl) Pirkl
1967	
Condon, Roxanne Louise *	Sylvester & Ethel (Schneider) Condon
Condon, Patricia Lynn **	Sylvester & Ethel (Schneider) Condon
Condon, Jacqueline Yvonne ***	Sylvester & Ethel (Schneider) Condon
Condon, Brian Allan ****	Sylvester & Ethel (Schneider) Condon
Condon, Kimberly Marie *****	Sylvester & Ethel (Schneider) Condon
Condon, Ethel Jean ******	Louis & Dorothy (Hobein) Schneider
Mork, Megan Marie ********	Kenneth & Donna (Bollinger) Mork
Pete, Amy Marie	Joseph & Martha (Klecker) Pete
Larson, Tina Jean	George & Jean (Thiele) Larson
Mork, Jonas Bryan	Kenneth & Donna (Bollinger) Mork
* Age 7, Convert; ** Age 6, Convert ***Age 5, Convert **** Age, 2, Convert ***** Age 1, Convert Donald & Dorothy Morgan Sponsors	
****** Infant, lived one day.	

CORPUS CHRIST BAPTISMS

1968	
O'Neil, Dennis George	David & Marcella (Hart) O'Neil
1969	
Sutlief, Patrick John	David Wm & Sandra (Hager) Sutlief
Larson, Catherine Lynne	Robert & Joyce (Sawyer) Larson
Cole, James Scott	James A & Candace (MullenMaster) Cole
1970	
Miller, Betty JoAnn	Ronald & Sally (Haefs) Miller
Mlenek, Amy Marie	Lyle D. & Shirley Ann (Miller) Mlenek
Holmquist, Chad Eric	LeeAnn Holmquist
Quimby, Suzanne Lee *	Carl & Ethel (Fraska) Quimby
Lange, Noel Kent **	Earl & Earleen (Zaiser) Lange
Miller, Sally Lee (Haefs) ***	Alvin & Ruby (Mal) Haefs
Mlenek, Lyle David ****	Frank & Opal (Schwanke) Mlenek
Brown, John W *****	Russell & Irene (Suder) Brown
Brown, Betty Josephine	John W. & Susan (Schweisthal) Brown
Miller, Keith Ronald	Ronald & Sally (Haefs) Miller
1971	
Eustice, Monica Jo	Donald & Cynthia Kaye (Clark) Eustice
Larson, David Robert	Robert & Joyce (Sawyer) Larson
Lang, Shaun Joseph	James W. & Mary (Pete) Lang
1972	
Condon, Vickie Kay	Sylvester & Ethel (Schneider) Condon
Miller, Karen Ann	Ronald & Sally (Haefs) Miller
Sutlief, Joene Kay	David Wm & Sandra (Hager) Sutlief
Hager, Rondol Wayne	Eugene M & Christine F. (Anderson) Hager
VonRuden, Bradley Eugene	Eugene & Kathryn (Thurnau) VonRuden
Mlenek, Conny Alice	Lyle D. & Shirley Ann (Miller)Mlenek
Sammon, Jason Charles	Aldon & Diane (Morgan) Sammon
Wieczoreak, Joseph Michael	George & Sharon (Peterson) Wieczoreak
Brown, John Russell	John W. & Susan (Schweisthal) Brown
1973	
Eustice, Marsha Jane	Donald & Cynthia Kaye (Clark) Eustice
Condon, Valerie Ann	Donald & Carolyn (Barydis) Condon
Nelson, Matthew David	David & Lois (Heim) Nelson

* Baptized Lutheran, Convert Profession of faith 7/1/1970; Married Robert Wm Klukas

** Baptized Lutheran, Convert Profession of faith 6/6/1970; Married Edith Brady

*** Baptized Lutheran, Convert Profession of faith 6/4/1970; Married Ronald Miller

**** Baptized Lutheran, Convert Profession of faith 6/4/1970; Married Shirley Miller

***** Baptized Methodist, Convert Profession of Faith 6/5/70; Married Susan Schweisthal

CORPUS CHRIST BAPTISMS (1974-1981)

1974		
	Sutlief, Bernadette Ann	David William & Sandra (Hager) Sutlief
	Dulas, Judy Maria	Sylvester & Jacqueline (Beckel) Dulas
	Hager, Mark Joseph	Dennis & Rebekah (Kratt) Hager
	Brown, Tanny Rose Ann	John W. & Susan (Schweisthal) Brown
	Sammon, Steven Aldon	Aldon & Diane (Morgan) Sammon
1975		
	Goettl, Amy Ann	James & Terri (Sikel) Goettl
	Dulas, Jay Sylvester	Sylvester & Jacqueline (Beckel) Dulas
1976		
	VonRuden, Bernard Matthew	Eugene & Kathryn (Thurnau) VonRuden
	Thom, Melissa Ann	Michael & Sandra (Distad) Thom
1977		
1/1/77	Nelson, Sara Marie	David Nelson, Lois Heim
1/9/77	Condon, Merry Kris	Donald Condon, Carolyn Barzdis
2/5/77	Voegele, Mark Albert	Robert Voegele, Sharon Kari
2/5/77	Voegele, Clarence John	Robert Voegele, Sharon Kari
9/11/77	Dulas, Joel Thomas	Sylvester Dulas, Jacqueline Beckel
1978		
3/11/78	Sutlief, Brian David	David W Sutlief, Sandra T Hager
4/30/78	Brady, Erin Marie	Byron P Brady, Carla T Maas
5/28/78	Jewison, Preston Joseph	Timothy J Jewison, Holly Barbknecht
10/1/78	Karsten, Jason Charles	Charles F Karsten, Kimberly J Mielke
1979		
1/13/79	Gillis, Jason Paul	Paul Gillis, Jean Marie Langeslag
2/10/79	Redman, Nicholas John	Donald Redman, Susie Hager
2/18/79	Morgan, Jessica Lynn	Dennis J Morgan, Debra Clarice Kosanda
5/6/79	Brady, Byron Francis	Byron P Brady, Carla T Maas
9/8/79	Frederick, Jessica Lynne	Roberta Frederick
1980		
7/13/80	Brady, Moggie Ellen	Byron P Brady, Carla T Maas
7/13/80	Condon, Gregory Daniel	Donald Condon, Carolyn Barzdis
11/1/80	Larson, Matthew Lawrence	George Larson, Jean Thiele
1981		
1/31/81	Morgan, Dustin Leo	Dennis J Morgan, Debra Clarice Kosanda
2/22/81	Karsten, Brandon Joseph	Charles F Karsten, Kimberly J Mielke
5/10/81	Jewison, Garrett Bernhardt	Timothy J Jewison, Holly Barbknecht
11/1/81	Condon, Jeffrey Paul	Donald Condon, Carolyn Barzdis

CORPUS CHRIST BAPTISMS (1982-1991)

1982		
1/31/82	Brady, Emerson Paul	Byron P Brady, Carla T Maas
1983		
8/21/83	Brady, Janine Melissa	James A Brady, Judy J Spinler
9/25/83	Brady, Brent Charles	Patrick Brady, Connie Schmidt
9/25/83	Jewison, Shawn Marie	Timothy J Jewison, Holly Barbknecht
1984		
2/19/84	Brady, Cherisse Marie	Dennis Brady, Theresa VonRuden
4/29/84	Karsten, Trisha Mae Marie	Charles F Karsten, Kimberly J Mielke
8/19/84	O'Connor, Neil Christopher	Byron T O'Connor, Linda K Caron
9/8/84	Morgan, Randi Mae	Dennis J Morgan, Debra C Kosanda
10/7/84	Brady, Jennifer Lynn	James A Brady, Judy J Spinler
10/28/84	Brady, Anna Rose	Byron P Brady, Carla T Maas
11/18/84	Kuhlman, Mitch Gaylord	Timothy P Kuhlman, Joan R Keller
1985		
13/24/1985	Brady, Marissa Katherine	Patrick Brady, Connie Schmidt
1986		
4/20/86	O'Connor, Kate Mackenzie	Byron O'Connor, Linda Caron O'Connor
5/3/86	Hager, Alyse Marie	Richard Hager, Laura Gillis Hager
9/20/86	Brady, Jessica Juliana	James Brady, Judy Spinler Brady
1987		
2/1/87	Brady, Kristin Marie	Patrick Brady & Connie Schmidt
2/21/87	Mork, Ashley Marie	Megan Mork
2/14/87	Pete, Cassandra Marie	Francis Pete, Vicky Tesch
1988		
4/23/88	Hager, Wesley	Richard Hager, Laura Gillis Hager
7/17/88	O'Connor, Cailin	Byron O'Connor, Linda Caron O'Connor
8/20/88	Morgan, Cody	Dennis J Morgan, Debra Kosanda Morgan
1989		
2/29/89	Brady, Brandon	Patrick Brady & Connie Schmidt
1990		
3/31/90	O'Connor, Orion Glynn	Byron T O'Connor, Linda Caron O'Connor
1991		
6/30/91	Brady, Jordon Evelyn	James A Brady, Judy Spinler
8/25/91	Hellevik, Justin	Brian Hellevik, Amy (Pete) Hellevik

CORPUS CHRIST BAPTISMS (1992-2005)

1992		
7/26/92	O'Connor, Alyssa	Byron T O'Connor, Linda Caron O'Connor
1993		
2/21/93	Hellevik, Emma Bernice	Brian Hellevik, Amy (Pete) Hellevik
2/28/93	Gillis, John Paul	Richard Gillis , Kathryn Cassels
	Taddei, Nicole Suzanne	Dee Maas
1994		
11/20/94	Morgan, Nicole	Daniel Morgan, Donna Trnka Morgan
1995		
4/23/95	O'Connor, Sara McKenna	Byron T O'Connor, Linda Caron O'Connor
10/22/95	Hanson, Brandon	Thomas Hanson, Brenda Manderfeld
1996		
1/28/96	Holmquist, Kristine Marie	Ron Thomburg II, Jennifer Holmquist
9/1/96	Berg, Mariah Cary	Cary Berg, Jacqueline Sexton Berg
10/27/96	Hellevik, Jacob Brian	Brian Hellevik, Amy (Pete) Hellevik
1997		
7/13/97	O'Connor, Quinn Thomas	Byron T O'Connor, Linda Caron O'Connor
7/13/97	Holmquist, Tylor Victor	Ron Thomburg II, Jennifer Holmquist
1998		
11/29/98	Morgan, Danielle Rose	Daniel Morgan, Donna Trnka Morgan
1999		
10/2/99	Berg, Brody Wayne	Cary Wayne Berg, Jacqueline Sexton
2000		
4/2/00	Gillis, Ian Richard	Richard Gillis, Dee Maas
8/13/00	Hanson, Beth Ann Marie	Thomas Hanson, Brenda Manderfeld
2001		
7/15/01	Gillis, Meredith Frances	Richard Gillis, Dee Maas
2002		
5/18/02	Reuvers, Isabel Ceceil	Jay Reuvers, Jackie Gillis
11/23/02	Berg, Jenna Marie	Cary Wayne Berg, Jacqueline Sexton
2003		
9/14/03	O'Connor, Brianna Claire	Byron T O'Connor, Linda Caron O'Connor
10/12/03	Larson, Lynn Margerite	Tim Larson, Joanne Stene Larson
2005		
12/3/05	Brady, Carsyn Beth	Byron F. Brady, Elizabeth Peterson

CORPUS CHRIST BAPTISMS (2006-2014)

2006		
6/18/06	Dulas, Charles David	Joel Dulas, Rhynda Simonson
7/22/06	Reuvers, Zachary David	Jay Reuvers, Jackie Gillis
7/22/06	Reuvers, Isaac Paul	Jay Reuvers, Jackie Gillis
2007		
9/16/07	Brady, Giakobe David	Justin Parker, Marissa Brady
3/16/08	Martin, Laura Kay	William Martin, Vida Clickner
8/17/08	Dulas, Samuel Sylvester	Joel Dulas, Rhynda Simonson
11/28/08	Schmidt, Crosby Ray	Douglas Schmidt, Theresa Lang
2009		
2/1/09	Brady, Jules Ellen	Byron F Brady, Laura Kay Martin
2/7/09	Evans, Luke Francis	Jacob Evans, Moggie Brady
3/8/09	Schimek, Zachary Frederick	Randy J Schimek, Traci Hyatt
11/15/09	Brady, Taylor Elizabeth	Byron F Brady, Laura Kay Martin
7/11/10	Dulas, Jacob Thomas	Joel Dulas, Rhynda Simonson
2011		
4/11/11	Schmidt, Tanner Lang	Douglas Schmidt, Theresa Lang
2012		
2/19/12	Hager, Henry Richard	Bradley Hager, Janice Green
3/25/12	Mares, Averie Lynn	Jeffrey Mares, Anna R Brad;y
2014		
7/27/14	Hager William Paul	Bradley Hager, Janice Green
8/31/14	Mares, Declan Brady	Jeffrey Mares, Anna R Brady

Fr. Joe Pete with Justin Hellevik (Aug. 25, 1991)

Jules Brady Baptism (Feb. 1, 2009) w. Fr. Haberman

235

Corpus Christi First Communion Class (1938)
Raymond McGuire, Harlow Pirkl, Sylvester Condon, Richard Paquin, Yvonne Sammon, Barbara Jones, Joan Chambers. Father Raymond Snyder at back.

Corpus Christi First Communion Class (1943)
Homer Guimond is at the very far right. All others including the priest are not identified.
Photo submitted by Dorothy Hruska, Claremont, Minnesota.

FIRST HOLY COMMUNION

	Communicant	
1944	Gertrude Furr	8
	Rita Gillis	7
	Paul Hurt	8
	Neil Hager	8
	Bernard Kavitz	13
	Elizabeth Jane Ness	7
	Marjorie Ness	9
	John Sammon	8
	Charles Stangler	7
	Patricia Hoffman	
5/19/45	Paul Gillis	
	Gerald Kerrons	
	Marlys Kerrons	
	Eileen Sammon	
	Laurence Sammon	
	Roger Sammon	
	Patrick Voegele	
	Donald Hager	
5/4/46	Carol Hoffman	7
	Duane Lorenz	7
	Patricia Ann Mohs	6
	Leo Mullenmaster	6
	Albert Thomas O'Brien	6
	Henry Hankens	7
4/20/47	Anna Marie Le Mieux	6
	Raymond Chavie	9
	Raymond Leonard Sammon	8
	Ramona Anna Klebel	9
	Marg. Joan Langworthy	9
	Harvard Earl Nicholas Weber	8
	Joseph Sammon	
	Gerald Androli	8
	Yvonne Hoffman	

	Communicant	
5/2/48	David Hager	9
	Robert Klebel	8
	William Kvasniscka	7
	Laurence Langworthy	8
	Robert Larson	7
	Collette Rita Mullenmaster	7
	Laurence Paquette	7
4/17/49	Louis Stephen Hager	8
	Raymond Berthold Mohs	7
	Mary Jeanette Gostomczik	7
	Thomas Arthur Paquette	8
	Joseph George Langworthy	8
	Joseph Eugene Langworthy	7
4/29/50	Richard Allen Cole	7
	Dennis Joseph Hager	8
	Helen Pauline Hurt	7
	Alfred Joseph Judd	8
	Doris Marie Krenik	8
	Ann Marie Mullenmaster	7
	Clarence Gilbert Sammon	8
	Donald Elmer Mohs	7
	Howard Voegele	7
4/14/51	Rosanne Hager	8
	Paul Tobin	7
	Margaret (Peggy) Voegele	7
	Marjorie Weber	8
6/22/52	Douglas Bock	7
	Sharon Brady	8
	Paul Hager	8
	Harlan Holmquist	8
	Stephen Judd	8
	James William Lang	7
	Mary Mullenmaster	8
	Jerome Nusbaum	7
	Rose Mary Pirkl	8
	Henry Reyant	8

FIRST HOLY COMMUNION

	Communicant	Age			Communicant	Age
6/14/53	Carolyn Marie Brady	8		6/8/58	Jean Bergee	7
	Ronald Eustice	7			Kathleen Brady	8
	LeRoy Hoffman	8			Marjorie Eustice	8
	Kathleen Hurt	8			Philip Heim	8
	William Mullenmaster	7			James Klukas	8
	Katherine Stirens	8			Colleen Mullenmaster	8
	Evelyn Elsner	8			Joseph Pete	8
					Catherine Phillips	8
6/13/54	Daniel Carmichael	8			Catherine Tuve	8
	Barbara Jean Condon	8				
	Robert Eustice	8		5/24/59	Mark Condon	8
	Eugene Hager	8			Darlene Marie Dahle	8
	Glenn Miller	8			Dayle Ann Hager	7
	Janet Mohs	8			(Lloyd) Bernard Paul Heim	7
	John Webbe	9			Linda Holmquist	7
					Terrence Adolph Jewison	7
6/12/55	Constance Bock	7			Timothy Joseph Jewison	7
	Patrick Brady	7			Janine Ann Miller	7
	Donald Eustice	7			Diane Morgan	8
	Susan Hager	7			Elaine Mullenmaster	7
	Lawrence Mullenmaster	7			Richard Springer	8
	Michael Phillips	7				
	Dennis Voegele	7		5/8/60	Byron Paul Brady	8
	Robert Webber	8			Daniel Dahle	8
					Kay Morgan	7
6/10/56	James Cole	7			Carol Phillips	7
	Constance Hurt	7				
	Paul Kavitz	7		3/30/61	Joanne Heim	7
	Robert Klukas	7			Donna Morgan	7
	LeAnn Holmquist	7			Gregory Mullenmaster	8
	Candace Mullenmaster	7			Craig Hager	8
	Linda Phillips	7			Dale Kavitz	7
					Carol Phillips	8
6/9/57	Edith Brady	7				
	Nancy Dickison	8		4/19/62	Mary Brady	8
	Sandra Hager	7			Gary Holmquist	7
	Dale Miller	7			Monica Mullenmaster	7
	Mary Pete	8			Robert Pete	8
	Jane Phillips	7			Diane Springer	8

The First Communion Class in 1945 with Fr. Snyder in the background and the two Dominican Sisters. The boy in front of sisters, almost hidden is Lawrence Sammon, who became Corpus Christi's first priest. Others pictured are Paul Gillis, Gerald and Marlys Kerrons, Eileen and Roger Sammon, Patrick Voegele and Donald Hager.

Leo Mullemaster First Communion (May 4, 1946).
Pictured with Fr. Raymond Snyder in back are Leo Mullenmaster Sr., Leo Mullenmaster Jr., William Mullenmaster.

David Hager First Communion
(May 2, 1948)

First Communion Class (June 22, 1952)
Back Row: L-R: Mary Mullenmaster, Rosemary Pirkl, Paul Hager, Henry Reyant, James Lang.
Front Row, L-R; Sharon Brady, Harlan Holmquist, Douglas Bock, Jerry Nussbaum. Missing: Stephen Judd.

First Communion Class (June 14, 1953)
Front, l-R: William Mullenmaster, Carolyn Brady, Kathleen Hurt, Evelyn Elsner, Ronald Eustice.
Back Row: Fr. Harold Mountain, Katherine Stirens, Dominican Sister, LeRoy Hoffman.

First Holy Communion is considered one of the holiest and most important occasions in our lives because it is the first time that we receive the Sacrament of the Holy Eucharist. The Holy Eucharist refers to Christ's body, blood, soul and divinity – truly present in the consecrated bread and wine. Most Catholic children receive their First Holy Communion when they are 7 or 8 years old as this is considered the age of reason.

Corpus Christi

Let's Look Back . . .

The First Communion Suit

Anna Hager's Uncle John and Aunt Albertina (Liebing) Wesley had five sons - Roland, Robert, Claire, Albert and William. All five wore the same white shirt and white pants for their First Holy Communion in Elysian, Minnesota. Aunt Albertina then gave the shirt and pants to Anna and Henry Hager. All of their sons also wore the same outfit for their First Holy Communion. John's First Communion was at Holy Trinity Church in Wateville, Minnesota in 1942. He received the sacrament from Father McCormack. After moving to Blooming Grove Township in Waseca County, the family attended Corpus Christi Church in Deerfield Township in Steele County. Neil (1944), Donald (1945), David (1946), Louis (1949), Dennis (1950), and Paul (1952) received the sacrament from Father Snyder. Father Mountain preformed the sacrament for Gene in 1954.

John - 1942

Neil - 1944

Donald - 1945

David - 1946

Gene - 1954

Neil, John, Donald, David
Louis, Dennis and Paul

Gene - 1954

From the Henry & Anna Hager Annual Family Newsletter
Note: First Communion photos were not available for Louis, Dennis and Paul Hager.

Corpus Christi First Communion, June 13, 1954
Front Row, L-R: Barbara Jean Condon, Glenn Miller, Janet Mohs. Back Row: Dominican Sister, John Webb,
Robert Eustice, Eugene Hager, Daniel Carmichael, Fr. Harold Mountain

Corpus Christi First Communion Class June 12, 1955
Front Row, L-R: Donald Eustice, Dennis Voegele, Larry Mullenmaster, Patrick Brady.
Back Row: Robert Weber, Connie Bock, Susan Hager, Michael Phillips

First Communion (June 10, 1956)
Front Row, L-R: Connie Hurt, Linda Phillips, Candace Mullenmaster, LeeAnn Holmquist.
Second Row: James Cole, Paul Kavitz, Robert Klukas.
Back Row: Fr. Harold B. Mountain and Dominican Sister.

Corpus Christi First Communion Class (May 24, 1957)
Front Row, L-R: Sandra Hager, Nancy Dickison, Dale Miller, Edith Brady, Mary Pete.

Corpus Christi First Communion Class (June 8, 1958)
Back Row: Marjorie Eustice, Philip Heim, James Klukas, Joseph Pete, Coleen Mullenmaster.
Front, L-R: Catherine Phillips, Jean Burgee, Kathleen Brady, Catherine Tuve.

Corpus Christi First Communion Class (May 24, 1959)
Front Row, L-R: Richard Springer, Timothy Jewison, Terry Jewison, Lloyd Heim, Mark Condon.
Back Row; Janeen Miller, Elaine Mullenmaster, Linda Holmquist, Dayle Ann Hager, Darlene Dahle, Diane Sammon
(face hidden).

245

Corpus Christi First Communion Class (1960)
Dominican Sister, Daniel Dahle, Kaylynn Morgan, Carol Phillips, Byron Paul Brady, Father H. Mountain.

Corpus Christi First Communion (June 1963).
Back Row: Robin Kavitz, Barbara Dahle, Debra Hager, Rosemary Heim.
Front: Charles Condon, Thomas Mullenmaster

Corpus Christi First Communion (June 1964).
Front Row: Daniel Filan, Brian Mullenmaster, Mary Jo Condon, Susan Dahle.
Back Row: Michael Pete, Charles Karsten, Pamela Peterson. In the back; Sister Luella.

Corpus Christi First Communion Class (1987)
Front, L-R: Nicolas Redman, Jason Gillis, Byron F
Brady, Jessica Morgan, Fr. Edward Mountain.

Corpus Christi First Communion Class (1975)
Front, L-R: Julie Hurst, Amy Pete, Megan Mork. Back;
Jerry Redman, John Dulas, Fr. Glynn, Sister Delores.

FIRST HOLY COMMUNION

	Communicant	Age
12/1962	Debra Hager	7
	Rosemary Heim	7
	Thomas Mullenmaster	7
	Robin Kavitz	7
	Communicant	**Age**
5/12/63	Charles Condon	8
	Barbara Dahle	9
	Communicant	**Age**
1964	Mary Jo Condon	7
	Susan Dahle	8
	Daniel Filan	7
	Charles Karsten	8
	Brian Mullenmaster	7
	Pamela Peterson	8
	Michael Pete	7
	Theresa Phillips	8
	Randy Springer	8
	Joyceann Dulas	7
	Roxanne Kniefel	7
	Mark Mullenmaster	7
	Monica Pete	7
	John Webbe	9
	Communicant	**Age**
1965	Dennis Brady	7
	Timmy Hager	7
	Dennis Morgan	7
	Communicant	**Age**
11/20/66	Leslie Scott Condon	7
	Tamara Irene Hager	7
	Patrick Joseph Heim	7
	Julie Ann Kuntz	7
	Marlys Mary Miller	7
	Maurice James Mullenmaster	7
	Rosemary Alice Phillips	7
	Curtis Frederick	7

	Communicant	Age
12/10/67	Victoria Frederick	7
	Cynthia Heim	7
	Wayne Karsten	7
	Scott Mullenmaster	7
	Francis Pete	8
	Communicant	**Age**
4/20/69	Charles Brady	8
	Patricia Condon	8
	Timothy Larson	8
	Douglas Morgan	7
	Lori Karsten	7
	Roberta Frederick	7
	Lori Karsten	7
	Communicant	**Age**
4/26/70	James Brady	
	Jacqueline Condon	
	Shareen Kuntz	7
	Richard Larson	
	Lawrence Pete	
	Debra Pirkl	
	Micke Pfeifer	7
	Jeff Voegele	7
	David Wenker	8
	Communicant	**Age**
4/25/71	Perry Frederick	8
	Jeanette Heim	8
	Dawn Kniefel	8
	Dawn Larson	8
	Mindy Hurst	8
	Communicant	**Age**
4/16/72	Brian Condon	7
	Penelope Frederick	8
	Daniel Hurst	8
	John Kniefel	8
	Janice Pete	7
	Kimberly Peterson	8
	Tim Pfeifer	8
	Mark Voegele	8
	Rhonda Wenker	8

FIRST HOLY COMMUNION

	Communicant	
4/8/73	Melissa Frederick	8
	Carmen Kuntz	8
	Charles Larson	8
	Michelle Larson	8
	Daniel Morgan	8
	Joshua Mork	8

	Communicant	Age
1974	Kimberly Condon	8
	Darla Morgan	8
	Mary Kuntz	8
	LaVonne Redman	7
	Tony Hager	7

	Communicant	
1975	Pete, Amy Marie	
	Mork, Megan Marie	
	Julie Hurst	
	John Dulas	
	Jerry Redman	

	Communicant	
1976	Larson, Trina	
	Mork, Jonas Bryan	

	Communicant	
4/7/77	Lori Hurst	
	Catherin Lynne Larson	
	Lori Hurst	

	Communicant	
4/16/78	Michael Nelson	
	Lynn Sehnert	
	Kari Sehnert	

	Communicant	Age
4/27/80	Patrick Condon	
	Vickie Condon	8
	Jason Sammon	7
	Angie Thom	
	Shane Thom	
	Brad Von Ruden	7

	Communicant	
4/ 26/1981	Valerie Condon	7
	Matthew Nelson	7
	Carrie Redman	7

	Communicant	
1982	Dulas, Judy	8

	Communicant	
1984	Dulas, Jay	

	Communicant	
4/26/70	Sara Nelson	

	Communicant	
1986	Brady, Erin	7
	Dulas, Joel	
	Jewison, Preston	
	O'Connor, Shaun	

	Communicant	
1987	Gillis, Jason	7
	Redman, Nicholas	8
	Morgan, Jessica	
	Brady, Byron F.	

	Communicant	
1988	Holmquist, Jeff	9
	Brady, Moggie	
	O'Connor Tara	7
	Turner, Jessica	

	Communicant	
1989	Jewison, Garett	8
	Larson, Matthew	8
	Morgan, Dustin	

	Communicant	
1990	Brady, Emerson	
	Kuhlman, Blaine	

	Communicant	
1991	Brady, Janine Melissa	
	Hager, Brad Richard	
	Brady, Brent	
	Sontheimer, Brian	
	Stadler, Mary	

Corpus Christi First Communion Class (1989)
L-R; Matt Larson, Garrett Jewison, Dustin Morgan, with Fr. Edward Mountain.

FIRST HOLY COMMUNION

	Communicant
1992	Brady, Cherisse Marie
	Morgan, Randi Mae
	Jewison, Shawn Marie
	Communicant
1993	Brady, Jennifer
	Brady, Anna
	Kuhlman, Mitchell
	O'Connor, Neil
	Stadler, Mindy
	Communicant
1994	Brady, Jessica
	O'Connor Kate
	Hager Alyse
	Pete, Francis
	Communicant
1995	Pete, Cassandra
	Communicant
1996	Hager, Wesley
	Mork, Ashley
	O'Connor, Caitlin
	Stadler, Megan
	Communicant
1998	Morgan, Tyler
	O'Connor, Orion
	Communicant
1999	Brady, Jordan
	Taddei, Monica
	Communicant
2000	Hellevik, Justin
	Communicant
2002	Larson, Daniel
	Communicant
2003	Hanson, Brandon
	O'Connor, Sara
	Morgan, Nicole
	Communicant
2004	Berg, Cary Wayne (adult)
	Berg, Mariah
	Schimek, Miranda
	Simonson, Rhynda Jane (adult)

	Communicant
2005	Hellevik, Jacob
	Larson, Mariah
	O'Connor Quinn
	Communicant
2006	DeWolfe-Gillis, Madison
	Communicant
2007	Larson, Holly Arlene
	Morgan, Danielle Rose
	Sontheimer, Brian Paul
	Communicant
2008	Berg, Brody Wayne
	Gillis, Ian Richard
	Hanson, Beth Ann
	Martin-Brady, Isabel Kay
	Communicant
2009	Gillis, Meredith Frances
	List, Devan Gregory
	Schimek, Hannah Christine
	Schimek, Isaiah Nicholas
	Communicant
2010	Reuvers, Isabel Ceceil
	List, Reily Owen
	Communicant
2011	Berg, Jenna Marie
	O'Connor, Brianne Claire
	Communicant
2012	Larson, Lynn
	Communicant
2014	Brady, Carsyn Beth
	Reuvers, Isaac Paul
	Reuvers, Zachary David
	Schimek, Zach
	Final First Communion at Corpus Christi Parish
	Communicant
5/7/17	Jules Ellen Brady
	Communicant
5/6/18	Taylor Elizabeth Brady

FIRST HOLY COMMUNION CLASSES (1986-1999)

Corpus Christi First Communion Class (1986)
Preston Jewison, Joel Dulas, Shaun O'Connor, Erin Brady

Corpus Christi First Communion Class (1996)
Megan Stadler and Ashley Mork

Corpus Christi First Communion Class (1991)
L-R: Brad Hager, Mary Stadler, Brent Brady, Janine Brady,
Brian Sontheimer, Back: Janis Simon, Fr. Ernster, Patti Wencl

Corpus Christi First Communion Class (1998)
Front, L-R: Martha Arnold, Orion O'Connor;
Tyler Morgan; Janice Simon, Father Herman.

Corpus Christi First Communion Class (1999)
Janice Simon, Jordan Brady, Monica Taddei, Martha Arnold.

FIRST HOLY COMMUNION CLASSES (1993-2000s)

Corpus Christi First Communion (May 2, 1993)
Back Row, L-R: Anna Brady, Mindy Stadler, Jennifer
Brady. Front: Mitch Kuhlman and Neil O'Connor.

Corpus Christi First Communion Class (May 4, 2008)
Front, L-R: Brody Berg, Ian Gillis, Isabel Martin, Beth Ann
Hanson. Back: Deb Sontheimer & Martha Arnold.

Corpus Christi First Communion Class (2005)
Quinn O'Connor, Jacob Hellevik, Mariah Larson.

First Communion (2006)
Madison DeWolfe Gillis with Fr. Herman

First Communion (2010)
Isabel Reuvers and Reily List

CONFIRMATION

Communicant Name	Age	Confirmation Name		Communicant Name	Age	Confirmation Name
July 3, 1944				1949		
Gillis, Patricia	13	Bernadette		Stearns, Marion	13	Sarah
Hager, John	10	Anthony		Larson, Josephine Anne	13	Marie
Hallinger, Dorothy	12	Cecilia		Hoffmann, Patricia	12	Magdalen
Kerrins, Nordine	12	Rose		Hager, Neil	13	Albert
Kerrins, Robert	13	Charles		Sammon, Lawrence	11	Patrick
Kniefel, Anthony	10	Cletus		Hurt, Paul	12	Francis
Maleska, Roman	11	Anthony		Hurt, Genevieve	11	Anne
Nusbaum, David	13	George		Reyant, Frank	12	Theodore
Nusbaum, Donald	11	James		Ness, Elizabeth	11	Frances
O'Brien, Grace	11	Ann		Ness, Marjorie	13	Josephine
O'Brien, Patricia	12	Theresa		Larson, George	11	Richard
Pirkl, Harlow	13	Louis		Voegele, Patrick	11	Peter
Pirkl, Raymond	11	Joseph		Hager, Donald	11	William
Sammon, Eugene	10	Christopher		Mohs, Patricia	9	Bernadette
Sammon, Joseph	11	Joseph		Larson, Mr. Adolph	44	John
Sammon, Patricia	10	Mary		Androli, Mrs. Mable		Mary
Sammon, William	11	Francis		Whitesk, Mrs.Adema		Mary
Syzmanski, Robert	11	John				
Vogele, Walter	10	Peter				
Sammon, Richard	10	Francis				
Holmquist, Bernard	33	Henry				
Gasner, Margaret	24	Ellen				
Morgan, Dorothy	22	Bernadine				
Nusbaum, Shirley	20	Louise				
Klinkhammer, Jane	19	Bernadette				

Administered by Bishop Leo Binz, D.D.

Administered by Bishop Leo Binz, D.D.

Confirmation is one of the sacraments of the Catholic Church. Together with Baptism and the Eucharist, it constitutes the set of "the sacraments of Christian initiation," that is, sacraments whose reception is necessary for the fullness of the grace we receive in Baptism.

Leo Binz, Co-adjutor Bishop (1942-1949)

CONFIRMATION

1952				1955		
Communicant Name	**Age**	**Confirmation Name**		**Communicant Name**	**Age**	**Confirmation Name**
Hurt, Pauline	9	Marie		Bock, Douglas		Robert
Hurt, JoAnne	12	Catherine		Condon, James		Leo
Krenik, Doris	11	Rita		Eustice, Ronald	10	Stephen
Le Mieux, Anna Marie	12	Leona		Hager, Paul	11	Peter
Hoffmann, La Vonne	12	Elizabeth		Hoffman, Leroy	10	John
Hoffmann, Carol	13	Constance		Holmquist, Harlan	11	Ernest
Mullenmaster, Collette	12	Kathleen		Lang, William	10	Joseph
Mullenmaster, Anne Marie	10			Mullenmaster, William	10	Leo
Hurt, Agnes	13	Rita		Reyant, Henry		Henry
Kvasnicka, William	11	James		Brady, Caroline	10	Ann
Hager, Louis	11	Peter		Brady, Sharon	11	Maria
Hager, Dennis	10	Patrick		Hager, Rosanne	12	Theresa
Hager, David	13	Thomas		Hurt, Kathleen		Christine
Cole, Richard	10	Edward		Mohs, Janet	9	Ann
Larson, Robert	12	Michael		Mullenmaster, Mary	11	Ann
Voegel, Howard	10	John		Pirkl, Rosemarie	11	Lucille
Mohs, Bert	11	John		Voegele, Margaret		Mary
Mohs, Donald	9	Patrick		Weber, Marjorie		Mary
Sammon, Clarence	10	Joseph		Davis, Donald		Joseph
Sammon, Joseph	13					
Mullenmaster, Leo		John				
Condon, Sylvester		Patrick				
Mork, Donna		Michaele				
Morgan, Dorothy						

Administered by Bishop Edward A. FitzGerald (1955 column)

Administered by Bishop Edward A. FitzGerald (1952 column)

Bishop Edward FitzGerald and Fr. Harold Mountain with Corpus Christi Confirmation Class (November 3, 1955).

Most Reverend Edward A. FitzGerald

CONFIRMATION

1958		
Communicant Name	**Age**	**Confirmation Name**
Brady, Patrick	10	Brian
Cole, James	10	Joseph
Eustice, Donald	10	Joseph
Eustice, Robert	11	Mark
Hager, Gene	12	John
Kavitz, Paul	9	Michael
Klukas, Robert	12	Paul
Miller, Glenn	12	Joseph
Mullenmaster, Lawrence	11	Maurice
Phillips, Michael	11	John
Condon, Barbara	12	Mary
Dickison, Nancy	10	Anne
Hager, Susan	11	Mary
Heim, Lois	11	Bernadette
Mullenmaster, Candace	9	Mary
Phillips, Linda	9	Mary
Heim, Elaine	9	Anne
Holmquist, LeAnn	10	Louise
Hager, Mrs. Neil (Donna)		Marie
Hurt, Constance	10	Marie
Voegele, Dennis	10	Gregory
Weber, Robert	11	Peter
Mork, Donna		Michaele
Morgan, Dorothy		
Shirley Hager		

Administered by Bishop Edward A. FitzGerald

1961		
Communicant Name	**Age**	**Confirmation Name**
Brady, Byron	9	James
Dahle, Danny	9	Joseph
Jewison, Terrance	10	John
Jewison, Timothy	10	Leo
Phillips, Carol	9	Marie
Condon, Mark	10	Joseph
Dahle, Darlene	10	Carol
Hager, Dayle	10	Theresa
Heim, Lloyd	10	Peter
Holmquist, Linda	10	Albina
Miller, Janeen	10	Mary
Morgan, Diane	10	Elizabeth
Mullenmaster, Elaine	10	Colette
Brady, Kathleen	11	Rose
Heim, Phillip	11	Tarcisius
Mullenmaster, Colleen	11	Mary
Pete, Joseph	11	Dominic
Phillips, Catherine	11	Marie
Tuve, Catherine	11	Edna
Klukas, James	11	Joseph
Eustice, Margie	11	Theodora
Brady, Edith	12	Bernadette
Hager, Sandra	12	Ann
Miller, Dale	12	Anthony
Pete, Mary	12	Amy
Phillips, Jane	11	Mary
Mr. Wayne Barbknecht	21	John
Mrs. John Bruender	20	Marie

Administered by Bishop Edward A. FitzGerald

CONFIRMATION (1964-1967)

1964		
Communicant Name	**Age**	**Confirmation Name**
Brady, Mary	10	Theresa
Filan, Michael	9	Joseph
Holmquist, Gary	9	Bernard
Mullenmaster, Monica	9	Ann
Pete, Robert	9	John
Phillips, Michael	9	Mathew
Springer, Diane	10	Mary
Filan, Gerianne	11	Elizabeth
Heim, JoAnne	10	Theresa
Morgan, Donna	10	Rose
Mullenmaster, Gregory	11	Leo
Hager, Craig	10	James
Kavitz, Dale	10	John
Phillips, Carol		Ruth
Peterson, Roberta		Marie
Miller, Phillip	17	Joseph

Administered by Bishop George Speltz

1967		
Communicant Name	**Age**	**Confirmation Name**
Hager, Debra	12	Marie
Heim, Rosemary	11	Maria
Kavitz, Robin E	11	Bridget
Mullenmaster, Thomas	11	William
Phillips, Theresa	12	Marie
Karsten, Charles	12	John
Kuntz, Thomas Mark	12	David
Morgan, Mary Lou	12	Theresa
Mullenmaster, Brian	10	Maurice
Pete, Michael	10	Albert
Brady, Dennis	10	Paul
Dulas, Joyceann	10	Patricia
Hager, Timothy	9	Andrew
Karsten, Curtis	10	Paul
Kniefel, Roxanne	10	Frances
Morgan, Dennis	9	John
Mullenmaster, Mark	10	Joseph
Pete, Monica	10	Veronica

Administered by Bishop Loris J. Waters

1969		
Communicant Name	**Age**	**Confirmation Name**
Peterson, Pamela	15	
Peterson, Kimberly	13	

Administered by Bishop Loris J. Waters

Most Reverend George H. Speltz

CONFIRMATION

1970		
Communicant Name	**Age**	**Confirmation Name**
Condon, Roxanne	11	Coleen
Heim, Patrick	11	Joseph
Phillips, Rosemary	11	Veronica
Wenker, Brian	11	Kenneth
Kuntz, Julie	11	Coleen
Brady, Kevin	12	Paul
Heim, Christine	12	Florence
Kniefel, Mark	12	Richard
Kuntz, Gerald	12	Leo
Morgan, Dawn	12	Catherine
Condon, Leslie		Scott
Frederick, Curtis		James
Karsten, Dennis		Michael
Miller, Marly		Mary
Wenker, Connie		Theresa
Wenker, Diane		Carol
Peterson, Elizabeth		Marie
Peterson, Pamela		Marie
Peterson, Roxanne		Victoria

Administered by Bishop Loris J. Waters

1973
Communicant Name
Heim, Cindy
Hurst, Jody
Voegele, Greg
Larson, Timothy
Morgan, Douglas
Hurst, Angela
Brady, Charles
Pete, Francis
Condon, Patricia
Hager, Terry
Frederick, Roberta
Frederick, Vicky
Karsten, Lori
Karsten, Wayne
Morgan, Pam
Morgan, Patrick

1978
Communicant Name
Condon, Brian
Frederick, Missy
Frederick, Penny
Hurst, Daniel
Kniefel, John
Kuntz, Carmen
Larson, Charles
Morgan, Daniel
Mork, Joshua
Pete, Janice
Peterson, Kimberly

Administered by Bishop Loris J. Waters

Most Reverend Loris J. Waters

CONFIRMATION (1981-1999)

June 3, 1981
Communicant Name
Redman, Jerry
Dulas, John
Hurst, Julie
Pirkl, Kristi
Mork, Megan
Pete, Amy
Morgan, Darla
Kuntz, Mary
Condon Kim
Redman, La Vonne
VonRuden, Anne
VonRuden, Thomas
Administered by *Bishop Loris J. Waters*

March 19, 1983
Frederick, Earl
Hackett, Elizabeth
Hurst, Lori
Larson, Catherine
Larson, Trina
Mork, Jonas
Valek, Charles
Administered by *Bishop Loris J. Waters*

March 23, 1985
Larson, David
Administered by *Bishop Loris J. Waters*

April 10, 1988
Communicant Name
Condon, Vicki
Nelson, Matthes
Redman, Carrie
Sammon, Jason
Sammon, Steven
Administered by *Bishop Loris J. Waters*

March 4, 1990
Communicant Name
Dulas, Judy
Administered by *Bishop Loris J. Waters*

March 7, 1992
Holmquist, Jennifer
Dulas, Jay
Administered by *Bishop Loris J. Waters*

March 3, 1993
Brady, Erin
Dulas, Joel
Jewison, Preston
Nelson, Sara
O'Connor, Shawn
Administered by *Bishop Loris J. Waters*

April 30, 1995
Gillis, Jason Paul
Redman, Nicholas John
Morgan, Jessica Lynn
Brady, Moggie
Holmquist, Jeff
O'Connor, Tara
Administered by *Bishop Loris J. Waters*

April 19, 1997
Communicant Name
Brady, Emerson
Kuhlman, Blaine
Jewison, Garett
Larson, Matthew
Morgan, Dustin
Schmitz, Matthew
Schmitz, Scott
Administered by *Bishop Loris J. Waters*

May 8, 1999
Communicant Name
Last Confirmation at Christ The King
Brady, Janine Melissa
Brady, Cherisse Marie
Morgan, Randi Mae
Jewison, Shawn Marie
Hager, Brad Richard

Administered by
Bishop Bernard Harrington
Last Confirmation at Christ
The King, Medford.

CONFIRMATION (2001-2008)

(All confirmations were at Church of St. Joseph, Owatonna).

May 10 , 2001
Communicant Name
Brady, Jennifer
Brady, Anna
Kuhlman, Mitchell
O'Connor, Neil
Administered by *Bishop Bernard Harrington*
May 17, 2002
Brady, Jessica
Hager, Alyse
O'Connor, Kate
Administered by *Bishop Bernard Harrington*
May 1, 2004
Hager, Wesley
O'Connor, Cailin
Administered by *Bishop Bernard Harrington*
April 16, 2005
Cody Morgan
Administered by *Bishop Bernard Harrington*
May 21, 2006
Morgan, Tyler
O'Connor, Orion
Administered by *Bishop Bernard Harrington*
May 4, 2007
Brady, Jordan
Taddei, Monica
Administered by *Bishop Bernard Harrington*

March 5, 2008
Communicant Name
Hellevik, Justin
O'Connor, Alyssa

Administered by
Bishop Bernard Harrington

Bishop Bernard Harrington

CONFIRMATION (2009-2024)

May 2, 2009
Communicant Name
Hellevik, Emma Bernice
Gillis, John Paul
Morgan, Chelsea Ann
Schimek, Courtney Lynn
Taddei, Nicole Suzanne
Larson, Katelyn Joanne
Administered by *Bishop John Quinn*

April 19, 2010
Larson, Daniel Timothy
Administered by *Bishop John Quinn*

May 7, 2011
Hanson, Brandon
Morgan, Nicole
O'Connor, Sara
Administered by *Bishop Bernard Harrington*

May 4, 2012
Berg, Mariah Jerome
Schimek, Miranda
Administered by *Bishop John Quinn*

April 27, 2014
Hellevik, Jacob
Larson, Mariah
O'Connor Quinn
Administered by *Bishop John Quinn*

May 15, 2015
Larson, Holly Arlene
Morgan, Sanielle Rose
Sontheimer, Brian *(Confirmed at New Richland)*
Administered by *Bishop John Quinn*

April 30, 2016
Berg, Brody Wayne
Brady, Isabel Kay
Gillis, Ian
Hanson Beth Ann

April 28, 2017
Gillis, Meredith Frances
Administered by *Bishop Bernard Harrington*

May 5, 2018
Communicant Name
List, Reilly Owen
Reuvers, Isabel Ceceil
Administered by *Bishop John Quinn*

May 18, 2019
Berg, Jenna Marie
O'Connor, Brianna Claire
Administered by *Bishop John Quinn*

October 7, 2020
Larson, Lynn Marguerite

May 23, 2021
Communicant Name
List, Adalia Kathryn
Administered by *Bishop John Quinn*

April 30, 2022
Communicant Name
Reuvers, Isaac
Reuvers, Zach
Administered by *Bishop John Quinn*

April 17, 2024
Communicant Name
Brady, Jules Ellen
Administered by *Bishop Robert Barron*

Bishop John Quinn

Bishop Robert Barron

SOME CORPUS CHRISTI MARRIAGES (EARLY)

NAME	DATE	GROOM	BRIDE	WITNESSES	PRIEST
MULLENMASTER & CROMER	Oct. 1, 1907	William Mullenmaster	Otilia Cromer	Arthur Mullenmaster & Jennie Cromer	J.J. Slevin IC; Faribault
PIRKL & O'NEILL	Nov. 23, 1920	Henry E. Pirkl	Margaret O'Neill	George O'Neill & Emma Pirkl	J. J. Slevin IC; Faribault
McGLAUGHLIN & WHEELER	Sept. 30,	Dennis McGlaughlin	Ann Wheeler	Maurice Wheeler & Jennie Mc-Laughlin	J. J. Slevin IC; Faribault
SWINTEK & BRUZANT	1938	Thomas Swintek	Margaret Bruzant		Corpus Christi
KVASNISCHKA & PELKEY	1939	Lawrence Kvasnischka	Easter Pelkey		Corpus Christi
BRADY & ELLINGSON	Feb. 24, 1942	Byron Brady	Jane Ellingson		Corpus Christi
CONDON & O'NEILL	Feb. 14, 1942	Philip Condon	Kathleen O'Neill	*Note: Per obituary. Kathleen died Nov. 17, 1999 (Dalby Database)*	
WEBB & CONDON	Oct. 20, 1942	Rudy Webb	Frances Condon	*Ancestry.com*	

Note that this is an incomplete list. We were not allowed to access records at Sacred Heart Church in Waseca where Father Raymond Snyder kept Corpus Christi records from 1938 through 1943.

Marriage of Rudy Webb & Frances Condon (October 20, 1942 at Corpus Christi)
L-R: Pat Condon, Rudy Webb, Frances Condon, Fritz Condon, Rita Condon, Agnes DeGroot, Don Morgan, Altar Boys are Bud Morgan and Harlow Pirkl. Father Snyder at far right.

CORPUS CHRISTI MARRIAGES

	Married Couple	Location	Date	Religion	Priest
1	Krueger, Ernest Morgan, Helen	Married at Sacred Heart, Waseca	2/22/44	Lutheran Catholic	Snyder
2	Kniefel, Robert Jensen, Jeanne Harriet	Married Corpus Christi, Deerfield	10/11/45	Catholic Catholic	Snyder
3	Judd, David M Pete, Clara A	Married Corpus Christi, Deerfield	5/2/46	Catholic Catholic	Snyder
4	Walters, Joseph E Chavie, Lorraine	Married Corpus Christi, Deerfield	5/17/46	Catholic Catholic	Snyder
5	Lorenz, Albert F Batou, Dorothy	Married Corpus Christi, Deerfield.	6/21/46	Catholic Catholic	Snyder
6	Walters, Lennard J Hoffelt, Marie	Married Corpus Christi, Deerfield	8/4/46	Catholic Catholic	Snyder
7	Androli, Herbert Brunken, Myrtle Emma	Married Christ The King Medford	12/21/46	Catholic Catholic	Snyder
8	Schwartz, Vernon Hager, Loretta	Married Corpus Christi, Deerfield	4/22/47	Catholic Catholic	Snyder
9	Chambers, Richard W Miller, Mary Ann	Married Corpus Christi, Deerfield	11/8/47	Catholic Catholic	Snyder
10	Wochnick, Felix John Broughten, Bonnette Jeanne	Married Corpus Christi, Deerfield	2/3/48	Catholic Catholic	Snyder
11	Feller, Bernard V Kniefel, Bernadine V	Married Corpus Christi, Deerfield	6/2/48	Catholic Catholic	Snyder
12	Morgan, Donald Bakken, Dorothy	Married Corpus Christi, Deerfield	8/16/50	Catholic Catholic	Snyder
13	Nusbaum, David Kelmer, Arline	Married Corpus Christi, Deerfield	6/2/51	Catholic Catholic	Snyder
14	Kaderlick, Ervin J Sammon, Yvonne	Married Corpus Christi, Deerfield	6/12/51	Catholic Catholic	Snyder
15	Nusbaum, Wm. James Iverson, Betty Ann	Married Corpus Christi, Deerfield	6/16/51	Catholic Catholic	Snyder
16	Gontarek, Michael Kaupa, Florence	Parish House Medford	8/4/51	Catholic Other	Snyder
17	Morgan, John Edward Buscho, Charlette Rae	Married Corpus Christi, Deerfield	1/5/52	Catholic Catholic	Snyder
18	Spolarich, Thomas Condon, Rita	Married Corpus Christi, Deerfield	4/24/52	Catholic Catholic	H. Mountain
19	Karsten, Willard Hager, Helen Marie	Christ The King Medford	9/27/52	Mixed	H. Mountain
20	Sammon, Richard L Zitzmann, Betty	Christ The King Medford	7/21/53	Mixed	H. Mountain

CORPUS CHRISTI MARRIAGES

	Married Couple	Location	Date	Religion	Priest
21	Reyant, Theresa Davis, Donald	Christ The King Medford	9/26/53	Catholic Catholic	H.Mountain
22	Kavitz, Marvin Zackorska, Donna	Christ The King Medford	12/12/53		H.Mountain
23	Brown, James Carol Voegele	Married Corpus Christi, Deerfield	9/1/56	Catholic Catholic	H.Mountain
24	Kratt, Donna R. Hager, Neil A	Married Corpus Christi, Deerfield	10/27/56	Catholic Catholic	H. Mountain
25	Ness, Elizabeth Manderfeld, William	Christ The King Medford	6/28/58	Catholic Catholic	H. Mountain
26	Shinozaki, Miyoko Dickison, Richard	Christ The King Medford	9/21/58	mixed	H. Mountain
27	Mohs, Patricia Jones, James	Christ The King Medford	2/7/59	Mixed	H. Mountain
28	Hurt, Rose Anne McMinimon, Edward J	Christ The King Medford	6/6/59	Catholic Catholic	H. Mountain
29	Hager, John Henry Conrath, Shirley Ann	Married Corpus Christi, Deerfield	9/30/59	Mixed	H. Mountain
30	Christenson, Julia Kvasnicka, William	Christ The King Medford	2/24/62	Catholic Catholic	H. Mountain
31	Breck, Kay Sammon, Joseph	Married Corpus Christi, Deerfield	10/13/62	mixed	H. Mountain
32	Sammon, Ruth Condon, Lewis James	Married Corpus Christi, Deerfield	Dec-54		H. Mountain
33	Weber, Marjorie Jones, William	Christ The King Medford	11/24/62	Catholic Catholic	H. Mountain
34	Nusbaum, Anna Dushek, Joseph	Married Corpus Christi, Deerfield	7/20/63	Catholic Catholic	H. Mountain
35	Tobin, Loretta Storlie, Oscar	Christ The King Medford	12/29/64	Mixed	H. Mountain
36	Kratt, Rebekah Hager, Dennis	Married Corpus Christi, Deerfield	8/26/65	Mixed	H. Mountain
37	Heim, Elaine Johnston, B. Carl	Married Corpus Christi, Deerfield.	8/26/67	Mixed	H. Mountain
38	Hager, Sandra Theresa Sutlief, David Wm	Married Corpus Christi, Deerfield	7/27/68	Mixed	H. Mountain
39	Kuntz, Carol Karsten, Steven	Married Corpus Christi, Deerfield	1/17/70	Mixed	F Glynn
40	Haefs, Sally Lee Miller, Ronald S	Married Corpus Christi, Deerfield	6/4/70		F Glynn

CORPUS CHRISTI MARRIAGES

	Married Couple	Location	Date	Religion	Priest
41	Miller, Shirley Ann Mlenek, Lyle David	Married Corpus Christi, Deerfield	6/6/70	Catholic Catholic	F Glynn
42	Schweisthal, Susan M Brown, John W	Married Corpus Christi, Deerfield	6/6/70	Catholic Catholic	F Glynn
43	Klukas, Robert Wm Quimby, Suzanne L.	Christ The King Medford	7/18/70	Catholic Catholic	F Glynn
44	Lang, James W. Pete, Mary M.	Christ The King Medford	8/29/70	Catholic Catholic	F Glynn
45	Lange, Noel K. Brady, Edith A	Christ The King Medford	9/12/70	Catholic Catholic	F Glynn
46	Morgan, Diane Marie Sammon, Aldon Joseph	Christ The King Medford	10/3/70	Catholic Catholic	L. Sammon
47	Purrier, Marvin John Morgan, Kay Lynn	Christ The King Medford	10/3/70	Mixed	F Glynn
48	Carlock, Randel Scott Brady, Kathleen Mae	Married Corpus Christi, Deerfield	4/3/71		F Glynn
49	Wieczoreak, George Wm Peterson, Sharon	Christ The King Medford	4/17/71		F Glynn
50	Glovka, Larry D. Phillips Catherine A	Christ The King Medford	9/4/71		F Glynn
51	Hager, Eugene M Anderson, Christina	Married Trinity Lutheran Owatonna	12/26/71	Mixed	Paul La Fontaine
52	O'Neil, Karen M Dragsten, John P	Married Corpus Christi, Deerfield	7/1/72	Mixed	F Glynn
53	Phillips, Linda L Blevor, Nikalai	Married Corpus Christi, Deerfield	9/3/72	Mixed	F Glynn
54	Johnson, Gordon Lewis Hager, Debra Jane	Married Corpus Christi, Deerfield	7/21/73		F. Glynn
55	Hinchley, Robert Wayne Peterson, Pamela Jean	Christ The King Medford	8/24/74	Mixed	F. Glynn
56	Caron, Michael Albert Peterson, Roberta Susan	Christ The King Medford	9/20/75		F. Glynn
57	Kratt, Michael John Schweisthal, Rosemond Ann	Christ The King Medford	1/4/75	Mixed	F. Glynn
58	Tuve, Catherine M Sigafur, Robert A	Married Corpus Christi, Deerfield	2/14/75	Mixed	F. Glynn
59	Miller, John C Bah, Sandra J	Christ The King Medford	7/19/75		F. Glynn
60	Racek, Robert Allan Heim, JoAnne Laraine	Christ The King Medford	8/9/75	Mixed	F. Glynn

CORPUS CHRISTI MARRIAGES

	Married Couple	Location	Date	Religion	Priest
1977	Brady, Byron Maas, Carla	Christ The King	June 17, 1977	Catholic	Joseph Pete John Cody Warren Ryan
1978	Lamont, David Hurst, Terry	Christ The King Medford	1978	Mixed	Cody
1978	Jewison, Terrence	Methodist Church, Waseca	8/27/78	Mixed	
1979	Brady, Dennis Von Ruden, Theresa (Terri)	St. Lawrence, Faribault	7/7/1979	Catholic	
1979	Morgan, Patrick Hurst, Angela	Married Corpus Christi, Deerfield	1979	Catholic	Cody
1982	Brady, James (Jamie) Spinler, Judy	Christ The King	2/13/1982	Catholic	Cody
1982	Brady, Patrick Schmidt, Connie	Christ The King	9/18/1982	Catholic	Cody
1984	Malterer, Randy J Heim, Jeannette L	Married Corpus Christi, Deerfield	1984		Cody
1990	Mork, Joshua Insley, Kathleen	Married Corpus Christi, Deerfield	6/9/1990		Ernster
1994	Larson, David Robert Lucero, Rose Marie	Married Corpus Christi, Deerfield	8/5/1994		Herman
2006	Larson, Mathew Pound, Ashley Renee	Married Corpus Christi, Deerfield	9/30/2006		Haberman
2007	Twaddle, Blair James Pete, Jessica Alice	Married Corpus Christi, Deerfield	11/4/2007		Haberman
2008	Maas, Ronald Edward Stoeckle, Nancy Ann	Married Corpus Christi, Deerfield	8/1/2008		Haberman
2009	Brady, Byron Francis Martin, Laura Kay	Married Corpus Christi, Deerfield	6/19/2009		Haberman

Note: On the following pages are photographs of couples married at Corpus Christi Church. Many marriages were also celebrated at Christ The King in Medford, but only pictures of some of those which took place at Deerfield are included.

*Wedding of Leo Thomas Sammon (1904–1975) & Margaret Lucille Fitzpatrick (1907-1981).
Leo and Margaret were married February 26, 1930 at Corpus Christ Church, Deerfield.
(Attendants at the wedding were Hilary Sammon and Agnes Bridget Fitzpatrick, standing).*

Leo & Margaret (Fitzpatrick) Sammon
(50th Wedding Anniversary --- 1980)

Lawrence Kvasnischka and Easter Pelkey were married at Corpus Christi Church in 1939.
They were the second couple to be married at Corpus Christi following the reopening in 1938.
(The first couple married at Corpus Christi after re-opening was Thomas Swintek and Margaret Bruzant in 1938).

Marriage of Loretta Hager and Vernon Schwartz
(Married April 22, 1947 at Corpus Christi Church)
Loretta was the daughter of Henry and Anna (Hollinger) Hager.
Photograph taken at Hager family home following the wedding.

Marriage of Bonnette 'Bonnie' Jeanne (Broughten) and Felix John Wochnick
(Married at Corpus Christi February 3, 1948. The priest officiating at their wedding was Father Raymond Snyder)

At the time of their marriage, Felix and Bonnie Wochnick were a hired couple working on Ted and Adeline (Gasner) Stiren's farm.

Mom, Dad, my husband Les, our two daughters, Melanie & Heidi and I attended Mass at Corpus Christi church on February 3, 2008 to celebrate their 60th anniversary. Mom and Dad saw some people they knew. One person asked them why they were attending Mass there (they knew that Mom and Dad were members of Sacred Heart in Owatonna) -- Dad's reply, "This is where it all started 60 years ago." I was baptized in 1948 at Corpus Christi by Father Snyder. Shirley Jeanne (Wochnick) Abraham

Bonnie and Felix Wochnick 60th Wedding anniversary picture.
Sunday, February 3, 2008 (inside Corpus Christi church)

271

Donald & Dorothy (Bakken) Morgan Wedding
(Married August 16, 1950 at Corpus Christi Church, Deerfield)
Donald Morgan, son of John and Mary (Ost) Morgan was born May 2, 1925. He married Dorothy Bakken at Corpus Christi Church on August 16, 1950 in a ceremony performed by Father Raymond Snyder.

DOROTHY ANN BAKKEN BECOMES THE BRIDE OF DONALD MORGAN

The Corpus Christi church of Deerfield was the scene of the wedding of Miss Dorothy Ann Bakken, daughter of Mr. and Mrs. Alfred Bakken of Rochester, to Donald S. Morgan, son of Mr. and Mrs. John Morgan of Morrrtown on Wednesday, August 16.

The Reverend Raymond Snyder performed the double ring ceremony at 9:30 am in the presence of a large number of family and friends. Baskets of gladioli were used to decorate the church.

Mrs. Bernard Holmquist played the wedding march. Songs sung by relatives of the bridegroom were "Ave Maria," "Oh, This Day," "Beautiful Mother," and "Oh Lord, I am Not Worthy."

White Net Over Satin
Miss Bakken wore a gown of white net over satin. It was styled with pointed sleeves and a high neck line and the skirt extended into a full train. The bride carried a bouquet of white gladioli. She chose as her maid of honor, Miss Evelyn Van Orsow, a cousin of the bridegroom. Miss Alvira Bakken, the bride's sister served as bridesmaid. Both wore white organdy dresses and carried bouquets of white gladioli.

Virginia Morgan, in a dress styled like the bride's served as flower girl. Virginia is a niece of the bridegroom. Ronald Krueger, nephew of the bridegroom, served as the ring bearer. He was dressed in a dark brown suit.

Mr. & Mrs. Donald Morgan

Attended By His Brother
Mr. Morgan was attended by his brother, Cpl. Everett Morgan of Fort Story, Virginia, and by Albert Maas.

A breakfast was given by the bridal party in the church hall by the parents of the bridegroom. About 75 guests attended the wedding dinner served by the bridegroom's parents at their home in Deerfield. A five-tier wedding cake decorated the table. In the afternoon a reception was held at the home of the bride's parents in Rochester at 2 o'clock. Miss Marlene Haseth poured.

Two bridal showers were given for the bride-elect. One was given by her mother and the other by Women of School District 42 and 2 and by the women of Corpus Christi Church in Deerfield.

Mrs. Morgan is a graduate of Kasson High School and of Mankato Teacher's College. Mr. and Mrs. Morgan are now at home on the Henry Ehlert farm, following a Wedding trip to Northern Minnesota.
Courtesy of Jeanine Sammon

273

Yvonne Sammon & Ervin Kaderlik Wedding
(Married June 12, 1951 at Corpus Christi Church, Deerfield)
Yvonne Sammon, daughter of Leo and Margaret (FitzPatrick) Sammon, married Ervin Kaderlik of Lonsdale
at Corpus Christi Church on June 12, 1951 in a ceremony performed by Father Raymond Snyder.

Yvonne Sammon & Ervin Kaderlik Wedding
(Married June 12, 1951 at Corpus Christi Church, Deerfield)
View from the belfry showing the pre-Vatican II position of altar with communion rail and Mass being said
with the priest with his back to the congregation.

John Edward "Bud" Morgan & Charlotte Rae Busho
(Married January 5, 1952 at Corpus Christi Church, Deerfield, Minnesota)

Neill Hager & Donna Kratt
(Married October 27, 1956 at Corpus Christi, Deerfield)
Neil was the son of Henry and Anna (Hollinger) Hager.

FATHER JOHN CODY'S COMICAL COMMENTS & WORDS OF WISDOM

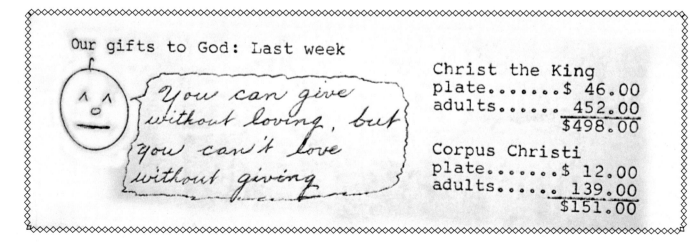

Weekly Bulletin (April 23, 1978)

John & Shirley (Conrath) Hager
(Married September 30, 1959)
This was the first time a "mixed" marriage was performed at the altar at Corpus Christi Church.

Marriage of Joseph Sammon & Kay Breck
(October 13, 1962)

Joseph Sammon was the son of Leo and Margaret (FitzPatrick) Sammon married Kay Breck at Corpus Christi Catholic Church on October 13, 1962. Pictured left to right are Maynard Breck, Florence (Paquin) Caron, Kay Breck, Joseph Sammon, William Sammon, Robert Delasky Note: Florence Paquin's mother was a Sammon.

FATHER CODY'S HUMOR FROM THE BULLETIN

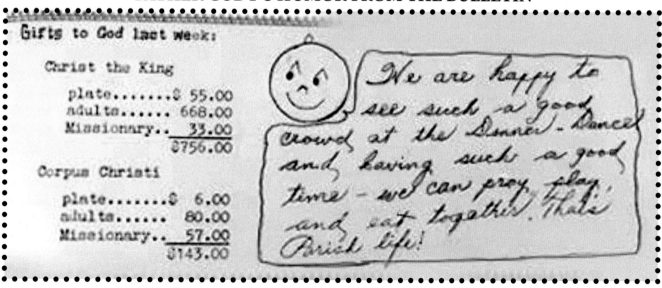

Sunday, January 27, 1980

Dennis Hager & Rebekah Kratt
(Married at Corpus Christi on August 26, 1965)

Sandra Hager & David Sutlief with Fr. Harold B. Mountain in front.
(Married July 27, 1968 at Corpus Christi Church, Deerfield)
Pictured are Back Row; L-R: Paul, Gene, Neil, David, Donald, John.
Middle Row; Dennis, Louis, Debbie, Helen, Anna, Henry, Loretta, Susan (bridesmaid), Roseanne.

Elaine Heim and B. Carl Johnston
(Married Aug. 26, 1967 at Corpus Christi).
(Daughter of Bernard and Luella (Gillen) Heim)

Randy Malterer and Jeannette Heim
(Married at Corpus Christi in 1984)
(Daughter of Bernard and Luella (Gillen) Heim)

Kathleen Mae Brady Wedding (April 3, 1971).
Front: Caroline, Dennis, Jamie, Patrick. Back: James M.,
Kathleen, and Evelyn.

Byron F. "Buzz" Brady & Laura Kay Martin Wedding
(Corpus Christi Church; June 19, 2009).

Catherine Tuve and Robert Sigafus
(Married at Corpus Christi on February 14, 1975)

Catherine Tuve, daughter of Edwin and Marie (Cifra) Tuve was born September 9, 1950 and raised on a farm in Deerfield. Catherine was baptized at Corpus Christi in 1950 and received her first communion there on June 8, 1958. Catherine married Bob Sigafus at Corpus Christi on St. Valentine's Day, February 14, 1975. Father Francis Glynn peformed the marriage ceremony.

View From The Choir Loft
Catherine Tuve and Robert Sigafus
(Married at Corpus Christi on February 14, 1975)

CORPUS CHRISTI DEATHS & BURIALS (EARLY)

NAME	RESIDENCE	AGE	NEXT OF KIN COMMENTS	DEATH	BURIAL
WERTZLER, Mary/ Mariane	Deerfield	58/59	Andrew (husband)	Oct. 31, 1878	Corpus Christi
STADLER, John F.	Deerfield	12	Nicolas C. Stadler Sr. & Anna Smith	1885	Corpus Christi (See Memory Section)
HAMENTIEN, Joseph	Deerfield	22 years	Claude Hamentine	May 26, 1886	Corpus Christi
STIRENS, Maria	Deerfield	15 years		Nov. 21, 1878	Corpus Christi
FAIT, Alice	Blooming Grove	6 years	Vincent and Philomena Fait; nine siblings.	Feb. 19, 1902	Corpus Christi
STIRENS, Gertrude	Deerfield	1 mo.		Aug. 15, 1905	Corpus Christi
STERINS, Theodore	Deerfield	76 years		May 11, 1906	
BLOOMER, Margaret *nee* Brady	Deerfield			Sept. 6, 1912	Corpus Christi
WERTZLER, Johanna nee Hennesey	Deerfield	49 years	Leonard Wertzler	10-23-1913	Corpus Christi
STIRENS, Ambrose	Deerfield	4 years	Died in barn fire	May 25, 1914	Corpus Christi
BRADY, Catherine	Deerfield		Thomas Brady, husband	April 2, 1919	Corpus Christi
STIRENS, Peter	Deerfield		Wife, Anna Fait	1938	Corpus Christi
WERTZLER, Leonard	Deerfield	80 years		July 20, 1938	Corpus Christi
LINDER, Mrs. W. (Esther)		31 years		1941	Corpus Christi
STIRENS, Anna nee Fait	Deerfield			October 30, 1942	Corpus Christi
SCHULLER, Jacqueline				1942	Corpus Christi
FITZPATRICK, Anna	Deerfield	62 yrs.	Margaret (Mrs. Leo) Sammon, Morristown	December 11, 1943	Calvary Cemetery, Faribault
O'BRIEN, Rosamond		39 years	Husband, Stephen O'Brien	1948	Corpus Christi
O'BRIEN, Baby			Stephen & Rosamond O"Brien	1948	Corpus Christi
PAUL, Charles		52 yrs.		Mar. 8, 1941	Corpus Christi

Funeral Rites Held Dec. 11 For Mrs. Fitzpatrick

Funeral services were held on Monday, December 13 at the Corpus Christi Catholic Church in Deerfield for Mrs. Michael Fitzpatrick, 62, who passed away at her home on Saturday, December 11, at 12:15 a.m.

Rev. Raymond Snyder, pastor of the church, officiated at the 10 o'clock requiem high mass and interment was made in Calvary Cemetery at Faribault.

Pallbearers were Henry Eisert, Morristown, William Nusbaum, Medford, S. J. Leahy, William, Ed, and Vernon Sammon of Faribault.

Mrs. Fitzpatrick nee Anna Novak was born in Veseli, the daughter of Frank and Catherine Novak, on January 1, 1881. She grew to young womanhood and attended school there. On February 8, 1902, she was united in marriage to Michael Fitzpatrick of Wheatland. The young couple took up farming as their life work and established their home in Deerfield. To this union was born three children, a son, Joseph, and twin daughters, Agnes of Morristown and Mrs. Leo Sammon (Margaret) of Morristown. The family continued to live on the farm until the death of Mr. Fitzpatrick, after which Mrs. Fitzpatrick moved to Faribault where she resided for 10 years. Mrs. Fitzpatrick and family then moved back to their farm in Deerfield. She has been in failing health for the past three years. Had she lived until January 1st, she would have been 63 years old. Mrs. Fitzpatrick was a devout Catholic and a faithful member of the Corpus Christi Church at Deerfield.

She is survived by her son and two daughters and seven grandchildren, Ruth, Yvonne, William, Richard, Lawrence, Joseph and Clarence Sammon, one brother, Frank W. Novak, Lonsdale, three sisters, Mrs. Mary Novotny, Lonsdale, Mrs. Frank Lands and Mrs. Frank Smisek of Lowry. She was preceded in death by her husband, her parents, one brother and two sisters and one grandchild.

Relatives from away who attended the fuenral were Mrs. Frank Smisek, Mrs. Frank Lands of Lowry, Frank Novak, Mrs. Helen Novotny and Robert Novak of Lonsdale, Mrs. Glen Himler and Mrs. William Walker of Minneapolis.

Keep on Backing the Attack with your purchases of WAR BONDS. Give War Bonds for Christmas.

Faribault Daily News (December 23, 1943)

CORPUS CHRISTI DEATHS & BURIALS (1944-1976)

NAME	RESIDENCE	AGE	NEXT OF KIN	DEATH	PRIEST	BURIAL
GILLIS, Martin	Deerfield	50	Mike Gillen, Brother	Aug. 16, 1944	R .J. Snyder	Faribault, Calvary
SWINTEK Richard	Deerfield	1 Day	Thomas Swintek Father	Aug. 26, 1944	R .J. Snyder	Corpus Christi
O'NEILL, John	Deerfield	82	George O'Neill, Son	Feb. 4, 1946	R .J. Snyder	Calvary, Faribault
O'CONNOR, Kathleen M.	Deerfield	15 mo.	Floyd O'Connor	Aug. 9, 1947	R .J. Snyder	Calvary, Faribault
WHITICK, Edward	Deerfield	60	Adina Whitick	Jan. 6, 1949	R .J. Snyder	Elysian, Cedar Hill
NUSSBAUM, Wm.	Deerfield	54	Ann Nussbaum	Apr. 15, 1950	R .J. Snyder	Faribault, St. Lawrence
HANSON, Arvid	Kenyon	31	Dorothy Hanson	June 14, 1950	R .J. Snyder	Corpus Christi
SAMMON, Baby Girl	Deerfield	1 hr.	Ruth Sammon	Jan. 5. 1951	R .J. Snyder	Faribault, Calvary
STIRENS, Peter	Deerfield	49	Mildred Stirens	April 19, 1951	R .J. Snyder	Corpus Christi
MULLENMASTER, Atilia	Deerfield	79	William Mullen-master	May 24, 1951	R .J. Snyder	Owatonna, Sacred Heart
MULLENMASTER, William	Deerfield	75	Leo Mullenmaster, Son	Aug. 9, 1951	R .J. Snyder	Owatonna, Sacred Heart
PIRKL, Henry	Deerfield	NA	Died in Morris-town, Corpus Christi Parishioner	NA	H. Mountain	Corpus Christi
PHILLIPS, Nick	Deerfield	74	Gene Phillips, Son	Feb, 21, 1956	H. Mountain	Corpus Christi
KNIEFEL, Ethel	Deerfield	60	Anton Kniefel	June 1956	H. Mountain	Owatonna
HURT, Alma	Deerfield	53	James Hurt, Hus-band	March 20, 1958	H. Mountain	Corpus Christi
HENTGES, Josephine	Deerfield	74	NA	Dec. 18, 1959	H. Mountain	Resurrection
PIRKL, Frank	Deerfield	69	Single; Brother to Charles Pirkl and Ella Schmanski.	June 12, 1959	H. Mountain	Corpus Christi
BRADY, James F.	Deerfield	84	Amelia, Wife	Sept. 29, 1960	H. Mountain	Faribault, Calvary
PIRKL, Charles	Deerfield	62	Mabel, Wife	Jan, 2, 1961	H. Mountain	Corpus Christi
NESS, Bernard	Deerfield	63	Anne Morgan, Wife	March 1, 1961	H. Mountain	Resurrection
PHILLIPS, Catherine	Owatonna	81	None	Jan. 7, 1963	H. Mountain	Corpus Christi
HOLMQUIST, Bernard	Deerfield	50	Loretta Holmquist	May 16, 1963	H. Mountain	Corpus Christi

CORPUS CHRISTI DEATHS & BURIALS (1944-1976)

NAME	RESIDENCE	AGE	NEXT OF KIN	DEATH	PRIEST	BURIAL
BARBKNECHT, John William	Deerfield	1 Day	Wayne & Roseann Barbknect. Parents	May 29, 1963	H. Mountain	Calvary, Faribault
VOEGELE, Dennis	Deerfield	15.	Mr. & Mrs. Art Voegele	Sept. 8, 1963	H. Mountain	Corpus Christi
MORK, Tracy John	Deerfield	1 Day	Mr. & Mrs. Kenneth Mork	Dec. 27, 1963	H. Mountain	Corpus Christi
WALKOWIAK, Agnes	Deerfield	77	Husband, Joseph; Son George.	Feb. 27, 1964	H. Mountain	Corpus Christi
MORGAN, Mary	Deerfield	76	Dorothy Hanson, Ann, Donald, Ed-waed & Robert	Sept. 24, 1965	H. Mountain	Resurrection, Medford
KLUKAS, William	Deerfield	54	Mary	Feb. 26, 1966	H. Mountain	Waseca, Sacred Heart
O'NEILL, George	Deerfield	68	Eleanor	Jan. 2, 1967	H. Mountain	Faribault, Meadow Ridge (Jan. 5, 1967)
WALKOWIAK, Joseph	Deerfield	78	Son, George.	Jan. 20, 1967	Ft. Brandel	Corpus Christi
CONDON, Patrick	Morristown	94	Son, Sylvester.	July 25, 1967	Mark Farrell	Fsribault, Calvary
RYSHAVY, Emma	Morristown	68	Sister, Ella Schman-ski.	1968	H. Mountain	Owatonna, Sacred Heart
DAWS, Charlie	Deerfield	70	None	Feb, 21, 1956	H. Mountain	Place of Death: Farib-ault, Meadow Ridge
BRUZANT, Richard E.	Parents: Joseph J. & Mary M. (Marsolek) Bruzant	49	Wife: Ila Mae Bu-scho. Richard was a brother to Irene Schmanski.	Dec. 12, 1964		Corpus Christ
BRADY, Rose	Medford	82	Charles Brady, Med-ford, son	March 18, 1969		Corpus Christi (March 20, 1969)
SCHMANSKI, Elizabeth nee Pirkl	Deerfield	74	Anton Schmans-ki, Husband; Ella Schmanski, sister.	Aug. 13, 1970	Francis Glynn	Corpus Christi
PIRKL, Justina	Deerfield	87	Louis, Son	Nov. 19, 1970	Francis Glynn	Sacred Heart, Owa-tonna (Nov. 23, 1970)
LARSON, George Jr.	Deerfield	3 Days	George & Jean Lar-son, Parents	June 8, 1971	Francis Glynn	Corpus Christi
COLE, Bonita Jean	State Hospital, Faribault	24 Yrs.	Corliss & Marian Cole, Parents	May 12, 1972	Francis Glynn	Corpus Christi
MORGAN, John J.	Deerfield	96	Children; Ann, Don-ald, Ed, Robert	Aug. 2, 1972	Franci Glynn	Resurrection, Med-ford
GOETTL Lori	Morristown	1 Day	James & Terri Goettl, Parents	Dec. 15, 1973	Francis Glynn	Corpus Christi
SCHMANSKI, Anton R.	Deerfield	82	Ed Schmanski, Son	April 29,1974	Fr.Glynn	Corpus Christi
O'BRIEN, Margaret	Medford	69	Steve O'Brien, hus-band	June 25, 1974	Francis Glynn	Resurrection, Med-ford; Died Car Crash
SAMMON, Leo T	Deerfield	70	Margaret, Wife	May 29, 1975	John Cody	Faribault, Calvary

CORPUS CHRISTI DEATHS & BURIALS (1976-1993)

NAME	RESIDENCE	AGE	NEXT OF KIN	DEATH	PRIEST	BURIAL
PIRKL, Louis	Deerfield	67	Lucille Curran, Wife	Mar. 16, 1976	Fr.Glynn	Owatonna, Sacred Heart
BRADY, Melvin	Rochester State Hospital	32	James & Evelyn Brady, Parents	June 22, 1976		Corpus Christi
VOEGELE, Baby			Robert Voegele	Feb. 25, 1977	Fr. Glynn	Corpus Christi
JEWISON, Baby	Deerfield	Stillborn	Timothy & Holly	April 26, 1977	Fr. Glynn	Corpus Christi
KAVITZ, Marvin	Medford	53	husband, divorced	Feb. 6, 1978	Fr. Cody	Faribault; Died house fire
PFIEFFER, Helen	Deerfield	67	Wife	Feb., 11, 1978	Fr. Cody	Waseca; Cancer
BRADY, Amelia nee Dusbabek	Deerfield	93	Wife	May 19, 1978	Fr. Cody	Calvary Cemetery in Faribault.
PHILIPS, Gene	Deerfield (Vet's Hospital)	61	Husband	June 26, 1979	Fr. Cody	Corpus Christi; Cancer
LARSON, Adolph	Deerfield	77	Husband	Feb., 11, 1980	Fr. Cody	Medford, Stroke
SZYMANSKI, Theodore	Deerfield	93	Husband	December 10, 1980	Fr. Cody	Sacred Heart, Owatonna; Heart Attack
PHILIPS, Florence	St. Paul	60	Widow of Gene Philips; died in 1979	Jan. 11 1983	Fr. Cody	Corpus Christi; Buried in spring; Cancer
HAGER, David	Medford	44	Lived with mother	July 9, 1983	Fr. Cody	Corpus Christi
SCHMANSKI, Irene	Medford	67	67; Wife and School Cook.	April 11, 1985	Fr. Cody	Corpus Christi loyal to cleaning church
O'BRIEN, Stephen	Medford	84	Retired farmer; Four sons, seven daughters	July 25, 1985	Frs. Cody & H. Mountain	Corpus Christi; Cancer
PIRKL, Lucille	Deerfield	76	Wife of Louis; deceased	Jan., 12, 1987	E. Mountain	Owatonna, Sacred Heart
LANG, Joseph	Deerfield	79	wife Margaret, son James	Dec. 8, 1987	E. Mountain	Corpus Christi
HURT, James	Deerfield	88	Children	June 25, 1988	E. Mountain	Deerfield
SCHMANSKI, Edward			August 1988			Corpus Christi
HAGER, Neil	Medford	53		Feb. 11, 1990	Milo Ernster	Medford
BRADY, Byron	Medford	77	Wife Jane	March 24, 1991		Corpus Christi, Deerfield (3/27/91)
SWINTEK, Thomas	Minneapolis	77	Wife, Margaret Bruzant; Foster son of Anton & Elizabeth Schmanski.	Feb. 6, 1990	Holy Cross, Minneapolis	Corpus Christi Cemetery
BRADY, Patrick	Deerfield	45	Wife Donna	Nov. 9, 1991	Fr. Ernster	Deerfield
VOEGELE, Arthur	Deerfield	84	Wife	Nov. 26, 1991	Fr. Ernster	Deerfield (11/30/91)
LARSON, George	Deerfield	54	Wife, Jean	April 22, 1992	Fr. Ernster	Deerfield (4/25/92)
HOFFMAN, Clarence	Medford/Deerfield	84	Wife, Edith	January 6, 1993	Robert Herman	Medford (1/9/93) Alzheimers

CORPUS CHRISTI DEATHS & BURIALS (1993-2003)

NAME	RESIDENCE	AGE	NEXT OF KIN	DEATH	PRIEST	BURIAL
VOEGELE, John Robert	Faribault	11	Father Robert, mother & siblings	Janaury 21, 1993	Robert Herman	Funeral Christ The King; Burial Calvary Faribault; Heart Failure
NESS, Ann Amelia	Medford	82	Widow, two daughters; Marjorie Ness and Betty Manderfeld	February 24, 1993	Robert Herman	Resurrection Cemetery, Medford (2/27/93)
REYANT, Francis	Medford/Deerfield	56	Widow, Teresa Steinbauer	June 5, 1993	Robert Herman	Funeral Christ The King Burial Corpus Christi
HEIM, Bernard	Medford	79	Wife Luella; Ten Choldren	November 17, 1993	Robert Herman	Corpus Christi (11/20/93)
MORK, Kenneth	Deerfield	65	Widow Donna & Children	Feb. 9, 1994	Robert Herman	Corpus Christi (2/14/94); Cancer
VOEGELE, Mary A.	Faribault	88	Widow of Arthur	March 11, 1995	Robert. Herman	Funeral Christ The King Burial Corpus Christi
HAGER, Anna Sarah	Medford	89	Large Family	April 18, 1996	Robert. Herman	Funeral Christ The King Burial Corpus Christi
VOEGELE, Sharon L.	Deerfield/Rice County	45	Husband Robert, Children	Jan. 25, 1997	Robert. Herman	Funeral Christ The King Burial Calvary, Faribault/Cancer
PIRKL, Mabel	Medford	94	Widow	Dec. 20, 1997	Robert. Herman	Medford
HOLMQUIST, Ellen Rose	Waseca	86	Husband Ernest Holmquist	March 22, 1999	Robert. Herman	Funeral Christ The King Burial Corpus Christi
HOLMQUIST Loretta	Waseca	82	Widow; four children	July 6, 1999	Robert. Herman	Funeral Christ The King Burial Corpus Christi
WEBER, Lucille	Medford	88	Husband; Joe	Nov, 21, 1999	Robert. Herman	Funeral Christ The King; Burial Medford
HOFFMAN, Edith	Medford	85	Children, Grandchildren, Great Grandchildren	March 28, 2000	Robert. Herman	Funeral Christ The King; Burial Medford
HAGER, Louis	Waseca	59		Oct. 28, 2000	Robert. Herman	Funeral Christ The King Burial Corpus Christi
EUSTICE, Donald F.	Waseca	81	Wife, Alice, Children Ronald, Robert, Donald & Marjorie	July 3, 2000	Robert Herman	Funeral Christ The King; Burial Corpus Christi
PETE, Joseph Philip	Medford	78	Wife, Martha V. Klecker; 9 Children	March 29, 2003	Robert Herman	Funeral Christ The King; Burial Corpus Christi
HOLMQUIST, Ernest William	Waseca County	92	Wife Ellen (Deceased), Foster Sons, Timothy & Terry Jewison	June 30, 2003	Robert Herman	Funeral Christ The King; Burial Corpus Christi

CORPUS CHRISTI DEATHS & BURIALS (2004-2009)

NAME	RESIDENCE	AGE	NEXT OF KIN	DEATH	PRIEST	BURIAL
CONDON, Sylvester Charles	Steele County	72	Wife, Ethel Schneider; Children: Roxanne, Patricia, Jacqueline, Brian, Kimberly, Vicky.	February 9, 2004	Clayton Haberman	Funeral @Christ The King
BRADY, James	Medford	88	Wife, Evelyn Maas; Children, Carolyn, Pat, Kathleen, James, Dennis	March 31, 2005	E. Mountain/ Clayton Haberman	Funeral Christ The King Burial Corpus Christi
BRUENING, Monica Jo nee Eustice	Rochester, MN	35	Children, Jared & Paige	August 13, 2006	Clayton Haberman	Funeral Christ The King; Burial Corpus Christi
PIRKL, Harlow	Medford	74	Wife, Joan; Daughters, Kristi & Debbie	October 15, 2006	Edward Mountain	Burial Resurrection, Medford
LARSON, Marguerite M.	Owatonna	94	Sons; George (deceased), Bob, Daughter Josephine Matz	April 18, 2007	Clayton Haberman	Burial Resurrection, Medford
DULAS. Sylvester	Rural Medford	76	Wife, Jackie; Children; Joyceann, John, Jay, Judy & Joel	September 4, 2007	Clayton Haberman	Funeral Christ The King Burial Corpus Christi
BRADY, Jane Delores	Rural Medford	87	Husband, Byron; Children: Sharon, Edith, Byron, Kevin, Mary, Charles	December 26, 2007	Robert Herman, Joseph Pete, Mark Pavlik	Funeral Christ The King Burial Corpus Christ (January 2, 2008)
MORGAN, Charlotte Rae (nee Busho)	Morristown	84	Husband, John; Children: Kay, Gordon, Mary Lou, Marilyn, Pam, Patrick, Patty,	March 24, 2008	Robert Herman	Christ The King/ Resurrection
EUSTICE, Alice Mae (Perron)	Faribault	85	Husband, Donald (Deceased); Children: Ronald, Robert, Donald & Marjorie	July 7, 2008	Joseph Pete	Funeral Christ The King Burial Corpus Christ (July 11, 2008)
BRADY, Evelyn (nee Maas)	Medford	84	Husband, James; (Deceased 2005) Children: Patrick, Dennis, James,	October 4, 2008	Edward Mountain Joseph Pete	Funeral Christ The King Burial Corpus Christ (October 7, 2008)
WEBER, Joseph C.	Medford	94	Wife, Lucille (dec. 1999); Children, Marge Wadekamp, Robert Weber.	January 3, 2009	Joseph Pete	Funeral Christ The King Burial Resurrection (January 7, 2009)
PETE, Martha Veronica	Medford	86	Husband, Joseph (deceased 1993; Children: Mary, Joe, Bob, Mike, Monica, Frank, Larry, Janice, Amy,	August 26, 2009	Bishop John Quinn, Fr. Robert Herman, Fr. Edw. Mountain, Fr. Clayton Haberman	Corpus Christi, Deerfield (August 31, 2009)
HACKETT, George	Morristown	83	Wife, Cathy; Children: Mike, Ann, Mary, Elizabeth, Patricia, Christine.	September 16, 2009	Clayton Haberman	Corpus Christi, Deerfield (September 16, 2009)

CORPUS CHRISTI DEATHS & BURIALS (2011-2021)

NAME	RESIDENCE	AGE	NEXT OF KIN	DEATH	PRIEST	BURIAL
MORK, (Bolinger) Donna	Owatonna	81	Kenneth (deceased 1999), Children: Josh, Jonas, Megan	August 21, 2011	Edward Mountain	Funeral at Christ The King on August 25, 2011; Burial at Corpus Christi, Deerfield
JOHNSON, Robert	Reno, Nevada	80	Wife; Maureen O'Brien	September 6, 2010	Edward Mountain	Corpus Christi
MULLENMASTER, Colette Rita	Plainview, Minnesota	80	Wife; Elizabeth Flanary; Siblings, Ann Marie, Bill Candace Elaine, Greg, Monica, Brian, Maurice and Scott Mullenmaster	August 11, 2021	Private family gathering held at Corpus Christi church in Deerfield.	Burial Corpus Christi Cemetery
HEIM, Luella	Medford Senior Care Center	100	Lois (David) Nelson, Elaine Johnston, Philip (Gail) Heim, Lloyd Heim, Rosemary Heim, Christine Heim, Patrick (Tracy) Heim, Cynthia (Richard) Smith, and Jeannette (Randy) Malterer; seventeen grandchildren; twenty-two great grandchildren and three great great grandchildren; siblings, Joanne (Jim) Cortese and Adrian Gillen; son-in-law, Robert Racek	September 28, 2021	Fr. Jim Starasinich/ Fr. Matthew Wagner	Funeral at Christ The King on October 4, 2021; Burial at Corpus Christi, Deerfield

FATHER JOHN CODY'S COMICAL COMMENTS & WORDS OF WISDOM

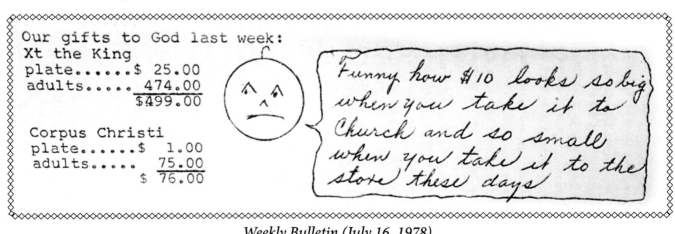

Weekly Bulletin (July 16, 1978)

CHAPTER VIII

VOCATIONS

FATHER LAWRENCE SAMMON

Lawrence T. Sammon

Lawrence T. Sammon, son of Leo and Margaret Sammon, became Corpus Christi's first "son" to be ordained a priest. After he had begun his education in Rural District 42 in Deerfield Township, he attended Bethlehem Academy in Faribault, where he graduated. Following that, he went to the Society of the Divine Word Seminary in Epworth, Iowa, having enrolled in 1955. His ordination took place there on January 15, 1966. His First Solemn Mass was celebrated at Christ the King Church in Medford on June 12, 1966.

Father Harold Mountain was pastor at that time and he assisted as Arch Priest at the Mass along with classmates of Father Sammon's from the Divine Word headquarters in Techny, Illinois and their seminary in Epworth Iowa. It was a day of celebration for the whole community. The 4th degree Knights of Columbus formed an honor guard at Mass and a delegation of Knights lined the sidewalk outside of church in honor of the newly ordained.

Following Mass, the family and visiting clergy shared dinner at Johnson's Supper Club in Medford, prior to the Open-House Reception which was hosted in Corpus Christi Basement.

Father Lawrence must have taken the phrase "You Are A Priest Forever" to heart because he served as a missionary in Mexico for his entire priestly life.

On the few times that Father Lawrence returned to Deerfield to visit his family, we felt blessed to have him celebrate Mass with us. In 1976, his home visit was highlighted by a celebration for his 10th Anniversary in the priesthood. It was another 10 years when he was brought home for a funeral Mass and then he was buried at the cemetery in Techny, Illinois.

His life came to an abrupt and tragic end on November 17, 1986, when he died from an aneurysm at the age of forty-nine in Mexico City.

The Rev. Lawrence T. Sammon, 49, a former resident of the Morristown and Medford area, died Monday, Nov. 17, 1986 in Mexico City, Mexico. The Mass of Christian Burial was held at 10 a.m. Friday in the Church of Christ the King in Medford. The Rev. Michael Allard, provincial superior of the Mexican Province, Divine Word Missions, wwas the celebrant. Interment was in St. Mary's Cemetery, Techny, Ill.

Lawrence Thomas Sammon, the son of Leo and Margaret (Fitzpatrick) Sammon, was born in Faribault on Aug. 14, 1937. He graduated from Bethlehem Academy in 1955 and was ordained a priest from the Divine Word Seminary in Epworth, Iowa, in 1966. He served in the missions in Mexico. He was survived by two sisters, Mrs. Lewis (Ruth) Condon of Owatonna and Mrs. Ervin (Yvonne) Kaderlik of Faribault; four brothers, William of Faribault, Richard of Morristown, Joseph of Waseca and Clarence (Butch) of Faribault; and other relatives. He was preceded in death by his parents. Arrangements were by the Parker-Kohl Funeral Home.
Source: Faribault Daily News   19/Nov/1986

Sister Colette Mullenmaster and Father Lawrence Sammon.

COLETTE MULLENMASTER

Sister Colette Mullenmaster

The following is a complete list of her assignment locations as a member of the Franciscan Community beginning in 1959 and ending March 1987 when she was given dispensation from her vows.

*Assisi Heights, Rochester, MN
*St. Margaret Mary's, Golden Valley, MN
*St Peters in North St. Paul, MN
*St. Johns in Rochester, MN
*St. Charles in St. Charles, MN
*Chicago at the Cook County Jail, Chicago, IL
*Assisi Heights, Christian Community Center/Retreat Center, Rochester, MN
*St. Croix Catholic School, Stillwater, Stillwater, MN

Colette enjoyed reading, writing, singing, telling stories, watching football, and riding horses. Colette Rita Mullenmaster, age 80 of Plainview, passed away on Wednesday, August 11, 2021 at the Green Prairie Rehabilitation Center in Plainview, Minnesota. A private family gathering was held at Corpus Christi church in Deerfield, with interment at Corpus Christi Cemetery.

Colette Rita Mullenmaster
(1940-2021)

Collette Mullenmaster, the daughter of Leo Cyril Mullenmaster and Creta Irene (Lonergan) Mullenmaster, was born in Owatonna on October 31, 1940, As a child, she attended Corpus Christi Church and District 19 country school before graduating from Medford High School. She then continued her education at the College of St. Teresa in Winona, where she earned a teaching certificate.

Following a teaching assignment in Golden Valley, she returned to St. Teresa's where she earned a Bachelor's degree in elementary education. Colette entered the convent of the Sisters of St. Francis on January 20, 1959 at Assisi Heights, Rochester, Minnesota. Colette devoted much of her life to her calling as a teacher, and positively impacted many lives over the years.

During her 28+ years as a Sister, her service was primarily directed to teaching elementary and middle school children. She directed and facilitated retreats at the retreat center at Assisi Heights during her assignment there. While serving at St. Charles in St. Charles, MN she held the position of Parish Pastoral Director. She worked one full year at the Cook County Jail in Chicago Illinois as a teacher to the women inmates.

FATHER JOSEPH PETE

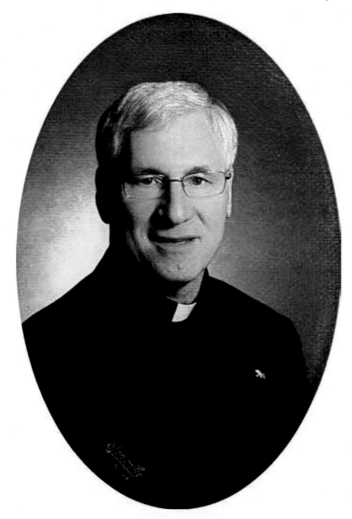

Father Joseph Pete

Father Joe Pete was ordained a priest at Winona on May 21, 1976 and celebrated his first Mass on May 23, 1976, at Christ the King Church with a reception following in the church basement with Corpus Christi CCW serving as host under Rita Kuntz, President at that time. Other familiar names who assisted in the day's celebration were the organist at Mass, Mary Phillips, and the guitarist, Nancy Hurst.

Father Joe was initially assigned to St. Mary's parish at Caledonia and St. Olaf's parish at Mabel. He later served parishes in Rochester, Worthington, Currie, St. Joseph the Worker Church, Mankato and Holy Family Church, Lake Crystal. He is currently in his 48th year of priesthood in the Diocese of Winona.

The following article was published in the Medford Shopper in May of 1976. Joseph Pete was just an ordinary Joe. He grew up on his parent's farm in Deerfield Township. Joe Pete was a country boy. When Jo·e was just a little "squirt" a baby of a few days old, he was baptized by Father Snyder. In baptism, Joe's parents asked that God bless this little boy that he may grow up with a love of Christ and all that He taught. Mr. & Mrs. Joe Pete, Sr. had no idea at that time that they were baptizing one who would be called to be a Catholic priest.

Joe attended Medford High School and graduated in 1968. After graduation, he attended St. Mary's College in Winona. In the summer, Joe worked for Stockwell Construction of Owatonna. "Working with the Stockwell's was an education in itself," said Joe. "I can still list every hollow tree in Steele County which might have a coon in it. And when they were not talking about coon hunting, one could always get an education on some other facet of life".

This spring, Joe graduated from St. Paul Seminary. Our "Ordinary Joe" became Father Joseph Pete on May 2, 1976, when he was ordained a priest by Bishop Loras J. Watters at Winona.

Father Pete says, "The role of the priest is to bring God to the people and to bring the people to God. Through the sacraments, in prayer, and in the way we live, we come into contact with God.".

"Another important job for the priest is that he must work to affirm the people. He must help everyone to see that in the eyes of God, everyone is important. God loves all people."

Father Pete is very optimistic about the Church. since Vatican II, the Church has reached a far more stable ground. The Church has found that it must develop an interdependence with society. As such, the church must be willing and able to be a leader, while at the same time not becoming to secularized in a materialistic world.

Joseph Pete
(First Holy Communion --- June 7, 1958)

Fr. Joe Pete
(Ordination to the Priesthood --- May 21, 1976

Joseph Pete is the son of Joseph and Martha (Klecker) Pete. He was born on June 1, 1950 and grew up on his parent's farm in Deerfield Township. He attended Brady School # 63, an elementary school in Deerfield Township and graduated from Medford High School in 1968. After graduation, he attended St. Mary's College in Winona. In the summer, Joe worked for Stockwell Construction of Owatonna. He attended St. Paul Seminary and was ordained a priest by Bishop Loris Watters at Winona on May 2, 1976. Following ordination, he served parishes in Caledonia, Rochester, Worthington, Currie, St. Joseph the Worker parish, Mankato and Holy Family Church, Lake Crystal. He is currently in his 48th year of priesthood in the Diocese of Winona and lives in Faribault.

Joseph Pete
(Medford High School Graduation--- June 1968)

REMEMBERING FATHER JOE PETE'S FIRST MASS

Joseph & Martha Pete Family at Fr. Joe's first Mass Front Row, R-L: Janice, Larry, Amy. Back Row: Michael, Martha, Fr. joe, Joe Sr., Mary, Monica, Robert, and Francis. Fr. Joe's first Mass was celebrated May 23, 1976 at the Church of Christ The King, Medford.

Fr. Joe Pete following his first Mass on May 23, 1976
L-R: Janice Pete and Richard Gillis, Fr. Joe, Amy Pete, Bob & Bernadette Webber with children.

The Joseph & Martha Pete Family; Front Row, L-R: Lawrence, Francis, Martha, Joe,Sr., Amy, Janice. Back Row: Monica, Michael, Father Joe, Mary (Mrs. James Lang), and Robert.

2016 CORPUS CHRISTI PARISH MEMBERSHIP
(FINAL ROSTER)

B

Berg, Cary & Jackie
Brady, Byron & Carla
Brady, Byron F. & Laura
Brady, Dennis & Theresa
Brady, James & Judy
Brady, Patrick

D

Dulas, Jackie
Dulas, Joel & Rhynda

G

Gillis, Dick & Dee Maas Gillis, Paul & Jean & Jason

H

Hackett, Cathy
Hager, Richard & Laurie
Hager, Brad & Jancie
Heim, Luella
Huxford, Kim

K

Kuhlman, Tim & Joan

L

Larson, Jean
Larson, Robert
Larson, Tim & Joanne
List, David & Janie, Concepcion

M

Manderfeld, Brenda
Morgan, Daniel & Donna
Morgan, Dennis & Debra
Morgan, Dorothy
Morgan Douglas

N

Nagel, Owen & Helen Mary
Nelson, Lois & Dave

O

O'Brien, Patricia
O'Connor Byron & Linda

P

Phillips, Michael
Pittman, Gregory

R

Reuvers, Jay & Jackie

S

Sammon, Aldon & Diane
Paul & Debbie

T

Thompson, Renee

V

Valek, Leonard

EXAMPLES OF FATHER CODY'S CHURCH BULLETIN HUMOR

```
Our gifts to God last week:
Christ the King
plate...... $ 132.00
adults..... 1385.00
Holyland...    50.00
Rice Bowl..   225.78
            $1792.78

Corpus Christi
plate...... $  14.00
adults.....   462.00
Holyland...    18.00
Rice Bowl..    24.69
             $518.69
```

Oh that every Sunday could be Easter Sunday

From The Church Bulletin (April 22, 1979)

Bittersweet Celebration At Deerfield

More than 100 parishioners attend the 145th anniversary celebration of Corpus Christi Catholic Church on Sept. 11, 2016 in Deerfield Township. The church closed for Sunday Mass effective Oct. 1, 2016. (Ashley Stewart/People's Press).

CHAPTER VII
THE END OF AN ERA:

BITTERSWEET CELEBRATION AT DEERFIELD: SEPT. 11, 2016

Corpus Christi Catholic Church celebrates 160 years of memories, parishioners

Some of more than 100 parishioners who attended the 160th anniversary celebration of Corpus Christi Catholic Church on Sept. 11, 2016. Marjorie (Eustice) Root, Margaret and Ronald Eustice are seated at the table.

DEERFIELD: Smiles and laughter graced the lawn of Corpus Christi Catholic Church in Deerfield Township as more than 100 current and former parishioners gathered for its 160th anniversary celebration. But for many, the anniversary was bittersweet.

"This has been my home for many years, but it's been a long time coming," said Luella Heim, a nearly 60-year parishioner of Corpus Christi. She recalls an all-parish reunion in 1996 - 20 years ago -when the congregation didn't think the church would remain open much longer.

On Sept. 11, parishioners received final notice in their bulletins that the church would be closing after Mass on Sept. 25, this upcoming Sunday.

That comes more than a year after the Diocese of Winona released a plan, titled Vision 2016, in February 2015 that detailed the closing of 21 smaller parishes across the diocese and the merging of them with other congregations in the area.

Corpus Christi was one of five local parishes recommended to close based on factors such as fewer priests, variations of sacramental trends and demographic shifts of both growth and decline in areas of the diocese.

Other parishes named were St. Aidan of Ellendale, St. Mary's of Geneva, St. Francis de Sales in Claremont and St. Vincent de Paul in West Concord.

At the time of the announcement, Joel Hennessy, the director of mission advancement and communication, said the diocese had about 100 priests, half of whom were retired. That left just 50 active priests to serve the diocese's 114 parishes, meaning many of the priests served multiple parishes known as clusters. And, Hennessy said, that the number was projected to decline slightly in the next five years as more priests retire and fewer come up the ranks.

Technically, the 21 smaller parishes won't be closed but moved to what the diocese calls "oratory status:' That means once the parish is merged with another parish - Corpus Christi with Christ the King in Medford, for example -the church building will no longer be used for Sunday or Vigil Masses. The building could, however, be used for Catholic weddings, funerals and local prayer until a time when the congregation can no longer maintain the facility and decides to close it altogether and dispose of the property.

The parishes that were selected to be closed and merged with other parishes were places where the demographics are projected to show no growth or even a decline in the residency in future years and where participation has shown 70 people or fewer attending Mass on a weekly basis, Hennessy said.

Heim, who has been a church greeter for the past couple years, said the size of the Corpus Christi congregation has "definitely dwindled over the years;" but that wasn't apparent Sept. 11, when more than 100 people squeezed into 10 rows of pews - on the main level and in the balcony - for a con-celebrated Mass with Bishop John M. Quinn.

"That's how I remember it as a kid,' said Leo Stirens, who attended the church as a child. "It seemed a lot bigger than this though."

Stirens said he and his family lived two farms from Corpus Christi and now, a resident of St. Paul with his wife, Suzie, admits its been eight years since he last attended the parish.

"I knew the closing was coming one of these days, but I had no clue when," he said. And although, he doesn't attend church regularly, his wife says he talks frequently of his years at Corpus Christi. "He's proud of it," Suzie Stirens said.

After Mass, parishioners filed out the doors of Corpus Christi to a large white tent on the northeast side of the church for a pancake and sausage breakfast provided by members of the Trinity Lutheran Church congregation of Medford.

Howard Schoenfeld, one of the five Trinity Lutheran Church volunteers, said he was approached earlier in the year about cooking for the celebration. "It's one set of Christian brothers and sisters helping another in a time of need," he said, acknowledging that it takes the burden of parishioners from cooking so they can enjoy the event.

Schoenfeld, although not a Catholic, said he's sad to see the church close because he grew up down the road from it and knew quite a few people who belonged to the congregation.

Parishioners mingled in the church and on the lawn lined with mature trees, tall grasses and crop fields as well as a dirt road and County Road 12- both lined with dozens of vehicles.

Corpus Christi, which was built in 1869, is one of the oldest faith communities in Steele County, and like many parishes at the time, it was built with farming communities in mind.

Heim, a mother of 10 children, lived on a farm two miles from the church, and she recalls how big families were when she started attending the church in 1957.

"Everyone had such big families, so one pew didn't accommodate them all she said. "Now it does."

Heim said, like Mass on Sept. 11 when flowers adorned the ends of the pews, she tended to a "huge garden" on the farm to decorate the pews with fresh flowers every week, something she's no longer responsible for because she resides in Medford.

Many of those who attended the anniversary celebration, like Heim, recalled memories at the church and others snapped photos with mobile phones and cameras to capture the moment.

That was the case for the Hager family as eleven of them lined the steps of the church for a photograph. "We were raised in this church," said Gene Hager of Owatonna. Gene Hager, one of 16 children born to Henry and Anna Hager, attended the anniversary celebration with his nine remaining brothers and sisters, many of whom married their spouses in the church.

Loretta Schwartz of Waterville is one of them. She married her husband, Vernon, 69 years ago at Corpus Christi. "I hate to see it close," she said.

Henry Hager started the grounds keeping of the cemetery and the parish in 1951, and after he died, his son, John Hager, took over. "I still mow it, and I'll continue to do so until I can't anymore," John Hager said.

Carla Brady, a current parishioner at Corpus Christi, joined the parish after she married her husband, Byron, who grew up as a parishioner in the church. There, the couple raised three daughters and two sons and Brady sang in the choir and served as president of the church ladies.

"It's been home for 39 years,' she said. That's what made the anniversary celebration emotional, but Carla Brady said she was happy to see so many people come out for the event, much of which she coordinated.

Brady sat across from the Rev. Robert Herman, who retired as a local priest in 2002 and was given a special tribute Sept. 11.

Father Herman - now a resident in Buffalo City, Wisconsin - has returned to Christ the King in Medford and Corpus Christi in Deerfield to offer Sunday Masses for more than a decade.

"They needed me,' he said. "This church was going to close and Medford was only going to have one service. I kept it open. I continued to do so as long as I could." And, Father Herman said it was something he enjoyed.. "There are good people here at Deerfield and in Medford," he said.

Under the Winona Diocese plan, Corpus Christi will merge with Christ the King on October 1st.
By Ashley Stewart
astewart@owatonna.com
Owatonna People's Press
(September 20, 2016)

THE 145TH ANNIVERSARY CELEBRATION AT CORPUS CHRISTI ON SEPTEMBER 11, 2016.

L-R: Fr. Robert Herman, Bishop John Quinn, Deacon Pat Fagan.

ECUMENICAL HELP

After final Sunday Mass, parishioners filed out the doors of Corpus Christi to a large white tent on the northeast side of the church for a pancake and sausage breakfast prepared by members of the Trinity Lutheran Church congregation of Medford; Howard and Mary Jo Schoenfeld, Steve Drewitz, Vern Owens, and Kevin Lindquist

Howard Schoenfeld, one of the five Trinity Lutheran Church volunteers, said he was approached earlier in the year about cooking for the celebration. "It's one set of Christian brothers and sisters helping another in a time of need," he said, acknowledging that it takes the burden of parishioners from cooking so they can enjoy the event.

Ronald & Margaret Eustice

Mary & Michael Phillips

Jamie & Judy (Spinler) Brady

Donald & Dorothy (Bakken) Morgan Family

Henry & Anna (Hollinger) Hager Family

This stained-glass window is located over the south front entry doors of the church. It was damaged by vandalism in 2010 and the repairs were covered by insurance. It now has protective glass over it on the outside.

Fr. Mountain purchased the crucified Christ figurine (above) in the holy land, he commissioned Mr. Panos of Medford to make the cross and attached the figure to it. This hangs on the back wall of the sanctuary today.

Martha Pete maintained the Hostas in front of the Grotto for many years.

1992

THANK YOU!!!
A SPECIAL THANK YOU GOES OUT
TO MARK AND MARLENE STADLER FOR
DONATING THE MARY STATUE FOR THE
GROTTO OUTSIDE OF CORPUS CHRISTI
CHURCH.

CHAPTER VIII

CORPUS CHRISTI MEMORIES

A BIT OF EARLY HISTORY FROM THE PARISH BULLETIN
(JULY 14, 1985)
Fr. Edward Mountain

The property for Corpus Christi Church at Deerfield was obtained from Andrew Wertzler on August 27, 1873 and the cemetery plot was acquired from John Loehmer November 14, 1873. The properties were recorded in the name of Thomas Grace, Bishop of St. Paul on July 10, 1874. This was 18 years before the Diocese of Winona was established. It was reported that priests came from both the areas of Faribault and Mankato to say Mass at various farm homes.

The Church cost $300.00 to build and it was a most difficult time to raise the necessary money. The first priest to say Mass in the church was Father Slevin who came from Faribault on horseback. Through more than a century, the parish has been served by priests from Faribault, Claremont, Waseca and Medford.

Christ the King Parish of Medford can rightly be called a daughter parish of Corpus Christi. Had there been no Corpus Christi Parish, Father Snyder probably could never have gotten a start in Medford. Corpus Christi's financial help to Christ the King Parish in the beginning was truly great.

Fr. Edward Mountain

GROWING UP IN DEERFIELD WITH CORPUS CHRISTI AT THE CENTER OF OUR LIFE
By Amy (Pete) Hellevik

Joseph Sr. and Amy Pete purchased their farm in Deerfield in 1946 and became members of Corpus Christi. Two years later in 1948 Joseph Pete Jr. married Martha Klecker and moved onto the farm while Joseph Sr. and Amy moved to Medford. Along came nine children, Mary, Joseph, Robert, Michael, Monica, Francis, Lawrence, Janice and finally Amy.

We were all baptized and most of us confirmed at Corpus Christi. In 1976 Joseph was ordained a Priest.
Our family social life was Corpus Christi Church. Every Sunday we were seen in church with Dad and boys dressed in white shirts and all had freshly polished shoes. The girls were in pressed dresses and all had their hair curled.

All of the boys were altar servers and girls sang in the choir. In 1969 Corpus Christi was left without an organist. Mary was asked to play the organ for Sunday Masses and continued to play until she got married to Jim Lang in 1970 and they moved out of the community. Mary Phillips then took over and played until 1982 at which time Janice and Amy started playing as 6th and 9th graders. Jonas Mork joined them on guitar. As time went on, Amy continued and played until 2016.

The Pete sisters did have their share of surprises. We were alway welcoming mice into the choir loft. One week, Jim Lang set a mouse trap under the foot pedal of the organ thinking we would either trap a mouse or the trap would go off during practice. Surprise - it went off during Mass, with Mary yelping as the trap got her toe. Another time as Janice was playing the organ during Mass, a mouse ran out from under the organ and then went back under the organ causing quit a commotion in the choir loft. Brave Carla Brady stood guard ready to grab the mouse with her hands if it dare show itself again. But it did not.

Christmas was always something for a child to look forward to at church. In the church basement, we had an annual Christmas program with the Nativity acted out and children reciting passages and singing. This was followed with a potluck lunch and a movie of the "Song of Bernadette". We had popcorn balls, a real treat, and Donald Morgan always brought apples for each of us.

In the summer, we always enjoyed the K of C Picnic. Softball was played on the area east of the cemetery and there were games for the children and the women. Evelyn Brady seemed to always win the "peel the orange game" - - getting the longest peel. A real treat for us Pete children - - all the soda pop and ice cream we could eat!

After every special sacramental celebration, their was a social brunch in the basement of the church. When a girl who was a member of Corpus Christi was getting married the ladies of the Church would have a bridal shower for her in the church basement. All the women of the parish were invited. In the same way, when a girl got married the girls of the parish would wait on tables at her wedding dinner. Our life was very much centered around the activities in the church. *Amy (Pete) Hellevik*

SOME MEMORIES OF CORPUS CHRISTI, DEERFIELD

Fr. Joseph Pete

Corpus Christi Church has meant so much to me. I found there a community where all were involved and supported one another. In a small parish, all have to serve and support the parish. I have served in many large parishes. They do not have the community of Corpus Christi.

I have so many memories that I would like to share: I remember going to church riding in my parents 1949 Ford pick-up truck. When we got there we sat in the back pew. Sometimes I would talk with another child close-by when my dad would give me a stern look to be quiet.

I remember looking around church at the stained glass windows and the symbols. On the windows, I remember seeing St. Michael defeat Satan. I remember Christ the King and the Assumption of Mary. Also, Jesus at the First Eucharist. I remember the symbol of the lamb on the wall above the sanctuary. On the left front was a picture of a pelican with its chicks. I always wondered what this represented. A few years ago, I googled it. This was a symbol of redemption from early Christianity in Europe. The pelican fed it's young with fish. Some years when the fish were sparse, tender chicks were starving, the pelican would, with its beak, strike its breast until blood came out. The chicks would feed on the blood. Some legends said that the pelican died saving it's young. It was a reminder of Jesus giving his life for us. We are saved by his blood.

I remember after Mass, everyone took time to visit. In the summer all would stand on the lawn for long periods of time. Then we would head to Mork's Deerfield store where we continued to visit. The Catholic Church has talked so often about community. We had it all along.

I remember going to catechism two weeks during the summer. A high school girl taught us. I remember once she held up three matchsticks and lighting them, talked to us about the Trinity, three matchsticks and one fire. Three persons and one God. I remember once she tapped a child over the head with a rolled up poster when he was making noise.

I remember Sister Rose teaching us how to serve at mass. We memorized the Latin responses to the priest. I remember serving these masses until the liturgy changed when I was in high school. I remember that all teens were scheduled to usher, so I took my turn ushering which I enjoyed.

In the summer, we had a church picnic. That was time for all to socialize and play games. There was lots of fun and laughter. At Christmas we had a potluck party in the church basement. Santa would show up with a bag of peanuts and candy. We drew names for gift-sharing.

I recall how the large families, with many children and teens packed the church. When the church was filled, we sat in the room on the side of sanctuary. We called it the "crying room." We were packed in there also.

With the second Vatican Council in the 1960s, the Catholic Church was challenged to be a community. We were to reach out to one another, to live the Eucharist every day as we brought the body of Christ home with us. At Corpus Christi, we already had this. We were way ahead of our time. We were already community.

Father Joe

MEMORIES OF CORPUS CHRISTI
Father Robert Herman

I first encountered the wonderful people of Corpus Christi church in Deerfield in July of 1992. I believe it was the first Sunday in July. That was 24 years and 3 months. I like to round it up to 25 years, because I still am part of the lives of the people of the Parish, but in a different mode now that the Church itself has been deactivated.

I have been a priest now for 56 years, and almost one half of my priesthood has been shared with the people of Corpus Christi and Christ the King parishes. I think God has blessed me by giving me such a rich ending to my time as a priest. I feel that I have gained so much about the Church and what it means to have a relationship with God through like thinking people all on the same journey toward our eternal destiny with our Creator. The pains and trials of life are a constant in all our lives, but made bearable when shared with God through one another.

I have found joy just in the casual encounters we have as we meet together on Sunday to worship the Lord through the Sacrament of the Body and Blood of Christ. I have seen that same pleasure in the reactions of the congregation as we encounter one another through the service. This sense of belonging and connection with one another in worshiping and working together is a strength that we all have acquired during the 145 years that Corpus Christi Church has brought down upon us the bounty and blessings of God. Victor Hugo in his book *"Les Miserables"* writes, "To love another person is to see the face of God". This may be an overly sentimental statement, but when we think about this realistically, we have to admit its reality. It is through the people we encounter that bring us to know about the existence of the source of everything, God our Creator and Father. We first learn through our family and then friends, and for us in this Parish Community, from one another here in this House of God.

All life is a blessing given us by God. We gratefully cherish our own life, but also the lives we encounter on life's journey. The path on that journey is clearer and smoother because the people of Medford and Deerfield are all journeying together. The Parish of Corpus Christi is no more, but the people who spread out from this center of worship take the strength of their faith that they learned here for the good of all whom they encounter. The journey still continues, but with new companions.

Father Robert Herman

MEMORIES FROM A CORPUS CHRISTI DIRECTORY

After Christ the King was established and prior to the presence of the Sisters of Notre Dame from Mankato, Father Snyder arranged with the Dominican Sisters at Bethlehem Academy in Faribault for assistance with the religious training for our children. A parishioner from Medford would drive to Faribault on Saturday mornings and bring two Sisters to Christ the King where they would conduct classes for the children. Then a driver from Corpus Christi would call for them and escort them "out to the country". After working with the children at Corpus Christi, the Sisters would be returned to Faribault. A standing joke among the farm families was that this was one incentive for cleaning their car when it was their turn to transport the Sisters back to Faribault.

SAVING THE CORPUS CHRISTI CHURCH ALTAR AFTER VATICAN II
By James Lang

Corpus Christi Altar

In 1967, Jim Lang, son of Joseph and Margaret (Pfeiffer) Lang was back from the service. Father Harold B. Mountain was responsible for updating the church with a new wood altar to face the congregation as per Vatican II rules. He asked Jim Lang to save the art work on the front of the old altar which was an image of the Last Supper. Jim recounts how the old altar was dismantled into three parts. The base of the altar was 4 feet wide and 7 feet long.

The middle section of the altar housed the tabernacle, and the top section contained a cross.

The construction of the altar was pipe framing, covered with plaster, infused with horse hair to make it more durable. The base of the altar needed to be removed from Corpus Christi Church and transported to the Joseph Lang farm where the preservation could begin.

Jim backed his dad's farm truck up to the front steps of the church. Kenneth Mork provided pipe rollers to assist with the moving of the altar. Several parishioners, along with Jim and Kenneth, removed the top two sections from the base of the altar. The men slid the base of the altar across the pipe rollers, the length of the church and onto the truck bed. After getting the altar base home, Jim worked about two months cutting the base in half.

Jim Lang would work his way through the plaster and then when he encountered a pipe, he cut it with a hacksaw. After Jim had the base cut in half, he painted the base white and then trimmed the figures of the Last Supper with gold paint. Jim then brought the base of the altar back to the church. The same process to remove the base of the altar, was used again to move the altar from the back of church across the pipe rollers to the front.

The restored altar was placed against the north wall behind the new wood altar, facing the congregation, where it remains today. A piece of quarter inch plywood covers the top of the altar. A linen cloth then covered the plywood. The Tabernacle sat in the center of the back altar flanked on either side with brass candelabras.

There was enough room to place vases of flowers on either side in front of the candelabras.

Evelyn (Maas) Brady received the top section of the altar containing the cross. Agnes Reyant received the middle section of the altar containing the covering for the tabernacle. Frank and Theresa Reyant later inherited this section, which was then placed into storage in a chicken coop. Jim later located the middle section and received it back from the Reyants. When the Jerry Hurst family moved into the Deerfield area and purchased a place just south of the Deerfield store in the early 1970s, they made a chapel in their home. Jim Lang gave the middle section to the Hurst family for their at home chapel.

When the Hurst family left the area and were no longer members of Corpus Christi Church this section was given back to Jim Lang in the early 1980s where it is currently being preserved in his home in Austin.

Father James Starasinich removed the Tabernacle from Corpus Christi Church and is being used in his personal chapel at St. Joseph parish in Owatonna.

JAMES WILLIAM LANG REMEMBERS

Joseph and Margaret (Pfeiffer) Lang moved to Deerfield in the spring of 1947. Jim "Bill" was 2 years old. Jim made his First Communion in 1952, and was confirmed in 1955 at Corpus Christi. The following are memories Jim has.

The earliest memories are of the many summer Sunday dinners that took place to raise money. A large tent was pitched east of the cemetery. Every family provided chickens and garden produce for these events.

In the spring the families would gather to clean up the yard. Women and children would rake and the men would trim trees and cut wood for the fall and winter to heat the church with the wood burning stove. Once a year a bingo party would take place to raise money for the catechism program which took place 2 weeks in the summer.

Dominican Nuns from Bethlehem Academy at Faribault would come to teach the children.

Father Raymond Snyder boarded his horse at the Pete Stiren's farm located west of the Corpus Christi church. When I was still a very small boy, Father would ride his horse to our farm to visit and would give me rides.
On the Feast of Corpus Christi a procession with a portable altar would take place in the circle drive around the church. All would follow in prayer as the altar was moved from station to station.

Once on a trip to the Remagen Passion Play in Germany, Father Harold Mountain brought back a hand carved corpus. He had Stanley Panos make the cross. This is the crucifix that is now in the sanctuary of Corpus Christi.

In 1967, after Vatican II, the altar was reversed to face the people. The original altar was made of plaster and had a beautiful figure of the Last Supper.

The men moving in the new altar said the original altar was too heavy to move and needed to be broken up to get it out of the church. Father Mountain said "Jim can you save it?"

With the help of the others the original altar was loaded onto Jim's father Joe Lang's pickup and taken to the Lang garage. I was able to save it and the face of the original altar is now on the back wall of the sanctuary.

One of my earliest memories of Sunday Mass at Corpus Christi was seeing a lady on her knees praying the Rosary before Mass and the last one to leave her knees after Mass. Years later, that lady became my mother-in-law, Martha Pete.

James William Lang

MEMORIES OF CORPUS CHRISTI CATHOLIC CHURCH IN DEERFIELD

I remember the stained glass windows and especially the one my Grandpa and Grandma James F. Brady's name was on. I always looked for it coming into church and Grandpa and Grandma were sitting there.

I remember the summer picnics and the baseball games. Delicious food and fun! I remember the Christmas parties we had. I especially remember Father Mountain showing a movie called "Our Lady of Fatima." I still think of that movie. Santa always made a visit too. Great fun.

Everything was wonderful to me because that was our social activity. Mom and Dad always visited after church with the neighbors and they knew everyone.

I received First Communion from Father Mountain and I knew all the people in my class because we had religion on Saturdays during the school year and two weeks in the summer. We always had nuns who taught us. We had confirmation in 5th grade. They closed the country school I attended at the end of my 6th grade and I went to Medford. Religion classes were then taught on Wednesday release time at school.

Grandpa and Grandma Brady had their 50th Wedding Anniversary party in Deerfield. It was a great party with my aunts and uncles all home. The saddest day was the funeral of Grandpa Brady in 1960. He was buried in Faribault.

Father Mountain was there 17 years so I don't remember other priests.

Sharon Brady Popowski

SEVENTY YEARS OF HISTORY AT CORPUS CHRISTI PARISH

By Dorothy (Bakken) Morgan

When we were married in 1950 at Corpus Christi Church by Father Raymond Snyder, Don was already a member as were his parents John and Mary (Ost) Morgan. At that time the Mass was said in Latin and the priest had his back to the people while saying the mass.

The organ was in the balcony as was the choir, the confessional was under the stairway and our pews had kneelers that were not attached, so the kneelers fell over quite often. The "Mother's Room" was to the left side of the altar.

In the winters at that time card parties and dances were held in the church basement; we enjoyed both. In the summer, picnics were held at the east church lawn across the road from the church. The first summer after we were married, I received a letter about the annual picnic.

I was surprised at all the food I was told to prepare and bring to the picnic; several chickens, potatoes, vegetables, pies, butter and pickles. There were huge crowds for these picnics. In the afternoon there would be Bingo and other games. For all events held at the church, water was pumped by hand out of well beside the basement door.

Our seven children (Diane, Donna, Dennis, Dawn, Douglas, Daniel, and Darla) were baptized, had their First Communion and Confirmations at Corpus Christi.

Diane, Dennis, Douglas, and Daniel and their families are still members of Corpus Christi parish. Father Harold Mountain came to Corpus Christi in 1952 and was here for 16 years. He always said "They couldn't move a Mountain".

Donald died in 2012; he had been a Corpus Christi member for over 70 years and as this is written, I have been a member for 66 years. We saw a number of changes over the years, but a number of families have remained the same... just different generations.

Corpus Christi members always enjoy visiting with each other after Mass, sometimes that will last longer than the Mass did. The new status with Corpus Christi going to oratory status will be a big change for all.

Dorothy (Bakken) Morgan

After Mass gatherings were an important part of the Corpus Christi parish community. It was not uncommon to find parishioners visiting in front of the church up to an hour or more after Mass ended.

CARLA BRADY REMEMBERS:
PARISH PICNICS, ORANGE POP, STATIONS OF THE CROSS & FINGER FOOD
By Carla (Maas) Brady

I was born on a farm west of Medford, and I attended Christ the King Church where my family was a member. I was married at Christ the King church in June of 1977 to Byron P. Brady a member of Corpus Christi, at which time I officially became a member of Corpus Christi Church.

My first memories of Corpus Christi Church were the parish picnics held out at Deerfield. I remember the cow tanks with pop bottles (especially orange crush) which was truly a treat for me. I never had pop growing up except at the parish picnic. I remember the games and the big families (I had 4 brothers and 4 sisters) and that it was a lot of fun interacting at the picnics.

My first memory of church was coming for different Masses with my dad. I remember attending the stations of the cross at Corpus Christi during Lent on a Thursday evening, if for some reason we were unable to attend Wednesday afternoon or Friday services offered at Christ The King in Medford. The Corpus Christi church at Deerfield had a distinct aroma; it was country and cozy. I loved the stations of the cross on the wall, so different from Medford. Corpus Christi church was full, and the people were friendly.

I remember my bridal shower held in the Corpus Christi church basement. There were at least 40 women there and they were all invited to our wedding. Money was scarce in those days, I remember receiving household things for the kitchen, and I received an iron and ironing board. Back then, we ironed our shirts and dresses.

I remember attending Mass at Deerfield and was intrigued how everyone stayed around and visited after Mass and caught up with the latest news of the church "family." The ladies added me to a guild and they were not shy about asking for help with whatever the church needed. I was made to feel a full member of the church, with an understanding that I was expected to pull my weight.

For nearly the next 40 years, I was very involved in the church: choir, lector, officer for the ladies' group, teaching religion, working at May Crowning, Christmas programs, fund raising, decorating the church for Christmas and other duties as assigned. I loved my Corpus Christi Church community. It was the best part of the week, and I looked forward to attending Mass on the weekend to see everyone and catch up with the activities of Deerfield.

It was with great sadness that we saw the closing of our church for Sunday Masses, with the changing to oratory status in 2016. The church spirit that was present at Deerfield is greatly missed. I really enjoy the annual Mass(es) that we have and the get-together with the "finger-food" meal afterwards and bonfire since the church became an oratory in 2016. When we meet the music is still great (thank you Amy Hellevik) and Corpus Christi still feels like home.

Carla (Maas) Brady

****

MARK & MARLENE STADLER
(COPPER KETTLE)

It was in the passing of Arthur Voegele that Mark and Marlene stepped up to help with the funeral luncheon. There was an ice storm overnight and on November 29, 1991, we had no electricity to prepare the funeral luncheon at Christ the King Church basement. Mark was very gracious and brought over hot coffee for the funeral from the Copper Kettle. We had to forego the scalloped potatoes and ham, serving cold sandwiches, cake and salads. The warm coffee was so welcomed on that cold and blustery day.

GROWING UP IN DEERFIELD TOWNSHIP DURING THE 1950s & 1960s

By Ronald F. Eustice

Donald & Alice Mae Eustice and their three small boys Ronald, Robert and Donald Jr. moved from Faribault to a farm in southwest Deerfield Township in early 1948. Daughter Marjorie was born at Waseca in October 1950.

The Eustices joined Corpus Christi parish immediately after arrival. The parish was in a period of transition. Father Raymond Snyder, who had been the pastor from the time the church was re-opened in 1937 was completing more than a decade of service to the parish. He was much loved and highly respected. Fr. Harold B. Mountain became the new pastor in 1952. Here are a few of my memories:

Parish Festivals:
Father Snyder had been instrumental in organizing Parish Picnics in June and a Harvest Festivals in October. While promoted as social events, the objective was to raise money to support the parish. The last of the fall Festivals was in 1951. I remember army tents, a huge crowd, lots of food and hundreds of cars parked along the gravel road. There were games for the kids. I remember some kind of a game where a prize could be pulled out of a basket behind a curtain with a fishing pole. The fundraisers began in 1938, and were very successful, generated revenue for the parish and helped parishioners become acquainted. The size of the crowd was impressive considering that Deerfield is rather remote. I remember only two Sauerkraut Festivals and they were exciting events. It was also a huge commitment of time for the parishioners. The amount of donated food was substantial especially considering the parishioners were mostly farmers of modest means. The fall (Sauerkraut) Festivals were discontinued soon after 1951.

Religious Education:
Every Saturday, Fr. Harold Mountain drove to Faribault to pick up sisters from Bethlehem Academy. I remember that he drove a shiny black Buick Invicta. Father Mountain liked fancy cars.

In those days, the sisters wore veils and habits traditionally worn by members of their orders. I wish I had a picture of the sisters getting out of Father Mountain's big, black Buick on Saturday morning.

We had catechism classes from 8:30 until noon. The sisters were from the Sinisawa Dominican Order and taught at Bethlehem Academy in Faribault. In June, the School Sisters of Notre Dame at Good Counsel Academy, Mankato came to Deerfield for two weeks.

We learned a lot from the sisters. I specifically remember Sister Aquin from Good Counsel. Besides catechism, the sisters helped train the Mass servers and choir members. They also prepared us for the sacraments, our first confession and First Holy Communion.

I began to serve Mass in third grade (1953) and served my final Mass in 1963 when I was a senior in high school. Since this was before Vatican II, all Masses were in Latin with only the homily in English. I still remember my prayers in Latin. Those words still roll off my tongue some 70 years later. *Ad Deum qui laetificat juventutem meam etcetera.....* The sisters taught us well! May their souls rest in peace.

Special Memories:
On a few occasions movies were shown in the church basement. I remember seeing *The Song of St. Bernadette.*

Choir, Usher, Server Activities:
Father Mountain worked closely with the Knights of Columbus to organize special activities for the choir, ushers and Mass servers. There was a Christmas party every December and during the summer there was often a trip to Bloomington for a Minnesota Twins game.

The Twins played in the old stadium, which was just north of where the Mall of America now stands. We looked forward to these activities and they gave us an opportunity to spend more time with each other. It was especially nice for those of us who did not go to Medford schools to meet the young people from Medford.

I graduated from Owatonna High School in 1963 and went on to complete a Bachelor's Degree at the University of Minnesota. I returned to Corpus Christi in 1968 to give a slide presentation following my six-month stay in Uruguay, South America as a Farm Youth (IFYE) Exchange student.

Our parents continued to be members of Corpus Christi Parish for the remainder of their lives. Donald Eustice died July 3, 2002 and Alice died July 7, 2008. Both are buried in Corpus Christi Cemetery.

Donald & Alice Mae (Perron) Eustice Family (1953)
(Donald Jr., Donald Sr., Ronald, Robert, Marjorie and Alice Mae).

Donald & Alice Mae (Perron) Eustice Family (1983)
(Seated, L-R: Alice Mae, Robert, Donald Sr., Marjorie. Standing; Ronald & Donald Jr.)

EUSTICE FAMILY HISTORY

DONALD F. EUSTICE
(1921-2002)

Donald Francis Eustice was born July 16, 1921, on the family farm in Alton Township, Waseca County, to John W. and Mary Gertrude (Donelan) Eustice. He grew up in Alton Township and attended a one-room country school located just north of the family farm. He served in the US Army during 1942 and 1943 and was stationed at Ft. Cronkite, near San Francisco, CA. He was discharged in late 1943 when his father was injured in a farm accident. On November 17, 1944, he married Alice Mae Perron, daughter of Omer and Emma (Remillard) Perron at Sacred Heart Catholic Church, Faribault, MN. They began farming on rented land located south of his family's farm in Alton Township. They remained at this location until early in 1947 when they moved to Faribault; where Donald began work as a fieldman for Faribault Canning Company. In 1948 Donald and Alice Mae purchased 160 acres in Deerfield Township, Steele Co, and Bloomington Grove Township, Waseca County. It was on this farm north of Meriden they raised their family of four children. In retirement, Donald continued to live on the family farm, raise cattle and pursue his hobby of collecting antique John Deere tractors. Donald F. and Alice Eustice were members of Corpus Christi Catholic Church at Deerfield since they moved to the area.

Donald F. Eustice, a Steele County, Minnesota farmer died July 3, 2002 at Pleasant Manor Nursing Home in Faribault at age 81. He was suffering from complications associated with diabetes. Donald F. Eustice was survived by his wife; children, Ronald and wife Margaret (McAndrews) of Savage, Robert and wife Diane (Caulfield) of Byron, Donald Jr. and wife Kathy (Novak) of Faribault, and Marjorie and husband Michael Root of Austin, TX; grandchildren, Kevin Eustice of Los Angeles, John Eustice of Minneapolis and AnnMarie Eustice of Savage; Mark Eustice of the U.S. Marine Corps, Angela Deutsch of New Market, Malia Eustice of Mankato and Brent Eustice of Byron; Monica Bruening of Eyota, Marsha Fuller of Faribault and Megan Eustice of Dundas; great grandchildren, Jared Bruening, Paige Bruening; Anthony Fuller and Sandra Capri Fuller; Chasity Dawn Eustice, Shadie Rosalie Brooks and Mickayla Marie Eustice. He was also survived by brothers Herbert (Eileen) Eustice of Janesville and Eugene (Leona) Eustice of Waseca and numerous nieces and nephews. He was preceded in death by his father in 1956 and by his mother in 1983. A Mass of Christian Burial was held July 6th at 10:30 am. at Christ the King Catholic Church in Medford with Father Robert Herman officiating. Burial with military honors took place in the Corpus Christi Church Cemetery in rural Deerfield Township.

Source: Faribault Daily News; July 5, 2002 & Dalby Database

ALICE MAE (PERRON) EUSTICE
(1923-2008)

Alice Mae Perron, daughter of Omer Perron and Emma Remillard was born Feb. 22, 1923 in Faribault. Alice was a long time parishioner and member of the Rosary Society, St. Ann's Guild and the Women's sewing club at Corpus Christi Catholic Church in Deerfield Township. Her first language was French which at that time was spoken by her parents as well as her extended family. Alice Mae attended elementary school at Sacred Heart School in Faribault from 1929 until 1937. The family lived at 614 3rd Street in Faribault and on a farm in Cannon City Township before moving to a farm located on 9th Avenue outside of Faribault known as the "McDonald Place." As a child she helped her parents with chores on the farm but at a very early age developed a talent for sewing. She had the ability to take a piece of cloth and without a pattern make it into an attractive and very functional garment. As a young woman, Alice Mae worked at various jobs including serving as a waitress at the Faribault Hotel. She married Donald F. Eustice of Waseca on Nov. 17, 1944 at Sacred Heart Church in Faribault. Donald and Alice began farming by renting what was known as the "Christie Farm" located just south of the Eustice family farm in Alton Township, Waseca County. They remained there until 1947 when they moved to Faribault. In 1948, Donald and Alice purchased 160 acres known then as the "Leader Farm" located in Deerfield and Blooming Grove Townships on the Steele-Waseca County line just north of Meriden. During the late 1950s and 1960s, Alice worked as a housekeeper at motels in Waseca and Owatonna and was employed five years at E.F. Johnson Company in Waseca where she assembled radio parts. She also worked about five years at Randall's Bakery in Waseca and at Birdseye Foods in Waseca during canning season. In her final years, she was a resident of Pleasant Manor in Faribault. Alice M. Eustice, 85, of Faribault and formerly of rural Waseca died July 7, 2008 at St. Marys Hospital in Rochester. A Mass of Christian Burial was held Friday, July 11 at Christ the King Catholic Church in Medford. Interment took place at Corpus Christi Cemetery in Deerfield Township, rural Steele county. Alice Mae is survived by her four children; Ronald of Savage (Margaret McAndrews), Robert of Byron (Diane Caulfield), Donald of Faribault (Kathy Novak) and Marjorie Ann Root of Austin, Texas (Michael); her brother Richard Perron of Faribault; nine grandchildren, and ten great-grandchildren. Alice was preceded in death by her husband Donald, granddaughter Monica Bruening. Memorials are preferred to Christ the King Church or American Heart Association.

Source: Owatonna People's Press; July 9, 2008 & Dalby Database

LARSON FAMILY MEMORIES
By Jean (Thiele) Larson

George & Jean Larson Family

My name is Jean Ann Thiele. I attended country school and graduated from Owatonna high School as an Indian, they were later called the Huskies. I met George through 4-H and we were married Dec. 28th 1957. George had one more year in the Navy and was discharged with honor as a 2nd class electrician in late November of 1958. We purchased our 240 acre farm in Deerfield Township from George's folks. We milked cows, had sheep and hogs and took over the 1000 Hyline parent stock chickens. The folks moved to the farm that became Bob's later. They remodeled the barn there to three floors of layers for Hyline.

George was an original member of the Fr. Carlin Council of the Knights of Columbus. He was also a lector when it was allowed. For several years he also worked nights in maintenance at OTC and also Washington Scientific in Owatonna. We did all the farm work together from milking to field work. We were also blessed with six children. Tim is married to Joanne (Stene) and they have five children, Katie, Dan, Mariah, Holly and Lynn. Richard is married to Teri (Struck) and they have Will and Maggie. Chuck is married to Diane (Stene) and they have Lauren, Samantha, Cassandra, and Greg. Trina is married to Dean Schmelger and they have Jorge, Julia, John, and Catherine. Mathew is married to Ashly (Pound) and their sons are Tucker and Hunter. The three oldest sons are Ag instructors and FFA advisors. Trina's farm is in Owen-Withee, Wisconsin and Matt is a maintenance mechanic for Jerome Foods by Medford and has a motorcycle repair shop at their home. Our little angel George Jr. was born on the 1st Straight River Days and passed away at three days of age.

Fr. Harold Mountain was our first priest and he named the CCW officers every year. You didn't say no to him and he always gave us a lovely gift when we were through. Fr. Glynn was our priest when George Jr. was born and was on priest retreat in Winona but came and helped bury him and then returned to Winona. We were so grateful. Fr. Ryan was a retired Air Force Chaplain. George always said he was like the Navy Chaplains. Fr. Cody was with us as we had teen-agers. His sermons often referred to football, the Vikings . Mother Larson didn't care for this but when George would quiz the kids about what he was talking about, they always got it!

Fr. Edward Mountain was next and he was especially dear to me as he had handled the funerals at Sacred Heart, Owatonna of my grandma Diety, my mom and then my father. April 21st 1992 we were waiting for friends from Illinois to come and visit. It was a beautiful day and shortly after they arrived George collapsed outside the back-door of our home.

The next afternoon he was pronounced brain dead and we donated his organs to others as he wanted. George's cause of death was a massive brain hemorrhage. My neighbors and friends and family were a great support. But God sent us Matt when we had 4 teenagers.

George always said we had him for a special reason and you don't fall apart with a sad, sad, 12 year old that's just lost daddy. George was 54 years old and we would have been married 35 years in December 1992.

Jean (Thiele) Larson

319

Sylvester and Jacqueline (Beckel) Dulas Family
Front; L-R: Joel, Jay, Jackie, Sylvester, Judy.
Standing at Back; John, Joyceann.
Sylvester and Jacqueline Dulas moved to Deerfield from Mapleton, Blue Earth County with their five children in March 1962. Dulas farm was located 1 1/2 miles northeast of the church. Sylvester served as Corpus Christ custodian from 1975 until 2006. Jackie was involved with almost all women's activities and served as custodian from 2006 until 2008.

MEMORIES OF CORPUS CHRISTI PARISH, DEERFIELD
By Jackie (Beckel) Dulas

In November 1961, my husband Sylvester and I purchased a 60-acre farm in Deerfield Township about a mile and a half north-east of Corpus Christi church. We moved to the farm in early-March 1962 with our five-year-old daughter, Joyceann.

Corpus Christi was a vibrant parish and the small church was packed every Sunday. Sometimes we had to sit in the "mother's room" because the main church was too crowded. We felt very welcome in the parish and I became involved in the women's activities. As the years moved on, our children Joyceann, John, Judy, Jay and Joel arrived and the entire family attended Corpus Christi. As this is written in 2024, our son Joel has the farm and I live in an apartment adjacent to the main house.

I especially remember the Christmas celebrations. For several years a live manger scene was set up with children from the parish portraying the holy family. In 2006, our grandson Charlie Dulas played Jesus and two years later another grandson Sam Dulas played the same role. Following the Christmas program a potluck dinner was served.

Sylvester served as custodian and janitor from early 1976 until 2006. Jackie continued to serve the church as custodian when Sylvester's health began to fail retiring in 2008 when Sontheimers took over.

When we arrived at Deerfield in 1962, the Catholic Church was in a state of transition, however the changes made during Vatican II (1962-1965) had not taken effect.

The priest said Mass in Latin with his back to the congregation. Only the homily was in English. There were no Saturday afternoon Masses. The Altar servers were all boys and the choir was entirely made up of girls and young women. Mass began with the Prayers at the Foot of The Altar and ended with a series of prayers. Special prayers were said at the end of Mass and very few left early.

Women wore hats in church; We saw the occasional white handkerchief clipped to a woman's hair. At Easter, many women saw a good reason to purchase a new hat, and there were some fancy ones! It was almost like an Easter parade. Gender roles were structured and clearly defined. All nuns were dressed in a full habit.

Before the changes of Vatican II, fasting before communion from midnight was required, only water could be consumed. Very few went to the later Masses because fasting was required. There was a communion rail and everyone knelt to receive the host. Only the priest distributed communion and the altar server held a plate known as a paten to prevent the host from falling in case of a mishap. There were no Eucharistic ministers or deacons and only the priest was allowed to touch the host. The host was placed on the communicant's tongue and there was no communion in the hand.

Not everyone went to communion every Sunday; for some it was only at Christmas and Easter, and only after confession. At Easter and Christmas, there were long lines of people waiting to go to confession, as Catholics were expected to make their "Easter Duty." The confessional at Corpus Christi was a small cubicle under the stairway to the belfry.

Each family was given envelopes for the collection. Even children had their own envelopes and gave a few pennies each Sunday. An annual financial statement was published with donation amount to exact penny with names listed.

THE SECOND VATICAN COUNCIL
The Second Vatican Council or commonly known as Vatican II, met in Saint Peter's Basilica in Vatican City for four periods (or sessions), each lasting between 8 and 12 weeks, in the autumn of each of the four years, 1962 to 1965. Pope John XXIII called the council because he felt the Church needed "updating" (in Italian: *aggiornamento*). In order to better connect with people in an increasingly secularized world, some of the Church's practices needed to be improved and presented in a more understandable and relevant way.

Since Vatican II, many changes have occurred. We now have girls serving Mass. There are no more hats worn by the ladies during Mass. Almost every parish has a deacon and men and women serve as lectors and Eucharistic ministers.

Key Developments due to Vatican II:
1. New general orientations and basic themes found throughout the documents:
* The Church defined as People of God
* The Eucharist as center of the Church and its unity
* The primacy of Scripture in theory and in practice
* The beneficial nature of diversity: *ecclesial* (the Church as a communion of "churches"), liturgical, and theological (diversity "even in the theological elaborations of revealed truth")
* Other Christians understood as being in [imperfect] communion with the Church
* The concern for secular human values, with justice and peace.
2. Specific texts that contain a shift from pre-conciliar teaching:
* The statement that the unique Church of Christ "subsists" in the Catholic Church (*Lumen Gentium 8*)
* The statement that "the Churches of the East, as much as those of the West, fully enjoy the right to rule themselves" (*Orientalium Ecclesiarum 5* and *Unitatis Redintegratio 16*)
* The recognition and commendation of the ministry of married priests in the Eastern Churches (*Presbyterorum Ordinis 16*)
* The recognition that every person has the right to religious freedom (*Dignitatis humanae 2*)
* The condemnation of anti-Semitism (*Nostra aetate 4*)
* The condemnation of mass destruction in war (*Gaudium et spes 80*)
* The statement that "parents themselves should ultimately make the judgment" as to the size of their family (*Gaudium et Spes 50*).
3. Practical decisions requiring new institutions or new behavior:
* The use of the vernacular (local language) in the liturgy
* The restoration of communion under both kinds for the laity
* The restoration of con-celebration of the Mass
* The restoration of the diaconate as a permanent order open to married men
* The [limited] possibility of sharing in the worship (including communion) of a Church other than one's own
* The instruction to establish national or regional Episcopal Conferences with authority and responsibilities
* The recommendation to establish an agency of the universal Church to "foster progress in needy regions and social justice on the international scene"

BERNARD & LUELLA (GILLEN) HEIM FAMILY MEMORIES

By Lois (Heim) Nelson

Front Row, L-R: Luella, Jeanette, Bernard. Second Row: Joanne Racek, Cynthia Smith, Rose Heim, Lois Nelson, Elaine Johnston, Christine Heim. Back Row: Philip Heim, Lloyd Heim, Patrick Heim.

The Bernard and Luella family moved from Kenyon with their then, six children-Lois, Elaine, Philip, Lloyd, Joanne, and Rosemary-the late summer of 1957 to what was known in the neighborhood as the 'Wendt Place'. They were able to settle in just in time to attend country school, District 42-2, down the road and join the little country church of Corpus Christi the first Sunday in September. The school and church were quite a new experience... the school which included classes through the 6th grade so the four oldest walked down the road to a one room school house of about forty students with teacher, Mrs. George (Gladys) Powell. They often walked to church on Saturday mornings for 'religion class' with Sister Rose and Sister Luella. Sister Rose shared the spiritual enlightenment from the Baltimore Catechism with the older students.

Sister Luella was in the Mother's Room with the younger students. These Notre Dame Sisters brought and taught the Catholic Faith to many of the children for several years at Corpus Christi.

After religion class, Sister Rose would prep the altar area for the next day's Sunday Mass and work with the boys who were the altar servers with Fr. Harold Mountain. Sister Luella would have choir practice upstairs in the loft area--at that time, it was an all-girls choir. Her back at the organ was to the altar so for timing she had a mirror to make sure she and we were keeping up with Father Mountain.

There were other big families at church – the Leo Mullenmaster's with sixteen children; the Henry Hager's with sixteen children—the Heim family also grew with Christine, Patrick, Cynthia and Jeannette (born in 1963).

Family life often centered around our country parish. The Sewing Ladies met at various homes throughout the year for mission quilting. Nimble fingers meant at least 100 quilts a year which were then proudly displayed with after Mass brunch in the fall before the annual Diocesan Women's Convention where the many boxes would be delivered to be distributed to numerous organizations. These brunches held at numerous times throughout the year where families were encouraged to bring 'finger food' and everyone delighted in the goodies.

The annual Christmas parties in those early years were also special. Grandpa Hager and his sons would stoke up the wood-burning furnace the night before. Then, made sure the basement was warm...metal pieces were placed upstairs in front of the vents by the communion rail directing the heat downstairs. A movie would be set up – Kenny Mork was called upon for some of this effort. Santa also came so we could all sit on his lap with our Christmas wishes and given a paper bag of candy, peanuts and a little religious mementos.

Then, there was the summer picnics where the hayfield east of the cemetery was cut for the ballgame that adults and young people enjoyed. All following a potluck picnic that everyone felt was the best ever. There were children and adult games for those who did not play ball. It may have meant peeling an orange for the longest peel or winning the three-legged race with gunny sacks. There definitely was a parish 'family' feel to the forty plus families that supported the activities at Corpus Christi.

Weddings, communions, and funerals were a part of this parish family. If the event required more people in attendance, Christ the King was then the selected site of the event. The ladies at Corpus Christi often held a wedding shower for the new bride-to-be.

Lois (Heim) Nelson, still displays the nativity set given to her in the fall of 1967 before she and Dave were married. Weddings would often have the women fixing the dinner at whatever place was chosen for the reception. Often, the young girls were asked to be waitresses and given a special apron commemorating the day. Funerals, too, meant parish family support with the ladies fixing the food and families all helping in the serving and clean up.

Agnes Reyant brought Sunday bouquets to decorate the altar and statues of the Blessed Mother and St. Joseph. With Agnes' advancing age and moving from the farm, Luella, assumed the taking of bouquets to each Mass. Oftentimes, dividing the blooms with others in sharing their beauty. This continued until their move to the Medford Manor in 1990.

Two of the Heim daughters were married at Corpus Christi. Elaine and Carl Johnston on August 26, 1967. Much later, the youngest daughter, Jeannette was married to Randall Malterer, on September 29, 1984.

Many family celebrations were enjoyed around the Corpus Christi family. Tragedy too as on November 21, 1984, daughter Joanne was killed in a car accident on her way to work at Owatonna Tool Company. She was also pregnant with the Racek's first child. Losing them both, meant the support of neighbors and the families of Corpus Christi.

It was a coincidental conversation that Loretta Holmquist, now widowed and relocating to Brainerd with the closing of the State School in Owatonna, had asked the folks if any of their children would consider moving to her family farm right behind Corpus Christi. When Lois' husband, Dave, heard this, he encouraged the possibility since Lois had missed the country and the idea of a house versus the two-bedroom upstairs apartment was appealing. They moved to the farmstead with their young son, Michael. Membership at Corpus Christi was a given! The Women's Council was still very active-in fact, Lois was elected President and was not at the meeting! Anna Hager and others assured her that they would all be supportive and so it was.

When first moving to the country, the Nelsons made regular use of the Mother's Room as Mike was a noisy toddler. Then, Anna Hager, also assured the young couple to sit in the church proper as it was wonderful to hear happy noises. Son Matthew and daughter, Sara, were born in the winter months of February and December. The long driveway was of concern, but parish member, Sylvester Dulas, assured them, that his tractor and blower would be available to keep the long driveway open. Both children were born at the Owatonna hospital and the driveway was nicely open.

The Lois and David Nelson family bought their home in Medford in December, 1976, and continued their membership and activities at Corpus Christi until its official closing.

Even after their move to Medford, Bernie and Luella Heim also made their way to the church and 9:00 Mass. With Bernie's passing in November, 1993; Luella and Lois would continue to drive to Deerfield and church. It was their time of catching up on the week's events and then, celebrating the start of the week with Mass at Corpus Christi.

The children of many of the original families from 1957 grew up and left the area. Their parents and some of them have passed away and are buried in the cemetery across the road from the parish church.

So was the situation with Bernard and Luella Heim. Bernard passed away in November of 1993 and was interred in the cemetery. Luella passed away on September 28, 2021, two days before her 100th birthday and joined Bernard in her final resting place at Corpus Christi Cemetery.

Lois (Heim) Nelson

Bernard & Luella (Gillen) Heim Grave at Corpus Christi Cemetery

323

CORPUS CHRISTI HEIM FAMILY MEMORIES

By Luella Heim

Going back to the end of August 1957--- our family moved into the old farmhouse on the Wendt farm not knowing anyone in that Deerfield neighborhood. We had lived in Kenyon for a brief nine months previously but this was new territory. Being a Saturday, we were concerned about where or when we could attend Sunday Mass. Our landlord suggested calling Louie and Lucille Pirkl who were Catholic and attended the country parish of Corpus Christi. We were pleased to learn that were within two miles of the church and Sunday Mass was at 9:00 am.

We arrived at our new home late Saturday, and our possessions were still packed in moving cartons. I recall it was quite a scramble that morning to find the right boxes for church clothes. But, by 9:00am, the Heim family then consisting of Bernie, Luella Lois, Elaine, Phillip, Lloyd, Joanne and Rosemary all filed into that little country church in Deerfield. None of us had ever seen such a small church; and surely we must have been noticed as some "new family" as our children then ranged in age from 10 to two years old.

It was with a feeling of acceptance and warm hospitality that we were welcomed to the parish community. By Christmas time, our children became actors in the annual pageant. Mary Voegele was president of the ladies CCW and made sure to introduce us all around at the event that was a part of every Christmas to this day.

Fr. Harold Mountain was pastor and before long, both boys, Philip and Lloyd, became altar servers. In January, 1958, another daughter, Christine, was born. Her baptism took place after Sunday Mass in the little sacristy with Fr Mountain officiating.

Saturday morning, classes were conducted in church with two Notre Dame nuns-Sister Rose and Sister Luella with our children often walking to the little country parish. We added three more children to our family, Patrick, Cynthia and Jeannette as we joined other large families in the parish-especially the Mullenmasters and the Hagers who each had even larger families.

Sunday morning Mass found the pews filled. For awhile, the Heims and Mullenmasters filled the Mother's Room as the side entrance was open to the little room opposite the sacristy. Now, it is used for the confessional and storage. Two of our girls were married at Corpus Christi. Elaine and Carl Johnston in 1967 and Jeannette and Randall Malterer in 1984.

In 1990, as Bernie's health was failing, we moved into an apartment in Medford. At that time, there was much speculation about how long Corpus Christi would continue functioning. Bernie was very emphatic that while it was open, we would continue our membership so every Sunday we headed west on County Road 12 and I still make that trip this fall of 2015 . When Bernie died in 1993, our burial plot awaited him in the parish cemetery. Now, twenty-two years later, Corpus Christi is definitely changing as it moves to Oratory status. I live close to Christ the King and will continue my dedication to parish life.

Luella (Gillen) Heim

Note: Luella (Gillen) Heim passed away on Sept. 28, 2021 shortly after this was written, see obituary on the next page.

BERNARD L. HEIM
(1914-1993)

Bernard Leonard Heim, the son of John and Mary (Schabet) Heim, was born in Rockway Township, Steams County, Minnesota on Aug. 20, 1914. The youngest of nine children, he served in the U.S. Army during World War II from May 1942 through March 1946. When he returned from France, he resumed his work at the Faribult Woolen Mill Co., Faribault. On July 9, 1946, he married Luella Gillen at the St. Lawrence Catholic Church, Faribault. They lived in Wells Township where he became active in farming. In 1956, the family moved to Kenyon, then to rural Steele County a year later. Heim worked at the Owatonna Canning Co. for more than 22 years until his retirement in 1979. In 1990, he and Luella moved to Medford to reside at Medford Manor. He was an active member of the Corpus Christi Catholic Church, the Medford-Deerfield Knights of Columbus Council 4909, and the Rice County VFW.

Bernard L. Heim, 79, of Medford, died Wednesday, Nov. 17, 1993, at his home following an extended illness. Funeral services were held at Christ the King Catholic Church, Medford, with burial at Corpus Christi Cemetery, Deerfield Township, Steele County. Members of the Faribault Veterans Service Organizations provided military rites at the cemetery. He was survived by his wife, Luella; by six daughters, Lois (and Dave) Nelson of Medford, Elaine (and Carl) Johnston of Mesa, Ariz., Rosemary Heim of Grand Marais, Christine (and Randy) Dominquez of Hawthorne, N.J., Cynthia (and Richard) Smith of Apple Valley, and Jeannette (and Randall) Malterer of Waseca; by three sons:, Philip (and Gail) Heim of Medford, Lloyd (and Carolyn) Heim), of Owatonna, and Patrick (and Tracy) Heim of Raleigh, N.C.; by 14 grandchildren; by three great-grandchildren; and a sister, Kay Heim, of St. Paul.

LUELLA (GILLEN) HEIM
September 30, 1921 — September 28, 2021

Luella M. Heim, age 99 of Medford, MN passed away on Tuesday, September 28, 2021 at the Medford Senior Care following an extended illness, two days from her 100th Birthday.

Mass of Christian Burial was held on Monday, October 4, 2021, at Christ the King Catholic Church, 205 2nd Ave. NW, Medford, MN with Fr. Jim Starasinich and Fr. Matthew Wagner Con-celebrating. Interment was held at the Corpus Christi Cemetery in Deerfield Township. For those unable to attend the service was live-streamed through a link found on Luella's obituary page.

Visitation was held at Parker Kohl Funeral Home, 1725 Lyndale Ave. N. in Faribault on Sunday, October 3, 2021, from 4:00 to 7:00 p.m.

The family requested that those attending Luella's visitation and funeral be fully vaccinated and masks were required.

Luella Marie Heim, daughter of Sebastian and Cecilia (Wagner) Gillen, was born on September 30, 1921, on the family farm in Cannon City Township. She graduated from St. Lawrence School in 1935, attended her freshman year at Bethlehem Academy and obtained her G.E.D. many years later. As a young lady, Luella was available for domestic duties with families who needed assistance, making friends and memories along the way.

Before WWII, Luella met her future husband, Bernard Heim, who left for military service in 1942. She moved to Minneapolis to help in the war effort and was hired by Honeywell Corporation. She worked there until 1946 when Bernard returned from France.

While in Minneapolis, she volunteered with the American Red Cross even marching with their unit in the Aquatennial Parade.

She was united in marriage to Bernard (Bernie) Heim on July 9, 1946 and settled in rural Rice County. By 1957, the young family had taken up residence in Deerfield Township in Steele County, where they were active in the Corpus Christi Catholic Church.

All ten of their children attended Medford Public School. She was a master of recycling and re-purposing long before it was trendy. At an early age, Luella developed a love of horticulture and nature. She spent many hours gardening and tending to her flowers.

She created beautiful floral arrangements that regularly adorned the Corpus Christi church altar on Sundays. She was a devout Catholic and her faith and the love of family was extremely important to her.

Giving of one's time played a key role throughout Luella's life, and she was proud to volunteer as a 4-H leader and with the Faribault Chapter of Hospice and St. Vincent de Paul organizations. She treasured her membership in the Court St. Anne of Catholic Daughters and the Winona Council of Catholic Women, holding various leadership roles in both organizations.

For over 30 years, using her mother's Singer treadle sewing machine, she produced beautiful, pieced quilts and ditty bags that were distributed to missions around the world. She enjoyed reading and journaling. She was always up for a good game of cards and was hard to beat at Scrabble. She was a devoted Minnesota Twins fan; watching them play brought her hours of enjoyment.

Left to treasure the memories of Luella are her children, Lois (David) Nelson, Elaine Johnston, Philip (Gail) Heim, Lloyd Heim, Rosemary Heim, Christine Heim, Patrick (Tracy) Heim, Cynthia (Richard) Smith, and Jeannette (Randy) Malterer; seventeen grandchildren; twenty-two great grandchildren and three great great grandchildren; siblings, Joanne (Jim) Cortese and Adrian Gillen; son-in-law, Robert Racek and hundreds of extended family members.

MEMORIES ABOUT SISTER DELORES
By Amy (Pete) Hellevik

"My sister, Janice, cleaned the RE Classrooms every Tuesday after school. After she was done, Sister Delores would bring her home and would always have dinner with the Pete Family. As she would leave our home, Mom and Dad would slip her a couple beers for the week. As I WAS NOT one of her favorites (like Janice), Sister Deloros would always look at me every time and say, 'Don't you say a word to anyone about this.' "I feared her at the time and never talked about it but can chuckle about it today!"

During the the late 1950s, an agreement was arranged with the School Sisters of Notre Dame to assign sisters to teach religion classes at Medford as well as Deerfield and Janesville. Father Mountain said the first Mass at the new convent on August 22, 1958. Bishop FitzGerald came to bless the convent on September 7, 1958. Permission was granted by the Medford School Board to release all pupils for Religious Instruction at various times during the week.

Initially, there were several sisters residing in the convent, but by 1980, only Sister Delores remained. She is remembered for implementing Christmas pageants that provided young people of Corpus Christi and Christ The King with a meaningful understanding of Christmas and other church holy days. She was the leader in preparation of students for first holy communion and confirmation. After she left in 1980, these tasks were transferred to lay volunteers.

JUDY BRADY & CARLA BRADY REMEMBER SISTER DELORES

Judy Brady recalls when she was in elementary school, Sister Dolores would host an overnight at the convent for a bunch of girls. They would bring their sleeping bags and have a grand time in the convent basement.

Carla Brady remembers when she was in high school, and Sister Dolores was starting a student choir. Carol Hill was at the organ with Sister Dolores directing. I often got in trouble with her because I had a difficult time remaining quiet. I was surprised when sister Dolores recruited me to teach 3rd grade religion in the fall of 1980. Sister escorted me to several training courses held in Faribault and Austin to prepare me for this new endeavor. I had just given birth to my 3rd child, so my mother Georgette volunteered to watch my children (I think Sr. Dolores and my mother had it planned before she asked me). It took a village to teach our children. This was the beginning of more than 25 years of teaching religion for me.

MEMORIES: ERIN (BRADY) HESSE

Singing in the choir has always been a prominent memory for me at Corpus Christi. Amy Hellevik would play the piano and my mom and sisters would sing along with others. The early memories included singing up on the balcony. The choir moved to the front of the church when the new piano was purchased. Even after I had graduated, returning home at Christmas to sing in the choir was a huge part of the Holiday. It was so fun to do all the harmonies with my sisters Anna and Moggie and the rest of the choir.

Community is another prominent memory at Corpus Christi. It was very special playing tag with the other kids after every Sunday Mass while the parents visited on the front lawn of the church. I loved the potluck gatherings in the basement, especially after the Christmas program. We looked forward to church picnics in the summer. Everyone would come together for fall and spring cleanup. We would rake leaves and pick up sticks and then afterwards we would share treats and sometimes even have a wiener roast.

Another fond memory is the kids Christmas program that was a huge part of Corpus Christi's getting us in the Christmas spirit. I participated in the Christmas program as a child. After I was married and lived away, I was welcomed back with my children, and they were also able to participate in the Christmas pageant. My boys were little "sheep," and my daughter was baby Jesus. The children were able to experience the finger food brunch and the visit from Santa. Corpus Christi people are very special to me.

MEMORIES FROM CAROL PHILLIPS ANDERSON

Eldred & Mary (Trettel) Phillips lived several places after they married, and it wasn't until they purchased their farm in 1955 in Deerfield Township that they became members of Corpus Christi Church with three children in tow; Cathy, Carol, and Michael (age1). Rosemary Alice was born and baptized in 1959 completing their family. Mary was active in the church guild, doing her part for the CCW. She was also a long-time member of the Catholic Daughters. Mary was the organist for more than 10 years while having both adult and youth choirs. The last few years that she played, she combined forces with Nancy Hurst on her guitar. Mary was so generous with her time and talents.

Sister Delores had been cleaning and pressing altar linens for the Corpus Christi altar. In 1977, She decided that it was time to replace the linens, so she bought material and gave it to Mary Phillips to sew, indicating the new altar linens would be easier to care for. Evelyn Brady helped to sew & hem the linens. After this, the Corpus Christi women were in charge of caring for the linens for the church.

Eldred was very involved in the church activities. He was a lector and usher. He was an active member in the Medford Deerfield Knights of Columbus. It was under the direction of Fr Cody that Eldred was called to act to assist with shipping ground corn to Tanzania

At first, the knights were going to each donate corn for the project, however after consideration of the logistics, it was decided that the corn would all come from one farm (Eldred's and Mike's) and the other knights could help by donating money for the corn or additional funds for shipping. This would provide for a uniform corn product. The corn needed to be dried further from 13% moisture to about 11% to avoid spoilage during shipping.

As the story goes (told by Aldon Sammon) Aldon drove his semi tractor to the cities to get the shipping container that would hold 40,000 lbs. (roughly 700 bu.) of ground corn. The container was purchased by Brother Regis Fust who worked with the Salvatorian Mission Warehouse out of Holstein Wisconsin who had a connection with shipping items to Tanzania.

The container was placed on a lowboy trailer that was rented and brought to the Phillip's farm. Some brother knights came to Eldred's farm to help with the project. Using the hammer-mill that ground pig feed at the farm, they ran some corn through it to clear out the previous feed. Then the mill was set to the finest setting and the corn was ground. As it came out of the mill it was placed in plain paper feed sacks and then stitched shut. The sacks were loaded into the container (20 ft. long and 8 ft wide) until it was nearly full. The container was then taken to Faribault and weighed at the Land-O-Lakes milk plant to verify the container was within perimeters. After adding a couple more bags to meet weight, a combination padlock sealed the container shut. The container was shipped out of the cities and was labeled medical supplies. This was to prevent the confiscation of the corn when it reached the port in Africa, which was a problem with past shipments of this kind. It was exciting news when word was received that the container with the Deerfield corn had reached its destination with the padlock intact. Great act of humanity by the local church men. *(See the Knights of Columbus ship much-needed corn to Tanzania news article on next page.)*

Eldred and Mary moved into Owatonna when son Michael took over the farm in 1983-84. They always came back to support our church events and remained active KC and CDA members until their deaths.

Carol recalls one time driving home from church, and Mary said "Eldred, don't sing so loud." Eldred replied: "God gave me this voice, so he can listen to it." Carol remembers singing in the Choir, but how scary it was due to the slant of the choir loft. She also remembers the special services: Christmas, Easter, the stations of the cross. She remembers the picnics, helping with setting up tables and chairs as well as taking them back down again. She remembers how special it was that she had been remembered with a wedding shower even though she had been gone from Deerfield for over 13 years. The shower was well attended, and she even remembered some of the gifts she received. Carol remembers wearing a round doily on her head when attending mass.

On several occasions, when she forgot her headwear, she sported a Kleenex, as a girl was never to have her head uncovered. Carol remembers the bingo parties in the little church basement. The many sandwiches and bars, and the high school girls were asked to serve at the event. It was great fun. Those were special times!

Carol (Phillips) Anderson

KNIGHTS OF COLUMBUS SHIP MUCH-NEEDED CORN TO TANZANIA

OWATONNA - Recent television scenes of starving people in Ethiopia and other nations in Africa have made Americans realize they must help ease the hunger in the world. yet, as the check is written, many contributors never know if the money will be used to buy food for starving millions or be diverted by government red tape.

But several local Knights of Columbus members need not wonder. In mid-October, a shipment almost 40,000 pounds of ground corn from southern Minnesota reached the city of Shinyanga, Tanzania, and was distributed to the people who needed the food to live.

None of the Knights ever sat down and decided to ship food to the starving Africans, according to Eldred Phillips, a member of the group. It just happened.

It all began with a celebration. It was the 30th anniversary of the ordination of the Rev. Nicholas Cody, brother of Rev. John Cody, pastor at Christ the King Catholic Church in Medford.

Nicholas Cody received about $3,000 in gifts from his parishioners at St. Therese parish in St. Paul. Cody knew of the plight of the Tanzanian people through messages received from the Rev. John Lange, a pastor living in Kibaha, Tanzania.

Nicholas Cody contacted his brother, John, and asked if he could arrange for the purchase and transportation of corn from southern Minnesota to the people of Tanzania. It was time for John Cody to call on area farmers who were members of the Knights of Columbus.

Cody called Eldred Phillips. The farmer said he had corn in his bin, but said it was already sold on contract. Through the help of a Knight who is a grain buyer, Phillips was able to arrange to fill the contract and still have the corn available to ship to the Africans.
While the corn was sufficiently dry by Minnesota standards, it wasn't dry enough for the humid African climate.

The corn was dried to 11 percent moisture, and then it was ground. The grinding and bagging were done by a group of Knights, using equipment owned by Phillips and Gene Von Ruden. But getting the corn from here to there was the next difficult step. Enter Brother Regis and the "container connection."

Brother Regis Fust works in the Salvatorian Mission Warehouse in New Holstein, Wis., a clearing house that has been sending supplies to missions in Tanzania for the past five years, according to the July 1984 Maryknoll News. Fust gathers and ships medicine, soap, food and other items needed by the Africans.

But the key to the shipments are the containers they are sent in - metal boxes 20 feet long by eight feet wide, which Fust buys second-hand from overseas shippers. Even used, the containers cost $850.

Once they arrive in Africa and are unloaded, the containers are used for classrooms and other shelters. Fust found a container in Milwaukee, Wis., which he purchased and had shipped by rail to Minneapolis. Aldon Sammon, a Knight who has a semi-truck, rented a flatbed to carry the container to Steele County where it was filled with 702 bushels of corn.

While Phillips and his son, Mike, offered the corn before they knew they'd be reimbursed, they have received either corn or money from Knights of Columbus members Jerry and Lloyd Kern, George Hackett, Francis Maas, Donald, Dennis, Doug and Dan Morgan, and the Fourth Degree Knights Council.

The container of corn was shipped back to the Twin Cities, where it was sent by rail to Montreal. Quebec. The corn was shipped out of Montreal in mid-July after Fust unraveled the paper-work required to allow the corn to be sent to Dar-es-Salaam, Tanzania.

Once in Africa, it still cost a great deal of money to have the corn sent about 700 miles into the country, Lange wrote. He also wrote of his hopes that the U.S. AID would pick up the tab.
Later, Lange mailed two letters, one to each of the Cody brothers. On Aug. 13, he wrote to John Cody:

"I just received a letter from Nick giving the good news that 20 tons of corn flour were just shipped by Brother Regis. Please be assured the corn will go to very hungry people. The drought in the country is bad. People were scrounging in for food even during the harvest season. I will do my best to see that the corn is shipped up-country by a rail. There it will be distributed by a committee of Maryknoll and diocesan priests.

I'm not in the real famine area. I used to live there and get many letters from people. Before, all I could do was send them money, but you can't eat that and the cost of food, if at all it can be found, would be about $60 per bushel."

In Lange's Nov. 7 letter to Nick Cody, he wrote: "l just received news from Fr. Marve Deutsch that the freight car arrived safely in about Oct. 20 and was quickly distributed. Most of it, 500 bags, went to Fr. Jim Travis's parish where people are in real bad shape. Even though things work slowly here, your food beat the food that is supposed to come from CRS (Catholic Relief Services). So, it was indeed food to save lives and much suffering."

Phillips said he didn't feel the task was anything more than the simple execution of duty.

"We weren't crusaders," he said."We were like the Good Samaritan.

This thing was kind of pushed on (Father John Cody) and he pushed it on to me and then I pushed it on to the Knights.

Byron & Linda (Caron) O'Connor Family at the 160th anniversary celebration at Corpus Christi on September 11, 2016.

RAISING TEN CHILDREN AT CORPUS CHRISTI PARISH
By Linda & Byron O'Connor

We moved to the Steele County-Deerfield area in December 1983. I was pregnant with our third child. The neighbor lady, Carla Brady, stopped by our house to welcome us to the neighborhood. She, too, was expecting.

Carla invited us to join the Corpus Christi Parish. It wasn't long, and we started going and joined Corpus Christi. We belonged to Immaculate Conception Church in Faribault, so this was a big change, but we loved the small country church. We felt very welcome by everyone and there were a lot of people with families about the same ages as our family.

We had seven more children while members of the Corpus Christi Parish. All eight had their Baptism while at Corpus Christi. All ten of our children had their First Communion at Corpus Christi, and nine of the children had their Confirmation as members of Corpus Christi.

Now, many of them return to visit and attend Mass in Deerfield. This tradition was missed by our huge family when Corpus Christi was changed to oratory status. We like to fill several pews during Christmas service and listen to the beautiful music and the large, extended family of Corpus Christi-Deerfield Parish.

Linda was the pre-school through Kindergarten religion teacher for many years. Our family attended and helped in the many events that our parish had. We especially enjoyed Bingo parties, Fun Fests, church picnics out at Corpus Christi, after Mass brunches, Spring church clean-ups (indoors and outdoors), church paintings, rehabs, WCCW, National Day of Prayer, etc. The quaint-no frills-church, parish community at Corpus Christi, and attitude really is all anybody would ever need.

MEMORIES OF CORPUS CHRISTI PARISH

By Philip Heim

Our family moved to Deerfield Township late in the summer of 1957. Our family of eventually 10 children, became one of the several large families that belonged to the Corpus Christi Parish. Some of the familiar family names were the Hagers, Holmquists, Morgans, Hurts, Bradys, Hoffmans, Mullenmasters, Phillips, Coles, Langs, Millers, Eustices, Dulas, Larsons, Jewisons, Ambergs, Smiths, Karstens, Morks, Klukas, Petes and several others.

We younger boys were to wear our white shirts, black slacks and shoes and crowd together in the front pew on the right side. I remember on one hot humid Sunday, I passed out and came to with two of the Hager boys, who were ushers, carrying me out of the church with one of them under each of my arms.

At the time of my First Communion, Father Harold Mountain asked me if I thought the nun who was my First Communion instructor ever sinned. I figured she probably had like the rest of us but I didn't want to accuse her so I said "No, I didn't think she did." That got a good laugh out of the congregation.

After I enlisted in the Air Force in 1969, I always appreciated the support I received when I came home on leave. Many people serving in the military at that time were disrespected because of the anti-Viet Nam War protests. I always appreciated the friendliness and welcoming of Corpus Christi parishioners.

When my wife, Gail and I were married in 1982, the parish members gave us a bridal shower, Jim and Mary Fredericks were the hosts. The Christmas parties, Easter Egg Hunts, and the Knights of Columbus parish picnics are a few of the many good memories I have of the Corpus Christi Parish.

Philip Heim

CORPUS CHRISTI MEMORIES BY JAMES AND JUDY (SPINLER) BRADY

I first came to Corpus Christi in 1982 after marrying James Brady, and I remember being reluctant. Christ the King in Medford had been my church since childhood. We always attended the 7:00 AM Mass on Sunday mornings. To my surprise, Corpus Christi was like a big family gathering to worship. Over the years, our daughters attended preschool catechism after Mass as we stood around and talked on the lawn in front of the church. Our daughters were able to perform different parts in the annual Christmas pageant throughout the years and were servers and ushers as well. The fellowship after Mass was great catching up with neighbors and friends. The kids looked forward to the service ending, Kenny Mork (known as the candy man) would hand out treats to them all, and weather permitting he even brought ice cream treats.

A few times a year we would bring finger foods (anything that you eat with your fingers) for gatherings in the basement of the church. There was always plenty of food and great coffee and fellowship. We each took our turn helping with things, and we knew we could count on each other to get the work done that needed to be done. We worked well as a big parish family. If a need was identified, the families took care of it, usually at no cost to the parish.

It was a very sad day when our church closed, going to oratory status in September 2016. For our last celebration we had a big brunch after Mass celebrated by the bishop, with great fellowship. I miss our little country church, the people, and Mass every Sunday morning. I do enjoy getting back to our Oratory Mass when they are held. It feels like home when we come back together to celebrate, the same smell and music.

James & Judy Brady

James remembers as a kid going to church, the Pete family would take up a whole pew and if one of the kids acted up Joe would tap them on the head to behave. Another memory was the Knights of Columbus picnics at Corpus Christi with a big ice filled cow tank with soda pop and participation in all the kids' games. Great fun.

James & Judy (Spinler) Brady

MULLENMASTER FAMILY MEMORIES

By Monica (Mullenmaster) Nelson

I have so many fond memories of growing up in Deerfield and belonging to Corpus Christi parish. The Christmas season was one of the most joyous times of the year. Viewing the statues in the nativity scene and singing Christmas carols together with our friends made us feel like a true family loved by everyone in the community. We learned about Jesus Christ and the unconditional love of God.

The summer parish picnics were such fun for us children. I especially remember competitions such as the "gunny sack" races, floating pop bottles in a water tank, and trying to see how far we could carry an egg in a spoon before it dropped.

Mullenmaster Sisters in 2024 on Roberds Lake, Faribault.
L-R: Elaine, Monica, Coleen and Candace.

At Thanksgiving, we gathered in the church basement and played Bingo. I remember how thrilled I was one Thanksgiving when I played Bingo and won my first Thanksgiving turkey. My parents were so happy and proud of me!

I remember that at Christmas there was a huge parish party in the church basement. Santa Claus always arrived so we could all sit on his lap and tell him our Christmas wishes and we were given a paper bag of candy, peanuts and a little religious memento.

First Communions were a very special time of celebration. An annual event was May Crowning when one of the girls was chosen to crown the Blessed Mother. Lilacs were always in bloom during this season. The pleasant lilac aroma was everywhere.

We grew up in a very large family with sixteen children. All of the children were baptized at Corpus Christi; most of us also received our first communion there as well. Traveling to Sunday Mass took a special effort.

Our farm was located about three miles from church, too far to walk, especially in cold Minnesota winters.

Mom and Dad owned a station wagon, and we all fit into it. Mom, Dad, a baby and the smallest child sat in the front seat. Half of the children "layered" in the middle while the larger kids sat in the back of the station wagon "horse shoe" style. I remember Byron Brady Sr. counting us as we got out of the car. Somehow, no one ever got left behind. Once we arrived at Mass, a decision had to made about where to sit. We did not all fit into one pew. The older girls sang in the choir and each of the boys served Mass, but only one at a time.

The altar was small and there was room only for two servers and the priest. Many times our family sat in the "Mother's Room" which had a separate entrance and was located on the west side of the altar. There was limited space in this room and it was usually crowded.

One of the highlights each year was when the Knights of Columbus sponsored a trip to see the Minnesota Twins play at the stadium which was then in Bloomington where the Mall of America now is. Only the altar boys were invited. I was so disappointed when I learned that the choir girls couldn't go. It wasn't fair!

Monica (Mullenmaster) Nelson

PAMELA (PETERSON) HINCHLEY MEMORIES:

I really liked the friendly, small church feeling and how everyone would visit outside after the service and then sometimes we would get to stop at Mork's Store for a treat on the way home. I thought it was kind of cute how families would sit in the same pew every Sunday, we never did though.

I received my first Holy Communion and my confirmation at Deerfield. My younger sister Kim, and I were confirmed at the same time. The bishop came on a weeknight, we were 15 and 13 years of age.

When I got engaged to Bob Hinchley, the church ladies gave me a bridal shower in the church basement. I remember lots of gifts and yummy food. When I was younger, I thought the balcony was cool and the way the choir would come down for communion, so I joined the choir when I got older. Mary Phillips was the organist. After I got married and moved to Medford, on Sunday mornings I would often come to visit my parents, so I would attend Corpus Christi church. I would always feel so welcome by everyone.

Pamela (Peterson) Hinchley

****

MEMORIES BY SHIRLEY (WOCHNICK) ABRAHAM

My parents, were married at Corpus Christi on February 3, 1948. My father was working as a hired man on a farm owned by Theodore Stirens Jr. in Blooming Grove Township, Waseca County. I was born in late 1948 and baptized at Corpus Christi Church. I was 2 1/2 years old when our family moved to Faribault. As a very small child I remember getting sick during a funeral at Corpus Christi when the priest was placing incense on the coffin before the body of the deceased was taken to the cemetery. I do not remember whose funeral it was, but I do remember my dad holding his hand over my mouth as we made a speedy exit from the church.

Shirley (Wochnick) Abraham

****

PAUL GILLIS CORPUS CHRISTI MEMORIES:

I remember going to church at Deerfield. I received my first Holy Communion there. There were large families in attendance. In the summer, I remember my dad dropping me off at Corpus Christi with the other children by 9:00. We would have our religion class, and it would be over by noon. However, we were not picked up as our parents were busy trying to make a living. The group of us would start out from the church heading east. We would walk by different farms and the kids would go home, O"Brien, Stirens, Mohs, Hoffman, and finally Gillis. My family had to walk the farthest as we lived on County Road 23, one mile north of the church and about 4.5 miles east. I remember Rosamond O'Brien playing organ for the Masses.

When Medford was beginning to have Mass, I remember going to church sometimes at the Diers basement. After that the Medford church moved to Teeters Garage. I also remember the procession over to the dedication groundbreaking for the new Christ the King Church.

My dad died when I was very young, so I helped out with the farming. Later I got married and belonged to Christ the King Church for many years. After some time, I returned to Corpus Christi because the Mass time worked out better for us as we were milking cows. Our youngest son Jason received all his sacraments at Corpus Christi.

As a family we sat in the same pew at Corpus Christi, 3 rows from the back on the right-hand side of the church. It was the pew with the post that holds up the choir loft.

Both of my daughters Laura Hager, Jackie Reuvers became members of Corpus Christi with their families and were very active in the church as well. My grandson Brad mows both the church and cemetery taking over for his grandpa John Hager. Corpus Christi holds a very special place in my heart. It was always fun to catch up after church
Note: Paul Gillis is the son of Michael and Gertrude (Blais) Gillis

Paul Gillis

Michael & Gertrude (Blais) Gillis Family (2008)
Rita Halpin, Paul Gillis, Joyce Rath, Janice Paro, Raymond, Larry, Victor

Paul & Jean (Langeslag) Gillis ---- 50th Wedding Anniversary at Corpus Christi (2008)
Jackie Reuvers, Jeff, Carolyn Schroeder, Paul, Jean, Richard "Dick", Laura Hager, Jason.

PAUL & JEAN (LANGESLAG) GILLIS FAMILY

Descendants of Paul & Jean (Langeslag) Gillis (2008)

Richard "Dick" & Deloris "Dee" Maas Family
Back: Monica Taddei, John Gillis, Nikki Taddei.
Front, Meredith Gillis, Dee, Dick, Ian Gillis

Richard 'Rick" & Laura (Gillis) Hager Family
Children, L-R: Brad, Wesley, Alyse (Hager) Miller

MEMORIES FROM THE DECEMBER 10, 1978 CHRISTMAS PARTY

The 1978 Christmas party was held December 10th at 3:00 pm in the church basement. Diane Sammon, Mary Fredericks and daughters took care of program. Penny Frederick announced the program, Santa Claus came, and the bags were made by the Knights of Columbus. Don Morgan and family generously donated delicious apples for everyone attending. Don Morgan and Aldon Sammon fixed the stage. Evelyn Brady fixed a Christmas tree she brought from home and decorated. Brunch was served and all had a good time."

PAT O'BRIEN'S MEMORIES OF CORPUS CHRISTI

Father Snyder was a wonderful man and family friend. We loved him. We moved to Deerfield in 1942, when I was nine years old. My dad, Steve O'Brien was a farmer, and we rented the Helen and Clifford Schoenfeld farm.

Father Snyder came to call on our family and welcome us to the Corpus Christi Church. I was raised in a very large family (4 boys, 5 girls); Leonard, Rita (Kuntz), Patricia, Grace (Skalicky), Maurice, Albert, Maureen (Johnson), Frances (Ahlman), and Michael.

My mother Rosamond (Rousseau) could play the organ. After Father Snyder found this out, whenever he was performing a funeral, he would pick my mother up to play the organ in the choir loft, that way he could collect additional money for the funeral mass. They became great friends.

I remember one Sunday our 1940 Plymouth wouldn't start so Dad got the buckboard, and Mom heated bricks which we stood on to stay warm. We had lots of blankets and we made our way to church. It was a wonderful adventure. Some of the church-goers helped us get home.

My first real job making good money was picking beans on the Charlie Parrish farm in Deerfield. There was 3 acres of string beans!! We picked with the Henry Hager family leaving home very early in the morning, bringing a pail lunch. They told me I was a good bean picker. With my money, I purchased my first boughten coat.

My mother was suffering with cancer, but we were not told as children. From April through September of 1948, my mother was in Rochester. She came home twice. The last time she left the farm, they laid table boards on the back seat and drove her back to the hospital that way. She was in a lot of pain.

Before she left, us kids filed through the car in one door and out the other to kiss and say goodbye to her. Father Snyder would visit her and say "Ro," I have converted another one because of your suffering.

My mother never came home again, passing away that year at the age of 39 years from cancer, along with the baby girl O'Brien.

Things were tough for our family after mother's death. We moved after that to the other side of Medford. I remember Fr. Snyder visiting us older girls and talking to us how hard it was on our father. He had met a very nice women, Margaret (Eastman) and he asked us girls to accept her into the family. We agreed we would, and so Steve was remarried in June of 1951. There were always good people at the church of Corpus Christi. I rejoined the Corpus Church after I moved to Morristown. Now, I am back home.

Descendants of Stephen and Rosamond (Rousseau) O'Brien gathered at Corpus Christi on July 16, 2024 for the funeral of Grace O'Brien Skalicky. On the left is Patricia O'Brien, age 91. On the right is the family of Ernest and Rita (O'Brien) Kuntz along with Rita's sister Maureen (O"Brien) Johnson. Patricia, Rita and Maureen are daughters of Stephen and Rosemond O'Brien. (See page 93 for more O'Brien family information).

ANNA & HENRY HAGER MEMORIES

By Susan (Hager) Redman and Roseann (Hager) Barbknecht

Anna and Henry Hager moved from Waterville, Minnesota to the Deerfield area in the fall of 1943 with 11 children. The family first planned to attend the November 7th service, but a snowstorm upset the plans. Henry and Anna continued to attend and be active members of the Corpus Christi Church until our mother moved off the farm.

We remember that Father Snyder had a horse that he boarded at the Hager farm. Each Sunday afternoon he would come to ride it just before supper time. He would give Sue Hager a ride on his horse. She now thinks of just how much of a "holy moment" it was.

Anna would invite Father Snyder for supper, and she would say you are more than welcome to stay for supper but all we have is baked beans and fresh bread. He would always stay and say Anna that food sounds like a feast.

Each year at Corpus Christi, a summer school was held for two weeks in early June. The Dominican nuns would come to Deerfield from Faribault, Bethlehem Academy to teach. We would start in the morning with Mass, so we would take some lunch along to eat after Mass. Summer school would end by noon, and we would walk home with the James and Alma Hurt family. It was a fun time.

Each year, there was a Christmas program and John Hager would be Santa Claus. One year, John came to the party in regular dress. He had fooled the crowd by getting our cousin Jack to play Santa. Santa always came to give every child treats; a bag of candy, maybe an apple or an orange.

Father Harold Mountain was our pastor in Medford and Deerfield from 1952-1968. He was a dear friend. When he passed away, I discovered that Sue was in his will. He left me his writing desk which had belonged to his mother (it's a treasure.) She also received some of his rosaries and statues of the Holy Mother.

Sue Hager remembers that sister Debbie was born in December of 1954. Mother did not tell anyone from the church that she was expecting. After Mass on Sunday, Dad told Susan to take Sandy and go back to the sacristy and tell Father Mountain that Anna had a little baby girl the previous night. So, my sister and I went back to the sacristy to tell Father Mountain.

Father Mountain was removing his vestments and he turned around (remember Father was over 6 feet tall) and he said sternly "Yes, what do you girls want?" Sue stammered and said, "Dad said to come back and tell you that Mom had a little baby girl last night." Father Mountain looked at us and said, "Little girls that lie go straight to Hell!" I was scared when I hear the word Hell and I started to cry. Dad came up the steps and wanted to know what happened. Father Mountain said "Hank they are trying to tell me Anna had a baby." My dad said, "That's right Father, a baby girl." Father Mountain shook his head and said, "Well I'll be damned!"

Most of our brothers served Mass. One Sunday morning when Louis was serving for Mass, he fell asleep during Father Mountain's homily. When it was time to stand up after the homily Louis sat there sleeping and Dennis did the serving. Louis blamed it on our brother-in-law, Willard Karsten as he gotten up early to do the morning milking and the chores for him. Father had to wake Louis. That only happened once.

Henry Hager served as custodian at Corpus Christi more than 25 years until he died suddenly in 1975. The church was heated by a wood burning furnace and the wood used to heat the church came from trees on our farm.

Ellen (Mrs. Ernest) Holmquist sold religious articles after Mass every Sunday. These included rosaries, prayer books, statues of the Holy Family, Mary, and the saints. This was a convenient and wonderful source for religious articles at that time.

HENRY & ANNA (HOLLINGER) HAGER FAMILY MARRIAGES:
1). Loretta and Vernon Schwartz; April 22, 1947 at Deerfield
2). Helen and Willard Karsten, married September 27, 1952 at Medford Parish House
3). John and Shirley Conrath; September 30, 1959 at Deerfield
4). Neil and Donna Kratt October 27, 1956 at Deerfield
5). Dennis and Becky Kratt; August 28, 1965 at Deerfield
6). Rosanne and Wayne Barbknecht August 26, 1961 at Christ the King, Medford
7). Susie and Donnie Redman, August 14, 1965 at Medford
8). Sandy and David Sutlief July 27, 1968 at Corpus Christi Deerfield
9). Debbie and Gordy Johnson; July 21, 1973 at Deerfiield

REACHING BACK: JOHN HAGER REMEMBERS CORPUS CHRISTI PARISH 1940-60

By Carla Brady

John Hager
(1934-2022)

John Hager, son of Henry and Anna (Holinger) Hager was born at Waterville, August 5, 1934. John moved from rural Waterville to a farm in Blooming Grove Township just across the Deerfield Township line with his parents and siblings in 1943 when he was 9 years old. He was the 5th child of a family which eventually included 8 brothers and 7 sisters.

On the farm, he remembers they had 18 cows, 200 pigs in the summer and about 100 in the winter months. They also had about 1,000 chickens. He said, "that was a large number of livestock for those days."

His first memory of Deerfield was in 1944 when Fr. Snyder had no altar boys. So, Richard Sammon, Wally Voegele, Anthony Kniefel and John Hager were trained to serve Mass. They needed to learn Latin which took many hours of practicing to get it right. John told me about one time these altar boys had gotten to church early and thought it would be a good idea to test the wine. Thank goodness they left some for consecration.

John recalled that until the 1960s and Vatican II, the women's head was always covered while in church. All Masses were in Latin. The altar servers never touched the chalice. He remembers the bishop coming to the parish to confirm the children who were usually ten or 11 years old.

John said he remember the organists: Merle Gostomczik, Loretta Holmquist, Mrs. Steve O'Brien, and later Mary Phillips. The custodian for the church was Peter Sterins when John moved to Deerfield. John's father, Henry Hager took over in 1951, at which time they began mowing the church lawns and cemeteries for Corpus Christi and later for Christ the King. In 1975, Kenny Mork held the position on an interim basis after Henry suddenly passed away. Sylvester Dulas took over in early 1976.

John recalled that in the winter of 1951, church services were canceled for 3 weeks due to huge winter snowstorms. John rode "Barney" the Hager family's big draft horse to church, and tied him to the water pump. John filled the wood burner with wood, then waited a half hour and filled again and then rode back home.

John remembers how every June for 2 weeks, from 9:00 am until 3pm, Fr. Snyder would bring Dominican nuns from Bethlehem Academy in Faribault to provide the children with religious training.

There was no indoor plumbing at Corpus Christi, just two outhouses, a his and hers. For entertainment back then, 5-6 families would get together on Friday evenings a little later in the evenings to say the rosary, and then the families would enjoy each other's company.

John recalls in 1952 until about 1954, that square dancing was held in the Corpus Christi Church basement. A man from Faribault would come and do the calling for the dance. Sometimes Henry Hager would be his substitute, and when he was, John would dance with his mother.

John's wife, Shirley assured me that John was indeed a good dancer. John also remembers in the 1950s, one Sunday a month they played a card game called Pfeffer and the wives would provide lunch.

John Hager remained active at Corpus Christi until 1959 when he was united in marriage to Shirley Conrath, at which time they moved to Medford and became members of Christ the King Church.

John married Shirley Conrath on September 30, 1959 at Corpus Christi Church. They were married 63 years. John Hager passed away December 15, 2022 at Medford.

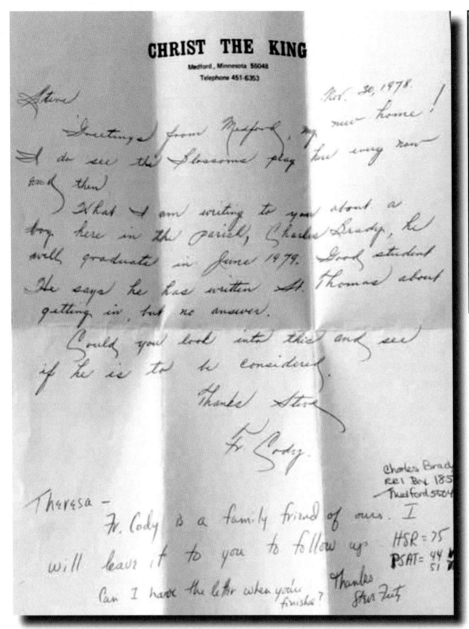

Charles Brady

Father Cody's letter that helped Charles Brady gain acceptance at St. Thomas.

St Thomas application left me unsettled. Fr. Cody, who had become my counsel, my confident, my friend, met my recitation of challenges and offered his belief that St. Thomas was an outstanding college which would be an excellent experience for me - exactly what I wanted to hear.

He sought to assure me that all would work out. For a 17-year old faced with perceived life-altering challenges, leaving it in God's hands - as I interpreted Fr. Cody's advise to be - can feel more like resignation than a sound strategy.

Within weeks, I received a letter informing me of my acceptance to become a student at the College of St. Thomas. Once I had received that letter, no other options were remotely considered. Attending St. Thomas turned out to be among my rewarding life-choices.

In 2016, I serendipitously met two regular visitors to the Island of Kauai (my home for several years), Steve and Beverly Fritz. Steve was St. Thomas' Head Basketball Coach while I attended the college.

In 2016, Steve was still employed St. Thomas (now as the Athletic Director) and he, Bev and I became good friends through our shared St Thomas experiences and our mutual admiration of Fr. John Cody who had been Steve's parish priest during his days in Blooming Prairie.

Steve retired from his role at St. Thomas in 2019 after 52 years at the University. As he and Bev worked through the half-century of memories in his office, they came across a note on Christ The King letterhead they thought I may be especially interested in. Steve had filed it away long ago and forgot of its existence.

I had no idea Fr. Cody personally knew someone at St. Thomas and I had no idea he had written this note, he never mentioned it. While I regret I did not have the chance to thank him in person for this special intervention, Fr. Cody is a constant in my prayers of gratitude and holds and prominent place in my memories of Corpus Christi.

RECOLLECTIONS BY GREG PITTMAN

I moved to our home at 13390 420th Avenue in rural Waseca in 2001 from Montgomery, Minnesota and was looking for a welcoming Catholic church to attend and join.

I have a son, Tim and his wife who live in Savage and a daughter, Tracy and her husband with three children who live in New Market. I have brought my grandchildren with me a number of times to Corpus Christi. My wife, Jolaine, who I have been married to for 15 years attends Grace Lutheran in Waseca.

A relative mentioned a Catholic church just 5 miles straight east of my home, so I started attending Sunday Mass at Corpus Christi and found the parishioners to be friendly and very welcoming. I joined the church and enjoyed singing the songs the choir was singing.

The Dulas family, Sylvester and Jackie, were especially welcoming. There was another lady who approached me one Sunday after Mass and told me that I sing really well and that I should join the choir. I found out that she was Martha Pete, the piano player's mother. I previously sang in the choir when I lived at Montgomery. I eventually approached Amy (Pete) Hellevik, the piano player and introduced myself.

She was excited to have me join her small choir and I have been singing at Corpus Christi ever since. I have enjoyed getting to know the parishioners and I especially have enjoyed Father Herman. When Corpus Christi closes I do not know where I will attend Mass. I may remain as a member for a while and try out other parishes like Sacred Heart in Waseca. *Greg Pittman*

Corpus Christi Christmas Creche (c1958)
L-R: Monica, Greg (partially hidden), Elaine and Coleen Mullenmaster, children of Leo and Creta Mullenmaster. The Nativity scene (creche) was built by Joseph Weber.(picture is c1958).

339

CORPUS CHRISTI CEMETERY TRUSTEES & VOLUNTEER CUSTODIANS (1954-2024)

James "Jamie" Brady

CEMETERY TRUSTEES:
1954-1961:
Ernest Holmquist & George Miller
1962-1973:
Ernest Holmquist & Corliss Cole
1974-1978:
Ernest Holmquist & Kenny Mork
1979-1993
Byron Brady & Kenny Mork
1994-2000:
Byron Brady & Byron O'Connor
2001-2020:
Byron Brady & Dick Gillis
2021-Current:
Byron Brady & James "Jamie" Brady

Byron P. Brady

The church has been well maintained. The care and love of the church is still apparent today. James "Jamie" and Byron P. Brady are the trustees of the Corpus Christi Cemetery. They look after the church facility, cleaning and maintaining, winterizing and make sure that the fuel is sufficient for heating the church during the cold winter months to prevent damage from frost. James Brady takes on extra duties for maintaining the outside property and the cemetery through brush mowing, and snow removal. Brad Hager is currently handling the mowing of the church property and cemetery. Donations from parishioners help with the costs of maintaining and mowing grounds, electricity, insurance and purchasing fuel. All donations are welcome and appreciated. Expenses for the oratory run about $4,100 per year. Some of the last major improvements to the property include:

* 2005 new roof and gutters
* 2007 new furnace
* 2008 new carpet, capped the well (no longer any water on premise)
* 2008 new concrete driveway, done by CEI Construction Greg Wencl,3 basement windows
* 2009 – additional windows
* 2010 -added gutter guards
* 2014-basement remove asbestos tiles, remove kitchen cupboards
* 2018-concrete steps at the church entrance-CEI Construction Greg Wencl
* 2018-new front door to the church-donated by Paul and Jean Gillis
**all improvements were paid for as they were completed.

> *Fr. Harold Mountain wrote back in 1955: (still true today)*
> I wish to thank all those that contributed so generously to the support of Corpus Christi parish during the past year. Our property is in first rate shape now, and it is our obligation to always keep it that way.
> **In making your will, be sure to leave at least a small sum to Corpus Christi to assure the future of our parish. We leave sums to others that we love, and everyone loves the parish to which they have been related spiritually for a period in their lives. May God bless you for your kindness and generosity.

If you are reading this book, sometime in the future, and you wish to donate to help preserve Corpus Christi as an oratory, donations can be made to:
Corpus Christi Church Oratory in care of St. Joseph's Catholic Church,
512 S. Elm Ave., Owatonna MN. 55060

Byron P. Brady with the new cross (2000).

Jacob Hellevik

By the year 2000, the woodpeckers had done a number on the old wooden cross at the cemetery. The body of Jesus was hanging precariously on the cross. Byron P. Brady, as trustee of the cemetery sought to rectify the situation. He went to see Scott Svenby of Svenby Milling just northeast of Medford. Scott had a Ponderosa pine log that he was able to mill for the project, donating the lumber and services.

Byron assembled the cross. It was then moved to Dennis Morgan's farm where it was coated with tar. Kyle Brendemuehl fabricated end caps for the cross. Jack Schwab, Dennis Morgan, Dick Gillis and Byron Brady installed the new cross at the cemetery. Ervin Jeno made new brackets to the cement base to hold the cross in place. Jesus was repainted and attached to the cross. The other statues were painted in the following spring. At the same time, the southwest end of the cemetery was drained with tile donated by Jack Schwab.

In 2014, the stone pillars at the entrance to the Corpus Christi Cemetery were disintegrating. Jacob Hellevik offered to assist with the repairs to gain his Eagle Scout Award. Byron and Jacob Hellevik removed the old cement around the fieldstone. Jacob mixed the cement and then the cement grout was replaced between the stones. They worked in the late afternoon after school for Jacob, and after work for Byron, for several days to complete the project. Jacob and Brian Hellevik also removed the shrubs along the north side of the cemetery. They were then replaced with shrubs purchased through Michael Pete Landscaping in Wadena, Minnesota at wholesale cost, and paid with cemetery funds. The following April, Jacob received his Eagle Scout Award.

CARLA REMEMBERS CHRISTMAS AT CORPUS CHRISTI

The altar decorated for Christmas at Corpus Christi.

Another tradition at Christmas was the setting up of the manger scene and decorating the church. The CCW officers oversaw the decorating which included putting up the advent wreath, prior to Christmas. Then setting up the Christmas tree and setting up the manger. The manger was stored under the stairs to the choir loft. In the early years, the crib was to the left of the Altar. After the Choir moved downstairs, the crib was moved to under the altar. We must give Joe Weber credit for building our creche/Nativity scene (see previous page) that we enjoyed for so many years up until our last Christmas celebration.

I believe that Fr. Mountain was responsible for purchasing the figurines. Over the years, some became damaged, Evelyn Brady came to the rescue in making the repairs with her sculpting abilities.

Christmas decorating was done after the last Sunday of Advent. The crib remained in place until the wisemen came. Each of the windowsills were decorated with garland and a red glass candle. Live wreaths were purchased through MCCL (Minnesota Concerned Citizens for Life) and hung between the windows. (Jean Gillis always donated funds to purchase the wreaths). The Stations of the Cross were taken down while the church sported the Christmas decorations. Live evergreen boughs were placed on the top of the crib. The altar was transformed for the Christmas service with red candles in the candelabras, and on the altar, and wreaths hung on the sacristy wall. Silk poinsettia flower arrangements were used on the altar, as the church was not heated during the week. I started decorating the church for Christmas in about 1991 and it was my task after that. I would decorate while we held Choir practice for the Christmas Mass and the

choir assisted in the undertaking. The music was the best. We sang harmony, songs that the congregation knew. The music swelled to the rafters. It was a tradition that most of the parishioners would come at least 20 minutes prior to the service to hear the Christmas carols before mass. As a special musical treat; bells, violins and solos were added to make the music really special.

Children were welcome to sing a few numbers as well. Fr. Robert Herman joined the action before Mass, singing his song with Brian Hellevik. He would also sing the Our Father during the service. After Mass many Merry Christmas wishes were shared before we headed home to have our own family Christmas.

Carla Brady

FATHER ERNSTER (1989-1992) THREATENS TO CLOSE CORPUS CHRISTI

By Carla Brady and Judy Brady

Bishop John George Vlazny distributing Holy Communion at Corpus Christi in 1991.
Father Ernster apologized and is sitting on the altar in the corner.

In late 1990, Fr. Ernster announced from the pulpit that Corpus Christi parish was going to be closed. This sounded the alarm for all our Corpus Christi families. Fr. Edward Mountain preceded Fr. Ernster, so I turned to him for spiritual guidance, asking him what we should do.

Fr. Mountain gave me encouraging news, saying that he had not heard anything like that from the bishop's office. He urged us to contact members of the parish and encourage them to write letters to Bishop Vlazny telling him what our church meant to us, so we did. Almost every family wrote letters which were personally delivered by parishioner Cathy Hackett during a Winona Council of Catholic Women board meeting that Bishop Vlazny was attending.

The Bishop did not accept our letters, so each was returned by mail to us.

Within a few days, we were informed that Bishop Vlazny would be coming on August 5th to celebrate Sunday Mass at Corpus Christi. We held a CCW meeting and decided that we would show Bishop Vlazny our church hospitality. We organized a finger food brunch and had our display of the sewing articles that the women had worked on over the last year.

We prepared ourselves for the worst, for we knew that someday Corpus Christi would be closed, but we prayed that the time had not arrived. If we were to be closed, we wanted to hear it directly from the bishop.

Bishop Vlazny arrived as planned on August 5th for Mass. During his homily, he assured us that we were would not be closed. He said Fr. Ernster did not have authority to close Corpus Christi and had him publicly apologized to the entire parish.

The church family was relieved, our beloved church could carry on with Sunday Masses for another 25 years.

We declared a truce with Fr. Ernster and moved ahead. It was in the spring of 1991, Fr. Ernster decided that if Corpus Christi was to stay open, the church needed to be painted to brighten it up. The last painting had been done during the 1960s, under Fr. Harold Mountain.

343

During painting in 1992, chairs were placed in the church for Mass since the pews were stored in the semi-trailer.

Father Ernster chose the colors and purchased the paint, and the Corpus Christi families got to work. After Sunday Mass, parishioner Aldon Sammon brought a semi-trailer on sight and the pews were removed from the church proper and placed in the trailer.

The red drapes behind the altar and the statues were removed permanently. Scaffolding was brought in by George Hackett, while families brought paint brushes and rollers. Working alongside Fr. Ernster, we began painting. The parishioners who did not paint provided food and refreshments for the workers.

We took shifts so that we were not on top of each other, with many painting in the evening after they had completed our day jobs. Kenny Mork and others brought additional lighting into the church so that we were able to paint well into the evening hours.

The following Sunday, chairs were placed in the church for Mass celebration since the pews were still in the semi-trailer. That gave us one more week to get our church back in order. We purchased new carpet for the sanctuary and the center aisle.

Fr. Ernster saw how we worked together, and that we were truly a church community. We did not have enough time to do anything to the sacristy or the mother's room. We were very pleased with the transformation of our worship space and our beautiful little church.

The CCW ladies decided that for Father's Day in June, 1992, we would spruce up the sacristy and the mother's room. We came in and painted, added curtains to the windows and freshened up both areas. Right before the final song, at Mass we dropped a banner over the choir loft wishing Fr. Ernster "Happy Father's Day."

Shortly after that Sunday, we received word that Fr. Ernster was being moved and we would be receiving Fr. Robert Herman as our pastor.

Since Corpus Christi became an oratory in 2016, Mass has been celebrated twice annually and on special occasions.

Mass at Corpus Christi Church (May 30, 2024)
(Con-celebrated by Monsignor Cook & Fr. Joe Pete)

CORPUS CHRISTI CHRONOLOGY

1849   The Minnesota Territory was formed on March 3, 1849. Approximately 5,000 settlers lived in the Territory.

1855   The first settlement in Deerfield township was made May 12, 1855, by Edward McCartney,

1856   Andrew Wuertzler emigrated from Bavaria to Illinois and moved to Deerfield in 1856.

1857   Deerfield Township was first created on April 6, 1857.

1858   Minnesota was admitted to the Union on May 11, 1858, as the 32nd state.

1859   On January 8, 1859, Fr. George Keller performed the marriage of John Woods to Ellen Conlin of Deerfield.

1868   The site for the church was donated by Andrew and Mary Wuertzler. The cemetery site was donated by the John and Veronica Loemer family.

1869   The Corpus Christi church structure was built in 1869.

1870   Mission Pastors between 1870 and 1923 included Rev. James Cotter, Rev. George Keller, Rev. Patrick Kiernan, Mgsr. John Pivo, and Rev. Francis Pribyl.

1873   The Corpus Christi church property was officially obtained by the Diocese of Winona on Aug. 27, 1873.

1874   The Deed was recorded on July 10, 1874 by Rev. Thomas L. Grace, Bishop of the St. Paul Archdiocese.

1891   Father John Pivo became the pastor of Sacred Heart, Owatonna, and of Corpus Christi.

1898   The Deerfield creamery built on land donated by James F. Brady, began receiving cream on April 1, 1898.

1903   Rev. John Meyers became pastor and served until 1909.

1909   Various priests from Claremont served Corpus Christi until 1935. There were no Masses or parish activities from 1935 until 1938.

1916   During the pastorate of Father McCarthy (1916-21), improvements were made on the Corpus Christi church and the choir loft was added.

1923   Corpus Christi was officially transferred to the Winona Diocese, and incorporated on July 20, 1923.

1935   Corpus Christi was closed from about 1935 until 1938.

1938   Bishop Francis Kelly announced at a Knights of Columbus meeting in Waseca that Fr. Raymond Snyder, then at St. Hyacinthe parish, Owatonna would be assigned to Deerfield. Father Snyder offered the first Mass at Corpus Christi on Pentecost Sunday June 5, 1938.

1939   During the Corpus Christi church building was physically moved back north and west from the road right of way to higher ground. Volunteers used horses and scoops to dig a basement, establish the foundation and physically move the entire building. Sunday Masses were held in the church cemetery for several months during the process.

1942   In 1942 Father Snyder was appointed to a pastorate at Fountain and Wykoff, southeast Minnesota.

1942   Rev. Alois Quillin served as pastor for about one year until 1943.

1943   The parish of Christ the King, Medford, was established. Rev. Raymond Snyder returned to serve as pastor of Corpus Christi and Christ The King and remained until 1952.

1949   Christ The King church at Medford built.

1952   Father Harold Mountain was appointed pastor in 1952 and remained at Corpus Christi and Christ The King until 1968.

1968   Rev. Francis Glynn appointed pastor; he served until 1976. The new organ was purchased in 1968 and that same year William Francl made and donated the small outdoor grotto of the Blessed Virgin.

1976   Msgr. Warren Ryan appointed pastor and served until 1977.

1977   Pastorate of Rev. John Cody who served until 1985.

1985   Rev. Edward Mountain appointed pastor and served until 1989.

1989   Rev. Milo Ernster was appointed pastor and remained until 1992

1992   Rev. Robert Herman served as pastor until 2002

2002   Rev. Robert Herman became priest moderator in 2002 and served until 2007. Father Herman, although retired, continued to serve Corpus Christi until 2016.

2016   Bishop John M. Quinn con-celebrated Mass at Corpus Christi on September 11, 2016 with Fr. Robert Herman and officially established the church as an oratory. Approximately one-hundred parishioners, past and present, attended a Mass and a pancake breakfast prepared by members of Trinity Lutheran Church, Medford.

2024   The parish of Corpus Christi in the small township of Deerfield, Steele County, Minnesota continues as an oratory with Masses on special occasions. The history of this vibrant parish tells the story of 160 years of faith, family and friendships. History of Corpus Christi Parish is published.

STATIONS OF THE CROSS AT CORPUS CHRISTI CHURCH

Jesus Is Condemned to Death

Jesus Falls the First Time under the Cross

Jesus Falls the First Time under the Cross

Jesus Meets His Afflicted Mother

347

The Cyrenian helps Jesus to Carry his Cross

Veronica Wipes the Face of Jesus

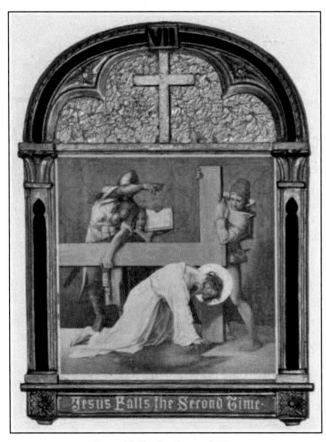

Jesus Falls the Second Time

Jesus Speaks to the Daughters of Jerusalem

Jesus Falls the Third Time

Jesus is Stripped of His Garments

Jesus is Nailed to the Cross

Jesus Dies on the Cross

Jesus is Taken Down from the Cross

Jesus is Placed in the Sepulchre

The Stations of the Cross or the Way of the Cross, also known as the Way of Sorrows or the *Via Crucis,* are a series of images depicting Jesus Christ on the day of his crucifixion and accompanying prayers. The stations grew out of imitations of the Via Dolorosa in Jerusalem, which is a traditional processional route symbolizing the path Jesus walked to Mount Calvary. The objective of the stations is to help the Christian faithful to make a spiritual pilgrimage through contemplation of the Passion of Christ. It has become one of the most popular devotions and the stations can be found in many Western Christian churches, including those in the Roman Catholic, Lutheran, Anglican, and Methodist traditions.

Commonly, a series of 14 images will be arranged in numbered order along a path, along which worshipers—individually or in a procession—move in order, stopping at each station to say prayers and engage in reflections associated with that station.

These devotions are most common during Lent, especially on Good Friday, and reflect a spirit of reparation for the sufferings and insults that Jesus endured during his passion. As a physical devotion involving standing, kneeling and genuflections, the Stations of the Cross are tied with the Christian themes of repentance and mortification of the flesh.

EPILOGUE

THE CORPUS CHRISTI HISTORY BOOK has finally been published. It has turned out to be a much larger project than anyone anticipated and has taken many long hours collecting arranging and editing material. This has truly been a "team" effort. The book will serve as a historic record of the main events which have happened over more than 160 years. The book will be a historical record for our children, their children, and generations to come... the extended community of Corpus Christi Catholic Church.

This book is a series of snapshots in time and includes information and photographs available to the authors prior to publication. As we researched the history of Corpus Christi, it seemed that new discoveries surfaced with every inquiry. If names or events have been omitted, we beg your forgiveness. We can assure you that any omissions are unintentional, and caused by lack of availability. We have included all pertinent information which we remember or was provided to us.

We especially wish to thank Father James Starasinich, formerly Pastor of St. Joseph Parish, Owatonna for his encouragement and providing access to early Corpus Christi records. Renee Thompson did early work on graphics and provided photographs. Linda (Caron) O'Connor provided some of the photographs. Amy (Pete) Hellevik, provided support, access to records and historical information for the book. We also wish to thank Jacqueline Dulas for sharing Corpus Christi history books from previous years.

Lois (Heim) Nelson, Diane (Morgan) Sammon, Susan (Hager) Redman, Roseanne (Hager) Barbknecht, Rosemary (Pirkl) Meyer and Paul Pirkl, as well as the Mullenmaster sisters; Candace, Coleen, Elaine and Monica, provided photographs and information on their families. Jeanine (Sammon) Swanson provided photographs, news clippings and other valuable information on the Sammon, Condon and Fitzpatrick families. Lori (Kaderlik) Hatfield, a Sammon descendant, provided news clippings from the first Corpus Christi picnics. Lois (Heim) Nelson and Judy (Spinler) Brady diligently proofread several versions of the manuscript and offered many helpful suggestions. We are extremely grateful to Scott Cody who provided the front cover photo taken with a drone.

The work on this book has had its rewards. We have renewed friendships, and made many interesting contacts. We have met people and talked with them about Corpus Christi and the families that worshiped there through many decades and generations. We have enjoyed working on the book, and we hope you and future generations will appreciate and treasure it. Enjoy!

Carla (Maas) Brady & Ronald F. Eustice
2024

This book can be purchased at Amazon.com.

In 1950, an altar and large crucifix were erected, which added much to our beautiful cemetery, nestled against a wooded background, which is also church property. The wood for the original cross was donated by William Mullenmaster. Pictured above is the updated cross which was made by Byron P. Brady with wood donated by Svenby Milling Company.

This statue of an angel stands as a serene and silent sentinel on the east side of Corpus Christi Cemetery. The statue was purchased through Nagel Sod Company in Medford with funds contributed by Jackie Dulas in honor of her late husband Sylvester.

It Takes a Lifetime

It takes a lifetime to learn how to live,
How to share and how to give.
How to face tragedy that comes your way,
How to find courage to face each new day.
How to smile when your heart is sore,
How to go on when you can take no more.
How to laugh when you want to cry,
How to be brave when you say goodbye.
How to still love when your loss is so great,
How to forgive when your urge is to hate.
How to be sure that God's really there,
How to find Him, seek Him in prayer.

CORPUS CHRIST: THE BODY OF CHRIST

The name 'Corpus Christi' is Latin for 'the body of Christ'. This jubilant festival is celebrated by Roman Catholics and other Christians to proclaim the truth of the transubstantiation of bread and wine into the actual body and blood of Christ during Mass.

The feast of Corpus Christi was proposed by Thomas Aquinas, Doctor of the Church, to Pope Urban IV, in order to create a feast focused solely on the Holy Eucharist, emphasizing the joy of the Eucharist being the Body of Christ.

The feast is liturgically celebrated on the Thursday after Trinity Sunday or, "where the Solemnity of The Most Holy Body and Blood of Christ is not a holy day of obligation, it is assigned to the Sunday after the Most Holy Trinity as its proper day."

At the end of Holy Mass, there is often a procession of the Blessed Sacrament, generally displayed in a monstrance. The procession is followed by the Benediction of the Blessed Sacrament.

 A notable Eucharistic procession is that presided over by the Pope each year in Rome, where it begins at the Archbasilica of St. John Lateran and passes to the Basilica of Saint Mary Major, where it concludes with the aforementioned Benediction. Corpus Christi wreaths, which are made of flowers, are hung on the doors and windows of the Christian faithful, in addition to being erected in gardens and fields.

SOME OF FATHER CODY'S COMICAL COMMENTS & WORDS OF WISDOM

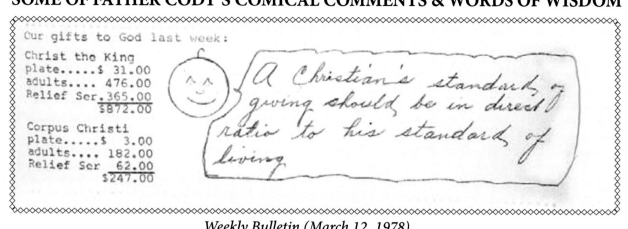

Weekly Bulletin (March 12, 1978)

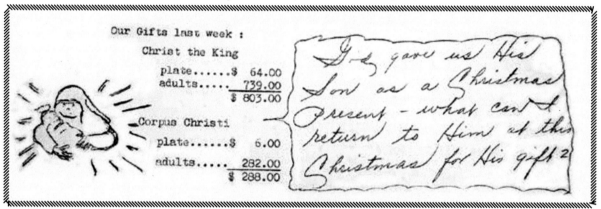

Weekly Bulletin (December 21, 1981)

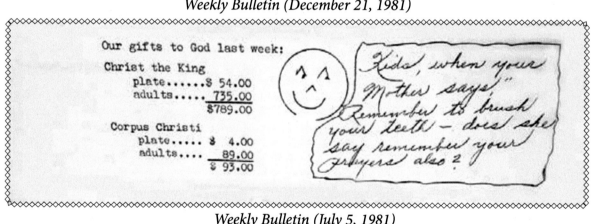

Weekly Bulletin (July 5, 1981)

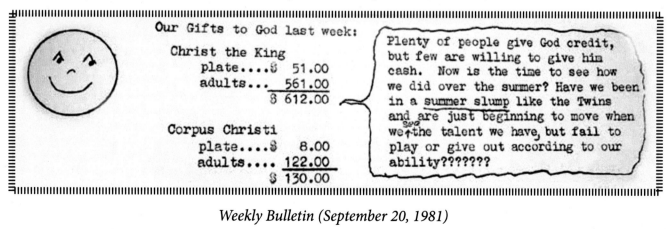

Weekly Bulletin (September 20, 1981)

Made in the USA
Monee, IL
24 November 2024

71148986R00219